A History of Methodism in

Kentucky

Volume 1: From 1783 to 1820

by

William Erastus Arnold

First Fruits Press
Wilmore, Kentucky
c2012

asburyseminary.edu
800.2ASBURY
204 North Lexington Avenue
Wilmore, Kentucky 40390

First Fruits
THE ACADEMIC OPEN PRESS OF ASBURY SEMINARY

ISBN: 9780984738687 (Vol. 1)

A History of Methodism in Kentucky, by William Erastus Arnold.
First Fruits Press, © 2012
Pentecostal Publishing Company, © 1921

Digital version at http://place.asburyseminary.edu/firstfruitsheritagematerial/8/

Arnold, William Erastus.
    A history of Methodism in Kentucky / by William Erastus Arnold.
    Wilmore, Ky. : First Fruits Press, c2012.
    2 v. ; 21 cm.
    Reprint. Previously published: Previously published: Louisville, Ky. :
    Pentecostal Publishing Company, c1935.
    Vol. 1. From 1783 to 1820 – v. 2. From 1820 to 1845.
    ISBN: 9780984738687 (pbk. : v. 1)
    ISBN: 9780914368908 (pbk. : v. 2)
    1. Methodist Church -- Kentucky. 2. Methodist Episcopal Church –
    Kentucky. 3. Methodist Church – Kentucky – Clergy – Biography. 4.
    Kentucky – Church history. I. Title.
    BX8248 .K4 A7 2012

Cover design by Haley Hill

asburyseminary.edu
800.2ASBURY
204 North Lexington Avenue
Wilmore, Kentucky 40390

John Wesley

A
HISTORY OF METHODISM
IN
KENTUCKY

BY

REV. W. E. ARNOLD, D. D.
**Member of the Kentucky Conference of the
Methodist Episcopal Church, South**

VOLUME I

FROM 1783 TO 1820

HERALD PRESS

1935

DEDICATION

Three persons have greatly influenced my life. My parents died when I was but an infant. My mother's brother, F. M. Henkle, and his good wife, Mrs. Casandra Henkle, took me into their home, and were father and mother to me as long as they lived. Their home was a truly religious home. At their family altar, some of my earliest and most lasting religious impressions were received. Through such influences, I became a church member before I was seven years of age, and had sought and obtained a definite religious experience at eighteen. During my childhood, my uncle was a subscriber to the church papers, and he bought and read aloud to us Redford's History of Methodism in Kentucky. Here I received my first interest in this subject. These good foster-parents have long since passed on to a better world.

My devoted wife, Elizabeth Strother Arnold, has for nearly half a century walked by my side, strengthening me by her prayers and lending encouragement in every good work. Her grandfather, George Strother, was one of Kentucky's greatest local preachers. Her father, Jeremiah Strother, was for many years a member of the Kentucky Conference. Her brother, J. P. Strother, and her nephew, William Bruce Strother, are now members of this body. Thus four generations of the Strother family have been Methodist preachers. Our daughter, Miss Katharine Arnold, is a deaconess, working under the Woman's Council of our Church.

To these three persons who have so greatly influenced my life, I affectionately dedicate this volume.

THE AUTHOR.

PREFACE

Between 1868 and 1876, Rev. Albert H. Redford, D. D., issued four volumes bearing on the History of Methodism in Kentucky down to 1844. These volumes are bulky,—containing over two thousand pages,—and have been out of print for more than fifty years. Persons of the present generation could not obtain these volumes if they so desired, and if they could obtain them, they would find that they contain no history of Kentucky Methodism for nearly a century. Dr. Redford was a tireless collector of historical data, and any future historian will be greatly indebted to him; but as his work covers less than half of our history, and as his volumes are not obtainable, the historian of the present is under the necessity of going back to the beginning, and of re-writing the history of the period covered by Redford, if he would get before the present generation an account of the heroic men and thrilling events of early Methodism in this State.

I gladly acknowledge my indebtedness to Dr. Redford. The present volume covers the period from the planting of the first Methodist society in Kentucky to the setting up of the Kentucky Conference—a period which Redford covered in two volumes. But the reader will find that I have not merely re-written Redford. Recent research has brought to light much that Redford knew nothing about. True, he had advantages that are forever denied the present and future historians. He knew men who took an active part in the work during

those early days, who told him many things about
the toils and sacrifices and difficulties of this work.
Then, many of these pioneers kept diaries and made
careful record of their experiences and of the events
that transpired around them. Redford quotes freely
from the unpublished journals that were in his hands,
but, unfortunately, these manuscripts have been de-
stroyed,—or lost—and no trace of them can now be
found. But recent research has added much to the
information he possessed, and has corrected many errors and misconceptions common to the historians of
his day. The present writer has carried his independent researches as far as time and opportunity would
permit; has tried to verify all statements of fact; and
has made an earnest effort to be accurate in all that the
following pages contain.

Credit for important quotations and statements on
the authority of others is usually given in the body of
this book, and the reader is saved the distraction and
annoyance of having to refer so frequently to foot
notes. The foot notes that are found on these pages
are intended to add details or to further explain matters that could not well be embodied in the text. I
think they will be found informing, and worthy the
attention of the reader.

What purports to be history is often little else than
annals—a mere recitation of facts, in chronological order, without story and without interest to the average
reader. On the other hand, history is sometimes so
loaded down with details and with comments of the
author that it is wearisome. However well or
poorly I have succeeded, I have tried to avoid both of
these dangers. I have been sparing of *preachments*
and *moralizings*, leaving the reader to draw his own

inferences and reach his own conclusions. I have tried to give enough concerning the men and events of our history to make them *live* before the minds of those who read. My greatest embarrassment has been to eliminate and condense. There is a surprising wealth of material in the sources from which I have drawn. Many incidents and anecdotes had to be omitted for want of space. Perhaps, if life and health are given me, I will, at some time, give to the public a book of Sketches that will more adequately present the men and the times in which they lived.

I am not presenting a Bibliography with this volume. Suffice it to say that I have consulted every authority I could get my hands upon,—histories of Kentucky and of the West, histories of sister denominations, General Conference Journals, General Minutes of the Conferences, biographies, magazine articles, files of old church papers, etc. I am greatly indebted to William Burke, Lewis Garrett, Jonathan Stamper, James B. Finley, John B. McFerrin, R. N. Price, and others who have written largely upon the history of Methodism in the early days of our country. But next to Redford, I owe more to Dr. W. W. Sweet, formerly of Depauw, but now of Chicago University, than to any other man. His "Rise of Methodism in the West," in which he publishes the Journal of the old Western Conference, and his "Circuit Rider Days Along the Ohio," in which he publishes the Journal of the Ohio Conference, have been invaluable to me. Other books of his have been very helpful.

I trust I shall be able to bring out Volume II of this History within the next year. It will deal with the Kentucky Conference as it was from 1820 to about 1846, when the Louisville Conference was set off from the Kentucky. Some very notable men and some very important events are to be treated in that Volume. I trust the reader of this number will be sufficiently interested to follow through the series.

THE AUTHOR.

Winchester, Ky.,
September 1, 1935.

CONTENTS

A HISTORY OF METHODISM IN KENTUCKY.

CHAPTER I

RELIGIOUS BEGINNINGS IN KENTUCKY

According to our best information, the first public religious service ever held in Kentucky was held at Boonesboro, May 28, 1775. The preacher was the Rev. John Lythe, of the Church of England. The service was held under the spreading branches of a magnificent elm, which stood about fifty yards to the south of the then unfinished fort built by Judge Richard Henderson. This fort was erected near the mouth of Otter Creek, in what is now Madison county, Kentucky, at a place on the Kentucky river selected for a settlement. The congregation, as Judge Henderson informs us, was made up, in part, at least, of "a set of scoundrels who scarcely believed in God or feared a devil."

The occasion of this first public religious service is quite interesting. The Transylvania Company, of which Judge Richard Henderson was promoter and head, had just purchased from the Cherokee Indians their claim to all the land lying between the Ohio and Cumberland rivers, and west of the Kentucky—a vast tract of more than twenty million acres—and was now opening it for settlement. Daniel Boone, who had long been in the employ of Henderson, was sent with a party of axemen to cut a road from the Cumberland Gap to some point on the banks of the Kentucky river, where a town could be laid out and Company headquarters established. He reached the mouth of Otter Creek on April 1, 1775, selected a site, and at once began the erection of a rude fort. Henderson, with a party of

1

forty men and boys (including a few Negro slaves), followed soon after, reaching the place of settlement on April 20th.

But James Harrod and others were already in this part of Kentucky. During the previous year, Harrod had built cabins at Harrodsburg, and, though these cabins were temporarily abandoned on account of Indian hostilities, Harrod and a party of thirty men had returned to them only a few days before Boone reached the mouth of Otter Creek. Besides reoccupying the cabins built in 1774, Harrod proceeded to establish another station at Boiling Spring, five or six miles away. About the same time, Benjamin Logan established a station at St. Asaph's, now Stanford.

All these stations were upon the land purchased by Henderson and his company from the Cherokees, and, by virtue of this purchase, the land was claimed by the Transylvania Company. An adjustment of titles was necessary. It was not difficult for Henderson to come to terms with Harrod and Logan, but a tide of immigration was setting in and bold adventurers were arriving every day. The Transylvania purchase would soon have many hardy settlers upon it. Evidently they must have a government to protect both the Company and the people in their rights and to regulate their affairs. Henderson promptly adopted a plan. He ordered an election of delegates in each of the settlements, and fixed a date for a legislative assembly—the first that was ever held in all the great West. The day fixed upon was May 23rd, and at that time the delegates assembled. Boonesboro had six delegates, and Harrodsburg, Boiling Spring, and St. Asaph's four each. Among the delegates from Harrodsburg was the Rev. John Lythe.

With all the formality of a British Parliament they proceeded to open the Assembly and to enact laws for the government of the territory. Lythe opened the Assembly with "divine service," which doubtless means that he offered prayer, invoking God's blessing upon the session. Their work as a legislative body was completed on Saturday, May 27th, but most of the delegates remained for divine worship on Sunday. Both the legislative Assembly and the religious service were held under that magnificent elm. In his Journal of May 14, two weeks before the time of this service, Henderson says:

No divine service our church not being finished—that is to say, about fifty yards from the place where I am writing and right before me to the South, (the river about 50 yards behind my camp and a fine spring a little to the west) stands one of the finest elms that perhaps nature ever produced in any region. . . This divine tree, or rather one of the many proofs of the existence from all eternity of its Divine Author, is to be our church, statehouse, council chamber, etc., and having many things on our hands we have not had time to erect pulpit, seats, etc., but hope by Sunday sennight (a week) to perform divine service for the first time—in a public manner and that to a set of scoundrels who scarcely believe in God or fear a devil, if we were to judge from most of their looks, words and actions.

When the first public service to which Judge Henderson looked forward was held, the legislators from Harrodsburg, Boiling Spring and St. Asaph's mingled with this motley crew from Boonesboro. Under date of Sunday, May 28, 1775, Henderson's Journal reads: *"Divine service for the first time by Rev. John Lythe, minister of the gospel, of England."*

Whether the Rev. John Lythe came to Harrodsburg with Harrod when he returned to that place in March, 1775, or came later, we do not know. Neither do we know whether or not he conducted any public religious service at Harrodsburg before going to Boonesboro as a legislative delegate. He may have done so, but we have no proof of it. He did not remain long in Kentucky. While a member of Henderson's Legislature, he was on some important committees, and got through that body a law against profane swearing and Sabbath breaking. He came from Virginia, and returned to the southwestern part of that State. His will is on record and a copy is found in the "Annals of Southwestern Virginia." Col. William Preston was administrator of his estate. He became a chaplain in a Virginia regiment led by Col. Russell,* and thus served in the American army in the Revolutionary War. There is a tradition that, while on an expedition against the Cherokee Indians, he was killed and scalped by them.

The Baptists were the first of the denominations to establish themselves in Kentucky. When Daniel Boone came into this trackless wilderness on his first expedition, in 1769, he stayed so long that his brother, Squire Boone, was sent in search of him and to bring a supply of flour, salt, and ammunition. They met, and for months roamed the wilds together, hunting the elk, the buffalo and the bear. Five years later, when Daniel Boone led the party of axemen to open the road from Cumberland Gap to Boonesboro, Squire Boone was one of the party. He was, therefore, one of the very first to reach the State for the purpose of settlement. When Henderson's Legislature met at Boonesboro, he was one of the six delegates from that place. He remained here

---

*Mrs. Russell was a sister of Patrick Henry. She and her husband were early converts to Methodism, and were pillars in the Church in Southwestern Virginia.

until some time in 1781, when he removed his family to Shelby county, and there established "Squire Boone's Station."

Now, besides being a skilful hunter and an expert gunsmith, Squire Boone was a Baptist preacher. It does not seem that, at this time, he was very zealous in the Master's cause, for although he had been at Boonesboro for nearly two months before the meeting of the "Legislature," there is no record of his holding any sort of religious service. Judge Henderson says that the service held by John Lythe was the first held at that place. So it appears that Boone allowed two months to pass without any effort to reach his rough and wicked fellow-pioneers with the gospel. It is a matter of record, however, that, on August 7, 1776, he officiated in the first wedding to take place on Kentucky soil, uniting in marriage Samuel Henderson, a younger brother of Judge Richard Henderson, and Betsy Calloway, the daughter of that redoubtable old pioneer, Col. Richard Calloway.*

*Many of our readers are familiar with the thrilling story of the capture by the Indians of Betsy Calloway, her sister Frances, and Jemima Boone, daughter of Daniel Boone, while rowing a canoe on the Kentucky river, not far from the fort at Boonesboro. The fathers of the girls immediately organized a party and pursued the Indians. They were overtaken when near the Blue Lick Springs, and the girls were rescued. Samuel Henderson, who was one of the rescuing party, was Betsy Calloway's sweetheart, and they were married two weeks after the rescue. They were the grandparents of Rev. R. H. Rivers, D. D., so well known throughout the M. E. Church, South, and for several years a member of the Louisville Conference.

It is not possible, at this late date, to determine the church affiliations, if any, of many of the first settlers of Kentucky. Judge Henderson, Benjamin Logan, and the McAfee brothers were Presbyterians. The Boones, Calloways, Bryants, and others were Baptists. Daniel Boone was never a member of any church, though his family were members of the old Dutchman's Creek Regular Baptist Church, in North Carolina. As already stated, his brother was a Baptist preacher. In a letter to his sister-in-law, dated October 17, 1816, Daniel Boone says: "All the relegan I have is to love and fear God, believe in Jeses Christ, Dow all the good to my nighbors and my Self I can and Do as little harm as I can help and trust on God's marcy for the rest." One of his biographers says of him: "He worshipped, as he often said, the Great Spirit—for the woods were his books and his temple; and the creed of the Red Men naturally became his." Several of the Boones of later generations became Baptist preachers.

The Yadkin country, in North Carolina, from which the Boones, and other families came, was a Baptist stronghold. Besides the old Dutchman's Creek church, to which the Boones, Bryants, and others of the pioneers belonged, the Sandy Creek church, in the same section, had, at one time, as many as 606 members. We are not surprised, therefore, that so many of the first comers were of the Baptist persuasion, and that these were the first of the denominations to establish churches in the new territory.

The soil into which the early pioneer preacher in Kentucky cast the gospel seed was not a propitious soil. It gave but little promise of an immediate or an abundant harvest. The first comers were a mixed multitude. Among them were families which were the equals of

any in the old settlements, and who became the progeni-
tors of some of the State's best citizenry. But many others were from the "back countries" of Virginia and the
Carolinas,—that border land between the civilization
of the colonies and the Indian country to the West.
Describing the educational and cultural conditions of
this border land, one writer says: "In that country at
that time there were no schools, no churches or par-
sons, or doctors or lawyers; no stores, groceries, or tav-
erns; nor do I recollect during the first two years any
officer, ecclesiastical, civil or military, except a justice
of the peace, a constable, and two or three itinerant
preachers." In this same backwoods country, one
boasted that "he had never worn a shirt, been at a fair,
heard a sermon, or seen a minister in all his life." The
bear hunter, the Indian fighter, and the criminal had
much to do in pushing back the frontier. "The settler
speedily followed in the hunter's wake. In his wake
also went many rude and lawless characters of the border, horse-thieves and criminals of different sorts, who
sought to hide their delinquencies in the merciful liber-
ality of the wilderness."—(Conquest of the Old Southwest, p. xvi). A large number of this ignorant, uncouth, and lawless class drifted into Kentucky at an
early day. Henderson speaks of his own party as a
"set of scoundrels who scarcely believe in God or fear
a devil." He and Boone had great difficulty in holding
their wild and restless comrades in place long enough
to complete the fort so necessary to their protection
from the Indians. After the Revolutionary War, a
better element began to arrive. The home seeker had
followed in the wake of the adventurer, and these furnished a more congenial soil for the gospel seed.

Except Squire Boone, whose zeal does not seem to

have been excessive, the first Baptist preacher to arrive
in Kentucky was the Rev. Thomas Tinsley. As early as
the spring of 1776, a year after the services by John
Lythe at Boonesboro, we find Tinsley at Harrodsburg,
preaching every Sunday to the settlers at that place.
Beyond the fact that he was in Harrodsburg in the
spring of 1776, preaching regularly on the Sabbath
days, but little is known of him. In a narrative of his
"Life and Travels," William Hickman, who visited Harrodsburg at this time, and who afterwards became an
eminent minister among the Baptists of the State,
says:

> We got to Harrodstown the first day of April. . . . My-
> self, Brother Thomas Tinsley* and my old friend, Mr. Morton,
> took our lodgings at Mr. John Gordon's, four miles from town.
> Mr. Tinsley was a good old preacher, Mr. Morton a good, pious
> Presbyterian, and love and friendship abounded among us. We
> went nearly every Sunday to town to hear Mr. Tinsley preach.
> I generally concluded his meetings. One Sunday morning, sit-
> ting at the head of a spring at this place, he laid his Bible on
> my thigh and said to me, 'you must preach today.' He said if
> I did not, he would not. I knew he would not draw back. I
> took the book and turned to the 23rd chapter of Numbers, 10th
> verse: 'Let me die the death of the righteous, and let my last
> end be like his.' I suppose I spoke fifteen or twenty minutes,
> a good deal scared, thinking if I had left any gaps down, he
> would put them up. He followed me with a good discourse,
> and never mentioned my blunders.

Thus began the long and useful ministry of William
Hickman, and thus we find that Thomas Tinsley was at
Harrodsburg as early as April, 1776. Spencer, the author of "A History of Kentucky Baptists," from whom
the above quotation is made, further says:

---

*Some historians give the name Peter Tinsley. But as Hick-
man was so intimately associated with him, his statement that
the name was Thomas, must be correct.

What is contained in the above paragraph is all that can now be known of the first Baptist preacher that ever preached in Kentucky, or, as far as known, in any part of the great West. At what time he came to Kentucky, or where from, is not known. He did not come with Mr. Hickman; for the latter gives the names of all who left Virginia with him, and Mr. Tinsley's is not among them. He either fell in with Mr. Hickman's party on the way, or was at Harrodsburg when the latter reached that village. However curious we may be to know more of the good old soldier of the cross, who first bore the tidings of salvation to this great valley, we shall probably never be gratified until we meet with him in the house of many mansions.

The tide of immigration from Virginia and North Carolina which set in toward the close of the Revolutionary War, bore upon its bosom many families who were Baptists, and along with them came quite a number of Baptist preachers. With Hickman in the spring of 1776 had come George Stokes Smith, "a distinguished pioneer preacher among the Baptists . . . probably going to Boonesboro." (Spencer, Pg. 14). In the fall of 1779, John Taylor arrived, and was followed the next spring by Joseph Redding. William Marshall, (an uncle of Chief Justice John Marshall), came either in 1779 or 1780, and settled first in Lincoln county, then in Shelby. Joseph Barnett, John Whitaker, and John Garrard soon followed and located in Hardin county. The three Craig brothers, Lewis, Elijah, and Joseph, were in Kentucky early in the Eighties.

The first Baptist church in Kentucky (and this means the first church of any kind) was constituted at Severn's Valley, about half a mile from the present limits of Elizabethtown, on June 18, 1781. The organization took place under the shade of a sugar tree, and there were thirty-seven members enrolled. On July 4th, a little more than two weeks later, Cedar

Creek church, in Nelson county, was constituted. This church was about five miles southwest of Bardstown. The third Baptist church in the State was the Gilbert's Creek church, about two-and-a-half miles from Lancaster, in what is now Garrard county. This was not the first church in Kentucky, as is erroneously stated by several historians. When dates are consulted the error is quickly disclosed. But the history of this church is very interesting. It was first constituted in Virginia, but was afterwards moved to Kentucky *as a church*. It was known in Virginia as the Upper Spottsylvania church, but in the latter part of 1781, almost the entire membership, together with the pastor, Lewis Craig, emigrated to Kentucky in a body. They came as an organized church—organized when they started, and the organization remained intact throughout the journey. They transacted church business while on the road. This "traveling church" reached the Gilbert's Creek neighborhood late in the year 1781. "About the 1st of December they passed through Cumberland Gap . . . and on the second Lord's Day in December, 1781, they arrived in Lincoln (now Garrard) county, and met as a Baptist church of Christ at Gilbert's Creek. Old William Marshall preached to them, with their pastor, the first Sunday after their arrival." (Dr. S. H. Ford, in the Christian Repository, March, 1856).*

---

*One of the most remarkable migrations in our history was that of the Traveling Church, a body of six hundred souls, who left their homes in Spottsylvania county, Va., near Fredericksburg, September, 1781, and came bringing their live-stock and the treasures of their church for which they had suffered so terribly, their books, records, communion service, and even their Bible from the pulpit as they followed their Moses into this land of Canaan. They were cheered along the way by their happy hearted slaves, who picked their banjoes and sang their

Other Baptist churches followed in rapid succession. "In 1781, three Regular Baptist churches were organized. At the close of the year 1785, there had been constituted in Kentucky eighteen churches—eleven Regular Baptists, and seven Separate Baptists. There were in the new country, at the same period, at least nineteen Regular Baptist preachers, and seven Separate Baptist preachers. These churches and preachers occupied the whole of the country then settled. Wherever there was a settlement formed, some of these valiant soldiers of Christ hastened to occupy it in the name of the Master." (Spencer, p. 103). Thus early and thus completely did the Baptist church entrench itself among the pioneers of our State.

The number of Baptists who came into Kentucky with the first influx of population was large, and the number of Baptist preachers coming at that early date was surprisingly so. Under their ministry many of the most prominent families became Baptists before any other denomination was on the ground. It is not to be

merry tunes or rested the tired little children by "toting" them on their shoulders as they plodded along their weary way, week after week, holding divine worship, singing hymns, ministering to the sick, burying the dead, comforting the sorrowing, protecting the helpless, and finally establishing the Baptist Church in the wilderness.

The leadership of this great body was in the hands of the Rev. Lewis Craig and Capt. William Ellis, but the story would be incomplete without that of "Old Captain" or Peter, who belonged to Joseph Craig, and ministered to his own colored brethren. In later years, he hired himself to John Maxwell and lived in his cabin at the Maxwell Springs (on what is now the campus of the University of Kentucky) at Lexington. He organized the first African Baptist Church at Lexington, and ministered unto it until his death in 1823."—Mrs. W. T. Lafferty.

wondered at that this denomination early acquired a lead in members, ministers, and congregations, or that it has held that lead to the present day. While we doubt the statement that they have more members in Kentucky today than all the other denominations put together, they do have much the largest membership of any, and they have filled an important place in the religious life of the State. They have always been active in promoting revivals and in evangelizing new communities. The first revival of religion in Kentucky was among the Baptists of old Providence church, in Clark county, not far from Boonesboro. It is worthy of note that, in 1786, a Baptist church was established by Lewis Craig at Bryant's Station, a few miles from Lexington, and that Ambrose Dudley became its first pastor. He was elected to this place in August, 1786, and ministered to the congregation for fifty years. He was succeeded by his son, Thomas P. Dudley, who held the position until his death in 1886. Thus father and son were pastors of this church for one hundred years.

The Presbyterians were the next to enter this new field. Mention has already been made of the fact that Judge Henderson, Benjamin Logan, the McAfees, and others were "Blue Stocking Presbyterians." Quite a number of other prominent families holding to this religious order had established homes about Danville, Harrodsburg, on Cane Run, and in the Forks of Dick's river. Rev. Tera Templin arrived at an early date, and preached in various places, but at this time he was only a licentiate, unordained, and he established no churches. He received ordination later at the hands of the first Presbytery that met in Kentucky, in 1786, preached for a number of years, and lies buried at Bardstown, Kentucky.

David Rice, known as the Father of Presbyterianism in Kentucky, visited the State in 1782. He was from Virginia. The child of poor parents, he struggled against great odds in his efforts to secure an education. At last, with the help of friends, he graduated from Princeton College, and entered the ministry. He preached for a while in North Carolina, then returned to Virginia and took charge of a congregation to whom he preached for four or five years. He finally took charge of three congregations in Bedford county, one of which was The Peaks of Otter, where he remained for several years.

Having married, a large family sprang up about him, and he felt keenly the obligation to care for them. With a view to securing land, the better to provide for those dependent upon him, he came to Kentucky and spent some time in looking over the situation. He preached as he had opportunity, but bought no land. He says:

I saw that the spirit of speculation was flowing in such a torrent that it would bear down every obstacle that stood in its way. I looked forward to fifty or sixty years, and saw the inhabitants engaged in very expensive and demoralizing litigation about their landed property. I knew the make of my own mind, that I could not enjoy the happiness of life if engaged in disputes and lawsuits. I therefore resolved to return home without securing a single foot of land.

As he returned to Virginia, he met upwards of a thousand people moving to Kentucky, so great was the migration in this direction. It was not long until he received a petition, signed by three hundred men, asking him to come back to this State and officiate as a minister here. He put the matter before his Presbytery and they thought it a call of Providence. He decided to accept the invitation, and reached Kentucky with his family in October, 1783. He found the people greatly demoralized and in wretched spiritual condition. He says:

> After I had been here some weeks and had preached at several places, I found scarcely one man and but a few women who supported a creditable profession of religion. Some were grossly ignorant of the first principles of religion, some given to quarrelling and fighting, some to profane swearing, some to intemperance, and perhaps most of them totally negligent of the forms of religion in their homes. Thinking it unwise to form a church out of such material, he decided to wait a year before doing so, in the meantime preaching and laboring with the people to bring them to a better spiritual state. At the commencement of the second year all was to begin anew. With a good deal of difficulty, however, a congregation was organized in what is now Mercer county, with as much formality as their distance from other regular churches and other disadvantages would admit. They had three places of worship which were known by the names of Danville, Cane Run, and the Forks of Dick's river.

If these quotations are to be relied upon, it was not until 1784 that the first Presbyterian church in Kentucky was organized, though several preaching places had been established as early as 1783. The quotations are taken from "An Outline of the History of the Church in the State of Kentucky During a Period of Forty Years, Containing the Memoirs of Rev. David Rice." The book is by Prof. Robert H. Bishop, Professor of History in Transylvania University, published in 1824, and its statements may be accepted as correct. This first church of this denomination was the Cane Run church, in Mercer county, near where Burgin now stands. Father Rice was a man of considerable ability, somewhat irascible and impatient, but a good man and did a noble work in laying the foundations of Presbyterianism in Kentucky. He finally left Danville and moved to Greensburg, where he died.

On October 1, 1784, Rev. Adam Rankin arrived in Lexington. Quite a number of Presbyterians had preceded him to that place, and he at once found himself surrounded by a considerable congregation. Soon afterwards, he took charge of a congregation gathered at Pisgah, just over the line in Woodford county; and in a little while he had organized churches at Paint Lick, in Garrard, and at Salem, in Clark county. Unfortunately, Mr. Rankin became deeply involved in the controversy over the use in the Presbyterian churches, of Watt's version of the Psalms, taking such extreme ground that he denied the right of communion to all who used this version instead of the old version. Several congregations in Kentucky divided over this controversy, and, the Presbytery having issued a process against him embracing several charges, Mr. Rankin renounced the jurisdiction of the Presbytery, led a faction of seceders, and finally gave strong evidence of an unbalanced mind.

While there were not so many Presbyterian as Baptist preachers in the State, they were exceedingly zealous, and, by 1786, there were almost as many Presbyterian churches in Kentucky as there were Baptist churches, though as a rule they were not so large. Perhaps the Presbyterians never made the popular appeal to the masses of the people that the Baptists did. By this time they were ready for the organization of a Presbytery, and, on Oct. 17, 1786, five ministers and several lay representatives from twelve Presbyterian churches, met in the Court House at Danville, and organized the Transylvania Presbytery. David Rice was Moderator and Andrew McClure, of Paris, was Clerk. The Presbyterian church in Kentucky has not grown as might have been expected. Perhaps there are not at this time as many as fifty thousand Presbyterians in all the branches of that Church in the State. They have done a great work, however, not only by their ministry, but by promoting educational interests in the State. The first session of Transylvania Academy, afterwards Transylvania University, was taught in the home of David Rice, between Harrodsburg and Danville, and while it was not, for several years, a church institution, he was Chairman of its Board of Trustees. Another academy was established at an early date at Pisgah, in Woodford county, but was later merged with Transylvania. Through Transylvania University, Centre College, and other colleges and academies, they have done a notable work for the intellectual life of the State, as well as in other departments of Christian service.

Prior to the American Revolution, the Church of England supplied Virginia and some other colonies with a ministry, and the churches they served constituted the Established Church in these colonies. But during the long struggle for independence, nearly all these clergymen, being from England and sympathizing with the British cause, found it so uncomfortable here that they fled to the Mother Country, leaving the churches in America not only in want of pastors, but with a strong prejudice against the Church on account of its Toryism. This was specially true in the new West, many of the people having suffered persecution at the hands of these clergymen while in Virginia prior to the beginning of the war.

It is not easy to give the exact date of the beginning of the Protestant Episcopal Church in Kentucky. This Church is not identical with the Church of England, but is a child of it. Marshall, in his History of Ken-

tucky, tells us that "there were in this country, and
chiefly from Virginia, many Episcopalians, but these
had formed no church, there being no parson or minister to take charge of such." Johnson's History is authority for the statement that the first Protestant Episcopal church in Kentucky was founded in 1794, "but
there was not an organized parish until 1809." This
church has never been strong in Kentucky. While
there are now two Episcopal dioceses in the State, outside of the larger cities their churches are few and
small.

A few Roman Catholics were in the party which accompanied James Harrod on his return to Harrodsburg
in the spring of 1775, and were, therefore, among the
earliest permanent settlers in the State. Rev. Thomas
J. Jenkins, of New Hope, Ky., long a priest of the Roman Catholic Church, in a letter to the author of "A
History of Kentucky and Kentuckians," says: "William
Cooms' family and Dr. Hart, with a small contingent
of Catholics, joined Harrod's party of forty, who descended the Kentucky river to found Oldtown (now
Harrodsburg), in 1774. Cooms and Hart removed close
to Bardstown, to be close to their Catholic brethren."
This statement can hardly be taken at face value. Harrod's party did not *descend* the Kentucky river in 1774
in order to found Oldtown"; and if by "Wm. Cooms'
family," Father Jenkins means to include Mrs.
Cooms, then the statement runs directly coun-
ter to the well-established fact that there were no
women in the new settlement prior to the fall of 1775.
Yet Mrs. Cooms was at Harrodsburg at an early date,
and taught the first school in Kentucky in 1776. Quite
a number of Catholics settled in Nelson county, and according to some of Kentucky's historians, built their

first church at Holy Cross, in 1792. Many other communicants of this church came at a later date, and took
up their homes in Nelson, Washington, and Marion
counties. They are perhaps the predominant religious
body in that section today, though outside the larger
cities they are not strong in other parts of the State.

The Cumberland Presbyterians, Disciples, Luther-
ans, and other denominations entered at later periods,
and each will receive notice when we come to treat of
the religious movements which lead to their organization. This brief account of the religious beginnings in
Kentucky, will enable us the better to understand the
environment and conditions under which Methodism
came into the State, and has carried forward its work.
All the denominations in this field have had their trou-
bles. Contentions and divisions have weakened and
discouraged them. There has been much denominational rivalry. Kentucky has not been an easy field for
cultivation by any of them, and the great difficulties
under which they have labored will become apparent as
we proceed with our history.

CHAPTER II

ENTER METHODISM

It would be interesting to know who was the first Methodist to come to Kentucky. But who he was, when he arrived, where he came from, and where he settled, are matters of history that lie forever buried in a forgotten past. Of one thing, however, we are certain: There were no Methodists among those first immigrants who came to Harrodsburg, Boonesboro and Saint Asaph's, for the very good reason that the pioneers of that migration were from the "back countries" of Virginia and North Carolina, and Methodism had not reached those "back countries" at that time. Methodism had its birth in England, when, on the night of May 24, 1738, John Wesley "felt his heart strangely warmed." Twenty-five years later the movement reached America. Robert Strawbridge, an Irish local preacher, came to this country and settled in Maryland. In 1763, he gathered together a group of fourteen persons and organized them into a Methodist "Society," the first to be organized in America. This was on Sam's Creek, (or Pipe Creek, as it was near that stream), in the then backwoods of Maryland.*

---

*While holding a Conference on Pipe Creek, in the neighborhood of the meeting house built by Strawbridge, Bishop Asbury says: "The settlement on Pipe Creek is the richest in the State. Here Mr. Strawbridge formed the first society in Maryland—and America."—Journal, April 30, 1801. There has been much discussion over the question whether this society or that

19

A rude log meeting house was erected, and for several years it was used by the Methodists as a place of worship.†

In 1766, Philip Embury, another Irish local preacher, established old John Street Church, in the city of New York, the second Methodist "Society" in the new world. Thus it will be seen that, at the time Kentucky was first settled, Methodism had been in existence only thirty-seven years, and in this country only twelve years. The movement here, as in England, encountered fierce opposition from many sources, and its growth for a time was slow. When Kentucky first became the home of white men, there was but a handful of Methodists in America. There were only ten preachers and about two thousand members, and fully half of these were in Eastern Maryland. There were only three

of John Street, New York, was first organized. A commission appointed by the General Conferences of the M. E. Church, M. E. Church, South, and the Methodist Protestant Church, after gathering all possible evidence bearing on the question, unanimously decided in favor of the Sam's Creek organization. This should settle the question, though some in the M. E. Church refuse to be convinced.

†In the Western Christian Advocate of Nov. 11, 1836, there is a letter from Rev. James Quinn, in which he says: "In the first year of the present century I was admitted into full connection, and received deacon's orders as a member of the Baltimore Conference, which held its session that year on Pipe Creek, Md., in the very neighborhood where Robert Strawbridge preached and raised his first society. Some of his members were then living, and in 1827, I buried Daniel Stephenson, in Ohio, who made one of Strawbridge's fourteen members. He was grand uncle of Rev. E. Stephenson, of Kentucky, and great-grand uncle of Rev. Evan Stephenson, of Ohio Conference. So that Methodism has lived in that family for four generations. The last words of old father Strawbridge were: 'My work is done, and I go in peace.' "

hundred in Virginia, practically all of them along the Eastern shore. Middle and Western Virginia and North Carolina had none at all.

During the American Revolution, every form of religious faith suffered from the confusion and violent passions of the times. Unreasoning prejudices inflamed the minds of many, and lawless brute force ran riot throughout the land. Methodists were subjected to a most bitter and senseless persecution. Methodist preachers were mobbed and almost beaten to death. Freeborn Garretson was beaten into insensibility. Joseph Hartly was sent to jail. Caleb Pedicord was whipped and badly hurt, and carried his scars to his grave. One preacher was coated with tar and feathers. Others suffered many things at the hands of their persecutors. As a consequence, all of those preachers sent over from England by Mr. Wesley returned to their homeland, except Francis Asbury; and he was driven into hiding for about two years. Nevertheless, a native ministry was raised up, and considerable advancement was made. In 1782, just before the close of the war, and seven years after the settlement of Boonesboro, the Conference Minutes show in all America, a total of eighty-two preachers and a membership of 13,740. By this time zealous evangelists had pushed beyond the first mountain ranges and had laid the foundations of Methodism in the Valley of Virginia and in Middle and Western North Carolina. A constituency was thus created from which Methodism might draw in future migrations to the West.

The War of the Revolution ended in 1783. Peace having been made, and the Indians being temporarily off the war path, there was a great rush of emigrants from the colonies toward the western frontier. Thousands of families took up their journey to Kentucky. "Kentucky in 1779 had but one hundred and seventy-six white men, but by 1784, the population had gone far up into the thousands, and each month brought hundreds of new settlers, over the mountains from North Carolina, or down the Ohio from Pennsylvania and Virginia." (Sweet). It is estimated that, in 1783, there were 12,000 white people in this territory. In the following year something like 30,000 immigrants arrived. On the crest of this wave was borne, along with other adventurous souls, a number of Methodist families.

Among these Methodist families, and possibly first among them, were the families of Francis Clark and John Durham. They were from Mecklenburg county, Virginia. They had been neighbors and co-workers in the Old Dominion, and upon reaching Kentucky they bought land and settled in the same neighborhood in what was then Lincoln, now Boyle, county, about six miles west of Danville, on the road to Perryville. In removing to the new country they did not leave their religion behind them. Francis Clark was a local preacher, and John Durham was a class-leader in Virginia, and soon again they were working together in the Master's service. Redford, in his "History of Methodism in Kentucky," tells us that Clark was accompanied to Kentucky not only by his friend Durham, "but by others of his neighbors," and that "he immediately organized a class, the first in the far West." It is probable that some of these neighbors who came with him from Virginia were already Methodists, and that they formed the nucleus of the class which he gathered here in the wilderness. But a man of Clark's zeal could not be content merely to gather together those who were already converted; he must preach the gospel to the unsaved also. This he did and gathered new converts into the fold. As early as 1784, according to Redford, Mrs. Mary Davis, Redford's wife's grandmother, was converted under Clark's ministry, and joined this first society in the State. She remained a Methodist for seventy-four years. It is very probable that Mrs. James Harrod, wife of the founder of Harrodsburg, was also converted under Clark's ministry. She lived only two or three miles from his home, and it is known that she was converted as early as 1785 or 1786, when there were not more than two Methodist preachers in the State. She lived an ardent Methodist until 1843, when she died at the age of eighty-seven. Her house was a preaching place, and a home for the early Methodist itinerants.

Clark organized this first "society" in Kentucky some time during the year 1783. He was a man of good ability and possessed an abounding zeal for the cause of Christ. Speaking of him, William Burke, who has given us much of our information about early Methodism in this State, says:

Francis Clark, a local preacher from old Virginia, settled in the neighborhood of Danville, Mercer county [then Lincoln, now Boyle], and was among the first Methodists that emigrated to the country. He was a man of sound judgment, and well instructed in the doctrines of the Methodist Church. As a preacher he was successful, and was made the instrument of forming several societies, and lived many years to rejoice in the success of the cause he had been the instrument, under God, of commencing in the wilderness. He died in his own domicil, in the fall of 1799, in great peace, and in hope of a blessed immortality. I attended his funeral in connection with the Rev. Francis Poythress, and at his request I preached from these words: "For me to live is Christ, but to die is gain." (Sketches of Western Methodism, pg. 63).

In his "Pictures of Early Methodism in Ohio," Mr.
Samuel Williams tells us that the earliest Methodist
sermon "preached in the Southwest part of that State,
was preached by Francis Clark, a local preacher from
Danville, Ky., and the pioneer of Methodism in that
place. He visited Fort Washington (Cincinnati) in
1793; and, like Paul at Athens, 'his spirit was stirred
within him,' when he beheld the godlessness of the
troops, and the wickedness of the citizens. Through
the intervention of a friend, he obtained the privilege
of preaching in the Fort, where he delivered his message from God faithfully and fearlessly." (Page 38).
John Kobler is credited with being the first Methodist
preacher to visit Cincinnati, and John Collins with
preaching the first Methodist sermon in that place.
But this sermon by Francis Clark was preached five
years before Kobler's visit, and more than ten years
before Collins came to that city. Thus did Francis
Clark introduce Methodism, not only in Kentucky, but
also in southwestern Ohio. Though only a local preacher
and never ordained, he was abundant in labors, building up the kingdom of the Lord in this western country.
He was a good farmer, much interested in improving
the breed of stock in his neighborhood, and in every
sense a good and thrifty man. An inventory of his
estate, on record in the Clerk's office at Harrodsburg,
evidences the fact that he owned a good farm and several slaves, and that he prospered in the things of this
world as well as in spiritual affairs. "Not slothful in
business; fervent in spirit; serving the Lord."

It is to be regretted that we do not know more than
we do about John Durham, the class-leader, in whose
home this first society in the West was organized. It
is generally understood that he and Clark came to Ken-

tucky together, though Redford thinks he came in 1781, and Clark in 1783. They were friends and co-workers in Virginia, were close neighbors in Kentucky, and shared together the honors of establishing the cause of Christ in the community in which they established their homes. In the early days of Methodism, a class-leader was about as important as a preacher. Each "society" was divided into classes of about a dozen each, and a "leader" was appointed over them. It was his duty to meet his class at least once every two weeks, to question them closely as to their religious progress, and to instruct, reprove and exhort them in their efforts to live as Christians. He was the spiritual nursing-father of the young convert, and a faithful class-leader who cared for and nourished the converts was a close second to the preacher whose ministry had awakened and won those converts to Christ.

John Durham was the progenitor of a large and most excellent family. His son, Benjamin Durham, was one of the truly great laymen of his day, and to him as much as to any man, is due the rapid growth of Methodism in that section of the State. A grandson, the Hon. Milton J. Durham, was a Judge of the Circuit Court of his District, a member of Congress, and Comptroller of the Treasury under President Cleveland. A long line of descendants have added much to the sterling character of our country's citizenship, and have contributed much to the power and influence of the Church in this and other States. John Durham's home was, beyond doubt, the cradle of Methodism in the Great West. The "Society" gathered in his humble cabin, worshipped there for several years, and became the center about which was gathered the old Danville circuit. A few years later a log meeting house was

erected on Durham's land, and this, in turn, gave way
to a more pretentious building, known as "Durham's
Chapel," or "The White Meeting House." A great camp
meeting site was established on Durham's farm where
hundreds of souls were born into the Kingdom of God.
In 1858, after a gracious revival in the town of Perryville, less than three miles away, the congregation
which worshipped at Durham's Chapel was merged
with the congregation at Perryville, and thus that
church became the successor of this first "society" in
Kentucky.*

Not long after Clark and Durham began their labors in Kentucky, they were joined by the Rev. William
J. Thompson, who, though a native of Maryland, is said
to have come to Kentucky from Stokes county, North
Carolina. He settled in the neighborhood of Clark and
Durham, and was soon engaged with them in preaching
the gospel to the pioneers about them. He was an acceptable preacher, and was greatly blessed in building
up the infant Church in this part of the State. After
serving for several years as a local preacher, he was
ordained a deacon by Bishop Asbury in 1800, and in
1804, was admitted on trial in the old Western Confer-

*Mrs. J. H. Spilman, of Harrodsburg, Ky., so well known
throughout the Church and State for her brilliant service in
the pulpit and on the platform, is a great-great-granddaughter
of Rev. Francis Clark. She is one of the really great women of
the M. E. Church, South. Rev. Henry Clay Morrison, D. D.,
evangelistic preacher, editor, and college president, is a great-
great-grandson of John Durham. His reputation as a preacher
is world-wide. Many other splendid Christian men and women
have sprung from these two pioneers, and are still enriching
Methodism by their godly living and devoted service. Dr. W.
B. Godbey, evangelist and author of many books, married a
granddaughter of John Durham.

ence. For two years he served the Danville circuit, in the bounds of which he lived. He then located, and subsequently removed to Ohio; joined the Ohio Conference, and gave several years of successful service to building up the work of the Lord in that new territory. Doubtless it was to Clark and Thompson that David Rice refers when he tells us that "about the same time (1784) two Methodist preachers came to the country, who, though they were rather passionate in their addresses, they seemed to be men of tender catholic spirits, and advocates of good morals."

It is not certain that Willis Green was a Methodist before coming to Kentucky. He came at an early date. He was born and reared in the Shenandoah Valley, in Virginia, and came to Kentucky as a surveyor. He represented Kentucky in the Legislature of Virginia, and after Kentucky became a State, served in the Legislature here. He was for many years clerk of the court of Lincoln county and filled many offices of trust. He was one of the most valuable of the State's citizens in his day. He was one of the trustees of Transylvania Seminary. Afterwards he was one of the chief promoters of Bethel Academy, and a member of its Board of Trustees. His son, Rev. Lewis Warner Green, D. D., became a Presbyterian minister; was President first of Hampden-Sydney College, in Virginia, then of Transylvania College, which position he resigned in 1858 in order to become President of Center College at Danville. Willis Green was a devoted Methodist, and his home, in Lincoln county, was one of Asbury's stopping places and the home of many a weary itinerant preacher.

The Kavanaughs came at an early day to Madison county, and bore an important part in the beginnings

of Methodism in the State. Few families have given
more men to the Methodist ministry than has this family.

Another Methodist family came to Kentucky at an
early date—the family of Thomas Stevenson. They
came from Maryland. Daniel Stevenson, an uncle of
Thomas, was one of the fourteen Methodists gathered
by Robert Strawbridge into that first Methodist Society in America. Sarah Stevenson, wife of Thomas,
united under Strawbridge in 1768, and her husband ten
years later. Some time prior to 1786, they emigrated
to Kentucky, coming down the Ohio river and landing
at Limestone, now Maysville. They lived for several
months in Kenton's Station, three miles back of Maysville and a little north of the Lexington road. When,
in 1786, Benjamin Ogden, one of the two first Methodist missionaries sent to Kentucky, reached the State, he
soon found his way to Stevenson's cabin home, and at
his hospitable fireside, offered up the first prayer ever
made by a Methodist itinerant at a family altar in Kentucky. Stevenson later purchased a farm west of the
town of Washington, Mason county, where his home
became a regular preaching place, and where a great
camp meeting was held year after year, where hundreds of souls were born into the kingdom of God. The
home of Thomas Stevenson was undoubtedly the birth-
place of Methodism in Northern Kentucky.

When Francis Clark organized his society in 1783,
Kentucky was a part of Virginia, and did not become a
separate State until nine years later.

It is well also to remember that Methodism, when
it was introduced into Kentucky, was not a *Church;* its
groups were only "Societies," or associations of men

and women seeking their own salvation and the salvation of others. Mr. Wesley did not promote the Methodist movement with any idea of starting a new Church, but of reviving those already in existence. Membership in the Methodist "societies" was perfectly consistent with membership in any of the orthodox Churches. When the movement was brought to America, the groups gathered were only so many units of the Wesley movement, were connected with the societies in England and directed by Mr. Wesley the same as they. But the success of the American arms in the War of the Revolution changed the entire situation. The colonies were no longer bound to England. The people, in their political relations, were entirely severed from England, and were now an independent nation. It was utterly impossible to keep the societies here in connection with those beyond the sea. Besides, it was necessary that they have leaders of their own, and ministers who could freely administer the ordinances of Baptism and the Lord's Supper to the members. So Mr. Wesley himself authorized the establishing of a CHURCH in America, and the historic "Christmas Conference," held in Baltimore, December 24, 1784, organized the American "Societies" into "The Methodist Episcopal Church in America." Clark's organization in the home of John Durham, and other societies organized by him, were at first only *Methodist Societies;* but upon the organization of the Methodist Episcopal Church in America, they went, along with other societies, into that Church.*

It will enable us to better understand the task of Methodism in Kentucky if we pause long enough to consider the conditions under which it entered and prosecuted its work in this western field. Its triumphs were not easy. They were won only after the most stupendous difficulties were surmounted and the most persistent opposition was overcome.

1. The country was yet new and wild. Towns with which we are so familiar at the present day were not then in existence, or else were but small groups of wretched log cabins. Long stretches of unbroken forest lay between blockhouses and stations. Except for buffalo traces or blazed trails there were no roads. The only modes of travel were on foot and horse back. The woods abounded in bears and wolves, wild cats and panthers, while savages still lurked in the bushes and cane brakes to murder and rob. Men went to church with their rifles on their shoulders, and not infrequently they were ambushed on their way. Two of our preachers were murdered by the Indians. The messengers of God had to make their way through the wilderness at the peril of their lives* Seldom could they have an escort, but they rarely went armed. Often they were overtaken by night in the forest, and, weary and hungry, with saddle blanket for a bed and saddlebags for a pillow, were compelled to sleep under the stars, trusting God to keep them from the maw of wild beasts and from the scalping knives of savage men. In searching for the scattered cabins of the pioneers, long distances had to be traveled, dangerous streams had to be crossed, and hardships of every kind endured. An itinerant preacher, in serving his circuit one year, had to swim the Big Sandy river or its tributaries two

---

*The word "Society" was for a long time retained in Methodist parlance to designate a church or congregation of Methodists. It was not infrequently used by other denominations to designate their organizations.

hundred times. The average life of a pioneer preacher was less than seven years.

2. The moral conditions to be faced were indeed desperate. As already stated, there were among these early settlers some very excellent people, who brought with them from the older States a considerable degree of culture and refinement. But even these became woefully demoralized in the new country. David Rice has told us of the evil spirit of speculation and land-madness which had taken possession of the people, and how they had given themselves over to quarreling and fighting, Sabbath breaking, drinking, and such like, until he was unwilling to organize a church out of such material. Infidelity was very prevalent among the more educated, and beastliness was frightfully common among the ignorant and less refined.

It was with this mass of godlessness and spiritual deadness that Methodism had to contend. It had no compromise to make with sin. It unsparingly denounced the habit and love of wickedness, and imperiously demanded that the "wicked forsake his way, and the unrighteous man his thoughts; and let him return unto the Lord." But it held forth a gospel which was indeed the "power of God unto salvation to every one that believeth." It gave assurance that Christ died for all men, and that even the most desperately wicked would infallibly be saved if they would repent and believe on the Lord Jesus Christ. But they must repent

---

*Writing to Bishop Coke four years after this, James Haw, the first Methodist missionary to Kentucky, said: "Observe, No man must be appointed to this country that is afraid to die. For there is now war with the Indians, who frequently lurk behind the trees, shoot the travelers, then scalp them; and we have one society on the very frontiers of the Indian country."

and believe. This gospel of the love of God for lost sinners, and the universal redemption made by Christ on the Cross, broke the hard hearts of some wicked men and women, but aroused the intense hostility of others.

3. Besides this grapple with sin in its basest forms, and the necessity of breaking down the prevailing skepticism of the day, early Methodism had to battle fiercely with the extreme Calvinism of the Baptist and Presbyterian churches which were already on the field. These Churches were then intensely Calvinistic. Calvin taught that "Predestination" is "the eternal decree of God, by which He hath determined in himself what He would have to become of every individual of mankind. . . . Eternal life is foreordained for some, and eternal damnation for others." According to this system, God loved, and Christ died for, the elect, but not for reprobates; no salvation was provided for them. Nor did this mean that God merely *passed by* the non-elect, without foreordaining them to eternal damnation. As Calvin says, "this is puerile and absurd, because election itself could not exist without being opposed to reprobation; whom God passes by he therefore reprobates, and from no other cause than his determination to exclude them from the inheritance which he predestines for his children." When this doctrine was coupled, as it always was, with the doctrine of "Once in grace, always in grace," it can readily be seen that it begat no spiritual concern on the part of the sinner, nor did it minister to moral living on the part of the professed Christian. Doubtless the spiritual deadness and the outbreaking wickedness of the times were due, in some measure, to this sort of teaching.

The advocates of Calvinism very bitterly opposed

the teachers of Arminian doctrines. They inveighed against them from the pulpit and in private; they heaped upon them all sorts of misrepresentation and abuse. They cried out, "The false prophets are come!" Though he admitted that not all the believers in a universal atonement followed their system to what he considered its logical conclusion, here is Rice's formula of the downward progress: "The first step is from Calvinism to Arminianism; then from Arminianism to universalism; from universalism to Pelagianism; from Pelagianism to Semi-Pelagianism; from Semi-Pelagianism to Arianism; from Arianism to Socinianism; from Socinianism to deism; from deism to atheism!" These were the days of intense religious prejudices. Men racked their brains to find phrases and epithets strong enough to use in denouncing their opponents. What was thought to be heresy was, to these teachers, a greater sin than drunkenness or profanity. Proselyting was reduced to a fine art. Many of the converts at Methodist altars were, by one means or another, drawn into the membership of other churches."

Methodism had to fight its way against the protagonists of extreme Calvinism, and of exclusive immersion. Leaders of this new faith needed to be well grounded in the doctrines of their Church, and the works of Wesley and Fletcher were thoroughly mastered by every itinerant and local preacher. Doctrinal preaching was the staple preaching of these men. And without doubt, the progress of Methodism was due largely to their masterful expositions of the Scriptures bearing upon an unlimited atonement, and of Christ's willingness to save to the uttermost all who would believe.

Under such conditions did Methodism begin its work in Kentucky. But it had a message for the people of that day and time. The men who proclaimed that message had tested its truth and knew from their own experience that it was "the power of God unto salvation to every one that believeth." "A dispensation of the gospel was committed unto them," and they preached it without fear or favor. As they went forward, multitudes of men and women believed, and when these had "tasted of the good word of God," and had been delivered from their sins through the preaching of these men, they were bold in their testimony to the saving power of the truth. These people said: "Whereas we were blind, we now see." This kind of "case work" at last stopped the mouths of the gainsayers. Like the persecutors of the early disciples, "beholding the man which was healed standing with them, they could say nothing against it."

CHAPTER III.

COMING OF THE MISSIONARIES

The population of Kentucky was increasing by leaps and bounds. Its rich soil, its cheap lands, its abundance of game, its opportunities for building up an ample inheritance for their children, appealed to the people of the East, and they turned their faces toward this new Eldorado of the West. Thousands came, braving the dangers and hardships of the way. The eagle eye of Bishop Asbury, always scanning the horizon for new fields for Methodism, saw this rapid gathering of the multitudes in the Kentucky District, and he deemed it time to send missionaries into this field.

Accordingly, at the Conference held in Baltimore in 1786, a new circuit was created, called "Kentucky." James Haw and Benjamin Ogden were the men selected to enter the new field. Haw was the older of the two, and had had at least five years experience in the work of an itinerant. He was ordained an elder at that Conference, and was, therefore, authorized to administer the sacraments of the Church. Ogden was a young man from New Jersey, only twenty-two years of age, and just now admitted on trial. A missionary collection was taken, and money contributed to bear their expenses in reaching their new charge.

Just when they reached Kentucky, and how they came, we do not certainly know. As the Conference which sent them convened in May, we judge it must have been early in the summer that they arrived at their field of labor. We have somewhere seen the statement that they did not come together—that Haw came from Southern Virginia, (where he had served the preceding year), through Cumberland Gap and over the Wilderness Road, and would, therefore, reach the Kentucky settlements about Crab Orchard and Stanford. There can be but little doubt that Ogden came down the Ohio river, landing at Maysville. Thomas Stevenson and wife, Methodists from Maryland, had already reached Kentucky, and had taken up their residence at Simon Kenton's Station, about three miles to the Southwest. Ogden soon found his way to their cabin home. Their son, Dr. Edward Stevenson, tells us that "the first prayer ever presented to the throne of the heavenly grace, at a family altar in the District of Kentucky, by a Methodist preacher," (itinerant) "was in my father's cottage, in the Station above named, Benjamin Ogden officiating." He further tells us that Ogden "remained several days, preaching to the people by night, and visiting and praying with the families by day, while his labors were duly appreciated by all in the garrison." And he still further informs us that "a class was associated together in" Mr. Stevenson's "little apartment, while living in Kenton's Station, in 1786, by Mr. Ogden."

No mention is made of Mr. Haw. Had he been present, being the older man and an Elder, it is inconceivable that he should not have officiated at the family altar and organized the class instead of Mr. Ogden. This is a strong indication that they were not together at that time, and that they came to Kentucky by separate ways.

After a short stay at Kenton's Station, Ogden was guarded through the intervening wilderness to Central

Kentucky, and he and Haw soon met and plunged into the great task assigned them. We know they visited Fayette, Madison, Garrard, and Mercer counties, for they left converts behind them in each of these counties. In his "Recollections of the West," Rev. Lewis Garrett informs us that "a mighty revival of religion commenced" under their ministry, "and the flame spread 'like fire in dry stubble.'" Much of the year was spent in seeking out and locating the scattered Methodists, and in establishing preaching places in the humble homes of the people. At the end of the year they reported *ninety* members organized into classes.

Naturally the reader will want to know about these men, who first came as Methodist missionaries into this great Western region. We have no information as to when and where James Haw was born. It has been erroneously stated that he was *received on trial* by the Conference in 1782. The General Minutes do not say so. His name is not in the list of those received on trial that year, but it is specifically stated that he was then *"received into connection,"*—that is, he became a full member of the Conference at that time. There is no record when he was admitted on trial, but it is stated that, at the Conference of 1781, he was appointed, with Beverly Allen, to the Isle of Wight circuit, in Southwestern Virginia. Doubtless he was received on trial in 1781, and received into full connection at the end of his first year, as was frequently done in those early days.

Haw then served successively on the South Branch, Amelia, Bedford, and Brunswick circuits, all in Southern Virginia. As already stated, in 1786, he was ordained *Elder* (we are not told when he was made a deacon), and sent, with Ogden as a colleague, to Kentucky.

He is described as "a man of zeal, rather bordering on enthusiasm," and was very successful for a time in winning souls. He was very devout, and the people loved him. In 1787, the Kentucky circuit was divided, and two circuits, the Kentucky and the Cumberland, were formed out of it. Haw is still "Elder," and as such, had the supervision of the whole field. In 1788, the Kentucky circuit was again divided and became the Lexington and Danville circuits, Barnabas McHenry, referring to his own work this year, says: "Soon after I reached the Kentucky settlement, which was on the 11th of June, 1788, Brother Haw formed the design of placing me on Cumberland circuit, to which he intended to accompany me and make a short stay, but before he had executed his purpose he was superceded by Brother Poythress. The consequence was that Brothers Haw and Massie went to Cumberland and I continued in Kentucky." From this it appears that Haw was not continued as *Presiding* Elder, but was superceded by Francis Poythress, and Haw went to Cumberland as preacher-in-charge with Peter Massie as his colleague.

In 1789, he is on the Lexington circuit, but in 1790, he goes back to Cumberland. This closes his labors as an itinerant preacher, for at the Conference of 1791 he located. His location was doubtless due to the fact that, during that year, he had married. His wife was a sister of General Thomas, of Nelson county, Kentucky. Marriage, in those days, usually meant a speedy location. He took up his residence in Sumner county, Tennessee, "where the people were so taken with him, they purchased for him a six-hundred-and-forty-acre tract of land. He settled on it, and in return promised to serve them as a Methodist preacher as long as he lived."

Francis Asbury

Alas! for human frailties. It was but a little while after this promise was made, that Haw became dissatisfied with the government of the Methodist Episcopal Church, began preaching against it, and zealously endeavored to persuade its members to leave it and join another organization! As we shall be compelled to frequently refer to that lamentable defection, known as the O'Kelly schism, a brief account of it is in order here.

It was the first breach in the unity of American Methodism. It was brought on by James O'Kelly, a very prominent and popular preacher in southern Virginia. O'Kelly had joined the ranks of the itinerancy as early as 1778, and was one of the thirteen preachers selected by the Christmas Conference, in 1784, for the office of elder. From that time he had continuously presided over the "South District of Virginia." The author of "Memorials of Methodism in Virginia" tells us that "he exercised great influence over the preachers and people in that part of the work, and as a leader was regarded as hardly second to Asbury." One of his contemporaries describes him as "laborious in the ministry, and man of zeal and usefulness, an advocate of holiness, given to prayer and fasting, an able defender of the Methodist doctrine and faith, and hard against negro slavery." In this he differed very little from other Methodist preachers of his day.

The Christmas Conference which organized the Methodist Episcopal Church in America, made no provision for a General Conference. In order to deal with the inevitable problems which arose in the management of the growing Church, a plan was later worked out for a "Council," composed of the Bishops and Presiding Elders. Large powers were given to this Council.

While O'Kelly was a member of it, he clearly saw that this was not a democratic form of government, but government by an oligarchy. The Bishop, having the power to appoint the Presiding Elders, could, through them, completely dominate and control the affairs of the Council. More than any other man O'Kelly was responsible for doing away with it and for calling of a General Conference in 1792. Of course O'Kelly was a member of this body.

O'Kelly has been accused of an ambitious desire to be a Bishop and of jealousy toward any one who was invested with more power than himself; and being disappointed in this ambition, tried to destroy the episcopacy. Some things gave color to this accusation. But however true or false the accusation may be, he became antagonistic toward Bishop Asbury, and deliberately set himself to trim the episcopacy of some of its powers. In the General Conference of 1792, he brought forward a resolution providing that,

"After the Bishop appoints the preachers at Conference to their several circuits, if any one think himself injured by the appointment, he shall have liberty to appeal to the Conference and state his objections, and if the Conference approve his objections, the Bishop shall appoint him to another charge."

It requires but little acumen to see what confusion and what impossible situations this would bring about. The resolution was debated long and with great candor, and was defeated by a large majority. O'Kelly was greatly offended by the defeat of his resolution. He and a few adherents immediately withdrew from the Conference, and the next day sent a letter stating that, as their resolution had been rejected, they could no longer retain their seats in the body. All efforts at conciliation were unavailing, and the disaffected breth-

ren left for home in a huff. O'Kelly immediately began
to accuse Asbury of many things and was very bitter
in his denunciations of him. He professed to see great
danger threatening Methodism, and prophesied its
speedy disintegration and ruin. He soon began to
form societies of his own, and to draw into them from
the old societies all whom he could persuade. He organized them into what he called "The Republican
Methodist Church." Quite a number of preachers, itinerant and local, and several thousand members were
gathered into the new organization. Much bitterness
was indulged. "Families were rent asunder; brother
was opposed to brother; parents and children were ar-
rayed against each other; warm friends became open
enemies; the claims of Christian love were forgotten in
the hot disputes about Church government. The
means of grace were neglected; piety declined! religion
was wounded in the house of her friends, and the enemies of Christ exulted over many who had fallen away
from the faith." It was not long until, on the motion
of Rice Haggard, who had withdrawn with O'Kelly and
who was his right hand man in the organization of the
new Church, the name was changed from "The Republican Methodist" to "The Christian Church." It
looked for a time that the Methodist Episcopal Church
would suffer great damage from the new movement,
but the violence of its promoters, and the dissensions
which soon sprang up among themselves, brought
about a reaction, and O'Kelly lived to see his movement
almost entirely disappear. Even Rice Haggard came
to Kentucky and united with Barton W. Stone, and influenced him to give the name, "The Christian Church,"
to his movement here in Kentucky.

James Haw, having joined in the O'Kelly movement, was quite active in spreading the disaffection among the local preachers and members in the Cumberland country. He was very successful for a time. Several local preachers joined him, and several "Christian" churches were established both in Tennessee and Kentucky. But when William Burke was sent to the Cumberland circuit in 1795, he met Haw in debate, and the old man was so completely routed that he lost his influence and standing in that part of the country, and "sunk down into silence, until the great revival about 1801, when he seemed to revive, joined the Presbyterians, preached occasionally, and did, it is thought, make a good end." Burke saved every society in the Cumberland circuit, except one small one, and every local preacher except one.

During the great revival on 1801, the Cumberland Presbytery became quite irregular both in the matter of doctrines and in licensing to preach young men who had not taken the required seminary training. The Synod of Kentucky sent a commission to the Presbytery to look into the matter and, if possible, to bring back the erring Presbytery to the faith and rules of the Church. One part of their report is as follows:

On the second day of their session, they took under consideration the case of Mr. James Haw, and were unanimously of opinion that the Presbytery had acted illegally in receiving him, as a regular minister of the Methodist Republican Church, without examining upon divinity, or requiring him to adopt the Confession of Faith of the Presbyterian Church. (Rice's Memoirs, Pg. 122).

Learner Blackman says that, after joining the Presbyterian Church, Haw made a public retraction of his charges against Bishop Asbury and the Methodist Church; and that he, in a measure, regained the confidence of the people, and died in the faith of Jesus.

Undoubtedly Haw was a good man, but was led into a wrong attitude toward the Church he had served so well by one in whom he reposed the utmost confidence. His son, Rev. Uriel Haw, did not go with his father, but was an honored minister of the Methodist Episcopal Church, preaching for years in Kentucky and Missouri. His great-grandson, Rev. Marvin T. Haw, D. D., is one of the leading members of the Southwest Missouri Conference.

Benjamin Ogden was born in New Jersey in 1764. Though a mere boy he served in the American army during a part of the Revolutionary War. Converted in 1784, he was admitted on trial at the Conference of 1786, and his first appointment was to Kentucky. Putnam, in his History of Middle Tennessee, describes him as "a plain, strong, effective preacher, who did much in planting Methodism in the western wilds. He was much beloved by the people, a few of whom still remain, cherishing the memory of the venerable man."

He was brave and, nerved by moral courage, he entered upon the hazardous field, and planted the standard of the cross where no other messenger of salvation had ever lifted up his voice. He was inured to hardship, and knew what it was to suffer hunger and nakedness, to be in perils in the wilderness, and to be without any certain dwelling place. When now he became a soldier of the cross, he knew how to endure hardness, and to count not his life dear unto himself so that he might win souls to Christ. —(Redford).

As we have already seen, when he came down the Ohio river and landed at Maysville, he soon found his way to Kenton's Station, and there, in the home of Thomas Stevenson, organized the first Methodist Society in northern Kentucky. Stevenson and others then guarded him through the wilderness to central Kentucky, where he and Haw were soon laboring together.

The next year he was sent to Middle Tennessee, to organize the Cumberland circuit. At the end of the year he reported the circuit formed with sixty-three members.

This was the beginning of Methodism in Tennessee west of the mountains. At the close of this year, Mr. Ogden returned to Kentucky, and, on the first day of May, 1788, James Haw married him to Miss Nancy Puckett, of Mercer county. He then returned to Virginia, and was appointed to Brunswick circuit. Redford says that he was very much broken in health and went back East at the earnest solicitation of Bishop Asbury. His lungs were affected and he "was so completely prostrated that his life was despaired of." He located, and later returned to Kentucky. Peter Cartwright says that

"He backslid, quit preaching, kept a groggery, and became wicked, and raised his family to hate the Methodists. In the year 1813, when I was on the Wabash District, Tennessee Conference, in Breckinridge county, at a camp meeting in said circuit, B. Ogden attended. There was a glorious revival of religion, and Ogden got under strong conviction, and professed to be reclaimed, joined the Church again, was licensed to preach, was soon recommended and received into the traveling connection again, and lived and died a good Methodist preacher. He was saved by mercy, as all seceders from the Methodist Church will be, if saved at all."

Evidently Cartwright was biased against Ogden, and it was hard for him to do justice to anyone he disliked. He must have been entirely mistaken in saying that Ogden raised his family to hate the Methodists. His son, Stephen Fletcher Ogden, became a faithful local preacher in the Methodist Church, and others of his family were devoted members.*

We have but little information concerning Mr. Ogden's connection with the O'Kelly movement. He lived for many years at Leitchfield, Ky., where he was engaged, at least a part of the time, in business. In February, 1801, John Durham conveyed to him by deed 500 acres of land lying in Breckinridge county, for services rendered in surveying and clearing out of the land office 1,000 acres entered in the name of John Durham. Ogden was readmitted into the traveling connection in 1817, but his health soon gave way, and he was compelled to desist from traveling. He tried again in 1824 to do the work of an itinerant and for three years traveled hard fields. In 1827, his name went upon the list of superannuates, where it remained until his death, in November, 1834. His grave is near Princeton, Ky. The General Minutes say: "He appears to have been a man of good native intellect, and various attainments as a Christian minister, and especially well instructed and deeply imbued with the principles and spirit of his vocation. He expired in all the calmness and confidence of faith and hope."

*Mrs. G. N. Hobbs, of Covington, Ky., is a great-granddaughter of Benjamin Ogden. At the General Conference at Hot Springs, Ark., in 1922, it was my pleasure to introduce Rev. Marvin T. Haw, D. D., great-grandson of James Haw, to Mrs. Hobbs.

CHAPTER IV.

When James Haw and Benjamin Ogden were assigned to "Kentucky," it meant that they were turned loose in this vast territory, and were at liberty to go anywhere in the District, preaching and organizing "classes" wherever they could. To search out the few scattered Methodists who had at that time come to Kentucky; to get them together in societies wherever possible; to get sinners saved—these were the tasks to which they applied themselves. This they did with zeal and faithfulness, and their efforts were rewarded with reasonable success. They found the Stevensons, the Clarks, the Durhams, and others; they preached in cabins, in forts, in the open air, in bar-rooms, in any places that were open to them; had a goodly number of conversions, and, at the end of the year, they reported ninety members in society. In Fayette county, Richard and Sarah Masterson were among the first fruits of their ministry, and became most valuable assistants in building up the infant Church in this new country. Richard Masterson and Sarah Shore were married in Virginia, July 29, 1784, and soon after came to Kentucky. They established their home about five miles northwest of Lexington, near where Greendale is now located. This humble log dwelling became a home for the preachers and a place where class meetings and preaching services were held. Masterson built here the first Methodist meeting house in the State. It

46

was a plain log structure, but met the needs of the day. It was here that Bishop Asbury, in April, 1790, held the first Conference west of the Alleghany mountains, and at least five other Conferences were held here prior to 1800. About 1796, Masterson sold his Fayette county farm, and removed to what is now Carroll county, where he bought a large tract of land on the Ohio river about two miles above the present town of Carrollton. He farmed on a large scale and owned many slaves. His home again became a center of Methodist influence and a resting place for McKendree and the weary Methodist circuit riders. Both he and his wife were deeply religious. He lived until March 31, 1806, when he died in the faith. His wife lingered until September 12, 1834.

Another of the converts under Haw and Ogden was Peter Massie, the first Kentuckian to enter the Methodist itinerancy, and the first of the western itinerants to die. Mrs. Jane Stamper, then of Madison county, was also converted under their ministry. Her son, Rev. Jonathan Stamper, was one of the leading preachers in Kentucky.

At the Conference of 1787 this great western circuit was enlarged by the addition of Middle Tennessee. Two circuits appear in the Minutes of this year, the Kentucky and Cumberland. Haw remained as Elder, having supervision of both circuits, while Ogden was sent to the Cumberland. This circuit did not then include Western Kentucky as it afterwards did, but "embraced, besides Nashville, all the forts and settlements on the north side of Cumberland river, extending in the direction of where Clarksville now stands, and up the stream to Gallatin and beyond." (McFerrin). Ogden was the first missionary in that part of the

State, and, as already stated, organized a circuit, reporting sixty-three members at the end of the year.

On the Kentucky circuit for this second year, we find Thomas Williamson and Wilson Lee. We are sorry we do not know more about Williamson than we do. Redford says he was admitted on trial in 1785, and that he had traveled successively the Yadkin and Salisbury circuits in North Carolina, before coming West. "He was a young man of superior talents, as well as of prepossessing manners. He was an excellent preacher. In the pulpit he commanded not only respect, but the admiration of his hearers, and in the social circle he was remarkably popular." William Burke tells us that "Thomas Williamson was a very successful and laborious preacher. He literally wore himself out in traveling and preaching, but ended his days in peace in the State of Kentucky, not far from Lexington." After this year on the Kentucky circuit, he served the Lexington and Cumberland circuits, each one year, then came to the Danville circuit for two years. His health gave way, and soon his weary body sank to rest. He was in the service seven years.

One of the ablest and best men sent to the West in those early days was Wilson Lee. He had been admitted on trial in 1784, and had labored on the Alleghany circuit, in Virginia; the Redstone, in Pennsylvania; and the Talbot, in Maryland. When he came to Kentucky he was just twenty-six years old, and in the full strength of his manhood. His early advantages had been excellent.

Reared in the midst of refinement, and surrounded by the luxuries of life, his manners polished, and possessing talents of a high order, he might have achieved eminence in any profession. But God had called him to the work of the ministry, and, following the voice of duty, he cheerfully obeyed the summons. At seventeen years of age, he embraced religion and in the morning of life entered the ministry. Familiar with the teachings of Christianity, his address handsome, a well-trained and pleasant voice, and with zeal commensurate with the importance of the work to which he had been called—added to all this, he was truly devout, and an excellent singer—his preaching was 'with the demonstration of the Spirit and with power.' Whether in his vindication of the great truths of Christianity, or in the tremendous appeals he made to the conscience, the effect was overwhelming. Success crowned his labors, and through his instrumentality many were converted to God. (Redford).

Lee remained in this western field for six years, serving successively the Kentucky, the Danville, the Lexington, the Cumberland, the Salt River, and then the Danville circuit a second time. In all these places he was "a workman who needed not to be ashamed." Many were converted under his ministry and the Church was greatly strengthened. William Burke says of him:

Wilson Lee was one of the most successful preachers among those early adventurers. He was a man of fine talents, meek and humble, of a sweet disposition, and not only a Christian and Christian Minister, but much of a gentleman. During his stay in Kentucky, from 1787 to 1792, he traveled over all the settlements of Kentucky and Cumberland, much admired and beloved by saint and sinner. In the spring of 1792, in company with Bishop Asbury, he crossed the wilderness from Kentucky to Virginia, where I met him at Conference on Holston, and from thence to the eastward, and attended the first General Conference at Baltimore, November 1, 1792, and remained in the bounds of the New York, Philadelphia, and Baltimore Conferences till he departed this life, in 1804, at Walter Worthington's, Ann Arundel county, Maryland. The last time I had the pleasure of seeing him was in Georgetown, District of Columbia, on my way to the General Conference of May 1, 1804. He was then in very feeble condition. His affliction was hemorrhage of the lungs, of which he died. During the time he traveled in Kentucky, he passed through many sufferings and privations, in weariness and want, in hunger and nakedness; traveling from fort to fort, sometimes with a guard and sometimes alone; often exposing his life; for the savages were constantly in quest of plunder and of life, and scarcely a week passed without hearing of some one falling a prey to them; and what we say of Brother Lee may be said of all the traveling preachers, as it respects their exposure and suffering, till the year 1794—the year of Wayne's campaign—when the northern Indians were held in fear and finally subdued.

It is well for us to know that into this work of founding Methodism in Kentucky was lavishly poured some of the best lives and blood of the land. While we had some rough and ignorant men in the service in those days of roughness and ignorance, Asbury sent to us some of the choicest spirits to be found in all the East. They were men among men, men who faltered not at the greatest sacrifices and sufferings in order to reach and save the lost. From his Memoir in the General Minutes we find that, after leaving Kentucky, Lee was stationed for two years in New Jersey, then was sent to New York City; then was pastor for three years in Philadelphia, and Presiding Elder of the Baltimore District for three years. "Wilson Lee was very correct in the economy and discipline of himself and others, as an elder and a Presiding Elder; and showed himself a workman that needeth not to be ashamed." He "professed the justifying and sanctifying grace of God. He was neat in his dress, affable in his manners, fervent in spirit, energetic in his ministry, and his discourses were fitted to the cases and characters of his hearers." While visiting a sick person, he was taken with a violent hemorrhage of the lungs, and died a few moments thereafter. Thus passed one of the noblest spirits that ever traversed these western wilds. It is worthy of note that, while on the Cumberland circuit, he was instrumental in the conversion of General James Robertson and wife, who were the most prominent of the settlers about Nashville and Middle Tennessee.

At the end of the Conference year of 1787-8, these faithful men report 479 white, and 64 colored members. The Church is now ready for another advance. In the Minutes of 1788, three circuits appear instead of two— the Kentucky circuit beng divided into the Lexington and Danville. The appointments are:

Francis Poythress, James Haw, Elders.
Lexington—Thomas Williamson, Peter Massie, Benjamin Snelling.
Danville—Wilson Lee.
Cumberland—David Combs, Barnabas McHenry.

This according to the General Minutes. We have already seen in a previous chapter that Barnabas McHenry did not go to the Cumberland circuit, but remained in Kentucky. David Combs was taken sick and never reached his field of labor. Poythress superceded Haw in Kentucky, and Haw went to Cumberland as preacher in charge, taking with him, as assistant, Peter Massie, from the Lexington circuit. Besides the workers already in the field, we find this year that Francis Poythress, Barnabas McHenry, Peter Massie and Benjamin Snelling are added to the list. Of Snelling but little is known. He was admitted on trial in 1788, and sent to Lexington as assistant to Thomas Williamson. The next year his name appears in connection with the Fairfax circuit, in Virginia, and the following year we find him again in Kentucky, with Barnabas McHenry on the Madison circuit. His name then disappears, though Redford tells us that he settled in Bath county, Kentucky, where he died.

As we have already seen, Peter Massie was one of the earliest converts under the ministry of the missionaries to this State. He was admitted this year, and though assigned to Lexington circuit with Williamson and Snelling, he was removed to the Cumberland circuit and labored during the year with Haw. With Barnabas McHenry he served Danville in 1789, Cumberland again in 1790, and in 1791 he was sent to the Limestone charge, but during the year he made a visit to Cumberland, and died suddenly at the home of a Mr. Hodges, about four or six miles from Nashville.*

William Burke testifies that Peter Massie, "the weeping prophet," was made

—the instrument of great good wherever he went, scattering the holy fire. His labors were so great that his race was but short. He literally wore himself out in a few years. The zeal of God's house literally consumed him. He was great and mighty in prayer, and always wished that he might die suddenly, and without lingering in pain. He labored faithfully for three years; and on the 18th of December, 1791, he was sitting in his chair at Brother Hodges', a station six miles south of Nashville, Tennessee, where he suddenly expired, in the morning about nine o'clock. So ended the labors of Brother Massie. His remains lie near the Old Station, unhonored by a single stone, and to the present generation entirely unknown; but he rests from his labors in hope of a resurrection, while his immortal spirit is in the world of bliss and glory.

---

*In the Treasurer's Book for the old Limestone circuit, which is in the hands of the writer, it is recorded that, at the Quarterly Conference which met in July, 1791, "Brother Massey" was paid, "in cash and country produce," five pounds and his expenses. At the Quarterly Conference in October, it is again recorded that he was paid so much; but at the next Quarterly Conference which was held December 24th, "Brother Haggard" takes the place of Brother Massey. This was David Haggard, who evidently was transferred from the Lexington circuit to fill the vacancy occasioned by the death of Massey.

As Peter Massie was the first of the Kentuckians to
enter the itinerant ranks, we feel disposed to linger a
little longer in giving a brief sketch of the man.   He
was converted under the ministry of Haw and Ogden
in 1786.   He was soon impressed with the conviction
that he should preach the gospel, but was unwilling to
yield to his convictions in a matter of such tremendous
importance.   He lost his religious enjoyment, but continued a member of the Church.   While in this back-
slidden condition, he, with two companions, crossed the
Ohio river, and went into the Indian country to recover some horses.   They were pursued by the Indians,
who overtook them on the banks of the river, and at
their fire both his companions fell.   Massie sprang
into a sink, and hid himself in the weeds.   He could see
the savages butchering the two men who were with
him, whom they cut to pieces and scattered the pieces
around.   In this hour of great peril he turned to God,
and promised, if his life were spared, to hesitate no
longer about entering the ministry.   He faithfully kept
his promise.   "As often as he preached, he wept over
the people.   He was styled 'the weeping prophet.'   A
writer says: 'He was a feeling, pathetic preacher.   The
sympathetic tear often trickled down his manly cheek
while pointing his audience to the Lamb of God slain
for sinners.'   His talents as a preacher were fair; his
personal appearance attractive; his voice soft and
plaintive—a good singer; fascinating in his address,
and remarkable for his zeal."   Speaking of his death,
Redford says:

He died in the bounds of the Cumberland circuit, on which
he had traveled the previous year, and to which he had gone
probably on a visit to his friends.   On the evening of the 18th
of December, 1791, he reached the house of Mr. Hodges, four

miles west of Nashville. The family of Mr. Hodges was in the fort, for protection, and Mr. Hodges himself was in his cabin, alone, and quite ill. The only person in the cabin, besides, was a negro boy named Simeon, who had on that evening escaped from the Indians, and reached the house of Mr. Hodges. Simeon had become acquainted with the preacher on the Cumberland Circuit, and had been converted through his instrumentality. Mr. Massie was 'an afflicted man.' His constitution, always feeble, had become greatly impaired by his excessive labors, and, on reaching the house of his friend, he complained of indisposition. He suffered considerably during the night, but on the next morning was able to take his place at the table. While in conversation with Mr. Hodges, it was observed to him 'that he would soon be well enough to travel, if he recovered so fast.' To which he replied: 'If I am not well enough to travel, I am happy enough to die.' These were his last words. In a few moments he fell from his seat, and suddenly expired.

The name of Barnabas McHenry was a household word among the Methodists of Kentucky for many years. "Talent, piety, preaching power, and a long and useful life, have put music into the name." "It was generally conceded that no minister in the State, of whatever denomination, occupied higher intellectual or moral rank." A distinguished statesman of Kentucky is quoted as saying: "I have known and admired many ministers of different denominations, but the only man I have ever known who even reminded me of my ideal of an apostle was Barnabas McHenry." Born in North Carolina, December 6, 1767; the son of John McHenry; removing with his father to Washington county, Virginia, when he was about eight years old; converted at the age of fifteen, he united with the Methodist Church, and at the age of nineteen, entered the traveling ministry. He was admitted in 1787, and sent to the Yadkin circuit, in North Carolina. In 1788, his name appears in the General Minutes in connection with Cumberland

FIRST METHODIST CHURCH IN KENTUCKY
Built by Richard Masterson, about 1788, five miles from Lexington

circuit, though he himself explains that this is an error, and that he stayed in Kentucky that year, probably on the Lexington circuit. He traveled successively the Danville, Madison, and Cumberland circuits, and in 1792, at the age of 25, was made Presiding Elder of a District in the Holston country, consisting of the Green River, New River, and Russell circuits.* The following year a larger District was given him in Virginia, and in 1794 and 1795 we find that he has returned to Kentucky and is on the Salt River circuit. His excessive labors and the hard life he had lived while serving these circuits and Districts, broke down his health and he was compelled to locate in 1796. Location did not mean a cessation of work, for he preached nearly every Sunday, seeking out neglected places and forming churches where no one else occupied the field. When twenty-six years of age, he was married to Miss Sarah Hardin, the daughter of Col. John Hardin, a stalwart Methodist, who was killed by the Indians while on a mission of peace to them. While in the local ranks, he taught a school for two years in the city of Frankfort. He also taught for a time in Danville, and then for a while in Richmond. He re-entered the traveling connection in 1818, but in 1821 was placed on the list of supernumeraries, and was superannuated the following year. He removed to a farm not far from Springfield, Kentucky, where he remained until his death in 1833. It was not only as an itinerant, but as a local and superannuate preacher that he built himself so largely into the esteem and affections of the people. Jacob

---

*At this time, Districts were not named. The term "Presiding Elder," appears in the General Minutes for the first time in 1789 and the Districts were first named in 1801.

Young, who served the Salt River circuit in 1801-2, relating his visit to Springfield, says: "The most distinguished man I met was Barnabas McHenry. I may truly say he was a man by himself. He was, at least, fifty years before the time in which he lived. He had not a collegiate education, but was one of the best English scholars I ever saw. I feel myself greatly indebted to that good man for the instruction I received from him at that early period of my life." He numbered among his friends, associates and correspondents, many of the most influential men of the State. Wherever he was known his influence was felt and his character commanded respect. Bishop Bascom said of him: "He was early remarkable for an admirable acquaintance with theology and a felicitous use of language in the pulpit. In both his excellence was beyond dispute, and so conversant was he with the whole range of theology as usually taught in the pulpit, and so accurately acquainted with the laws and structure of the English language especially, that his judgments, with those who knew him, had the force of law on these subjects. In the Greek of the New Testament he subsequently became quite a proficient, while his less perfect knowledge of Hebrew and Latin enabled him to consult authorities with great facility."

His preaching was mainly expository and didactic. The whole style of his preaching denoted the confidence of history and experience. All seemed to be real and personal to him. The perfect simplicity, and yet clear, discriminating accuracy of his manner and language, made the impression that he was speaking only what he knew to be true. He spoke of everything as of a natural scene before him. There was an intensity of conception, a sustained sentiment of personal interest, which gave one a feeling of wonder and awe in listening to him. You could not doubt his right to guide and teach. One felt how safe and proper it was to follow such leading. His style was exceedingly rich, without being showy . . . . His language was always accurate, well chosen, strong, and clear. All his sermons, as delivered, were in this respect fit for the press—not only remarkably free from error on the score of thought, but from defect and fault of style, and language. His whole manner, too, was natural, dignified, and becoming. Good taste and sound judgment were his main mental characteristics. Of imagination proper he had but little, and still less of fancy. Reason, fitness and beauty were the perceptions by which he was influenced. The intrinsic value of things alone attracted him. The outward show of things made little or no impression upon him, under any circumstances. The inner man—the hidden things of the heart —controlled him in all his judgments and preferences. (Bascom).

Dr. Abel Stevens, in his History of American Methodism, says he was "one of the most influential men of his Church and State. He was low of stature, square built, with a Grecian rather than a Roman face, with heavy eyebrows, a sallow complexion, and a singularly frank, generous, and noble physiognomy."

Such was Barnabas McHenry. Persons of other denominations have assiduously tried to make it appear that the early Methodists were an ignorant people, but little versed in the learning and culture of the world. The truth is that the founders of Methodism in Kentucky were the equals of any other preachers of any other denomination in the field. And as for preaching ability, they were far superior to any others of whom we know. Barnabas McHenry, Wilson Lee, Thomas Williamson, and others of the pioneers of that early day, were the peers of any with whom they came into competition.

McHenry was a victim of cholera in 1833. He died on June 15th of that year. The dread disease "reached the village near where he lived on the 9th, and he went there the next day, and visited almost every person who was sick, and prayed with them. He was taken ill on the morning of the 14th, and died at one o'clock that night. He suffered no pain, but died as if a small vein had been opened, and his life had leaked out. There was no one present but a few of his own family. His wife was extremely ill, and died a few hours after. He appeared to wish to take as little attention as possible —did not talk at all, but to inquire how his wife was— said not a word about dying, but remarked to his daughter that he wanted to be buried by Susanna, (a daughter who had died some years before). He and his wife lived together thirty-nine years, and were buried in one grave." (From a letter from his daughter to Lewis Garrett). A daughter and a granddaughter were stricken the next day, and shared a common grave, while still another daughter died of the scourge three days later.

We pause with reverence before the name of Francis Poythress.

Among the eight pioneers of Methodism in Kentucky and Tennessee in the year 1788, the name of Francis Poythress stands pre-eminent. By those intrepid heroes of the cross the foundation of Methodism was laid in those States, on which others have since built, and others are now building. Their names ought to be held in grateful remembrance by all who love the Lord Jesus Christ in sincerity and truth; but among all, we are inclined to the opinion, there is not one of them to whom the members of our Church, in those States, owe a greater debt of gratitude than to Francis Poythress. (Rev. Thomas Scott.)

A Virginian by birth; of a wealthy family; the heir to a considerable estate; rather wild and reckless in youth; brought under deep conviction by the reproof of an intelligent and pious lady of his community, he determined to mend his ways, and began earnestly to seek the salvation of his soul. But who was there to instruct him? Those were the days when spirituality was low in the Established Church, the prevailing denomination in that part of Virginia. He read his Bible, examined himself severely and sought peace in many ways, but did not find it. Finally hearing of Devereaux Jarratt, the evangelical minister of the Church of England, he visited him, and was entertained for some time under his hospitable roof. At length he found the peace that he sought. He soon began assisting Mr. Jarratt as he could, taking part in the great revival then in progress in that part of Virginia under Mr. Jarratt's evangelical preaching. It was not long ere he was preaching the gospel. This was before the Methodists had come into those parts, and he knew nothing about them. On one of his preaching excursions, however, he fell in with one of their preachers, who furnished him with a copy of the doctrines and discipline of the Methodists. He read them, and being convinced that they were founded on the Holy Scriptures, he joined the Methodists and was soon preaching among them. His conversion took place in 1772, one year before the first Methodist Conference was held in America. He was admitted among the traveling preachers in 1776, and sent to Carolina. For some reason, we know not what, his name does not appear in the Minutes of 1777, but in 1778, he is listed as one of the "Assistants," and assigned to Hanover circuit. He served various circuits until 1786, when he was ordained an elder, and at once put in charge of a District. Two years later he was brought to Kentucky by Bishop Asbury and placed in charge of the work in this great field. He remained the elder in all this vast western territory until 1797, when, on account of failing health, he is placed for one year on the supernumerary list. In 1798, he is in charge of the District in the Holston country, but in 1799, he returns to Kentucky and resumes his work as Presiding Elder here. In 1800, he is put in charge of a very large District in North Carolina, but before the end of the year he came back to Kentucky so completely broken in health that he was never able to do work again.

Poythress is described as having "the bearing of one who had been well brought up, his deportment being very gentlemanly. He was disposed to melancholy. He was an acceptable preacher, though not of the first order of talents. He was greatly gifted in prayer; when he prayed he seemed to bring heaven and earth together." The Rev. John Carr, of Tennessee, tells this anecdote concerning him:

When traveling in Middle Tennessee, which was in 1793 and years following, he sometimes found the table fare very rough; but he was never heard to complain of what was set before him. Knowing the destitution of the people, and being delicate in health, he carried with him a canister of tea. At one place he gave the canister to a good sister, that she might prepare for him a good cup of tea. She emptied the whole canister into water and gave it a good boiling as so much greens, and brought it to the table with an apology for not being able to boil it down sufficiently, when Poythress kindly remarked: "Why, sister, you have spoiled all my tea; it was not the leaves, but the juice that I wanted."

Such ignorance was not uncommon among a people who had come in contact with so little of the world, and enjoyed so few of the luxuries of life. Many a pioneer lived to an old age without ever seeing coffee or tea.

Poythress was about five feet, eight inches high, and heavily built. In early life he was a powerful man, and even in extreme old age and suffering from the severest afflictions, his step was firm and his appearance commanding. He had a high sense of honor and obligation. Though he did not rank with the greatest preachers, he excelled as an administrator. Asbury once nominated him for election as Bishop.

During his stay in Kentucky, whenever Asbury could not be present, he always presided over the sessions of the Conference and stationed the preachers. He had been in this State but a little while until he saw the need of schools in this new country, and it was through his influence and efforts more than those of any other, that Bethel Academy was promoted and built. During his last year on this western District, he traveled over nearly all of Kentucky and Tennessee, and over parts of Ohio and Virginia. When he came to this field, he found in Kentucky and Tennessee a little over 500 members; and though his administration covered one of the most trying periods in our history, he left in these States about 2,500 members. It was he who directed the forces in this formative period of Methodism in Kentucky. He did indeed "endure hardness as a good soldier of Jesus Christ." His excessive labors; his exposure; his long rides on horseback; the rude accommodations he found in the cabins in the backwoods; the rough fare; the perils of the wilderness; the dangers from wild beasts and savage men—all these broke down his strong physique, wrecked his nervous system and left him at last hopelessly insane! Symptoms of his mental derangement had been noticed at times for several years. He would occasionally lapse into a state of melancholy, and would be afflicted with strange and unfounded hallucinations. His sister, Mrs. Susan Pryor, lived in Jessamine county, about twelve miles south of Lexington, and when the complete wreck of his noble mind had been wrought, he retired to her home, and there lingered until sometime in 1818, when death brought him a happy release. The Minutes of the old Western Conference testify to the love and esteem of his brethren. In the Minutes of 1801, we find this entry:

"Whereas Francis Poythress appears to be incapable of taking a station, it is agreed to by the Conference that his name shall stand on the Minutes among the Elders; and that he shall have a proportionable claim on the Conference for his support." At the next Conference we find this item: "The Conference proceeded to take into consideration the critical, deranged state of unaccountability which Francis Poythress at present is in, and judge it best, for the safety of the Connection that his name shall be left off of the General Minutes. But at the same time are tenderly concerned for his support and welfare—and therefore Resolved, that his name shall stand on our Journal; and that he shall have a proportionable claim on the Western Conference for his support; and further it is our opinion that his name should be perpetuated on the Journals of this Conference, for the same purpose." In 1803, the Journal states, "Francis Poythress stands on our Journal as a claimant for $80.00. But it appears that he is able to support himself, and does not expect or wish his support from us. We therefore judge that he should not be considered as dependent on us."

We have searched diligently for the grave of this good man, but have been unable to find it. It is somewhere in Jessamine county, though doubtless it is unmarked. If it can be found, the Methodists of Kentucky should place over his ashes a suitable monument to commemorate the services of one of its most laborious and efficient workers.

These men who came into this western wilderness in 1788 were men of mark. They had the grace of God in their hearts and iron in their blood. Their preaching was in power and demonstration of the Spirit.

They were not afraid in time of danger; they did not falter in the face of difficulties; they did not hesitate when sacrifices were required. To them, as to St. Paul, "to live was Christ, and to die was gain." A gracious revival sprang up in the wake of their labors. The flame was first kindled by Haw and Ogden, and continued to burn with greater intensity during this year. Burke says:

This band of young resolute soldiers of the cross united under two old and experienced veterans—Francis Poythress and James Haw. Providence opened their way, and they began to make some favorable impressions upon the minds and hearts of the people. They occupied the whole ground, and, with the assistance of the few local preachers who had been there before them, they carried the war into the camp of the enemy, and in a short time a powerful and extensive revival took place. Hundreds were added to the Church; and considering the situation of the country, surrounded by a wilderness, the Indians continually making depredations on the frontiers, and the people constantly harassed and penned up in forts and stations, it may be considered among the greatest revivals that was ever known. In this revival a number of wealthy and respectable citizens were added to the Church—the Hardins, Thomases, Hites, Lewises, Eastlands, Mastersons, Kavanaughs, Tuckers, Richardsons, Letemores, Browns, Garretts, Churchfields, Jefferses, Hoards, and numbers of others of respectable standing in society; and out of this revival was raised up some useful and promising young men, who entered the traveling connection, and many of them made full proof of their ministry, and lived many years to ornament the Church of God.

The General Minutes show that the membership was more than doubled this year—863 members in the Lexington and Danville circuits, and 225 in the Cumberland. During the progress of this gracious work, writing from the Cumberland country early in 1789, James Haw addressed a letter to Bishop Asbury, which, notwithstanding its length, we shall place before our readers. It gives the best possible insight both into the character of the man and of the work that was going on. He says:

"Good news from Zion: the work of God is going on rapidly in the new world; a glorious victory the Son of God has gained, and he is still going on conquering and to conquer. Shout, ye angels! Hell trembles and heaven rejoices daily over sinners that repent. At a quarterly meeting held in Bourbon county, Kentucky, July 19 and 20, 1788, the Lord poured out his Spirit in a wonderful manner, first on the Christians, and sanctified several of them powerfully and gloriously, and, as I charitably hope, wholly. The seekers also felt the power and presence of God, and cried for mercy as at the point of death. We prayed with and for them, till we had reason to believe that the Lord converted seventeen or eighteen precious souls. Hallelujah, praise the Lord!

As I went from that, through the circuit, to another quarterly meeting, the Lord converted two or three more. The Saturday and Sunday following, the Lord poured out his Spirit again. The work of sanctification among the believers broke out again at the Lord's table, and the Spirit of the Lord went through the assembly like a mighty rushing wind. Some fell; many cried for mercy. Sighs and groans proceeded from their hearts; tears of sorrow for sin ran streaming down their eyes. Their prayers reached to heaven, and the Spirit of the Lord entered into them and filled fourteen or fifteen with peace and joy in believing. 'Salvation! O the joyful sound! how the echo flies!' A few days after, Brother Poythress came, and went with me to another quarterly meeting. We had another gracious season round the Lord's table, but no remarkable stir till after preaching; when, under several exhortations, some burst out into tears, others trembled, and some fell. I sprang in among the people, and the Lord converted one more very powerfully, who praised the Lord with such acclamation of joy as I trust will never be forgotten. The Sunday following, I preached my farewell sermon, and met the class, and the Lord converted three more. Glory be to his holy name.

The first round I went on Cumberland, the Lord converted six precious souls, and I joined three gracious Baptists to our Church; and every round, I have reason to believe, some sinners

are awakened, some seekers joined to society, and some penitents converted to God. At our Cumberland quarterly meeting,
the Lord converted six souls the first day, and one the next.
Glory, honor, praise, and power be unto God for ever! The work
still goes on. I have joined two more serious Baptists since the
quarterly meeting. The Lord has converted several more precious souls in various parts of the circuit, and some more have
joined the society, so that we have one hundred and twelve disciples now in Cumberland—forty-seven of whom, I trust, have
received the gift of the Holy Ghost since they believed; and I
hope these are but the first of a universal harvest which God
will give us in this country. Brother Massie is with me, going
on weeping over sinners, and the Lord blesses his labors. A
letter from brother Williamson, dated November 10, 1788, informs me that the work is still going on rapidly in Kentucky;
that at two quarterly meetings since I came away, the Lord
poured out his Spirit, and converted ten penitents, and sanctified
five believers, at the first, and twenty more were converted at
the second; indeed, the wilderness and the solitary places are
glad, and the desert rejoices and blossoms as the rose, and, I
trust, will soon become as beautiful as Tirza and comely as
Jerusalem.

What shall I say more? Time would fail me to tell you all
the Lord's doings among us. It is marvelous in our eyes. To
him be glory, honor, praise, power, might, majesty, and dominion, both now and forever. Amen, and amen."

At the next Conference, that of 1789, the circuits
remain the same as the preceding year, and much the
same force is retained. The names of Benjamin Snelling and David Combs disappear, and those of Stephen
Brooks and Joshua Hartley take their places. Stephen
Brooks was no ordinary man. He was born on Cape
Hatteras, N. C., but in early life removed with his
father to Hyde county, in the same State. He was educated for a seaman's life, and spent some time on the
waters, receiving a captain's commission. Though
brought up a high-churchman, he was deeply convicted
under the instrumentality of a Methodist preacher.

and was converted while praying alone in his father's cornfield. He soon gave up his life on the sea, was licensed to preach, and admitted on trial at the Conference at Newbern, N. C., in 1789. It is told of him that, near the close of the Conference at Newbern, he approached Bishop Asbury and asked where he was to be sent. The Bishop asked his name, and, on learning it, put his arms about his neck and said, "You will go with me to Kentucky." When asked if he was not afraid the Indians would kill him, he replied: "If they kill one part, they can not kill the other."

While he traveled in Kentucky the Indians were very troublesome, killed many people, and did other mischief. He was often guarded from fort to fort to preach; but God mercifully preserved him, so that he never came in contact with the savages and never saw one. During the brief period of his itinerant work he was most of the time on the frontier, was much exposed, often camped out at night or slept in open houses. Hard labor and much exposure laid in his system the foundation of much suffering in after life. (Price's "Holston Methodism.")

When he reached Kentucky he was assigned to the Lexington circuit with James Haw and Wilson Lee. In 1790 he was appointed to the Danville circuit; 1791, his name, for some reason, does not appear in the Minutes; in 1792, he served the Greene circuit in East Tennessee, and in 1793 he located and took up his residence near Greenville, in that State. He was very active and useful in his local relation, and was a delegate to the convention which drafted the Constitution of Tennessee in 1796. Rev. John H. Bruner, who had visited in his home and had often heard him preach, is quoted by Dr. Price in his "Holston Methodism" as follows:

He was a man of fine appearance and easy manners. His mind was of superior mold and burnished by extensive reading. Hence he was often put forward on camp meeting and other

ρcρular occasions. He kept abreast of the discussions of his
day, and punctured with his polished lance the skeptical theories
that came into vogue then, as such notions have been coming and
disappearing all along the ages. At his home he was a model
conversationalist, never frivolous, but interesting to the last degree. His good sense and sincerity gave weight to all that he
said. Taking him all in all, he was a man of great moral excellence, and so were his children after him. A better example
of citizenship and piety it were hard to find in any age or clime.

Two of his sons, and three of his grand sons became preachers.

Of Joshua Hartley we know but little. He was
admitted on trial in 1785, and sent to the Salisbury circuit, with that mighty preacher, Hope Hull, as his
colleague. The next year he was on the New River
circuit, but his name does not appear in the Minutes
of 1787. In 1788, he is again among those admitted
on trial, and his appointment was to Bedford circuit,
in Virginia. The next year he was received into full
connection and sent to Cumberland to aid Thomas
Williamson. His name then disappears without any
statement as to how or why.

CHAPTER V.

The holding of the first Conference in Kentucky marked a period in the history of Methodism in the State. We have noted the fact that the first "Society" was organized by Clark and Durham in 1783. We have also seen that the first itinerants, Haw and Ogden, reached the State three years later, in 1786. We have noted further that the labors of these men began immediately to bear fruit in the conversion of sinners, the organization of churches, and the extension of the work into Middle Tennessee. We have seen the membership grow from a very few to more than a thousand in the four years since the coming of these missionaries. We have given brief sketches of the eleven men who braved the dangers, endured the toils, and invested their lives in the work of the Master in this great wilderness. There are now three immense circuits, reaching almost all the settlements in this State and in Middle Tennessee. Two or three log meeting houses have been built, homes have been thrown open to the preaching of the word, several influential families have been gathered into the infant Church, and the time is now ripe for still another step in advance.

By 1790, the population of Kentucky had grown to 73,673. Of these, a little more than 61,000 were white; the rest were negro slaves, or emancipated blacks. A cluster of settlements had been established in the northern part of the State, centering in Maysville. Another cluster, with Lexington as its center, occupied the rich

Blue ·Grass in the North-Central part. Still another gathered around Harrodsburg and Danville, in the South-Central part, and yet another was forming about Greensburg. Port William (Carrollton) and the Falls of Ohio (Louisville) were also small centers of population. Between these, great stretches of primitive forest intervened, seamed only by a few buffalo traces and a few trails blazed by the adventurous pioneers. While two or three itinerants were appointed to each of the great Lexington and Danville circuits, and several local preachers—who, by this time had come into Kentucky —were employed as helpers, it was impossible to reach and adequately serve all these groups of settlements. The Lexington circuit embraced everything north and east of the Kentucky river, and the Danville everything west and south of that stream. We are not sure that Methodism had at this time, established preaching places in any of the towns mentioned. Towns, in this early day in Kentucky, were of slow growth. The opportunities were in the country, and the people, for the most part, aspired to be owners of land.

We do not know the exact dates of the arrival of several local preachers who aided in building up the Church in this State, but it was about 1790 that they came. Besides Francis Clark and W. J. Thompson, who settled in Mercer county, Nathaniel Harris and Philip Taylor settled in Jessamine; Gabriel and Daniel Woodfield in Fayette; Joseph Ferguson in Nelson; Edward Tolbert in Shelby; William Forman in Bourbon, and others in various sections. These bore a conspicuous part in preaching the gospel in the scattered settlements. Some of these men were far above the ordinary. Nathaniel Harris was a preacher of splendid ability. He came from Virginia. Having a good

English education, he taught in Bethel Academy, and was the first Principal of that school. Col. Bennett Young, in his History of Jessamine County, says of him:

Few men have ever been better known in Jessamine county than Rev. Nathaniel Harris. He was born in Powattan county, Virginia, in 1759, of Presbyterian parentage. Being an only son, he was indulged in many things, which in the end proved hurtful. His intercourse with what was then known as the gentlemen of the day, caused him to become both profane and wicked. Shortly after his father removed from the old home place, he became a volunteer in the American army, and was in the battle of Guilford Court House, North Carolina. He was converted in August, 1783, and joined the Methodist Church, and the conviction forced itself on his mind that he was called to preach. He settled in Jessamine county in 1790, and was the Principal of the English department in the Bethel Academy. . . . He died on the 12th day of August, 1849, lacking only a few days of ninety years of age. He had been in the Methodist ministry for more than sixty years.

For more than half a century Nathaniel Harris was a local preacher in the central part of Kentucky, but his services were in great demand, and he was frequently called to preach in Lexington, Frankfort, Georgetown, Danville, and other places. He joined the Conference in 1819, and was sent to Lexington Station. We shall have occasion to refer to him frequently as we carry forward the story of Kentucky Methodism.

Gabriel Woodfield was another local preacher of more than ordinary ability. He came to Kentucky at an early day, and was very helpful in building up Methodism. He lived first in Fayette, then in Shelby county. He was said to be an excellent preacher, and a very useful man. Twice he entered the traveling connection and was appointed to the Lexington and Shelby circuits.

Edward Tolbert also lived in the bounds of the Shelby circuit, and built a church which was known as "Edward Tolbert's Meeting House." He was one of the first to cross the Ohio and preach in the Indiana Territory.

Joseph Ferguson was from Fairfax county, Virginia, and came to Kentucky at an early day. He settled in Nelson county and became the center of the Methodist movement in that section of the State. He was the chief promoter in building "Ferguson's Chapel," the first church of any kind in that part of Kentucky. It was built at Poplar Flat, Nelson county, and was a round-log structure, with clapboard roof. It was the nucleus around which the Salt River circuit was afterwards formed.

Philip Taylor came to Kentucky some time not far from 1790, and he, too, settled first in Fayette county, then removed to Shelby. He was a soldier in the Continental army, and was present at the siege of Yorktown and the surrender of Cornwallis. On his way to Kentucky, while descending the Ohio river, the boat he was in was attacked by the Indians, and Taylor's arm was shattered by an Indian bullet. It was ever afterwards useless to him. He was lead away, with other local preachers, by the Methodist Protestant movement about 1830, but was an able and useful man.

The local preacher has been an important factor in the economy of Methodism. Neither American nor Kentucky Methodism originated in missionary enterprise, but through the labors of immigrant local preachers. Robert Strawbridge in Maryland; Philip Embury in New York; and Francis Clark in Kentucky, were the founders of the Church in their respective sections. Local preachers have also been im-

portant factors in extending the work. They have
sought out destitute communities and established
churches in them. They have been promoters in building houses of worship, and have aided both the class-
leader and the traveling preacher in holding together
the classes; in ministering to the needs of the people;
and in pushing forward the work in all its branches.
One of McKendree's strongest points as a Presiding
Elder was his ability to call out and use local preachers.
The few itinerants in this great western field could
never have accomplished the work which was done
without the aid of the local preachers.

Bishop Asbury was keenly alive to the progress of
the work in every part of the land. Having reports of
the growing work here in the West, he planned to
visit the brethren in Kentucky and to hold a Conference in this new field. The time of the Conference
was April 15, 1790, and the place fixed upon was
Masterson's Station, in the vicinity of Lexington.

We have frequently mentioned Bishop Asbury, but
no particular account of him has been given. Many
of our readers are familiar with his history and do not
need further information, but to others he is known
only in a vague and indefinite way. For the sake of
these we here give a brief sketch of this remarkable
man.

Francis Asbury was an Englishman, born in
Handsworth, Staffordshire, August 20, 1745; had a
very pious mother; was converted when fourteen; began to hold meetings and to exhort when sixteen; licensed to preach when eighteen; preached under Wesley in England for four years; volunteered to come to
America in 1771; arrived at Philadelphia late in that
year; the following year, though only twenty-six years

of age, was appointed by Mr. Wesley as Superintendent
of the work in America. When Wesley ordained Coke
and sent him to America to organize a Church, he instructed him to ordain Asbury as Joint Superintendent,
but Asbury, knowing the temper of the American people, refused to be ordained unless elected by the Conference; he was elected unanimously, and was ordained a deacon one day, an elder the next, and a
Bishop on the third day. From that time until his
death in 1816, he traveled over the eastern half of the
United States as no other man ever did, and performed a service such as has been rendered by no
other before or since. The truth of these statements
will be verified as we go along. He was "in labors
more abundant;" "in journeyings often, in perils of
waters, in perils of robbers, in perils by his own coun-
trymen, in perils by the heathen, in perils in the city,
in perils in the wilderness, . . . in weariness and pain-
fulness, in watchings often, in hunger and thirst, in
fastings often, in cold and nakedness." Never did any
man more nearly approach to St. Paul in all these
marks of apostleship. He was indeed the apostle of
Methodism in America. Endowed by nature with a
clear, strong mind, thoughtful and studious, he made
himself a ripe scholar, reading with ease the Latin,
Greek, and Hebrew. His sermons were logical, sys-
tematically arranged, and delivered with great spiritual power. When stirred by a great theme or by a
great occasion, he was truly eloquent, and some times
overwhelming. But he excelled as an organizer and
administrator. Ranging from Maine to Western Tennessee, from the borders of Canada to Florida; riding
down horse after horse; visiting churches and camp-
meetings; holding Conferences and stationing preacn-

ers; pioneering new work and administering the rigid discipline of early Methodism, this apostolic man was the greatest figure known to the Church in America.

The spring of 1790 found Asbury in North Carolina. He had sent word that he would visit Kentucky and hold a Conference with the preachers laboring in that field. A guard of riflemen, consisting of Peter Massie, John Clark, Eli Garrett, and seven or eight others, met him at Cumberland Gap and accompanied him over the Wilderness Road to Crab Orchard and beyond. The Indians were, at that time, and for several years afterward, very troublesome. They lurked in the bushes and behind the rocks and trees along this mountain road, to murder and plunder the people on their way to and from Kentucky. The greatest vigilance was necessary. Asbury says of this journey:

> I was strangely outdone for want of sleep, having been greatly deprived of it in my journey through the wilderness—which is like being at sea in some respects, and in others worse. Our way is over mountains, steep hills, deep rivers, and muddy creeks—a thick growth of reeds for miles together, and no inhabitants but wild beasts and savage men. I slept about an hour the first night, and about two the last. We ate no regular meals; our bread grew short, and I was much spent.

Somewhere along the way he "saw the graves of the slain—twenty-four in one camp—who had a few nights previous, been murdered by the Indians." In the midst of such conditions, no wonder the good Bishop was "strangely outdone for want of sleep!"

After seven days spent on the trip from North Carolina, the party reached Richmond, where they rested for awhile, then went on to Lexington. Richard Whatcoat, (afterwards Bishop Whatcoat) ; Hope Hull, the great preacher from Georgia; and John Sewell, afterwards a missionary to this same region, accompanied Asbury as traveling companions. At Masterson's Station, they met with six preachers. viz., Francis Poythress, James Haw, Wilson Lee, Stephen Brooks, Barnabas McHenry, and Peter Massie. So it is stated, but it is certain that Thomas Williamson was there also, as he was ordained an Elder before the Conference closed. Many people attended. Lewis Garrett says that he went to "the first Western Conference, which was held at Masterson's Station, near the place where Georgetown is situated. Here I first looked upon the venerable form of Asbury, and heard the thunder tones of Hope Hull and John Seawell (Sewell), two men who were mighty in the Scriptures, and full of faith and the Holy Ghost, who accompanied Mr. Asbury to the Far West. Here a tolerably large log meeting house had been erected, which was crowded day and night with shouting converts or anxious inquirers. There were no altars or mourners' benches, but the floor was often covered with persons groaning for redemption, and the woods resounded with the shouts of the converted." A most gracious revival had been going on during the year, and this was a part of that wonderful outpouring of the Holy Spirit which followed the preaching of these poor but mighty preachers in the wilderness.

The Conference lasted two days. Asbury, in his Journal, gives the following account of it:

Our Conference was held at Brother Masterson's—a very comfortable house and kind people. We went through our business in great love and harmony. I ordained Wilson Lee, Thomas Williamson, and Barnabas McHenry, elders. We had preaching noon and night, and souls were converted, and the fallen restored. My soul has been blessed among these people, and I am

exceedingly pleased with them. I would not, for the worth of
all the place, have been prevented in this visit, having no doubt
that it will be for the good of the present and rising generations. It is true, such exertions of mind and body are trying;
but I am supported under it; if souls are saved it is enough.
Brother Poythress is much alive to God. We fixed a plan for a
school, and called it **Bethel**, and obtained a subscription of three
hundred pounds in land and money toward its establishment.

It will be seen that of the preachers appointed to
the West the preceding year, all were present at this
Conference except Joshua Hartley, who, on account of
illness, did not go to his appointment on the Cumberland circuit. There are no separate minutes of this
first Western Conference, and we have no means of
knowing what business was transacted, except as we
have it from the testimony of some one who was present. The characters of the preachers were passed, they
were assigned to their respective fields of labor, three
were ordained elders, the numbers in society were
taken, and a plan for a school was adopted. The appointments are as follows:

> Francis Poythress, Elder.
> Danville—Thomas Williamson, Stephen Brooks.
> Cumberland—Wilson Lee, James Haw, Peter Massie.
> Madison—Barnabas McHenry, Benjamin Snelling.
> Limestone—Samuel Tucker, Joseph Lillard.
> Lexington—Henry Birchett, David Haggard.

All who labored here the preceding year are re-
tained, and four other names are added to the list, viz.,
Samuel Tucker, Joseph Lillard, Henry Birchett, and
David Haggard. The numbers in society are given in
the General Minutes as 1265 whites, and 107 colored.
Two new circuits are added—Madison and Limestone.
The Limestone circuit lay north of the Licking river,
and included all the settlements between the Licking

and the Ohio. The Lexington was next on the South, and embraced everything between the Licking and the Kentucky rivers. The Madison circuit was south of the Kentucky river, and was, at that time, one of the roughest, most desperately wicked sections of the State. The Danville circuit included all that great area between the Kentucky and Green rivers, not embraced in Madison. A great stretch of treeless ground known as "The Barrens," lay between Green river and the Tennessee line and was then uninhabited. The Cumberland circuit southwest of The Barrens, continued to serve all the settlments in Middle Tennessee.

Of the preachers who appear in Kentucky this year for the first time, the career of Samuel Tucker was the briefest and most tragic. The story of his life and tragic death by the Indians, has gathered about it a great deal of error while passing from lip to lip, as such stories will. Having sifted all the accounts left us, we believe the following to be most reliable and freest from traditional glosses. In his very interesting Autobiography, telling of his year on the Marietta circuit, Jacob Young says:

We had a great and good quarterly meeting at Tucker's station, near Briceland's cross-roads, between Steubenville and Pittsburg. This was among the oldest stations west of the Alleghany mountains. Father Tucker was living here at the time that Adam Poe had his famous battle with the Wyandott chief, 'Big Foot.' . . . Father Tucker resided here during a long, dangerous, and bloody war with the Indians; raised a very large family, but one of whom distinguished himself; I think his name was William. (The General Minutes give his name as Samuel). His father might have said of him, as old Priam said of Hector, that William (Samuel) was the wisest and best of all his sons. He became pious when very young, and before he was twenty years of age commenced preaching the gospel. Although born and reared on the frontier, by close and constant application, he acquired a pretty good English education. He bore a very active and successful part in trying to civilize and christianize the people in the country where he resided. His zeal increased with his years; and while he was yet a young man, he volunteered as a missionary to go to Kentucky; he well knew the danger to which he would be exposed—for the Indian war was raging at the time in its most dreadful form—but a desire to save souls elevated him above the fear of death. While he was going down the Ohio river, the boat in which he descended was attacked by a large company of Indians, and as he was well acquainted with the mode of Indian warfare, he took the supervision of all the boats in the company, and had them all lashed together with ropes. Taking his stand in the middle boat, that the whole company might hear the voice of command, he ordered the women and children to keep close to the bottom of the boats, lest the Indians might shoot them, and directed the men to arm themselves with axes and bars of iron, etc., so that if the Indians attempted to come on board they might mash their fingers and hands. In this way they crippled many of their warriors, and defended themselves for a long time. At length the cunning Indians found out where the commander stood, and in a canoe, got round to the end of the boat where the steering-oar works, and shot him through the hole. He saw that he had received his death wound. He advised them all to get into one boat, leave their property, and try to save their lives. Having given them the best direction he could, he kneeled down, made his last prayer, and expired. They made their escape from the Indians, and landed at Limestone, where they buried their beloved minister. I have stood and looked at his grave with mingled feelings. I will here say, that I received this minute information through an uncle of mine, who owned one of the boats, and was an eyewitness of the whole scene."

Redford and other writers think this was while Tucker was on his first trip to Kentucky, and that he did not reach the field assigned him. Others say that he came to the Limestone circuit, served for some time, then returned to his old home to attend to some business or to bring some of his kindred and friends to Kentucky, and that his death occurred while he was returning to his labors. The writer has in his hands the Treasurer's Book of the old Limestone circuit, for the years 1790 to 1805. In it is the record of moneys paid to "Brother Tucker," showing beyond doubt that he was in Kentucky and labored for some time on this circuit. He was the only itinerant who met death by the hands of the Indians here in Kentucky, though a local preacher, bearing the same name of Tucker, was murdered by them in the Green river country.

Joseph Lillard, who was received on trial this year, is said to have been a native Kentuckian, born not far from Harrodsburg. There must be some mistake as to this, for there was no settlement in Kentucky prior to 1775, and no women reached the District until the fall of that year. If he had been born in Kentucky, he could not have been over fourteen years of age when assigned to the Limestone circuit, with Samuel Tucker. We are sure, therefore, that he was born elsewhere. His second year in the Conference was spent on the Salt River circuit as the colleague of Wilson Lee. His name then disappears from the Minutes, and he dropped back into the local ranks. He did not, however, cease to labor. In his "Cyclopedia of Methodism," Bishop Simpson informs us that the first Methodist preacher in the State of Illinois was Joseph Lillard, and that he organized in St. Clair county, the first class in that State. Later, he made his home in Mercer county, Kentucky, a few miles from Harrodsburg, and in the community where he lived there stands a church called "Joseph's Chapel," founded by Joseph Lillard and named in his honor. He is said to have been an ordinary preacher, but a good man, though somewhat eccentric. He died while on his way from Missouri to his home in Kentucky, and his family always thought he was murdered.

Henry Birchett was from Brunswick county, Virginia. He was admitted on trial in 1788, and served in succession the Camden and Bertie circuits in that State. When transferred to Kentucky in 1790, he was sent to Lexington circuit, where he remained two years. After a year on the Salt River circuit, he went to Cumberland, where he died in February, 1794. From the brief memoir in the General Minutes, we find that he was

a gracious, happy, useful man, who freely offered himself for four years' service on the dangerous stations of Kentucky and Cumberland. He might have returned at the Kentucky Conference, 1793, but finding there was a probability of Cumberland being vacated by the preachers, notwithstanding the pain in his breast, and spitting blood, the danger of the Indians, the prevalence of small pox, he went a willing martyr, after asking the consent of the Bishop and the Conference. We hoped that his life would have been preserved, but report saith, he departed in much peace, at Cumberland, on the western waters, in February, 1794. His ashes sleep in an old graveyard, overgrown with briars and bushes, in the midst of a large field, about three miles below Nashville, Tenn. A simple tombstone, inscribed with his initials, was erected by some kind hand and marks his final resting place.

David Haggard was admitted in 1787, spent three years in Virginia, then came to Kentucky, where he was appointed to the Lexington circuit with Henry Birchett. Both men were assigned to this circuit for two years, but during his second year Haggard was removed to Limestone to take the place of Peter Massie, who died in December of that year. He then returned to Virginia, and for one year was on the New River circuit in that State, then for one year on the Salisbury circuit, in North Carolina. Sometime during this year, he withdrew from the Methodist Episcopal

Church and joined O'Kelly. He returned to Kentucky some time later, and when the followers of O'Kelly and Stone coalesced under the name of "The Christian Church," (the New Lights), he became a minister in that organization. He seems to have lived in or near Burkesville, Ky., as we have in our possession a copy of the action of the County Court of Cumberland county, granting him license to solemnize the rites of matrimony, as a minister of that Church. While he remained a Methodist preacher, he was both faithful and useful, and his character above reproach.

The oft-told story of Bethel Academy remains to be told again. Let it be remembered that the plan for this school was adopted in 1790, two years before Kentucky became a State. The number of Methodists in this Territory at the time was but a little more than one thousand. The towns then in existence were few and small, while the country was very sparsely settled. But immigrants were coming rapidly, and the future development of Kentucky was assured. Schools were needed, and though the Methodists were few and poor. they were willing to make the sacrifices necessary to provide an institution for the education of the coming generations. No other Church had, at this time, undertaken such an enterprise. Transylvania Seminary had been established by the Legislature of Virginia by a grant of escheated lands, but it was not then a church enterprise. The Methodists, acting through their first Conference in Kentucky, were the first to enter upon this ambitious undertaking.

At the Conference held in North Carolina, in 1789, Dr. Coke, alluding to some letters from Kentucky, says, 'Our friends in that country earnestly entreat us to have a college built for the education of their youth, offering to give, or purchase, three or four thousand acres of good land for its support. We debated the point, and sent them word, that if they would provide five thousand acres of fertile land, and settle it upon such trustees as we should mention under the direction of the Conference, we will undertake to build a college for that part of our connection within ten years.' This project was not carried out according to the plan of Dr. Coke. Subsequently, Mr. Lewis, of Jessamine county, donated 100 acres of land for the site of an academy. Collections were made in different circuits, and a building was erected 80 by 40 feet, three stories high; the lower part of the building was finished and a school was commenced. The Legislature of the State afterwards gave a donation of 6,000 acres of land to Bethel Academy. The land was located in Christian county, south of Green River, and remained a long time unproductive. In 1802 the Academy was incorporated, with all the powers and privileges of a literary institution. In 1798. Rev. Valentine Cook was the first Principal of the Academic Department, though a primary school had previously been kept, and a number of students entered its halls. Unfortunately, some difficulties occurred, and Mr. Cook resigned.—(Cyclopedia of Methodism, by Bishop Simpson.)

William Burke is authority for the statement that this project of building a school originated with Mr. Asbury, Francis Poythress, then Presiding Elder of the Kentucky District; Mr. Isaac Hite, of Jefferson county; Col. Hinde, of Nelson; Willis Green, of Lincoln; Richard Masterson, of Fayette; and Mr. Lewis, of Jessamine. There is some confusion as to which "Mr. Lewis" donated the one hundred acres of land upon which to build. Col. Bennett Young, in his History of Jessamine County, says it was Mr. *Thomas* Lewis; but a report of a Committee appointed by the Kentucky Conference in 1845, to investigate the title and determine what interest the Church then had in the proceeds of the defunct institution, seems to have gone very thoroughly into the matter, and says it was Mr. *John* Lewis, who, in the year 1797, conveyed the

100 acres for the purpose of establishing the Academy.*

Bishop Simpson must be in error when he states that the institution was incorporated in 1802. There lies before me a copy of "An Act Establishing Bethel Academy and Incorporating the Trustees thereof," passed by the Legislature of Kentucky, and approved February 10, 1798. The trustees were, Rev. Francis Poythress, John Knobler (Kobler), Nathaniel Harris, John Metcalf, Barnabas McHenry, James Crutcher, James Hord, and Richard Masterson; and they are authorized "to execute all powers and privileges that are enjoyed by trustees, governors, or visitors of any college or university within this State."

In addition to the subscription of three hundred pounds "in land and money," taken at the Conference at Masterson's, the preachers, under the lead of Poythress, "were continually employed in begging for Bethel. The people were liberal, but they could do no more than they did. The country was new, and the unsettled state of the people, in consequence of the Indian wars and depredations, kept the country in a continual state of agitation." (Burke). How much was collected for the enterprise, we do not know. Land was about the cheapest and most plentiful commodity the people possessed, yet but little income could be expected from it. The grant of 6,000 acres by the Legislature, made February 10, 1798, was a liability rather than an asset. Money was exceedingly scarce in those

---

*Under date of May 17, 1790, Bishop Asbury in his Journal, says: "Rode to J. Lewis' on the bend of the Kentucky river. Lewis is an old acquaintance, from Leesburg, Va.; I was pleased to find that heaven and religion were not lost sight of in this family. Brother Lewis offered me one hundred acres of land for Bethel, on a good spot for building materials."

days, and it is marvelous that enough was gathered together to put up the large brick building that was erected.

Just when the first school was opened in this building we do not know. We think Nathaniel Harris was the first Master. Rev. Valentine Cook, the great preacher, the ripe scholar, and the excellent teacher, was brought to Kentucky in 1798, and made Presiding Elder of the Kentucky District; but he had not made more than one or two rounds until an order came from Bishop Asbury for him to take charge of Bethel Academy. What the trouble was that caused him to resign, or with whom the difficulty arose, we do not know, but at the end of one year he resigned, and became principal of an academy at Harrodsburg. Rev. John Metcalf took his place. Things had not gone well from the beginning. When, in 1792, Bishop Asbury visited Kentucky, he found it necessary to change the plan of the building in order to secure greater comfort for the students. The building was never completed. Undoubtedly the school was not a success under Metcalf, for he, without authority from the trustees, removed the school to Nicholasville, together with the furniture that was in the building. For this he was arraigned by the quarterly conference of the Lexington circuit, convicted and suspended from the ministry for twelve months!

For want of adequate records, the future history of the Academy is vague and uncertain. We know that the school did not prosper. Many things were against it. The fewness and poverty of the Methodists upon whom the support of the institution depended, and the dissensions which sprang up among them, made its success an impossibility. Bishop Asbury, who held a

Conference there in the fall of 1800, says:

I came to Bethel. . . . I was so dejected that I could say little, but weep. Here is Bethel—Cokesbury in miniature, eighty by thirty feet, three stories, with high roof, and finished below. Now we want a fund and an income of three hundred (pounds) per year to carry it on; without which it will be useless. But it is too far distant from public places; its being surrounded by the river Kentucky in part, we now find to be no benefit. Thus all our excellencies are turned into defects. Perhaps Brother Poythress and myself were as much overseen with this place as Dr. Coke was with the site of Cokesbury. But all is right that works right, and all is wrong that works wrong, and we must be blamed by men of slender sense for consequences impossible to foresee, and for other people's misconduct. Sabbath day, Monday, and Tuesday we were shut up in Bethel with the traveling and local preachers and the trustees that could be called together. . . . It was thought expedient to carry the first design of education into execution, and that we should employ a man of sterling qualifications, to be chosen by and under the direction of a select number of trustees and others, who should obligate themselves to see him paid, and take the profits, if any, arising from the establishment. Dr. Jennings was thought of, talked of, and written to."

The Dr. Jennings spoken of was Samuel Kennedy Jennings, M. D., a very popular and scholarly local preacher, then at the head of a school in Virginia, but afterwards a leader in the movement that ultimated in the organization of the Methodist Protestant Church. He did not come to Bethel. Valentine Cook had already resigned, and the Rev. John Metcalf became Principal. The school did not prosper under his management, and he removed it to Nicholasville. The building was suffered to fall into a dilapidated condition, and "the removal of the school to Nicholasville was considered a breach of trust, and thereupon the land reverted to the heirs of Lewis." Several efforts were made to revive and continue the school. Rev. Nathaniel Harris moved to the property, and for a time conducted a school for the neighborhood. As late as 1808, we find the Conference directing that about $33 from a charity fund be placed in the hands of William Burke for the use and benefit of the trustees of Bethel Academy. After a few years the building was torn down, and thus our first educational enterprise in Kentucky came to naught!*

The number of members reported at this Conference of 1790, was 1,024 white, and 66 colored in Kentucky, and 241 white, and 41 colored in Cumberland.

*In September, 1933, while the Kentucky Conference of the M. E. Church, South, was in session at Wilmore, Ky., a neat monument, built out of the foundation stones of Bethel was dedicated on the site of the Academy. This monument was erected by the Historical Society of the Kentucky Conference. A bronze tablet fitted into the stone, bears an inscription setting forth a brief history of the Institution.

CHAPTER VI.

1791 TO 1793

It is worthy of note that the foundations of Kentucky Methodism were laid by very young men. Benjamin Ogden was only twenty-two when he entered this field, and it was his first appointment. Peter Massie, Benjamin Snelling, Stephen Brooks, Samuel Tucker, and Joseph Lillard received their first appointments to circuits in this State. Barnabas McHenry was only twenty-one, and had only one year of service before he came to Kentucky. Henry Birchett had but two years, and David Haggard three. James Haw had served five years before he was appointed to Kentucky circuit, but he was not an old man. Francis Poythress was the only man among the whole number who could be called mature. Yet these young and inexperienced men, under the splendid leadership of the veteran Poythress, did a great work and firmly established a great Church in the wilderness. Most of them died or broke down under the toils and hardships they endured, and thus their period of service was short.

We have but little information concerning the Conference of 1791. Sweet includes it in a list of Conferences held at Masterson's, but gives no authority for so doing. In the General Minutes for 1790, under the question, "When and where shall the next Conferences be held?" none is appointed for Kentucky or East Tennessee for the year 1791. The nearest one to this field was at McKnight's, on the Yadkin river, in North Carolina, and this was held April 2nd. Bangs, in his History of Methodism, lists thirteen Conferences held this year, but neither Kentucky nor Tennessee is in the list. Redford, McFerrin, and Price are silent on the subject. As stated in a previous chapter, there were at that time, no geographical boundaries of the Conferences, and no separate minutes were kept. The Bishop determined both the time and place of meeting and could make the appointments for Kentucky from a Conference held in North Carolina or Baltimore as well as from any other place.

The General Minutes, however, supply us with the appointments in Kentucky for this year. They are as follows:

Francis Poythress, Elder.
Limestone—Peter Massie.
'Danville—Thomas Williamson, J. Tatman.
Salt River—Wilson Lee, Joseph Lillard.
Lexington—Henry Birchett, David Haggard.
Cumberland—Barnabas McHenry, James O'Cull.

Only two new names appear in this list, viz., J. Tatman and James O'Cull. Of Joseph Tatman but little is known. He located at the end of this year, married, and removed to Ohio. In 1812 he was admitted into the Ohio Conference and appointed to the Mad River circuit. In 1814 he again obtained a location.

Of James O'Cull, it is said that he was a native of Pennsylvania, and by birth and education a Roman Catholic. In early life he attended a Methodist meeting, was deeply convicted of sin, and graciously converted. He at once began to exhort others; was licensed to preach, and came to Kentucky as a local preached in 1789. After traveling two years under the Presiding Elder, he joined the Conference in 1791, bas McHenry. His constitution was not strong. He could not bear up under the terrific strain of the itinerancy, and was compelled to drop back into the local ranks at the close of the year. McHenry says of him:

·My helper on the Cumberland circuit, Brother O'Cull, labored with great zeal until sometime in the fall of 1791, when he broke himself down so entirely that he has never recovered to this day. True, he sometimes preaches—and preaches, I am told, in a very impressive strain—but he has to speak slowly and in a very soft tone of voice. Indeed, it is in this manner only that he can hold conversation. He resides in Fleming county, in the northern part of the State, and has reared a family, etc.

O'Cull was a very useful man in Fleming county, and when he was able to preach, he preached with wonderful effectiveness. Many were converted under his ministry, and he was a great stay to the Church in all that region of the country.

There was no change in the number of circuits from that of 1790, though there was some readjustment. The Madison circuit was absorbed by the Danville, and the name disappears from the list for several years. The Salt River circuit, embracing all that territory now in Green, Washington, Nelson, Jefferson, Taylor, Spencer, Bullitt, LaRue, Oldham, Henry, and Trimble counties, took its place. A few years later there were fifty-eight preaching places in this circuit. The revival that was in progress in 1790, was still attending the ministry of the Methodists, and the increase of members, including those in Cumberland, was four hundred and sixty-three.

The death of Mr. Wesley occurred on March the 2nd of this year, 1791, and American Methodism, as well as the Methodists in England, mourned his departure. No man in his generation so deeply impressed humanity as did this man. In the estimation of James Birrell, "No single figure influenced so many minds, no single voice touched so many hearts. No other man did such a life's work for England." The _Spectator,_ of London, expressed the opinion that, "it may well be doubted whether in the long course of her (England's) history, any one person has ever influenced her life in so direct, palpable, and powerful way as John Wesley .... If it be asked what is Wesley's supreme title to fame, the answer, we think, would be that he arrested the moral and spiritual decline of England, and that he was the chief agent in the renewal of her moral and spiritual life." The influence of that life had reached America and was destined to impress our own national life as much as it did that of England. The movement started by him was now blessing Kentucky, and our own people were being impressed as in other parts of the world. Even at this early period, Methodism, the product of Wesley's toil, had made for itself a record by its opposition to slavery, to the liquor traffic, to gambling, and to other evils of the day. "The circuit rider waged war with vice of every sort .... The Methodist Church was the original Temperance Society in the West, if not in the nation." (Sweet). Methodism has exerted no small influence upon the moral and spiritual life of Kentucky, and a full story of its work in leading the forces of reform, in ridding the State of evils and establishing the good, would, if told, be almost incredible. When the news of Wesley's death reached this distant part of the world, our people sorrowed along with other followers of this great man.

The year 1792 was an eventful year in both State and Church. Kentucky was this year admitted as a separate State into the Union. As early as 1784, the people of the Kentucky District began agitating for a State separate from Virginia. The Indians were exceedingly troublesome and it was estimated that, within seven years as many as fifteen hundred persons were killed or taken prisoners by them, and as many as twenty thousand horses were carried off. People seldom went without their guns, even to church. There was no safety anywhere at any time. Nevertheless, Virginia utterly failed to provide for the protection of the people in her back counties, not even providing for the legal organization of a militia by the Kentuckians, by which to protect themselves. The people very properly reasoned that what was not worth protecting was not worth claiming; so they very insistently demanded an organization of their own by means of which they might safe-guard themselves and their families. As many as ten conventions were held at Danville. looking to the establishing of a State independent of the Mother State.

On June 1, 1792, Kentucky became a State and on June 4th Isaac Shelby was inaugurated the first Governor. Of Welsh descent, a native of Maryland, a man of forceful character, he had distinguished himself as a soldier in the Revolutionary war. He came to Kentucky in 1783. A man of his character could not long remain out of public affairs, and he was soon put forward by the Kentuckians as their representative in various important matters. He was twice Governor of the State, and did a noble work in protecting the State from the Indians and in building up the best interests of the Commonwealth.

Prior to the admission of Kentucky into the Union as a separate State, nine counties had been formed, viz., Lincoln, Fayette, Jefferson, Nelson, Bourbon, Madison, Mercer, Woodford, and Mason. In 1792, the Legislature created six other counties, Green, Hardin, Scott, Logan, Shelby, and Washington. These fifteen counties covered the entire area of Kentucky east of the Tennessee river, and of course were much larger than the counties now bearing the same names.

The Conference of 1792 was held at Masterson's. Bishop Asbury presided. He again came on horseback, through Cumberland Gap and over the Wilderness Road. On his way through the mountains he and his party encountered heavy rains, and were compelled to swim the Laurel river to get to Rockcastle Station. Here he says "we found such a set of sinners as made it next to hell itself." Here they spent the night and, scarce as money was, paid a dollar a bushel for the corn with which to feed their horses. In the morning they had to swim Rockcastle river, also the West Fork of the same, and Asbury was "steeped in the water up to the waist." That night they reached Crab Orchard, and went at once to the home of Willis Green. Asbury says:

"How much I have suffered in this journey is only known to God and myself. What added much to its disagreeableness, is the extreme filthiness of the houses. I was seized with a severe flux which followed me eight days; for some of the time I kept up, but at last found myself under the necessity of taking my bed. I endured as severe pain as, perhaps, I ever felt. I made use of small portions of rhubarb, and also obtained some good claret, of which I drank a bottle in three days, and was almost well, so that on Sunday following I preached a sermon an hour long. I have had serious views of eternity, and was free from the fear of death. I stopped and lodged, during my illness, with Mr. Willis Green, who showed me all possible attention and kindness."

While here he wrote to David Rice "a commendation of his speech, delivered in a convention in Kentucky, on the natural rights of man," and also an address on behalf of Bethel school. He visited and preached at Clark's station, then came to Bethel, where he found it necessary "to change the plan of the house, to make it more comfortable to the scholars in cold weather." He says: "I am too much in company, and hear so much about Indians, convention, treaty, killing and scalping, that my attention is drawn to these things more than I could wish. I found it good to get alone in the woods and converse with God."

On April 25th, he met the Conference, and for some time was closely engaged with the preachers and leaders in the Conference business. He says: "I met the married men and women apart, and we had great consolation in the Lord. Vast crowds of people attended public worship. The spirit of matrimony is very prevalent here. In one circuit," (which was the Cumberland), "both preachers are settled. The land is good, the country new, and indeed all possible facilities to the comfortable maintenance of a family are offered to an industrious, prudent pair."

"**Monday, April 30,** Came to L's. An alarm was spreading of a depredation committed by the Indians, on the east and west frontiers of the settlement. In the former, report says one man was killed. In the latter, many men, women, and children. Everything is in motion. There having been so many about me at Conference, my rest was much broken. I hoped now to repair it, and get refreshed before I set out to return through the wilderness; but the continual arrival of people until midnight, the barking of dogs, and other annoyances prevented. Next night we reached the Crab Orchard, where thirty or forty people were compelled to crowd into one mean house. We could get no more rest here than we did in the wilderness. We came the old way by Scagg's Creek and Rockcastle, supposing it to be safer, as it was a road less frequented, and therefore less liable to be waylaid by the savages. My body, by this time, is well tried. I had a violent fever and pain in the head, such as I had not lately felt. I stretched myself on the cold ground, and borrowing clothes to keep me warm, by the mercy of God I slept four or five hours. Next morning we set off early, and passed beyond Richland creek. Here we were in danger if anywhere. I could have slept, but was afraid. Seeing the drowsiness of the company, I walked the encampment, and watched the sentries the whole night. Early next morning we made our way to Robinson's Station. We had the best company I ever met with—thirty-six good travelers, and a few warriors; but we had a pack-horse, some old men, and two tired horses—these were not the best part.

These quotations give us a vivid conception of the difficulties under which these pioneer preachers performed their work. There was no mission board behind them. Their salaries were only $64 per year and all of this was seldom paid. The salary of the Bishop was the same as that of the traveling preacher. The people they served were poor, just getting a start in a new country. Their log cabins were small and their furniture home-made and of the rudest type. The conditions under which most of them lived were wretched. These preachers could never be accused of preaching the gospel for the sake of ease or pecuniary advantage. "Traveling and preaching, night and day, in weariness and want; many days without the necessaries of life, and always without those comforts that are now enjoyed by traveling preachers; with worn and tattered garments, but happy and united like a band of brothers. The quarterly meetings and annual conferences were high times. When the pilgrims met they never met without embracing each other, and never parted at those seasons without weeping. Those were days that tried men's souls." It was on a future trip through the mountains that Asbury caught the itch!

The number of circuits in Kentucky this year was the same as that of the two preceding years. The appointments were as follows:

Francis Poythress, Elder.
Limestone—John Ray.
Lexington—John Sewell, Benjamin Northcutt, John Page.
Danville—Wilson Lee, Richard Bird.
Salt River—Henry Birchett, Isaac Hammer.
Cumberland—John Ball, Jonathan Stephenson.

Nearly all of these were new men in this great field, and most of them were just entering the traveling connection. Peter Massie had died during the year just past; Thomas Williamson had located on account of ill health; Joseph Tatman, Joseph Lillard, and James O'Cull had ceased traveling; David Haggard had returned to Virginia; Barnabas McHenry had been made Presiding Elder of a District in the western part of Virginia, and of those who labored here last year, only Wilson Lee and Henry Birchett remained. John Ray, John Sewell, Benjamin Northcutt, John Page, Richard Bird, Isaac Hammer, John Ball, and Jonathan Stephenson appear for the first time. Of Isaac Hammer we know nothing, except that he was appointed this year to the Salt River circuit as the colleague of Henry Birchett. Jonathan Stephenson traveled only one year, married, located, and lived on Red River, in the bounds of the Cumberland circuit. He went with James Haw into the O'Kelly movement, and was the only local preacher in the Cumberland circuit that was not won back to the Methodist Episcopal Church. John Ball was admitted on trial in 1790, and traveled five years; located and settled in the Cumberland country, where

for a good many years he served as a local preacher.
He is described as "a son of thunder. He smote with
his hands, and stamped with his feet. He warned the
people faithfully to flee from the wrath to come." "He
was firm, independent, and opinionated. He was regarded as a pious, useful minister, of the medium
grade, and was well received wherever he traveled. He
was a bold, intrepid man, who never turned his back
on an enemy."

John Sewell (or Seawell, as it is sometimes spelled),
accompanied Bishop Asbury on his first visit to Kentucky in 1790. He was then a local preacher, but, in
1791, was admitted on trial in the traveling ranks.
With Benjamin Northcutt and John Page, he served the
Lexington circuit this year, traveled the Danville circuit in 1793, and located at the end of that year. Not
long afterward, he established his home in Sumner
county, Tennessee, where he was an earnest and faithful local preacher until his death in 1804 or 1805. He
was a native of North Carolina, and out of one of the
best families in the land.· It is said that, when he came
to his death bed, his physician was a deist. Visiting
Sewell one day, the doctor saw that he was dying, and
started to leave. Brother Sewell said to him, "Stay,
doctor, and see a Christian die!" The remark made
a very deep impression on the skeptical doctor. A son,
Rev. Benjamin Sewell, was a Methodist minister.

Richard Bird, "a man of fair talent and education
and a very earnest preacher," was also a North Carolinian. He was admitted on trial in 1792, and traveled
six years; the Danville, Hinkstone, and Limestone in
Kentucky, then for three years in Virginia. He located, and made his home in North Carolina, where he
and his brother Jonathan were towers of strength and

usefulness. "He preached and exhorted with pungency and power, and he generally produced a religious sensation in his audiences."

The other three men who appeared upon the scene this year—John Ray, Benjamin Northcutt, and John Page—were all remarkable men. We will meet with them frequently as we go forward with this narrative. Few men have left a deeper impress upon Methodism in the West than they, and a more extended sketch of them will be appropriate here. The General Minutes of the Conferences, from which most of our information is drawn, are very defective. They do not tell us in what year John Ray was received on trial, though in the Minutes of 1791 his name stands among those who "remain on trial;" and in 1792, it is included among those who were received into full connection. The inference is that he was admitted in 1790, though his name is not among those receiving appointments that year, nor in 1791. This year, 1792, he is appointed to the Limestone circuit, where he remained for two years. He was a Virginian, born in 1768, and his early life was spent on the frontier, where he had no educational advantages. He is described as a "man of large stature—tall, well-proportioned, rather portly, erect, noble, and commanding in appearance." His complexion was dark, though not swarthy; his step firm and elastic; "benignant humor, independent boldness, uncompromising firmness, and biting sarcasm, were strongly written upon his countenance." He read but little, (except the Bible and the standards of Methodism), yet he thought much. His ideas were clear, his reasoning strong and logical. He had a strong and well modulated voice, and his language was usually in accord with the rules of grammar. He was an indefatigable worker, and many were converted under his ministry. After laboring for two years on the Limestone circuit, he was sent to East Tennessee, Virginia, and North Carolina, where, in 1801, under the hardships and excessive labors he broke down and was compelled to locate. He returned to Kentucky, and established a home about three miles east of Mt. Sterling, in Montgomery county, where he lived until 1831. We cannot do better than to quote his memoir from the General Minutes:

John Ray was born in 1768, in the state of Virginia; and while he was yet a youth his parents emigrated to the then wilds of Kentucky, where he, in the nineteenth year of his age, sought and found peace with God, and attached himself to the Methodist Episcopal Church. In 1790, he joined the traveling connection; and after laboring with great success in the states of Virginia and North Carolina, married, located, and returned to Kentucky. He there reared the standard of the cross, preached Christ crucified to sinners, and was instrumental in establishing the first Methodist societies that were formed in Montgomery county. In his located sphere Brother Ray was active and successful, and fully sustained the dignity of a gospel minister. In 1819 he again entered the itinerant field, by joining the Kentucky Conference, which he had seen grow from a few classes to an extensive Conference. Here he traveled successively the Lexington, Madison, Mount Sterling, and Hinkstone circuits. On this last circuit his health failed, and he retired, sustaining a superannuate relation. In 1833 he was transferred to the Indiana Conference, where he still continued to preach the blessed gospel as his health would permit, till God sent his messenger to call him home. The last acts of his life were to give fifty dollars for the redemption of Thompson, and fifty to the Colonization Society. He died in peace, May, 1837, and now reigns with God on high.

The reason for his transfer to Indiana was his intense hatred of slavery and his desire to get entirely away from it. "He became noted in Kentucky, in his day, for his strong opposition to slavery and was quite rough, and sometimes offensive, in the manner in which he obtruded that subject, especially upon people of the world. He would seldom lodge at the house of a slave-holder, if he could well avoid it. Often, in his appointments, when invited home with a stranger, his prompt interrogatory would be: 'Have you any negroes?' In the Annual Conference, whenever a preacher was proposed for admission, every eye would be turned to Father Ray, expecting him to arise, as was his custom, and say: 'Mr. President, has he any negroes?' "

Ray was an utter stranger to fear. He was very successful in commanding order and in taming ruffians who infested camp meetings. In these meetings in those days men and women sat apart. On one occasion, he requested some young men to leave the seats assigned to the ladies, and when they did not comply with his request, he left the stand and went toward them. As he approached, he heard one of them say: "If he comes to me, I'll knock him down." In perfect coolness Ray replied, "You are too light, young man," and taking him by the hand, led him to his appropriate seat.

Once a man in his neighborhood kidnaped some free negroes, and took them to Tennessee, where he sold them. Ray and a few others prosecuted the man, and compelled him to buy back the negroes at a considerable advance, and restore them to freedom. The man was very angry, and swore he would have revenge. Not long after that, Ray, with three ministerial companions, was returning from a Conference at Lexington, and, before they had traveled far, found that they were followed by five men, heavily armed with knives and pistols. When they reached a certain place, these men rode up, swearing they would be revenged by shedding Ray's heart's blood. Ray received them as coolly as if they had been harmless travelers. "If you think," said he, "to frighten me by this meneuver, you are mistaken. I know well that you are a set of cowards, or you would not come up armed against an unarmed man. It is dastardly. You are young men; I am an old man. Why all this parade?" Notwithstanding their rage, Ray's companions finally dissuaded them from attacking him, and they rode off. Ray was perfectly cool through it all, and was perhaps the calmest person in the group.

His wit and gift of repartee were fine. Many amusing anecdotes are told of him. One of his neighbors, familiarly known as "Raccoon John Smith," then a Baptist preacher, but afterwards a leader in the so-called "Reformation," was a great friend of Ray's. They had many a friendly rencounter of wits. One day they met in the road in the presence of some friends, Ray returning from a camp meeting and Smith from a Baptist Association. Smith accosted Ray: "How do you do, Brother Ray? You seem to be returning from camp meeting. I suppose you had the devil with you, as usual." Quick as a flash Ray responded, "No, sir, he had not time to leave the Association."

It is said that Ray usually rode a very fine horse. Once when he was going into Mount Sterling, a group of young lawyers and doctors were gathered in the shade of a building, and seeing Ray approaching, thought they would have some fun at his expense. One of them, who was chosen as their spokesman, greeted him as follows: "Father Ray, how is it that you are so much better than your Master? He had to ride on an ass, but you are mounted on a very fine horse. You must be proud. Why don't you ride as did your Master?" Without a moment's hesitation, Ray responded, "For the simple reason that there are no asses now to be obtained—they turned them all into lawyers and doctors!"

Brother Ray had a son who was greatly beloved as a Methodist minister. Edwin Ray was converted early in life, joined the Kentucky Conference in 1822, and after two years of successful service here, volunteered to go as a missionary to the new State of Illinois, where he was greatly blessed in his labors for the few years that he lived. Father Ray died at the home he had established in Putnam county, Indiana, a few miles north of Greencastle, in May, 1837.

Benjamin Northcutt gave but little time to the work as an itinerant, but was a very remarkable and a very useful man. He was born in North Carolina, January 16, 1770. In his nineteenth year he volunteered as one of a military guard to protect a party of emigrants to Kentucky. The Indians were still lurking along the path, and it was with great hazard that families came from the older states to the new country in the West. This party reached their destination without mishap, and, though he had expected to return to North Carolina, Northcutt remained in Kentucky. He soon found constant employment with his rifle, in procuring game for new comers while they were building cabins and getting ready their new homes. His educational advantages had been very limited, though he had acquired a sufficient knowledge of the fundamentals of an English education to enable him to read well, write a legible hand, and to transact the business of life. Many of the early preachers had but little opportunity to attend school, but they gave themselves so earnestly to reading and study that they became scholarly men. Even Bascom never attended school after he was twelve years of age. These men did not have chaffy newspapers and magazines upon which to fritter away their time; they read great books; they set for themselves regular courses of study, and held themselves to them; they thought about things, and mastered the subjects to which they gave attention. Schools are helps, but one who has the will to do it can study with or without schools.

Mr. Northcutt was converted about 1790, a little more than a year after coming to Kentucky.

His conversion was preceded by a clear conviction of sin and of his lost condition. He sought earnestly for pardon both in public and private, and while wrestling in prayer during the hours of the night, and alone in a dense cane-brake, the blessing was bestowed upon him in power. He often spoke of his conversion, and always as though it was as much a matter of fact to his consciousness as any other event of his life. No doubt was left on his mind as to the reality of the work and the certainty of his acceptance with God. ("Life of Benjamin Northcutt," by his son, Rev. H. C. Northcutt).

Almost at once the conviction came to him that he must preach the gospel. He was not a member of the Church, and as he was to give his life to this work, it was a matter of vital importance that he should connect himself with the right Church. He began a careful study of the doctrines of the different denominations and found himself in hearty accord with the teachings of Methodism. He was not clear upon some points in the government of that Church, but reasoned that it was better to have good doctrine with defective government, than to have good government with defective doctrine. So he united with the Methodist Episcopal Church, and was almost immediately licensed to preach. He was soon helping on the Lexington and Danville circuits, and in 1792 was admitted on trial in the Conference. With John Sewell as senior preacher, and John Page as a fellow helper, he was appointed to the Lexington circuit, and they had a year of considerable prosperity. The next year he was assigned to Limestone circuit—a large circuit, where he preached every day, sometimes twice a day, and often three times. Soon a revival broke out all over the circuit. It was customary in those days to have preaching on Christmas morning at day break. Accordingly, Mr. Northcutt had an appointment to preach that Christmas morning, and while preaching, a vocal chord gave way, and he was compelled at once to stop. Here ended his labors as an itinerant. For six months he was able to speak only in a whisper, and never did fully recover from the injury. He located, married Miss Jane Armstrong, of Fleming county, and established a home in that county, not far from Hillsboro, where he lived the rest of his life.

As soon as he had sufficiently recovered his voice, he resumed preaching, and, as a local preacher, labored incessantly, going far and near in order to minister to the needy people. He had a passion for preaching where no one else had preached, and was the instrument in establishing many societies in these neglected places. More than any other man, perhaps, it was Benjamin Northcutt who promoted the great revival in this part of Kentucky at the beginning of the nineteenth century. While this great work had begun a little earlier in the Cumberland country, its beginning in Northern Kentucky seems to have been entirely independent of the revival on Cumberland. In the year 1800, Mr. Northcutt and the Rev. Mr. Allen, pastor of the Presbyterian Church at Flemingsburg, arranged to hold a union meeting at old Union Meeting House, on the road between Flemingsburg and Poplar Plains. Denominational prejudices ran high in those days. When the people saw a Methodist and a Presbyterian join together in a meeting for the salvation of sinners, they said: These preachers are getting in earnest about saving souls when they can lay aside their prejudices and worship together in this way. The attendance upon this meeting was large and deep feeling was manifested from the beginning. "On Saturday afternoon, Mr. Northcutt delivered an exhortation of such power that strong men fell prostrate and helpless. The work was deep and genuine and many were converted and added to the Churches."

A few months after this, a meeting was appointed in the Presbyterian church, at Concord, Nicholas county, where Barton W. Stone was pastor. Mr. Northcutt was invited to attend and to assist in the meeting. It was Monday morning before he reached the church. Religious prejudice was so strong that the Presbyterian ministers thought it best that it should not be known that Northcutt, who was a stranger, was a Methodist. So a Presbyterian minister opened the services that day with a short sermon, and was followed by Northcutt. His text was, "Behold, ye despisers, and wonder, and perish," etc.

The Spirit's power came down like a hurricane upon the people. More than two hundred persons fell to the ground. Convictions were of the most pungent character. Penitents cried in agony for mercy as though they were dropping right into hell. The Presbyterian ministers were not fully prepared for such a scene. It was new to them. One of them, sitting in the pulpit behind the speaker, resisted the power that came upon him for some time. At last he could hold out no longer.

The blood gushed from his nose, and smiting his thigh violently with his hand, he cried vehemently, 'I yield! I yield! I yield!' The work went on for several days, and many were converted and added to the church.—(Life of Northcutt).

Mr. Northcutt was present and took a very prominent part in the great meeting at Cane Ridge, and at other places during the progress of this mighty work of grace. That the reader may have a better view of this truly great preacher, we are giving here a sketch of him, drawn by the Rev. Jonathan Stamper, in a series of papers entitled "Autumn Leaves," published many years ago in the "Home Circle:"

None among them gave me a heartier welcome (to the Maysville District) than did Benjamin Northcutt—as noble a spirit as ever lived. He was one of those who first preached the gospel in forts and blockhouses, and shared with the early settlers the dangers of the wilderness. After some three or four years spent in the itinerancy, ill health and family considerations compelled him to locate, and he settled in Fleming county, where he remained until removed by death. But although a local preacher, and compelled to provide for his family by the labor of his own hands, he preached a great deal, and was instrumental in doing much good. He was one of the most incessant laborers I have ever known in the local ranks. It was a matter of wonder to many how he could support a large and helpless family, and yet spend so much time in preaching and working for the Church, which he did without fee or reward. Not only were his Sabbaths devoted to preaching, but often whole weeks together were employed in attending meetings, far and near. Notwithstanding which, he prospered in the world, and always had a competency. The solving of the mystery is easy enough. The blessing of God was upon all that he did, because he did his duty, and trusted in the promise that his bread should be given him, and his water should be sure.

Father Northcutt was one of the most distinguished ministers in the great revival of 1800 to 1806. During this period he attended most of those extraordinary protracted camp meetings which have been the subject of so much wonder and speculation in later times, and was one of the few who knew how to carry them on to the best advantage. He was at Cane Ridge, at Indian Creek, at Sugar Grove, and many other places where these meetings were held, and on all occasions was looked up to as being wise in counsel, and powerful in word and doctrine. His voice was remarkable strong, yet clear and musical, and in the midst of the general uproar it could be heard above all others, directing sinners to the Lamb of God. He and William Burke were often together on these occasions, and were a host in themselves. It is not wronging others to say that Burke, Northcutt, Lakin, Ray, and Page were among the most efficient instruments in that work. The Presbyterian clergy were to a great extent astonished and confounded. They did not know what it meant. They had never seen the like before; but to the Methodists it was no new thing, and they knew at once what to do, and how to do it. Although it may not be readily admitted, yet it is none the less true, that our Presbyterian brethren were much indebted to those early Methodist preachers for the conduct and success of those extraordinary revivals.

Northcutt was continually busy. Now preaching to thousands, and again praying with mourners; there, rejoicing with the newly converted, and there exhorting impenitent sinners, he never tired of the blessed work; and even after whole nights spent in this way, seemed as strong and vigorous as when he commenced. . . . . . .

His superior talents, zeal, and Christian benevolence, rendered him very popular as a minister, and gave him ready access to all classes. Thus there was opened to him a field of usefulness such as is seldom presented to one man, and he failed not to improve these opportunities of doing good, to the extent of his ability. He buried the dead, baptized the children, and married the sons and daughters of his neighbors for one or two generations, and was regarded by all as the patriarch of the neighborhood. Few men have been permitted to live an age in one community, and go down to the grave with the universal testimony that their lives were of unimpeachable purity. Yet this was the lot of Benjamin Northcutt."

He died January 13, 1854, at his home in Fleming county, where he had lived for more than half a century. His son, Rev. Henry Clay Northcutt, was for many years an honored Methodist minister, and wrote a very interesting Life of his father. All his children were converted and became active members of the Church, and were among the most worthy citizens of the State.

Few men have served the Church longer or been more useful than John Page. He lived until he was in his ninety-third year, and was in the ministry nearly sixty-eight years. Born in Fauquier county, Virginia, Nov. 22, 1766; married to Miss Celia Douglass in 1791; he entered the traveling ministry in 1792. He was one of the very few of that day to be admitted as a married man. The life of an itinerant in those early times was so exacting, and he was compelled to spend so much of his time ranging over large circuits, that it was well nigh impossible for him to establish a home and care for a family. The salary he received was so small that the preacher himself could barely live upon it, and to feed and clothe a family was out of all question. When a preacher married it usually meant his immediate location, and John Page was one of the very first to enter the itinerancy after he had taken a wife.

This year, he was sent to the Lexington circuit as the colleague of Sewell and Northcutt. The next year he is on the Danville circuit, then on the Salt River, and after this on Limestone. After a year in East Tennessee, he comes back to Kentucky where he serves in succession the Hinkstone and Limestone circuits, then goes to the Cumberland. Except while he was Presiding Elder of the Cumberland District in 1803-4, which, at that time, reached over into Kentucky, his labors in this State were now at an end. After a very hard year on this District he was so worn down that he was compelled to locate. He continued in this relation until 1825, when he was readmitted into the Tennessee Conference, in which he served for eight years, then was placed on the retired list, on which he remained until his death, June 17, 1859.

Page is described as "a large, splendid looking man, of an open, manly countenance. He possessed a sound, discriminating judgment, and was regarded as an able, useful minister of the gospel wherever he traveled." Jacob Young speaks of him while on the Salt River circuit, as "a very superior man—he was acknowledged by all to be of the first order of talent." He took a very conspicuous part in the great revival of 1801, and in a letter written by him late in life, he states that this revival really began under his ministry on the Nashville circuit early in 1799, before the remarkable manifestations of divine power among the Presbyterians at Gasper and Muddy River. "He was ranked among the first order of preachers of his day. The Church was under stronger obligations to John Page than to any man I knew of in his day. He was a strong defender of the doctrines held by the Methodist Church; he possessed a great deal of originality, and was devoted to the itinerant system, and continued to travel and preach as long as he was able."* (Carr).

---

*Jacob Young, who was converted under Page's ministry, and in 1803, served under him while he was Presiding Elder of the Cumberland District, says: "I went to see my new presiding elder who was the Rev. John Page, my father in the gospel. He was a mill-wright, by trade, and was building mills and traveling, both at once."

This conscludes the list of those who entered upon the work in the West at the Conference of 1792. The year was, in some degree, a prosperous one, and closed with an increase of 251 white, and 15 colored members. In the four circuits of Kentucky and in the Cumberland, there were now 2059 white, and 176 colored communicants.

CHAPTER VII.

On November 1, 1792, a General Conference met in the city of Baltimore, all the preachers in full connection being entitled to membership therein. The plan of governing the Church by means of a Council, consisting of the Bishops and the Presiding Elders, who were the appointees of the Bishops, had not proved satisfactory, and by general agreement, a General Conference was called to meet at the time and place mentioned. The Christmas Conference had adopted a form of Discipline for the Church, but naturally changes and additions were necessary in order to meet the needs of a growing body such as Methodism. At this General Conference of 1792, "the entire Discipline of the Church came up for review and revision." But few of the changes made affected the work in the West to any great extent, and it is not necessary to dwell on the work done. It was here that O'Kelly failed to get through his scheme for an appeal by a preacher to the Conference when dissatisfied with the appointment given him by the Bishop. Failing to secure the adoption of the measure, he left the Conference in a huff, and soon after withdrew from the Methodist Episcopal Church, and organized his "Republican Methodist Church." Haw and Ogden were carried away by this movement, and disaffection and schism were produced among the Methodists of Kentucky. This same General Conference placed the restriction on the Bishop, forbidding him to appoint an Elder to preside over a given District for more than four years successively; forbade a preacher to "make a charge" for administering baptism; removed the ban on receiving fees for solemnizing matrimony, and provided that the wife of a married preacher should have an annual allowance equal to that of her husband, namely, sixty-four dollars. Except for the O'Kelly affair, Kentucky Methodism was affected but little by this General Conference. We do not think any of the Kentucky preachers were present except Wilson Lee, whom William Burke says he met in the spring of 1792, in company with Bishop Asbury, leaving Kentucky and going east, and that he attended the General Conference at Baltimore. It was in the spring of 1792 that Lee closed his ministry in Kentucky. He had been here for six years, and was now worn down, his health broken, and he was returning to the older settlements of the East in the hope of rest and recuperation. He remained in New York, Philadelphia and Baltimore until in 1804, when death ended his most useful career.

It was some time during this year, 1792, that Col. John Hardin was murdered by the Indians. He was out of one of the best families of Virginia. Brave, prudent, dependable, he had rendered distinguished service to his country during the War of Independence, and enjoyed the full confidence of all who knew him. Coming with his family to Kentucky in 1786, he settled in what is now Washington county, and was a tower of strength in defending the early settlers from the attacks of the Indians. In the spring of this year, he was sent by Gen. Wilkinson into the Indian country to the North on a mission of peace. Accompanied by an interpreter, he reached an Indian village, and spent the night with them. In the morning he was ruthlessly murdered. His fate was not known by his family and friends for several months, during which time they anxiously awaited his return. Finally the news was received that he was not a prisoner, but a victim of Indian treachery and thirst for blood. Not only was he a most upright and valuable citizen, but he was an earnest Christian. He embraced religion and joined the Methodist Church as early as 1787, and as long as he was at home, it was his habit to gather his family about the family altar night and morning and commend them to the goodness and mercy of God. The Church in Kentucky keenly felt the loss of this good man. He was the father-in-law of Rev. Barnabas McHenry.

The Conference in this section of the western country for the year 1793, was held at Masterson's Station, April 30th. Bishop Asbury was present. He had just held a Conference in East Tennessee, and with Henry Hill, his traveling companion, and Barnabas McHenry, James Ward and William Burke, he came again through Powell's valley, over the Cumberland Gap, and through the Wilderness to the seat of the Conference at Masterson's. Meeting up with some persons on Holston who were coming to Kentucky, the Bishop's party was swelled to sixteen, "all pretty well armed except the Bishop." The Indians were still on the warpath, and it was dangerous to travel over this haunted trail. William Burke now comes on the scene, and has left us a most interesting account of this trip. He says:

I will here introduce a plan that Mr. Asbury suggested before we left the settlements. It was to make a rope long enough to tie to the trees all around the camp when we stopped at night, except a small passage for us to retreat, should the Indians surprise us; the rope to be so fixed as to strike the Indians below the knee, in which case they would fall forward, and we would retreat into the dark and pour in a fire upon them from our rifles. We accordingly prepared ourselves with the rope, and placed it on our pack-horse. We had to pack on the horses we rode corn sufficient to feed them for three days, and our own provisions, besides our saddle-bags of clothes. Through the course of the day nothing material transpired till very late in the afternoon, say less than an hour before sunset, when passing up a stony hollow from Richland Creek, at the head of which was the war path from the Northern Indians to the Southern tribes, we heard, just over the point of a hill, a noise like a child crying in great distress. We soon discovered that there were Indians there, and the reason why they used that stratagem to decoy us was, that a few days before they had defeated a company, known for a long time as McFarland's defeat, and a number were killed, and several children supposed to be lost in the woods. We immediately put whip to our horses, and in a few minutes crossed the ridge and descended to Camp Creek about sunset, when we called a halt to consult on what was best to be done; and on putting it to vote whether we proceed on our journey, every one was for proceeding but one of the preachers, who said it would kill his horse to travel that night. The Bishop all this time was sitting on his horse in silence, and on the vote being taken he reined up his steed and said, 'Kill man, kill horse, kill horse first;' and in a few minutes we made our arrangements for the night. The night being dark, and nothing but a narrow path, we appointed two to proceed in front, to lead the way and keep the path, and two as a rear guard, to keep some distance behind and bring intelligence every half hour, that we might know whether they were in pursuit of us; for we could not go faster than a walk. They reported that they were following us till near twelve o'clock. We were then on the Big Laurel river. We agreed to proceed, and alighted from our horses and continued on foot till daybreak, when we arrived at the Hazel Patch, where we stopped and fed our horses, and took some refreshment. We were mounted and on our journey by the rising of the sun; but by this time we were all very much fatigued, and we had yet between forty and fifty miles before us for that day. That night about dark we arrived at our good friend Willis Green's, near Stanford, Lincoln Court House, having been on horseback nearly forty hours, and having traveled about one hundred and ten miles in that time. I perfectly recollect that at supper I handed my cup for a second cup of tea, and before it reached me I was fast asleep, and had to be waked up to receive it. Part of us remained at Mr. Green's over Sunday, and preached at several places in the neighborhood. The Bishop and brother McHenry proceeded on next morning to attend a quarterly meeting at brother Francis Clark's, on the waters of Salt River, six miles west of Danville.

1793. The session of the Conference of 1793 was a pleasant one, and closed "under the melting, praying, praising power of God." "Trustees were appointed for the school, (Bethel) and sundry regulations made relative thereto." The Discipline was read, section by section, but for what purpose Asbury does not inform us. After the Conference adjourned, Asbury visited Bethel, and held a meeting with the newly-appointed trustees, then held two or three quarterly conferences before he again crossed the Wilderness on his return to the East. Hinkstone, a new circuit, takes its place in the list of appointments this year. It takes its name, doubtless, from the stream which rises out of a big spring at Mount Sterling, and flows through the midst of the circuit. Hinkstone circuit embraced the present counties of Montgomery, Clark, and Bourbon, and parts of Bath. Nicholas and Harrison. It was bounded by the then uninhabited stretch of country lying along the Licking river on the north, by the Kentucky river on the south, and included all the settled territory east of the Lexington circuit. The appointments for this year are as follows:

Francis Poythress, Elder.
Cumberland—Henry Birchett.
Salt River—Jacob Lurton, James Ward.
Danville—William Burke, John Page, J. Sewell.

Lexington—John Ball, Gabriel Woodfield.
Hinkstone—Richard Bird
Limestone—Benjamin Northcutt.

Of the ten preachers who were appointed to the work in Kentucky and Cumberland this year, four of them are new; namely, Jacob Lurton, James Ward, William Burke, and Gabriel Woodfield. Jacob Lurton had been in the work for seven years before coming to Kentucky, serving charges in Virginia, Maryland, and Pennsylvania. He served the Salt River circuit this year, the largest and most difficult of all the circuits in the State. The following year he went to Cumberland, but here his health failed and in 1795 he located. Returning to Kentucky, he married a Miss Tooley, of Jefferson county, and for many years lived on Floyd's Fork of Salt River, laboring as best he could in the local sphere to build up the Church in that part of the State. He is described as "an original genius," and a "useful preacher." While on the Cumberland circuit, a gracious revival attended his ministry, and it was he who extended the bounds of the Cumberland circuit into Logan county, Kentucky. Late in life he removed to Illinois, near Alton, where he died in great peace.

James Ward accompanied Bishop Asbury on his journey to Kentucky this year. He was admitted on trial at Baltimore in 1792, and appointed to Holston circuit. After one year with Jacob Lurton on the Salt River circuit, he was transferred to other fields and it was not until 1807 that he returned to Kentucky. In 1808, when William McKendree was elected Bishop, Ward was taken from the Lexington circuit to succeed him on the Cumberland District. Besides a portion of Middle Tennessee and all of Southern Kentucky, this District at that time included the settled portions of the territories of Missouri, Illinois, and Indiana. Sometimes he was compelled to carry his provisions with him and to sleep out in the woods or on the broad prairies. His zeal was great, and wonderful displays of divine power attended his ministry. In 1809 and 1810, he was on the Kentucky District, and was equally zealous and equally successful. After a few years he was compelled by ill health and family interests to locate. He engaged in farming near where Crestwood, Ky., now stands. While in this local relation, he preached nearly every Sunday, and was always ready to do his part in promoting the interests of the kingdom of his Redeemer. Twice after this he took regular work in the Conference, but was able to serve only a few years. He lived until 1855, dying when in his eighty-fourth year, having been in the ministry nearly sixty-three years. He was a member of the General Conferences of 1804 and 1808, and was elected to that of 1812, but modestly declined to serve. When the Kentucky Conference adhered to the M. E. Church, South, in 1845, he refused to go with the Conference, but adhered to the M. E. Church. In 1848, he was duly transferred to the Baltimore Conference of that Church. It was here he had begun his ministry, and he died a member of that body. His son, Rev. Joseph G. Ward, was for many years a member of our Little Rock Conference.

Mention has already been made of Gabriel Woodfield as one of the local preachers who came, at an early date, to Kentucky. He came from Pennsylvania, and for several years made his home in Fayette county. He was said to have been a preacher of more than ordinary ability, and very useful in the local ranks.

While the General Minutes make no mention of his being admitted on trial, his name is this year found in the list of appointments as the colleague of John Ball on the Lexington circuit. Redford is in error in saying that "the name of Gabriel Woodfield appears only for the present year on the roll of the Conference." In 1802, he was appointed to the Shelby circuit, but for some reason resigned before the year was out, and Jacob Young supplied in his place. He had then removed to Henry county, and some years before his death, he removed to Indiana, not far from Madison, where he lived to a good old age.

This year, 1793, introduces William Burke to Kentucky. Next to William McKendree, he did more for Kentucky Methodism than any other who served in this great field. As a pioneer preacher, as a Presiding Elder, as a revivalist, as a defender of the doctrines and government of Episcopal Methodism, and finally as historian of the Church during those early days, he stands out as one of the most useful men Kentucky Methodism has ever had. He was born in Loudon county, Virginia, in 1770; was converted about the time he reached manhood, and soon after began preaching; was admitted on trial in 1792, and was appointed with Stephen Brooks to the Green circuit, on the line between East Tennessee and North Carolina. In 1793 Bishop Asbury brought him to Kentucky and appointed him to the Danville circuit, with John Page as helper. Concerning this circuit he tells us in his Autobio graphical sketch:

The circuit was in but poor condition. Discipline had been very much neglected, and numbers had their names on the class-papers who had not met their class for months. We applied ourselves to the discharge of our duty and enforced the discipline, and, during the course of the summer, disposed of upward of one hundred. We had some few additions, but, under God, laid the foundation for a glorious revival the next and following years. The bounds and extent of this circuit were large, including the counties of Mercer, Lincoln, Garrard, and Madison; the west part of the circuit including the head waters of Salt River and Chaplin; on the north, bounded by the Kentucky river; south and east, extending as far as the settlements—taking four weeks to perform the round. There were three log meeting-houses on the circuit; one in Madison county, called Proctor's Chapel; one in the Forks of Dix river, Garrett's meeting-house; and one on Shoenea Run, called Shoney Run, not far from Harrod's Station, in Mercer county. During the course of this year, a new meeting-house was erected in Garrard county, considered the best meeting-house in the country, and they named it Burke's Chapel.

The above quotation is made from an Autobiographical Sketch of Burke, written late in life, and published in "Sketches of Western Methodism," by Rev. James B. Finley. From this Sketch we get as much information concerning early Methodism in this State as we get from any other source. We shall have occasion to quote from it often, and as we are to meet with Burke so frequently in the course of this history, we shall not here attempt an extended account of the man or his labors. In 1794, Burke was sent to the Hinkstone circuit, but at his first quarterly meeting the Presiding Elder removed him to the Salt River circuit to take the place of one of the preachers who had left his charge. He remained here for about six months. This was a very large and difficult circuit, and it being the summer of Wayne's campaign against the Indians, many of the men from the counties embraced were away in this campaign. Things were in a turmoil, and there was but little opportunity to accomplish good. Money was not to be had. Burke says: "I was reduced to the last pinch. My clothes were nearly all gone. I had patch upon patch, and patch by patch, and I received only money sufficient to buy a waistcoat, and not enough of that to pay for the making, during the two quarters I remained on the circuit." After the second quarterly meeting, his Presiding Elder changed him to the Lexington circuit where he replenished his wardrobe and improved his condition generally. "Lexington was a four weeks' circuit, and tolerably compact. It included the counties of Fayette, Jessamine, Woodford, Franklin, Scott, and Harrison; bounded on the east and north by the Hinkstone circuit, on the west by the frontiers. Frankfort, now the seat of government, was then a frontier station. The southern boundary was the Kentucky river, which is peculiar for the high cliffs of limestone rocks, which present a wild and grand appearance, in many places from four to five hundred feet high." We shall have occasion later to refer to the services of Burke in winning back to the Church those who had gone off with the O'Kelly movement, his debates with the Baptists, his work as secretary of the Conference, his break-down in health, etc., so we leave him for the present.

Reference has been made to the enforcement of discipline on the Danville circuit, and the dropping of more than a hundred names from the class rolls. Methodism, in those early days, was aptly characterized as "Christianity in earnest." These early Methodist preachers were very zealous in trying to win souls from the ways of sin, but when one applied for membership in the societies, they expected him to be in earnest about it. They put him on probation for six months so as to be sure his action was not prompted by mere impulse that would soon pass away. When admitted to membership, they expected him to continue to manifest his sincerity by attending the meetings of his class, where he would receive spiritual instruction and help. They expected him to "walk worthy of the vocation wherewith he is called," and if he did not do these things, they judged that the purposes of his enrollment had failed, and he was put out of the society until such time as he made up his mind to be a Christian in deed and in truth. Numbers counted for little; it was souls they were after, and unless there was genuine salvation and a godly life, they deemed that the mere name of a careless and indifferent member was of no benefit to him, but was very hurtful to the Church. Much of their success was due to their rigid adherence to discipline. A church loaded down with an indifferent or immoral membership can neither be a strong church, nor command the respect of the outside world. The Church of the present day might improve its efficiency by ridding itself of its indifferent and unworthy members.

There was practically no gain in membership this year. According to the figures given in the General Minutes, the increase of white members in Kentucky and Cumberland was only twenty-three; while there was a loss of forty colored members.

1794. The Conference of 1794 was held at Lewis' Chapel, near the site of Bethel Academy. Bishop Asbury was not there. William Burke headed a company of twelve well-armed men to meet the Bishop beyond Cumberland Gap and guard him through the Wilderness, but Asbury was sick and could not come. At Crab Orchard, as they were starting on this trip, they fell in with about fifty others who were going back to the older States, and Burke was made commander of the whole party. On their way, they came to a place where four preachers, two Baptists and two Dunkards, had been killed by the Indians the day before. These preachers, leaving Crab Orchard the day before Burke's party started, accompanied a large party toward the East. "The company, with whom they traveled, had treated them in such an ungentlemanly and unchristian way during the first day and night, that on the morning of the second day they all four started in advance, and had not proceeded more than one mile before they were surprised by a party of Indians, and all four killed and scalped, and their horses and all they had taken off by the Indians." A sad commentary on the moral condition of that company, who were thus responsible for the death of these men. When Burke reached Bean's Station, in Powell's Valley, he received the news that Bishop Asbury was sick and unable to come to Kentucky.

Conference met on April 15th, with Francis Poythress in the chair. During the year Henry Birchett had died. Though in feeble health, he had asked the privilege of going to the Cumberland circuit the year before, and it was not long ere his strength failed him, and he found in death the rest he would not take while living. "He was one among the worthies who freely left safety, ease, and prosperity, to seek after and suffer faithfully for souls." John Sewell and Benjamin Northcutt had located, the first to settle in Sumner county Tennessee, and the latter, on account of the giving way of a vocal chord, to spend the rest of his life as a local preacher in Fleming county, Ky. John Ball also located and made his home in the Cumberland country. Gabriel Woodfield, too, dropped back

into the local ranks. Barnabas McHenry, after a year
as Presiding Elder of a District in western Virginia,
with health impaired, returns to Kentucky and is sent
to the Salt River charge. John Metcalf, Tobias Gibson, Thomas Scott, Moses Speer and Peter Guthrie appear as new men assigned to this field. The appointments are as follows:

Francis Poythress, Elder.
Lexington—John Metcalf, Tobias Gibson.
Danville—Thomas Scott.
Hinkstone—William Burke.
Limestone—Richard Bird.
Cumberland—Jacob Lurton, Moses Speer.
Salt River—Barnabas McHenry, John Page, Peter Guthrie.
"Barnabas McHenry and Jacob Lurton to exchange"

Of Peter Guthrie little is known beyond the fact
that he was admitted on trial this year and appointed
to the Salt River circuit as a helper to Barnabas Mc-
Henry and John Page; and that in 1795 he was appointed to Cumberland circuit as the colleague of William Burke. His name then disappears and we find no
further trace of him. Burke says he was "a man of
deep piety, but of slender preaching ability."

John Metcalf had been received on trial in 1790.
Three years he had spent on circuits in Virginia and
one in North Carolina before coming to Kentucky. He
is appointed this year to the Lexington circuit with
Tobias Gibson. After this his name disappears from
the Minutes with no explanation as to how or why he
did not continue as an itinerant. However, Burke
says that he had married and settled down, and that
he succeeded Valentine Cook as Principal of Bethel
Academy. His leaving Bethel Academy, to say the
least, was somewhat irregular. While we have already

mentioned the incident, the following from the old Quarterly Conference Record of the Lexington circuit, under date of May 19, 1804, will be found interesting:

"At a quarterly meeting for Lexington circuit, at J. Griffith's, the members of the Conference were the following: William McKendree, P. E., Learner Blackman, Thomas Wilkerson, Benj. Coleman, Jesse Griffith, David Robertson, Bryan McGrath, Benj. Vanpelt, Nathaniel Harris, William Rutter, Humphrey Lyons, Cornelius Ruddle, Jesse Rowland, Luke Hanson, Elias Johnson, Richard Demit, John Lair.

The case of John Metcalf, L. D., was brought forward from the Committee, who were Jesse Garner, Sl. Newman, Nathaniel Harris.

The charges were as follows, viz., Charge 1st. For removing the property of Bethel Academy without the knowledge or consent of the trustees of said Academy. Charge 2nd. In not giving information of s'd property, though inquired of in an official manner, 1st, before the Board of Trustees, and 2nd, by one of the Trustees alone. Charge 3rd. For not sending a full account of said property. Charge 4th. In not sending a true account of the time when, (nor by whom), s'd property was removed. This Conference, taking up the charges one by one, concur in judgment with the above named Committee, and finally give it as their judgment, that s'd J. Metcalf, be reduced to a state of trial, for the time of 12 months, from the present date, and deprived of the liberty of all official services in the Church, for the same term of 12 months.

Signed in behalf of Conference, By Nathaniel Harris.

How long he continued as Principal of Bethel we do not know. Cook gave up the Principalship in 1800 and this record of his trial and suspension is dated in May, 1804. We do know that he removed the furniture of the institution to Nicholasville, where it was used for school purposes. It is stated, but whether correct or not we can not say, that the removal of the property occurred in 1803, and that Metcalf taught a school in Nicholasville for eighteen years. A good man may become entangled in unfortunate affairs, and, acting upon his best judgment, he may conscientiously do things that do not seem right to others, who can not put themselves in his place or see things from his point of view. We suspect that Metcalf saw the hopelessness of Bethel and took the action he thought must be taken sooner or later. However this may be, Metcalf continued to preach after his sentence of suspension had expired, and for years he was the only professor of religion in Nicholasville. He preached all over Jessamine county and in surrounding communities, and was regraded by all as a most godly man. His wife was the niece of the Rev. Francis Poythress. He died in August, 1820, leaving a large number of descendants in Jessamine county.

Col. Bennett Young, in his "History of Jessamine County," says of him:

> To Rev. John Metcalf belongs the honor of laying off the county seat of Jessamine, and also of naming the town. He was a native of Southampton county, Va., and came to Kentucky in the spring of 1790, bringing with him, not only his credentials as a minister, but also a heart full of love to God. Bethel Academy was established in 1790, and was opened for the reception of pupils in January, 1794. It was the second institution of learning ever established by the Methodist Church in the United States, the one at Cokesburg (Cokesbury) being the first. The labors of Mr. Metcalf were confined largely to Jessamine county. He traveled a few circuits in Fayette and Mercer, but his life work was connected with Jessamine. He took charge of Bethel Academy at the request of Bishop Asbury. He began his work as founder and continued his labors there as principal of this school in the "wilderness." He infused his own earnest and enthusiastic spirit into the institution. He labored under tremendous disadvantages in his work, but he overcame most of them, and brought success where others would have had only failure.

"He was the first Methodist minister who ever preached a sermon in Lexington. . . . Plain, practical and earnest, he attracted attention and won hearts, and he generally drew large crowds of people, who were glad to hear him. He was largely instrumental in building up the Methodist Church in Jessamine county. He was born in 1758, and died at his home in Nicholasville, in 1820, having reached his sixty-first year. It was through his labors that the white frame Methodist church was first erected in Nicholasville, in 1799.

Tobias Gibson, according to the General Minutes, received two appointments this year,—to Union circuit, in North Carolina, for "one quarter;" and to Lexington without any limitation of time. We suppose that it was intended that he remain in North Carolina until he had served one quarter, then go on to Lexington, but we have no information from any source that he ever came to Lexington or rendered any service there. It is probable that he remained in the South throughout the year. He was not a strong man physically, and even now the strain of the itinerancy began to break down his feeble body. Yet he pressed on, refusing to cease his labors or take a rest. In 1799 he begged the privilege of going to Mississippi as a missionary, and for five years he toiled as he could to lay the foundations of Methodism in the Natchez country. He was truly the father of Methodism in Mississippi, where his name is still as ointment poured forth. His memoir says that "Tobias Gibson did for many years, preach, profess, possess and practise christian perfection." We may have occasion to refer to him again, but inasmuch as he did not labor in Kentucky, we shall not extend this sketch at the present time.*

---

*Tobias Gibson was highly connected, and several of his relations in Kentucky and New York are quite wealthy. The writer was called to see Mrs. C. D. Chenault, of Lexington, who was a

Thomas Scott, familiarly known as Judge Scott, because he was, for several years, one of the Judges of the Supreme Court of Ohio, was born in Maryland, embraced religion and became a member of the Methodist Church before he was fourteen years of age. When only sixteen-and-a-half years of age, he was admitted on trial in the Conference, and for five years served in Virginia and Pennsylvania. His parents had removed to Bracken county, Kentucky, and in the spring of 1794, acting under instructions from Asbury, he came to this State. He came down the Ohio river on a flat boat loaded with provisions for Wayne's Army, landed at Maysville, and made his way to Bethel Academy, near which the Conference was held. He was appointed to the Danville circuit. In order to attend to some important business in Pennsylvania, he located at the Conference of 1795, but sickness and other circumstances prevented his going to Pennsylvania. At the request of the Presiding Elder, Rev. Francis Poythress, he took charge of the Lexington circuit during the summer of that year, filling the place of Aquila Sugg, whose health had failed. In May, 1796, Scott was married to Miss Wood, of Mason county, and settled in the town of Washington as a clerk in a dry goods store. His employer failing in business, he began the study of law. After many difficulties had been overcome, he received license to practice, and moved to Flemingsburg, where he was appointed prosecuting attorney. After a year in this place he went to Chillicothe, Ohio, where he lived for more than fifty-one

---

distant relative, and greatly interested in a plan for these relatives to found a school somewhere in the mountains of Kentucky in honor of Tobias Gibson. But death overtook her before she could work out her plans.

years. In Ohio he filled many offices of trust; was clerk of the Court, Secretary of the Senate, Justice of the Peace, and, finally, in 1809, was elected a member of the Supreme Court of that State. He continued to preach as a local preacher, and was eminently useful in that sphere. He lived to be more than 80 years of age.

The older members of the Kentucky Conference will remember the Rev. Samuel W. Speer, D. D., who was for many years a member of the Louisville and Kentucky Conferences, and who died in 1900. He was the son of Moses Speer, whose name appears this year in connection with the Cumberland circuit. Born in Maryland, in 1766, Moses Speer came with his parents to the mouth of Bear Grass (Louisville), in 1780. Early in life he gave his heart to God, united with the Church, and not long afterwards, was licensed to preach. He is said to have been the first Protestant minister to preach the gospel in Indiana, though this honor has been claimed by others. Under the Presiding Elder, he labored for a while on the Hinkstone circuit, then in 1794, was admitted on trial in the Conference and sent to Cumberland. Here his labors were greatly blessed. During the year he was married to Miss Amelia Ewing, of Nashville. He located at the end of the year, and took up his home near Nashville, where he lived for more than forty years. He was very helpful as a local preacher, and aided Wm. Burke in holding the Methodists of that section to the Methodist Episcopal Church when Haw drew off and went with the Republican Methodists. "In his early ministry, he was the intimate friend of Haw, Ogden, McHenry, and Burke. He was among the first who were licensed to preach west of the mountains. He was also one of the brave band that was sent to meet Bishop Asbury near Cumberland Gap, and guard him through the wilderness into the settled portions of Kentucky. He contributed by his labors much toward the planting of Methodism in Logan county, Kentucky, and labored with the McGees in the great revival in 1799-1805." Dr. Redford tells us that, as late as 1839, when Speer was seventy-three years old, his name again appears upon the Conference roll, this time in the Mississippi Conference, and that he was appointed to Montgomery, in the San Augustin District, Texas, but before the year closed, he was called from labor to reward. Two of his sons entered the Methodist ministry, one of whom will be noticed at a later period in this narrative.

But little advancement was made this year in the way of membership. Several things might be given in explanation of the poor showing. The O'Kelly schism was just now reaching Kentucky and Middle Tennessee, and there was considerable disaffection, especially in the Cumberland country. Then, this was the year of Wayne's campaign against the Indians of the North, many of the members were away with him, and the preaching services suffered from their absence. Often their families could not attend without them. Until Wayne won the complete victory at The Fallen Timbers, the Indians were exceedingly troublesome to the Kentuckians. While no formidable invasions of the State were made by the savages, marauding parties were constantly skulking through the country, waylaying the roads, shooting down workers in the fields, attacking cabins in the night, and making life hideous for the settlers. This forced the people to live in forts or grouped near blockhouses in order to protect themselves, and but few had the hardihood to build their cabins at any great distance from communities of this sort. But when the Indians were so completely subdued by Wayne's Army, it removed the danger of Indian depredations and the people began at once to scatter everywhere and to occupy lands they had already pre-empted. This resulted in the breaking up of several societies and the weakening of others. The circuit-rider was under the necessity of following up the people, and of reorganizing the Church among them. This, besides the demoralization and wickedness which always follow upon war. It is not surprising that the increase during this period of demoralization and reconstruction was small.

1795. There is a disagreement among the writers from whom we get our information as to where the Conference of 1795 was held. But William Burke very explicitly states that "the Conference for the year 1795 met at Ebenezer, Earnest's neighborhood, on Nolachucky, the last week in April." He is very circumstantial in his account of what took place. He says that "most of the preachers from Kentucky met their brethren on Holston district;" that he was ordained elder at that Conference, and that his parchments bear date of April 30, 1795; that, at the request of Bishop Asbury, he preached the ordination sermon, etc. The meager records of the General Minutes give us no help in the matter. But inasmuch as Asbury's Journal under date of April 27, 1795, shows that Asbury was present at this Conference at Ernest's and that "six brethren from Kentucky met us," we must accept this as the place and date of the Conference.

The appointments made in the spring of 1795, are as follows:

Francis Poythress, Elder.
Cumberland—William Burke, Peter Guthrie.
Salt River—John Buxton, W. Duzan, B. McHenry.
Danville—Francis Acuff.
Lexington, Aquila Sugg.
Hinkstone—Thomas Wilkerson.
Limestone—John Page.

It will be seen that the preachers returning to this field for this year were Poythress, Burke, Guthrie, McHenry, and Page. Bird had been transferred back to Virginia. Gibson had not, so far as known, come to Kentucky. Metcalf, Scott, Speer, and Lurton had located. The new men are John Buxton, William Duzan, Francis Acuff, Aquila Sugg, and Thomas Wilkerson.

Burke gives us an interesting account of his trip from the seat of the Conference to his circuit. He says:

"I received my appointment this year to Cumberland, Mero district, Western Territory. The circuit included Davidson, Sumner, and Robinson counties in the territory, and part of Logan county, Kentucky, lying on the waters of Red River, and extending out to the neighborhood where Russellville now stands; in a word, it included all the settlements in that region of country. In order to reach my destination I had to return through Kentucky, and to take my colleague, who was a young man, . . . by the name of Peter Guthrie. He was a man of deep piety, but of slender preaching abilities. We made the best of our way for Cumberland, passed on from Lexington through Danville circuit and Salt River; and on the first night after we left the bounds of Salt River circuit, we stopped at the last house, on the edge of the barrens, on the south side of Green river, at Sidebottom's Ferry. After we had put our horses up, circumstances made it necessary, by an occurrence in the family, that we should camp out; and we accordingly made our fire in the woods, and laid us down to rest; and, all things considered, we had a comfortable night's rest. We now had a vast barren track to pass through of between eighty and ninety miles, with but one house —McFadden's Station, on Big Barren river, not far from where

Bowling Green is now situated. The next day we arrived in the settlement, on the waters of Red river. On the following day we arrived at Nashville, and in the evening at James Hockett's, about two miles west of town."

It was during this year that Burke held his debate with James Haw and won back this field from the followers of O'Kelly. We shall let Burke tell the story.

On inquiry I found that James Haw, who was one of the first preachers that came to Kentucky, had located and settled in Cumberland, and embraced the views of O'Kelly, and by his influence and address had brought over the traveling and every local preacher but one in the country to his views, and considerable dissatisfaction obtained in many of the societies. Under these circumstances I was considerably perplexed to know what course to take—a stranger to everybody in the country, a young preacher, and Haw an old and experienced preacher, well known, a popular man, and looked up to as one of the fathers of the Church, and one who had suffered much in planting Methodism in Kentucky and Cumberland. After much reflection and prayer to God for direction, I finally settled upon the following plan, viz.; to take the Discipline and examine it thoroughly, selecting all that was objected to by O'Kelly, and those who adhered to him, and then undertake an explanation and defense of the same. I accordingly met Brother Speer at Nashville, and after preaching requested the society to remain, and commenced my work. When I concluded my defense, I took the vote of the society, and they unanimously sustained the positions I had taken. Brother Speer also asked the privilege of making a few remarks. He stated to the society that he would consider the Church as a house that he lived in; and notwithstanding the door was not exactly in the place he should like it, or the chimney in the end that best pleased him, yet he could not throw away or pull down his house on that account; and therefore, he concluded that he would not throw away the Church, although some things, he thought, could be improved in the Discipline. In consequence of this victory of my first attempt, I took courage, and proceeded with my work in every society; and, to my utter astonishment, I succeeded in every place, and saved every society but one small class on Red River, where a local preacher lived, by the name of Jonathan Stevenson, who had traveled the circuit two years before, and located in that neighborhood. Haw and Stevenson appointed a meeting on Red river, and invited the Methodists all over the circuit to attend the meeting for the purpose of organizing the new Church. The result was, that only ten or twelve members offered themselves, and most of them had formerly belonged to the Baptist Church. Having failed in every attempt to break up the societies, the next step was to call me to a public debate. I accepted his challenge, and the day was appointed to meet at Station Camp, one of the most popular neighborhoods, and convenient to a number of large societies. Notwithstanding I accepted the challenge, I trembled for the cause. I was young in the ministry, and inexperienced in that kind of debate. He was an old minister, of long experience, and of high standing in the community. I summoned up all my courage, and, like young David with his sling, I went forth to meet the Goliath. The day arrived, and a great concourse of people attended. The preliminaries were settled, and I had the opening of the debate. The Lord stood by me. I had uncommon liberty, and before I concluded, many voices were heard in the congregation, saying, "Give us the old way!" Mr. Haw arose to make his reply very much agitated, and exhibited a very bad temper, being very much confused. He made some statement that called from me a denial, and the people rose up to sustain me, which was no sooner done than he was so confused that he picked up his saddle-bags, and walked off, and made no reply. This left me in possession of the whole field, and from that hour he lost his influence among the Methodists, and his usefulness as a preacher. In this situation he remained until 1801; and when the great revival began in Tennessee among the Presbyterians and Methodists, he connected himself with the former, and ended his days among them as a preacher.

After the difficulties with Haw had subsided, there was a considerable revival among the societies, and harmony prevailed throughout the charge. On the 9th of January, Burke, defying the prejudice against married preachers, and determining to brave all the difficulties of supporting a wife while doing the work of an itinerant, was married to Miss Rachel Cooper, of

Sumner county, Tenn. At the Conference that fall, Bishop Asbury facetiously remarked that Burke had that year accomplished two important things—he had defeated the O'Kellyites, and had married a wife!

Tall, thin, taciturn, and lacking in social qualities, was John Buxton, who this year was appointed to the Salt River circuit. But he was fervent in piety, and zealous and effective in his ministry. While in Kentucky he was greatly blessed in his work. He had traveled four years in Virginia and North Carolina before his transfer to the West. After one year in Kentucky, he was sent to Cumberland for one year, then was returned to East Tennessee and Virginia. But in 1798, we find him again in Kentucky, on the Lexington circuit, and the following year on Limestone. From this time until his location in 1814, he served various Districts in the Virginia Conference. He seems to have excelled as an administrator. He was a member of the General Conferences of 1804, 1808, and 1812.

"Small in stature, and of humble pretensions in the ministry," William Duzan was admitted this year and sent to the Salt River circuit with John Buxton and Barnabas McHenry. He traveled but three years —the Salt River, Cumberland and Holston circuits. He was living in Washington county, Kentucky, at the time he entered the ministry, and Redford thinks it likely that he was a convert of the revival of 1790. "A young man of unblemished reputation, pious, humble, deeply devoted to God, and greatly esteemed by all his acquaintances on account of his excellent qualities."*

---

*The father of Wm. Duzan lived in Fleming county—Burke. The statement that he lived in Washington county lacks confirmation.

Francis Acuff was born in Virginia, but his youth was spent in East Tennessee. He was in the itinerant work but little more than two years, the first spent on Greenbrier circuit, in Virginia, the second on Holston, and this year he was sent to the Danville circuit in Kentucky, but in August, 1795, a little more than three months after his appointment to Danville, he died. He was buried somewhere in the bounds of the then Danville circuit. This circuit at that time covered a very large territory, and we have no means of knowing the exact place of his burial. He was the son of Timothy Acuff, who gave the land on which to build the first Methodist church in Tennessee. It was called Acuff's Chapel. Francis Acuff was a young man of fine ability and gave great promise of usefulness, but was cut down when only in his twenty-fifth year. As an instance of the strong affection in which he was held, it is related that an Englishman, who had been greatly blessed under Acuff's ministry, when he heard of his death, determined to visit his grave. He walked for many miles through the dangerous wilderness in order to carry out his purpose, trusting God to protect him from Indians and wild beasts. Said he, "When I came to rivers I would wade them; or, if there were ferries, they would take me across; and when I was hungry, the travelers would give me a morsel of bread. When I came to Mr. Green's in Madison county, I inquired for our dear Mr. Acuff's grave. The people looked astonished, but directed me to it. I went to it; felt my soul happy; shouted over it, and praised the Lord."

In our brief sketch of Judge Thomas Scott, we mentioned the fact that, at the request of the Presiding Elder, he went to the Lexington circuit in 1795, and filled out the term of Aquila Sugg, whose health had failed. Aquila Sugg had been admitted on trial in 1788, and traveled in Virginia and the two Carolinas until this year, when he was transferred to Kentucky. He was appointed to the Lexington circuit, but at the end of three months he was compelled by ill health to give up his work and return to the home of his parents. Improving somewhat in health, and anxious to have a part in the great work of the Master, in the spring of 1796 he reported for service and was appointed to Logan circuit, which had just been created out of the old Cumberland circuit. But just before the close of the year, his health gave way so completely that he had to surrender a work that was dearer to him than life. He located at the Conference of 1797. Methodism in Western Kentucky had its beginning in Logan county, under the ministry of Jacob Lurton, but Aquila Sugg was the first pastor to serve a charge in that section of the State.

One of the men who stands out preeminent among the preachers of his day, was Thomas Wilkerson—

a man of well-balanced character, distinguished for a sound understanding, lively fancy, tender sympathies, and profound piety. As a preacher he was classed among the best of his day. To a thorough acquaintance with the Scriptures and Methodist theology, he added a deep knowledge of human nature, especially in its more profound and subjective experiences. Gentle and persuasive in manner, clear and logical in statement, his sermons were pleasing and instructive, and often overwhelmingly convincing. When inspired by his theme, he rose into the higher regions of pulpit eloquence. At such times he was one of the finest specimens of a gospel preacher ever heard in this country. He lived and died without the suspicion of a taint on his spotless character.—Rev. W .G. E. Cunningham.

Born in Amelia county, Virginia; without religious influences in childhood; convicted under Methodist preaching in boyhood; converted at eighteen, and preaching at twenty, he was admitted on trial in 1792. During a long life, he labored in Southwest Virginia, East and Middle Tennessee, Kentucky and Maryland. In the fall of 1794, he says: "There was a Macedonian call from Kentucky. Bishop Asbury would not take the responsibility on himself to appoint where life was to be in danger, but called for volunteers. John Buxton and I offered our services." He had been suffering from chills and fever, but was ready to start for his new field in the spring of 1795. His appointment was the Hinkstone circuit, including Mount Sterling, Winchester, Paris, and other points. In some articles published in *The Southwestern Christian Advocate,* in 1841, he has left an account of his trip and of his work in Kentucky. He says:

We had to pack our provisions for man and horse for nearly two hundred miles, lie on the ground at night, having a guard stationed around us. I was apprehensive such exposure would be fatal to me in my delicate state of health. In the evening before the first night, I lay without a bed—I had an ague, which was the last I ever had. What I thought would make much against me, was so overruled as to prove the means of my cure. My health rapidly improved; so that I was soon able to undergo the hardships of a pioneer. I now saw the excellency of the itinerant plan. We kept up with the frontier settlements, preached to the people in their forts and blockhouses. Here I met no D. D.'s to discuss doctrines, or to make out reports about moral wastes. We had nothing to contend with from without but Indians, the wild beasts, and smaller vermin. We thought ourselves quite well accommodated if we had a half-faced camp or a cabin to shelter us, and some wild meat to eat. It has been a matter of inquiry how we found such ready access to the frontier settlements. We followed the openings of providence, as did Mr. Wesley. Owing to the uncertainty of land titles, emigrants would squat down on the frontiers, where they could get permission. Our brethren, moving from the old settlements together, would settle in the same neighborhood. As soon as they could build some cabins, they would go in search of a preacher; and there would be a society raised. As soon as they became acquainted with the country, they would seek homes of their own, and, as lands were always cheapest on the frontiers, the class would scatter in different directions, and, as before, search out the preachers and invite them to their houses; so we had not to go in search of preaching places, but the people searched out the preachers.

Mr. Wilkerson served the Hinkstone circuit one year, then the Lexington, and then the Cumberland His health was poor. He was transferred to other fields for a few years, but returned to Kentucky in 1801, and was one of the outstanding workers in the great revival of that period. Upon returning to Kentucky, he traveled, during the summer, the Lexington circuit with William Burke. He says: "On this circuit we had a considerable revival. We found our Baptist friends a little troublesome. They brought their old proselyting engine to bear upon us; but Brother Burke met them so promptly, and so fully rebutted their arguments, that they failed to do the Church much harm."

The old story was here repeated—a good man wore himself out by excessive labors, exposures, privations and want, and was compelled to locate. He married, and made his home near Strawberry Plains, in East Tennessee. Here he lived for many years, serving the Church in the local ranks to the limit of his ability, greatly beloved and respected by all. Many interesting anecdotes are told of him, but we have not space to repeat them here. This little scrap from one of his articles in the *Southwestern* is worthy of transcription to our pages:

Mr. Editor, while on this subject I will answer another inquiry: How were the people first brought to receive the Methodist preachers and their doctrine? I can only answer for the neighborhood where I was raised. The novelty of their preaching produced great excitement. Some said they were good men; others said, nay, they deceive the people. Many, however, would go and hear for themselves, and the inherent power of gospel truth would arrest them; conviction for sin would cause them to inquire what they must do to be saved. This led to reading the Scriptures and examining the doctrines. (For there was much controversy). The following inquiries would take place: Are the Methodists, or some other denomination, right? If the Calvinists are right, and God, for the purposes of his own glory, did foreordain whatsoever comes to pass, then the Methodists cannot be wrong; for he ordained there should be Methodists, and that they should preach and act just as they do; but if the Methodists are right, and man is a free agent, the Calvinists must be wrong, and, by trusting to their election, may lose their souls. If the Antinomian is right, the Methodist Christian is safe; for his believing he can fall from grace, and using all diligence to make his calling and election sure, will not make him fall; but if the Methodists are right, the Antinomian must be dangerously wrong, and by trusting to his once being in grace may fall and perish forever. If the Universalian is right, the Methodist is safe; for if all are to be saved, the Methodist will be among them; but if the Methodist is right, they must be wrong, and their purgatory may last forever. If the infidel is right, the Methodist is on safe ground. If the whole system of religion is a mere farce, it is to the Christian a very safe and pleasing delusion; but if the Methodists are right, the infidel is dangerously wrong; for he that believeth not shall be damned. Hence, it was an easy matter for those who wished to save their souls and be on the safe side, to choose their future course, and none but such durst join the Methodist Church; for there was great persecution."

Wilkerson was the first pastor of the first *Station* in Kentucky. In 1803, Lexington had sent a petition to Bishop Asbury, asking that they be separated from the circuit. This was done, and Thomas Wilkerson was sent as their pastor. His health was very poor, and he saw but little fruit. He died near Abingdon, Va., in 1856, in the eighty-fourth year of his age.*

Owing to conditions already referred to, there was a decrease in membership this year, the white members numbering only 2,110 and the colored members, 111.

1796. The Conference held in the spring of 1796 was held again at Masterson's Station—the last that was held there. Masterson about this time sold his Fayette county home, and removed to what is now Carroll county, a mile or two above the mouth of the Kentucky river. Asbury was not present at this Conference, and Poythress presided. The appointments were as follows:

Francis Poythress, Elder.
Limestone—Henry Smith.
Lexington—Thomas Wilkerson.
Hinkstone—Aquila Jones.
Danville—Benjamin Lakin.
Salt River—John Watson.
Shelby—Jeremiah Lawson.
Logan—Aquila Sugg.

The reader will see that two new circuits appear in the list—Shelby and Logan,—Shelby being taken out of the Salt River circuit, and Logan out of the Cumberland. Poythress still leads the forces as Presiding Elder, though five of the seven men who labor in Kentucky under him, are new men. Acuff had died during the year; Guthrie and McHenry had located; Burke

---

*Bishop Paine, in his Life of McKendree, says that Wilkerson "was universally esteemed for his talents and piety. His simplicity of manners, his dignity, amiability, and remarkably good sense, gave him great influence among all classes, and particularly among the most intelligent. . . . I have often thought that, in his intellectual, moral, and social characteristics, he strikingly resembled Bishop Roberts."

had been sent to Guilford circuit, in North Carolina; Buxton and Duzan were on Cumberland, and only Wilkerson and Sugg remained to preach the gospel another year to the Kentuckians. The new men are Henry Smith, Aquila Jones, Benjamin Lakin, John Watson, and Jeremiah Lawson. The introduction of so many new men was due largely to the tremendous strain upon the workers in this hard field. Of those who remained in Kentucky, Aquila Sugg broke down before the year closed, and Wilkerson had to go to the local ranks a few years later. Poythress himself was on the verge of a complete breakdown.

Henry Smith, who was this year appointed to the Limestone circuit, was no ordinary man. He was born near Frederick City, Md., in 1769, of German parentage, and was baptized in infancy in the German Reformed Church. Convicted of sin under the preaching of Rev. Thomas Scott, when in his twenty-first year, he was soon after converted and called to preach. He served for two years in Virginia, then came to Kentucky, and was assigned to the Limestone circuit. The next year he was sent to Salt River, then after a year in East Tennessee, and two years in Ohio, he was returned to Kentucky and again appointed to the Limestone circuit. This was the last year that he spent in Kentucky. He was transferred to the Baltimore Conference, and continued in connection with it until his death. He lived to be a very old man, reaching his ninety-fourth year, having been a minister for nearly seventy years. Although a delicate man, he outlived all of his contemporaries. He was a fine preacher, a fine character, and was much beloved by all who knew him. He was buried near his home, at Hookstown, Md., but in the spring of 1863,

the Baltimore Conference removed his remains to
Mount Olivet cemetery, in the city of Baltimore, and
reburied them near the graves of Bishops Asbury,
George, Waugh, and Emory.

Aquila Jones entered the traveling connection in
1795, and remained in it only three years. After a
year on the Holston circuit, he served Hinkstone and
Limestone in Kentucky, then located in 1798. We
know nothing further about him.

Benjamin Lakin, who received Bishop Kavanaugh
and John P. Durbin into the Methodist Church, was a
native of Maryland, born in Montgomery county, August 23, 1767. His father died when he was nine
years old, and his mother moved to the Redstone country, in Pennsylvania; but dissatisfied there, she
brought her family to Kentucky, and settled on Bracken
Creek, near the Mason county line. Young Benjamin was converted under the ministry of Richard
Whatcoat when fourteen years of age, and entered the
ministry at seventeen, serving the Hinkstone circuit
under the Presiding Elder, Francis Poythress. Admitted on trial in 1795, he was appointed to Green circuit, in East Tennessee, then to Danville in 1796, and
to Lexington in 1797. During this year he was married, and, as was usual in those days, was compelled
to locate to care for his family. He was readmitted
in 1801, and sent to Limestone circuit, then for two
years his labors were in Ohio, on the Scioto and Miami
circuits. He then spent three years in Kentucky on
the Salt River, Danville, and Shelby circuits, after
which, in 1806, he returned to Ohio, and remained until 1814, when he came back to Kentucky, and on the
Hinkstone circuit was instrumental in bringing into
the Church one who became an honored Bishop, and

another who, in later years was one of the leading
men of American Methodism—H. H. Kavanaugh and
John P. Durbin. Health failing, in 1818 he is placed
on the retired list, upon which he remained until his
death. He lived sometime in Bourbon county, then
removed to Clermont county, Ohio, and made his home
near Felicity. In February, 1849, he entered upon
rest at God's right hand.

He had a clear intellect, and was a calm though earnest
thinker. He was distinguished by conscientiousness, by self-
sacrifice, by strong faith and burning zeal. He had industry
and methodical habits. He seemed to be steadily governed by
the rule of our Discipline, Never be unemployed; never be
triflingly employed. He was a great reader, and it was his
practice to make abstracts and write an analysis of the books
he studied. He thus accumulated large stores of knowledge. . . .
He had marked prudence, and his executive skill inspired confidence in his administration.

In the controversies over religious matters which
prevailed in Kentucky during his active ministry, Lakin
was preeminent in his defense and vindication of the
doctrines and polity of Methodism. Fluent in speech
and often truly eloquent, he beat back with great force
the attacks of all assailants. Few men have been
more loved and trusted by the Methodists of Kentucky
and Ohio than was Benjamin Lakin.

John Watson was this year on the Salt River circuit. He had been in the ministry four years before
coming to Kentucky, traveling in Virginia and Pennsylvania, and he spent only three years in this State,
serving Salt River. Hinkstone and Lexington. Returning East, he filled many important places both
as pastor and Presiding Elder, being at one time stationed in Washington City. It was with him as with
so many others among these early preachers—he wore
himself out in the service of the Church and was compelled to retire from his loved employ. He died near

Martinsburg, Va., in the summer of 1838.

Jeremiah Lawson located after three years of service on the Shelby, Danville, and Lexington circuits. Later, at the request of the Presiding Elder, he took the place on the Limestone circuit of William Algood, who failed to come to his charge. Lawson lived in the bounds of this circuit for many years, and his relatives still abide in this section of the State. His death occurred at the home of his son, who was an eminent physician in Cincinnati.

Thus we have passed under brief review the men who served the Church in this hard field during the quadrennium from 1792 to 1796. The country was still sparcely settled. During the greater part of the period, the Indian wars were raging and the people were in constant dread of massacre from the tribes both to the North and South of them. It was not until 1795 that the peace of Greenville, following the crushing defeat of the savages by Wayne, quieted the northern tribes; and the famous Nickajack expedition, carrying death and disaster to the Cherokees in the South, that the early settlers in Kentucky had any rest from these enemies. Then followed a scattering of the people to secure new homes and the pioneer preachers had to follow them and reorganize the work of the Church. It was not a fruitful period for the cause of Christ. Indeed, there was a serious loss of members during this time. In 1792, there were in Kentucky and Cumberland, 2,059 white members and 176 colored. In 1796 there were reported in this same field only 1,856 white, and 114 colored members, a loss of 203 white, and 52 colored communicants. It was a trying time on all the churches and we think it will be found that the Methodists only shared with others the casualties of a difficult period.

CHAPTER VIII.

FROM 1796 TO 1800

At the General Conference which met in Baltimore, October 20, 1796, several measures were adopted which affected the work in Kentucky. In the first place, it was ordered that there should be six yearly Conferences held, each within a specified boundary, viz., the New England, Philadelphia, Baltimore, Virginia, South Carolina, and the Western. This last was "for the States of Kentucky and Tennessee." The following explanatory note is appended:

"N. B. For several years the annual conferences were very small, consisting only of the preachers of a single district, or of two or three very small ones. This was attended with many inconveniences: 1. There were but few of the senior preachers whose years and experience had matured their judgments, who could be present at any one conference. 2. The conferences wanted that dignity which every religious synod should possess, and which always accompanies a large assembly of gospel ministers. 3. The itinerant plan was exceedingly cramped, from the difficulty of removing preachers from one district to another. All these inconveniences will, we trust, be removed on the present plan; and at the same time the conferences are so arranged that all the members respectively may attend with little difficulty.

To all which may be added, that the active, zealous, unmarried preachers may move on a larger scale, and preach the ever-blessed gospel far more extensively through the sixteen States, and other parts of the continent; while the married preachers, whose circumstances require them, in many instances, to be more located than the single men, will have a considerable field of action opened to them; and also the bishops will be able to attend the conferences with greater ease, and without injury to their health."

A form of deed was prepared in order to secure uniformity of titles and to secure all our church property to its proper use. This was very important and the "Trust Clause" has saved to us many pieces of real estate that otherwise would have been diverted from the uses for which they were intended.

Inasmuch as the Church was beginning to establish schools for the education of its young people, this General Conference drafted an address, setting forth the purposes of such schools, and proposing a set of rules for their management. As Bethel Academy was then operating in our bounds, these principles and rules had an important relation to this institution. It was declared that it is "our particular desire, that all who shall be educated in Methodist seminaries, be kept at the utmost distance as from vice in general, so in particular from softness and effeminacy of manners." This explains the selection of a site for Bethel—out in the country, away from any town, which was supposed to be a hot bed of evil, and on a farm, where habits of industry might be encouraged. Early rising is enjoined as a means of preserving the health of the body and of developing the mind. Play of every sort is strictly banned; "the students shall be indulged with nothing which the world calls PLAY. Let this rule be observed with the strictest nicety; for those who play when they are young, will play when they are old." A schedule is laid down for the student: Rising at five o'clock; public prayers at six; breakfast at seven; study from eight to twelve; from twelve to three, recreation and dining; dinner at one; from three to six, study; supper at six; public prayers at seven; recreation until bed-time, and "all in bed at nine o'clock, without fail." The recreations prescribed are "gardening, walking, riding, and bathing, without doors; and the carpenter's, joiner's, cabinet-maker's, or turner's business, within doors." The rule for bathing was, that "a master, or some proper person by him appointed, shall be always present at the time of bathing. Only one shall bathe at a time; and no one shall remain in the water above a minute." The ideas of education indicated by these rules, seem to us at the present day, rigid and unreasonable; but they were in accord with the prevailing ideas of that day. Both Locke and Rousseau are quoted in the Address as authorities in such matters.

Of course the attitude of the Church on both the questions of slavery and temperance was re-stated and emphasized. These enactments will be further discussed at a later period. The Conference also provided for a "Chartered Fund," for the aid of distressed preachers and their families, and for superannuates and the widows and orphans of preachers. A subscription was to be raised throughout the Church for the establishment of this Fund, and the interest was to be distributed annually among those for whom the Fund was established. It was further provided that the proceeds of the Book Concern, after its expenses were paid, should be added to this Fund. We see here the beginnings of our own Superannuate Endowment and Preachers' Aid Funds, and of the plan of using the proceeds of the Publishing House for the relief of conference claimants. The need of such provision was very urgent. The General Conference says: "It is to be lamented, if possible, with tears of blood, that we have lost scores of our most able married ministers—men who, like good householders, could, upon occasion, bring things new and old out of their treasury, but were obliged to retire from the general work, because they saw nothing before them for their wives and children, if they continued itinerants, but misery and ruin." The financial condition of the country was, at that time, deplorable. The whole monetary system was chaotic. Money was exceedingly scarce. In a new country, like Kentucky and Tennessee, almost none was to be had. The pittance of sixty-four dollars, the annual allowance of the preachers, whether pastors, presiding elders, or bishops, (all shared alike), was seldom paid. The sacrifices necessary in order to do the work of an itinerant preacher can hardly be understood at the present time. The Chartered Fund was of greatest benefit to the preachers of the West. It saved many a good man to the work.

1797. The Conference for 1797 was held at Bethel Academy. Bishop Asbury was not present, though he had sent on a plan for stationing the preachers. No separate minutes of the Conference were kept, but the old plan of combining the Minutes of all the Conferences was still followed, notwithstanding the division of the Church into six annual Conference areas. In the General Minutes the title, *Presiding* Elder, came into use this year—1797. It was not until 1801 that the Districts were designated *by names*, and they were not grouped under their respective Annual Conferences until 1802.

The appointments for Kentucky this year are as follows:

John Kobler, Presiding Elder.
Francis Poythress, supernumerary.
Limestone—Aquila Jones.
Hinkstone—John Page.
Lexington—Benjamin Lakin.
Danville—Jeremiah Lawson, Thomas Allen.
Salt River—Henry Smith, Williams Kavanaugh.

For ten years Francis Poythress had been presiding over the western District. Gradually its borders had been extended until in 1796, it included all of Kentucky, the Cumberland country, and one circuit in North Carolina. This faithful man had gone over this vast territory, riding horse-back, often sleeping in the woods or under the open sky on the "Barrens," living on the coarse and often poorly prepared food of the settler's cabins, preaching, singing, praying, holding class-meetings, visiting, counseling, calling out local preachers and placing them on circuits, promoting revivals, and supervising all the interests of the Church,—no wonder that his body was worn and his health impaired at the end of these ten years! Hence, we find him on the supernumerary list, and he is given a year's rest. We have no information as to where or how he spent this year, but it is probable that he was with his sister, Mrs. Pryor, in Jessamine county, and that he preached as often as opportunity presented and strength would permit.

He was succeeded on the District by John Kobler. Kobler was a native of Culpepper county, Virginia., born August 27, 1768. Under the teachings and influence of a pious mother, he was happily converted on Christmas Eve, 1787, and was soon in the ministry. He was admitted on trial in 1789. As soon as he was ordained an elder, he was appointed *Presiding* Elder of a District in Southwestern Virginia, and remained on that District for four years. This year he was transferred to Kentucky and succeeded the veteran, Poythress, on the Kentucky District, where he remained only one year. Ohio was now open to settlement and many Kentuckians crossed the river to find homes in the then Northwest Territory. Kobler was sent in 1798 to follow up these pioneers, and he established a circuit north of the Ohio. At the end of the year he reported the Miami circuit mapped out, with ninety-eight white and one colored member. In 1799 he is back in Kentucky on the Hinkstone circuit. 1800, he went back to Virginia, and after one year, located on account of broken health. As a preacher he was above the average, and seems to have had special adaptation to the work of the Presiding Eldership. He is said to have been a universal favorite.

Everywhere he went, listening crowds gathered around him, and communities where no Methodist churches had been organized invited his ministrations. At that period, no church had been planted in the town of Washington, then the county-seat of Mason, and no Methodist preacher had probably every preached in the place. Through the efforts of a few of the most influential citizens, the use of the court house was obtained, and Mr. Kobler was invited to preach. 'All the respectable citizens attended, and listened to his sermon with profound attention.' When the public services were over, the people insisted that he was wrongly named—that he was no cobbler, but a complete workman.

After his location, he lived for many years at Fredericksburg, Virginia, where he died, July 26, 1843.

Of Thomas Allen, who was appointed this year to Danville with Jeremiah Lawson, but little is known. We only know that he was admitted on trial this year, and served in succession the Danville, New River, Salt River and Shelby, and the Lexington circuits, and that he located in 1801.

The name now to be introduced is one of the most familiar names in Kentucky Methodism—*Kavanaugh.* Williams Kavanaugh, Jr. was the son of Williams Kavanaugh, Sr., and the father of four sons who became Methodist ministers—among them Bishop Hub-

bard Hinde Kavanaugh. Williams Kavanaugh, Jr. was
born near the dividing line between Virginia and Tennessee, August 3, 1775, while his parents were on their
way to Kentucky. The date, 1775, will be recognized
as the year when the first permanent settlement was
made in Kentucky. This settlement was in the spring,
and the Kavanaugh family came late that fall, and was,
therefore, among the first to come to the State. They
settled in Madison county, on Muddy Creek, about ten
miles northeast of Boonesboro, and were under the
immediate protection of Capt. Estill, of Estill's Station. His parents being religious, Williams Kavanaugh, while a mere boy, recognized the need of salvation and sought and found the pearl of great price.
When only nineteen years of age, he was received into
the Conference, (1794) and with Lewis Garrett, was
appointed to Green circuit, in East Tennessee. Both
Kavanaugh and Garrett were from the Danville circuit, and both were received at this Conference. They
went to their appointment together, and Garrett has
left us an interesting account of their trip through
the mountains. With a company of about sixty men,
six of whom were traveling preachers, they left Crab
Orchard, and the first night they encamped in the
woods, near a small fort that had been erected somewhere along the Wilderness road. The next day they
passed a gloomy spot where only a short time before,
a company of people had been massacred by the Indians, two of the dead being Baptist preachers. That
night they again built their camp-fires in the woods,
and John Ray, who was one of the company, held religious services. Kavanaugh and Garrett labored together during that year, and Garrett always spoke of
his colleague in terms of confidence and affection.

Rev. Valentine Cook, A. M.

For two years after this, Kavanaugh served the Brunswick and Cumberland circuits, both in Virginia, and in 1797, his name appears in connection with *two* circuits,—Franklin, in Virginia, and Salt River, in Kentucky. In those days, preachers were frequently changed at the end of six months, and doubtless it was understood that he was to spend the first six months in Virginia, then come to the Salt River circuit in Kentucky.

On March 29, 1798, Williams Kavanaugh was married to Hannah Hubbard Hinde, the daugher of Dr. Thomas Hinde, of Clark county, Kentucky. At the Conference which met on Holston a few weeks later, he asked for, and received a location. Of all the preachers who traveled in this western country up to that time, William Burke and John Page were the only two who continued in the work after their marriage. On circuits with as many as thirty preaching places, necessitating a horseback ride of from two to five hundred miles in order to reach all these places, preaching almost every day, visiting the classes and otherwise superintending the work, a preacher had very little time to remain with his family if he had one. Besides, the support was so meager that a man coulu barely maintain himself and the indispensable horse, and the support of a family was, in almost every case, impossible. Hence, the marriage of a preacher meant his location, and Kavanaugh located and took up his residence in Clark county. Here he taught a school. but his Sundays were employed in preaching and working for the Master in every way he could. His name stands as one of eight persons who formed the first class at Ebenezer, in Clark county. This old church was built about six miles from Winchester, on the road to Lexington, and Williams Kavanaugh gave it the name it bore.

But Kavanaugh was not happy in the local relation. He felt his call to the ministry, and could not rest out of active work. He was a brilliant man. As a preacher, "he was not boisterous, but fluent, ready, and his sermons smoothly delivered; his style perspicuous, and every word expressive of the idea intended." He was unwilling to spend his life and the talents God had given him in comparative inactivity, but longed for a wider field than that of a local preacher. An opportunity presented itself which he thought would solve his difficulty and enable him both to gain the larger field of usefulness, and care for his family. An offer came to him to unite with the Protestant Episcopal Church, and become the rector of a church in Lexington, and he accepted it. After remaining for a while in Lexington, he accepted a charge in Louisville, and then one in Henderson, Ky., where he died, Oct. 16, 1806. It is said that he carried with him to the end a reputation for piety and a zeal for the salvation of souls. Converted and trained in the Methodist Church, he never lost those characteristic qualities which so strongly marked our Methodism. It seems that none of his family went with him into the Episcopal Church. His widow remained a most devoted Methodist; was twice married afterwards; while his sons, LeRoy, Benjamin Taylor, Hubbard Hinde, and Williams Barbour, became ministers in the Methodist Episcopal Church. They will have due notice at the proper time.

As illustrative of the straights to which a married man was put in order to do the work of an itinerant, William Burke, who served the Cumberland circuit in 1799, says: "During this year I had to pay nearly a hundred dollars for a horse, and I found it hard to raise the money, and support myself, and pay the board of my wife; however, I economized in every way. I borrowed a blanket, and wore it instead of a great-coat through the winter, and by that means paid my debts." The following year on the Danville circuit his wife wrought with her own hands, doubtless in sewing, knitting and weaving, and made enough to pay her own board and clothe herself.

The Minutes for 1797 report a loss in member-ship in Kentucky of *one hundred and ninety-six.*

1798. The Conference for 1798 met on Holston. While Burke states that Asbury was present, Asbury's Journal says that, at this very time, he was at the Bal-timore Conference. Burke, who was a very old man when he wrote, slightly slipped in his recollections of the event. Who presided over the Conference we do not know. The appointments for Kentucky as given in the General Minutes, are as follows:

Valentine Cook, Presiding Elder.
Limestone—Jeremiah Lawson.
Hinkstone—John Watson.
Lexington—John Buxton.
Danville—Robert Wilkerson.
Salt River and Shelby—John Page.

Francis Poythress, who was on the supernumerary list the preceding year, had reported again for work, and was appointed, together with Jonathan Bird, as Presiding Elder of a District in southwestern Virginia. It was an unusual thing for two presiding elders to be appointed to one District, but we suspect that the health of Poythress was still uncertain, and that he was assigned to this work in order to lighten the bur-den that would rest upon his shoulders. Williams

Kavanaugh, Aquila Jones, and Benjamin Lakin had located, and Henry Smith had been sent to East Tennessee. But two new names appear in the appointments to the Kentucky field, viz., Valentine Cook and Robert Wilkerson.

Robert Wilkerson spent but one year in Kentucky. He was admitted on trial in 1797, and served the Green circuit, in East Tennessee. He located in 1801. He was the brother of Thomas Wilkerson, and though not regarded as his equal, yet he was reckoned a splendid preacher. Of his life after his location we are not informed.

We devoutly wish we could transmit to the reader some of the spirit of the learned and saintly man who was appointed this year to preside over this western district. We are embarrassed by limitation of space in which to tell of Valentine Cook. "In literary, scientific, and useful attainments, he was equalled by few, while in biblical learning and practical piety he was surpassed, perhaps, by none." "Circumstances beyond his control compelled him, at the close of the tenth year of his ministry, to retire from the itinerant field, and seek a position with his local brethren. Such, however, were his extraordinary endowments, mental, moral, and evangelical—such the strength of his faith, the fervency of his zeal, and the efficiency of his ministry—that no seclusion of place or obscurity of position could prevent the Church or the world from recognizing him as a great and good man, as well as an able, laborious, and eminently successful minister of the 'cross of Christ.' "

Valentine Cook, like Williams Kavanaugh, bore the full name of his father. He was some times spoken of as Valentine Cook, Jr. His grand-father was a first cousin of Captain James Cook, the famous English navigator, who discovered the Sandwich Islands. Valentine Cook, Sr., came to America, and for a time made his home in Pennsylvania, where Valentine, Jr., was born. The family removed to the "Greenbrier Country," not Monroe county, West Virginia, where young Cook grew to manhood. He was pious from childhood, but lacked the clear witness to his acceptance in Christ until he was nearly grown. He was noted from childhood for his eagerness to learn and for a remarkably acute mind. He became a student in Cokesbury College, where he remained for some time and greatly profited by the instruction he there received. He could write and speak the German language fluently, and during his after life he acquainted himself with several of the classic languages, and kept abreast of the discoveries of science and the attainments of the literary world. Like many of the preachers of that early period, he was a hard student as long as he lived.

When he returned from Cokesbury, about 1787, he began to exhort, and was instrumental in the awakening and conversion of many of his Virginia neighbors, who through life held him in great reverence and affection. He was received into the traveling connection in 1788, and for five years served important circuits in Maryland and Pennsylvania, until, in 1793, he was made a Presiding Elder. He was kept in this work in the East until 1798, when he was brought to the West and placed in charge of the work here. His districts in the East included Philadelphia and Pittsburg. It will be remembered that both Poythress and Bird had this year been appointed to the same District in Southwestern Virginia. Judge Scott, in his sketch of Francis Poythress, informs us that "shortly after brother

Cook's arrival in Kentucky—and we feel quite sure it was before he had completed one round on his district—he received instructions from Bishop Asbury to take charge of Bethel Academy, then on the decline for want of a suitable teacher, and brother Poythress was instructed to take charge of the District. Cook, therefore, took charge of the Academy, Poythress the District, and Bird remained on the station to which he had been appointed."

From this statement it appears that Cook's incumbency as Principal of Bethel Academy began during the summer of 1798. His biographer says that "a feeling of opposition had been very improperly awakened in the Church against the institution," which Cook "found it impossible to overcome." Who the opposers were, and what was the ground of their opposition, we are not informed. William Burke tells us that "Rev. Valentine Cook was the first that organized the academic department; and at first the prospect was flattering. A number of students were in attendance; but difficulties occurred which it would be needless to mention, as all the parties concerned have gone to give an account at a higher tribunal; but such was the effect that the school soon declined. and brother Cook abandoned the project."*

---

*Burke continues: "The Rev. John Metcalf, who had married and located, was next introduced, and kept a common school for some time. On his leaving the place vacant, Rev. Nathaniel Harris moved, with his family, and occupied the building as a dwelling, and kept a school for the neighborhood. On his leaving the premises, it was soon in a dilapidated state. The land on which it was built fell into the hands of Mr. Lewis' heirs, the house was taken down so that not one stone was left upon another, and the whole was transferred to Nicholasville, and incorporated into a county academy, which is still in operation;

Some time during the fall of 1798 or early in 1799, Cook was married to Miss Tabitha Slaughter, a niece of ex-governor Slaughter, of Kentucky. He located in 1800. Leaving Bethel, he went to Harrodsburg where for several years he conducted an academy.* He finally went to Logan county, bought a small farm about three miles north of Russellvile, and there lived the rest of his days. He taught school in Russellville, and also in the country at, or near, his home. As a teacher he was regarded as among the most competent and successful in the country.

Valentine Cook was a man of prayer.

The habit of praying in secret three times a day, which he formed at an early period of his Christian course, was never abandoned or even modified. . . . He seldom entered the pulpit without having previously retired to some secret place for the renewal of his commission and the strengthening of his faith. On many occasions his brethren and friends had to hunt him up and bring him from his knees to the sacred desk. He was so thoroughly convinced that without the agency of the Holy Spirit no merely human preparation could suffice for the successful proclamation of the gospel, that he was never willing to enter the sacred place without a conscious sense of the divine presence.†

---

but the Methodist Church have no more interest in it than other citizens of Jessamine county."

*In this we follow his biographer, Dr. Edward Stevenson. Records in the court house at Harrodsburg show that Cook officiated in several weddings in Mercer county as late as 1808. But Jonathan Stamper, in Number VII of his "Autumn Leaves," says that Cook was living at Bethel in 1812, and that he visited him often at that place. There is no doubt that he was at Harrodsburg, but just when he went there, or how long he remained, we do not know.

†Stamper says: "At Bethel Academy he had a place conse-

It was the custom of Methodist preachers in those days to spend hours in the woods, reading, meditating, and in prayer, when preparing for the work they were to do in the pulpit.

He was also a man of the Book. "The Bible was his constant companion, at home and abroad, in public and in private. Other books he read as opportunity served or occasion required, but the Bible he read every day. Whether found in his private study, the School room, the field, or the forest, he always had the precious volume at command. He was often observed poring over its sacred pages when traveling on horse-back, as well as on foot. . . . No passage could be called for that he was not able to repeat, or to which he could not turn in a few moments."

The effect of his preaching was tremendous. One wicked man declared that he could not get a comfortable night's sleep for at least a month after hearing one of his sermons. "He always says something that I can't forget!" On one occasion while he was preaching at a camp meeting in Southern Kentucky, a man sprang up crying, "Stop! stop until I get out of this place." He started out of the assembly, but fell prostrate on the ground crying aloud for mercy.

His biographer, Dr. Edward Stevenson, himself a great preacher, tells of a sermon he heard him preach in a private house not far from Lexington. He says:

The hour for preaching arrived. Mr. Cook took his position

crated to prayer and meditation. Just under the brow of the cliff upon which the house stood, the projecting rocks formed a sheltered as well as a retired spot, where he spent a portion of every day alone with his God. The ground was beaten smoothe by his frequent foot steps, and where he knelt to pray by a large rock, the prints of his knees were left in the earth."

by a small table upon which lay the "old family Bible." Resting his hand reverently on that blessed volume, he commenced
repeating, in a somewhat indistinct undertone, the affecting
hymn beginning with—

> "I saw one hanging on a tree
> In agony and blood;
> He fixed his lanquid eyes on me,
> As near the cross I stood."

Before he reached the last stanza, his voice had become perfectly clear, and so pathetic and impressive, many faces were
suffused with tears. After reading the hymn, he raised the tune
himself, and the audience united with him in the delightful exercise of singing. The prayer which followed was simple, solemn, and affecting. On rising from his knees, he straightened
himself up, and after looking around upon the congregation a
few moments, without opening the Bible, on which his right
hand again rested, he announced as his text, Mal. iv. 1: "For
behold, the day cometh." . . . . It is impossible to give more than
an imperfect outline of the discourse. Man's responsibility to
God was the leading thought. In the commencemeent, he dwelt
at some length and with great effect on the all-pervading presence of him with whom we have to do. Never until then had I
been so deeply impressed with the fact that God was all around
me, above me, beneath me, within me. The sinfulness of sin,
and its dreadful consequences, were portrayed in language and
imagery most powerful and startling. . . . In conclusion, the
great remedial scheme was brought to view. Jesus, with garments rolled in blood, was announced as the only hope of a
ruined world. We saw and felt, as under the clear light of
heaven itself, how God could be just through the intervention
and sacrificial death of his Son, and yet the justifier of penitent
believing sinners. The ability and willingness of Almighty God,
as revealed in Christ and him crucified, to save—to save now—
to the uttermost and forever—were presented in such strains
of simple, fervent, melting eloquence, that the entire assembly
was roused, excited, and overwhelmed. Some were pale with
fear; others radiant with hope. Prayer and praise, cries and
songs, were loudly commingled. While the wail of awakened
sinners was heard in various parts of the house, from other directions came the shouts of rejoicing saints. Christ, by his
Holy Spirit, had spoken through his minister to the under-

standings and hearts of the people. The midnight watch had come and gone before the people could be induced to leave the strangely consecrated place. Since that memorable night I have listened to many able and eloquent dissertations on this great doctrine of our holy religion; but such a sermon as that, for clearness, directness, power and effect, I have never heard.

On another occasion, while attending a camp meeting at Fountain Head, Tennessee, a spiritual deadness seemed to pervade the encampment, and there was not the slightest indication that any good would be done. No move of any kind had taken place. Cook made it a matter of earnest prayer, and felt that the Lord had heard and answered. He informed a friend that, notwithstanding appearances, they were going to have a gracious outpouring of the Spirit. He was appointed to preach on Monday morning. His text was, "If the righteous scarcely be saved, where shall the ungodly and the sinner appear?" Before he concluded, "the whole assembly was in tears; sinners were crying to God for mercy, while the saints of the Most High were shouting aloud for joy. Many precious souls were converted before the meeting closed. A great revival succeeded in all that section of the country. The fruits of that memorable discourse will doubtless be seen in the day of eternity."

When occasion demanded, Cook was a powerful polemic, a mighty defender of the faith. While a very young preacher in Pennsylvania, his preaching the doctrines of free grace and sanctification aroused the displeasure of the Scotch Seeders who were predominant in that section, and at length he was challenged to debate the issue with an old minister by the name of Jamieson, and accepted the challenge. Bishop Roberts, then a young man, was present and gives a very vivid account of the whole affair. Rev. Jamieson treated the young preacher with great contempt, would not consent to any rules of debate, but proposed to talk as long as he pleased, and then, "if the stripling had anything to say, he might say on." The old man ranted and raved for about two hours, then sat down, his voice about gone, and he almost physically exhausted. No prayer had been offered, no explanation of the debate had been made. Cook arose and offered a fervent prayer, then launched into his defense of the Wesleyan doctrines as contrasted with Calvinism. Before he had concluded, his opponent had fled the field. "Long before the mighty effort was brought to a close," says Bishop Roberts, "the whole assembly were on their feet, all eagerly listening, and insensibly pressing towards the speaker. . . . When Mr. Cook took his seat, all faces were upturned, and for the most part bathed in tears. The great multitude stood, for some time, like statues, no one appearing disposed to move, utter a word, or leave the place." It is said that, from that day, Methodism, in all that region, made rapid advancement both in numbers and influence. Cook had won the day. While living near Russellville, he had a controversy with a Baptist minister named Vardiman, on the subjects and mode of baptism, which opened the way for a gracious revival in that town, in which the Methodist church was greatly increased in numbers and strengthened both socially and materially.

Many interesting things are told of Father Cook which we can not here repeat. In personal appearance he is described as "without form or comeliness," and not without his eccentricities. Dr. Stevenson gives his impression of him as he first saw him:

Valentine Cook was slightly above the medium height and size. There was no symmetry in his figure; his limbs, being disproportionately long, seemed more like awkward appendages than well-fitted parts of a perfect whole. He was what is called stoop-shouldered to such a degree, that his long neck projected from between his shoulders almost at a right angle with the perpendicular of his chest. His head, which was of peculiar formation, being much longer than usual from the crown to the point of the chin, seemed rather suspended to than supported by the neck. A remarkably low forehead, small, deeply-sunken, hazel eyes, a prominent Roman nose, large mouth, thin lips, a dark, sallow complexion, coarse black hair, with here and there a thread of gray, formed the **tout ensemble** in which nature seemed to have paid no regard to order, strength, or beauty. His singularly eccentric appearance, his homely apparel, and humble attitude, as he slowly approached the house, are imprinted upon my mind as vividly now as when for the first time I looked upon him.

Such was Valentine Cook, both a good and a great man. He died at his home in Logan county, Kentucky, some time during the year 1821. Though he had for years sustained only a local relation, at the request of the Kentucky Conference, in session at Lexington, in 1822, a funeral sermon was preached by the Rev. John Johnson, and the Conference united in paying tribute to the memory of this most remarkable man. In July, 1934, the Louisville Conference Historical Society unveiled a marker, suitably inscribed, at his grave, on the little farm on which he lived and where sleeps the dust of this Father of Methodism in that section of the State.

1799. We know but little of the Conference of 1799, or of the year which followed it. Bethel Academy was the place, and May 1st was the time for holding the Conference. We do not know who presided, or what was done during the session. The appointments, as they appear in the General Minutes, are as follows:

Francis Poythress, Presiding Elder.

Lexington—John Watson.
Danville—William Burke.
Salt River and Shelby—Thomas Allen, Daniel Gossage.
Hinkstone—John Kobler.
Limestone—John Buxton.
Miami—Henry Smith.

Francis Poythress is again Presiding Elder of the District, and it proved to be his last year in the service to which he had given his life. As stated in a previous chapter, his nervous system had been so broken by excessive labors that he was fast hastening to a complete and permanent mental derangement. When this came, he retired to the home of his sister, Mrs. Susan Pryor, of Jessamine county, and remained with her until death brought him release in 1818.

Valentine Cook was at Bethel Academy; Robert Wilkerson was sent back to North Carolina; Jeremiah Lawson located, and John Page was assigned to Cumberland. But one new name is added to the list of workers in Kentucky—Daniel Gossage. We know nothing of him except that he was admitted on trial this year, and sent, with Thomas Allen, to the Salt River and Shelby circuit. Who he was, whence he came, and what became of him we do not know. His name disappears from the Minutes with no explanation of his discontinuance.

John Kobler and William Burke come back to Kentucky this year, the former going to the Hinkstone, and the latter to the Danville circuit. The Danville circuit was very large, including Boyle, Pulaski, Mercer, Garrard, Madison, Estill and Lincoln counties. Burke has left us a brief account of his labors this year. Henry Smith was his colleague. There was much objection on the part of some to a married preacher, and no provision was made for his wife. His

Presiding Elder advised him to locate, but this he was determined not to do, nor would his wife consent to it. She worked with her own hands and paid her board and clothed herself, while Burke divided the salary equally with his colleague. He says:

"This year began my war with the Baptists. Having had some small revival, the Baptists did all they could do to draw off our members and get them into the water; and I began with lecturing every time I baptized an infant, which greatly roused up the Baptists, so much so that I received a challenge from the Rev. Thomas Shelton, the champion of the whole Baptist denomination. I accepted the challenge, and the day was appointed at Irvin's Lick, in Madison county. We met according to appointment, and settled the preliminaries of debate, each to speak fifteen minutes. Brother John Watson was appointed by me to keep time and call to order, and a Baptist preacher was appointed by Mr. Shelton for the same purpose. We proceeded about four hours to debate the subject. I had the close, when Shelton observed to the immense congregation that he believed I was an honest but a mistaken man. I proceeded to administer the ordinance of baptism on the spot, and Mr. Shelton stood by and witnessed the same. From that day the tug of war began, and continued until 1811, when I left the State. At that meeting Elisha W. Bowman was present, a young speaker in the Methodist Church, who immediately entered upon the study of the subject and became a warm auxiliary in the cause. William J. Thompson also took up the subject. He was a strong man and rendered efficient service. After 1800 John Sale and William McKendree engaged with me in the contest. We kept up a constant fire upon the Baptists, and the Methodists began to gain confidence and to make a respectable stand among the denominations of Christians."

In Kentucky, Methodism has had to fight for every inch of ground she has gained, then has had to fight to hold it. Perhaps there is no section of the entire country where so many and such violent attacks have been made upon us as in this State. We doubt if there is any other place where proselyting has been carried on so persistently and boldly. The people of the present generation can have no conception of the bitterness with which we were assailed by Calvinists, immersionists, and anti-pedobaptists. This polemical war began almost as soon as we entered the field, and continued with scarcely any intermission until about 1880, when it can be truthfully said that we conquered a peace. Since that time, with but little exception, an era of good feeling among the denominations has prevailed. Methodism has been the broadest and most irenic of the denominations. Their emphasis has always been upon Christian experience and godly living, and they have put but little stress upon rites and forms that are merely incidental to Christianity. We have been willing "to think and let think," and to accord to each person liberty of conscience in these incidental matters. But narrowness and bigotry have not been content to let us alone in the exercise of our liberal views upon these matters, and time and again we have been under the necessity of defending ourselves against the onslaughts of those holding less liberal opinions. We think the statement will hardly be challenged that we have been the strongest influence to bring about Christian comity of any in the land, and it has not been our habit to inveigh against other denominations, except when it was necessary to defend ourselves against the aggressions of others.

The West was expanding and Methodism was following in the wake of the pioneers into new parts of the country. In 1798, the Spanish rule over the Mississippi Territory came to an end. In 1799, Tobias Gibson, then a member of the South Carolina Conference, was sent as a missionary to the Natchez Country. Randall Gibson, a cousin, and other relatives had preceded him, and he found a warm welcome upon his arrival. Leaving South Carolina, he rode horse-back through Kentucky to Nashville, a distance of six hundred miles; there sold his horse, purchased a canoe, and paddled his way down the Cumberland, out into the Ohio, then down the Mississippi to the scattered settlements around Natchez. Here he began his apostolic labors and in a few years laid down his life for the sake of souls. Ohio was rapidly filling up; Indiana was being opened to settlers, and Illinois was beginning to attract attention. All these States, with Missouri, Arkansas, and Louisiana, were soon included in the bounds of the Western Conference, and must receive notice if we would understand the history of Methodism in Kentucky.

There were two Conferences held for the West in 1800; one in April at a place called Dunworth, somewhere in the Holston country, but the exact location is not now known. It seems that Bishop Asbury was not present at this Conference. He was in bad health at the time, and was slowly making his way from the South toward Baltimore, where the next General Conference was to meet in May. Up to this time, the Conferences in the West had been held in the spring, but a change was now made to the fall, so another Conference was held at Bethel Academy, beginning October 6th. It appears that only temporary appointments were made at the Conference at Dunworth. The General Conference was to meet a few days later, and Bishop Asbury had planned then to secure an entire new force of workers for the West. Burke, with his usual clarity, thus explains the matter:

The year 1799 I expected would terminate my labors in the western country. At the request of Bishop Asbury, all the

William McKendree

preachers that had been in the west for any considerable time were to leave the country and attend the General Conference at Baltimore, on the sixth of May, 1800, and to receive their appointments in the old States, and a new set to be sent to the West. We all accordingly set out early in April. The following were the preachers that left: Francis Poythress, Thomas Wilkerson, John Page, John Watson, John Buxton, Henry Smith, John Kobler, and William Burke. Bishop Asbury had formed the intended plan of appointing a presiding elder to take charge of all the West in one district; viz., Kentucky, Tennessee, and all that part of Virginia west of New River and the Northwestern Territory, including the Miami and Scioto valleys. He used his utmost endeavors, during the General Conference, to engage a man for that purpose, but failed; for when they understood the extent of the territory they would have to travel over, they uniformly declined to undertake it. Before the close of the General Conference he applied to me to know if I would consent to return to Kentucky and take with me all the papers pertaining to the annual conference and Bethel Academy, and do the best I could for the work in that field. I consented, and he appointed to go with me John Sale, Hezekiah Harriman, William Algood, and Henry Smith; for the Holston country, James Hunter, John Watson, and John Page; and for Cumberland, William Lambeth. John Sale and H. Harriman proceeded with me immediately for Kentucky. Hezekiah Harriman was appointed to Danville circuit, John Sale to Salt River and Shelby, William Algood to Limestone. I was appointed to Hinkstone, and to superintend the quarterly meetings where there was no elder. William Algood never came to his appointment I prevailed on Jeremiah Lawson to supply his place on Limestone circuit, and I placed Lewis Hunt on Hinkstone, and spent most of my time on Lexington, Hinkstone and Limestone circuits. My labors, during the summer, were very arduous, and to accomplish my work I rode down two good horses."

Inasmuch as there had been a decrease in the membership in this great field for several years, it is likely that Asbury thought those men who had been laboring here had grown stale; that they needed a change and that the work would fare better with a new force.

This is often the case. Or, it is possible that he thought they had borne the strenuous labors of this hard field long enough, and that it was but right that some one else should share with them the hardship they had endured.

Of the men appointed to accompany Burke to the West, William Algood did not come. He remained in the East, laboring chiefly in North Carolina, until 1806, when he located.

For four or five years prior to this, Hezekiah Harriman had itinerated in Virginia. He served Danville circuit this year, then the Salt River and Hinkstone circuits. In 1803, he was sent to the Natchez country, in Mississippi, with Moses Floyd as a colleague. Here he was taken ill, and for several months his life was despaired of; but he finally recovered and went to Baltimore, where he labored for a year or two, and then was placed on the retired list. He suffered a stroke of paralysis in 1807, but lingered until 1818, when he peacefully passed away. His labors here in Kentucky were successful.

John Sale was a man of more than average ability. He was a Virginian, born in 1769, converted when about twenty years of age, but did not enter the itinerancy until 1796. After four years in North Carolina and Virginia, he volunteered for the work in the West and came with Burke to Kentucky. Here he served Salt River and Shelby, then the Danville circuit, after which he spent two years in Ohio on the Scioto and Miami circuits. He then returned to Kentucky, and was on the Lexington circuit for one year. After this he gave most of his life to service on Districts in Ohio and Kentucky, serving the Kentucky District from 1809 to 1813. He died in 1826. The

Hon. John McLean, of Ohio, has furnished a sketch of him in which he says:

He was a man of fine presence, of erect and manly form, and of great personal dignity. He was naturally of a social turn, and had excellent powers of conversation. . . . His mind could not be said to be brilliant, and yet he sometimes produced a very powerful effect by his preaching. His distinct enunciation, earnest manner, and appropriate and well-digested thoughts, always secured him the attention of his audience; but I have sometimes heard him when, rising with the dignity and fullness of his subject, he seemed to me one of the noblest personifications of eloquence in the pulpit. . . . In some of his more felicitous efforts, I think I have heard him with as much interest as I have heard any man. . . . Mr. Sale's life was an eminently useful one, and he adorned every relation that he sustained, and every sphere that he occupied.

In the General Minutes the name of Jonathan Kidwell appears as the colleague of Sale on the Salt River and Shelby circuit. His name does not appear again in the appointments, but he was afterwards a local preacher in Madison county.

CHAPTER IX.

The year 1790, which saw the holding of the first Methodist Conference in Kentucky, marked a period in the history of Kentucky Methodism. So did the year 1800. The great revival which was then sweeping the continent, was at its height. Thousands were being converted to God; the Church was taking on new life, and the whole social and religious structure of the country was undergoing a change for the better. Then the coming of William McKendree to the West at this time, gave to Methodism a leader who marshalled its forces and lead it to great victories. Having reached this period in our narrative, it will not be amiss to pause for a moment, look back over the way we have come, and take stock of our resources at the beginning of the new century.

When Francis Clark and John Durham organized the first Methodist society in Kentucky in 1783, the State was little else than a vast wilderness. The Indian and the wild beast roamed its mighty forests, and each fought to hold the land against the invasions of the white man. A few settlements had been established here and there but most of the settlers lived in forts and block-houses, or else had pitched their cabins close enough to these "cities of refuge" to flee to them for safety at the approach of the foe. Both Estill's defeat and the bloody battle of the Blue Licks had occurred only the year before. Kentucky was still a part of Virginia, and the population at that time was only a few thousand. But by 1800, this population had grown to 220,000. The Indian and the wild beasts had been subdued, and it was now safe to live in any part of the State.

Prior to 1783, the Methodists in Kentucky could have been counted on the fingers of your two hands. Notwithstanding the hard conditions against which the early Methodists had to contend, their numbers by 1800 had increased to nearly two thousand. This increase was not as great as it would have been under more normal conditions, but it compared favorably with that of other denominations laboring in the same field. Including the Cumberland country, there were now six circuits, while beginnings had been made in Ohio, Indiana, Illinois, and Mississippi.

The number of itinerant preachers was not large; but their labors were supplemented by a considerable force of local preachers who now resided in the territory, many of whom were men of fine ability, and were in the local ranks only because of impaired health or family cares. Their piety and zeal were great, and under the direction and encouragement of the Presiding Elder, they did much in planting the Church in Kentucky and Tennessee. No roster of the local preachers who came to Kentucky prior to 1800 is possible—would that it were possible, so that the present generation might know who they were and what service they performed. Their names are written in the Lamb's Book of Life.

Of these local preachers we have already mentioned Francis Clark and William J. Thompson, who lived in the bounds of the Danville circuit; Nathaniel Harris, Philip Taylor, Daniel and Gabriel Woodfield, in the Lexington circuit; Joseph Ferguson, Edward Talbot,

and others in the Salt River circuit, and William Forman in the Hinkstone circuit. Others had arrived and
were zealously pushing forward the work in their respective parts of the State. In 1791, Rev. Lawrence
Owen had emigrated from Maryland and settled in
Clark county, and about him a society had been gathered and a log meeting-house had been erected. This
church was a strong Methodist center for many years.

At an early day the father of Rev. Richard Durrett
obtained from Patrick Henry a grant for land "on the
waters of Limestone," in Mason county, not far from
the town of Washington, and as early as 1791, "Durrett's" became one of the preaching places on the
Limestone circuit.

Rev. John Whitaker, eccentric, vehement, but gen-
uinely pious and useful, settled in Harrison county,
and established what was then known as "Whitaker's
Settlement," now Oddville. He was the father of Rev.
Josiah Whitaker. His home was a preaching place,
and sent forth a gospel influence which radiated for
many miles in every direction.

The Woodfield brothers, with Philip Taylor and Edward Talbot, removed from Fayette to Shelby county,
and "Edward Talbot's Meeting-house," was a part of
the Salt River circuit. Charles Sherman and Elijah
Sparks, "both lawyer and preacher," also settled in
this part of the State, and did their part in establishing Methodism in their respective neighborhoods.
Sparks afterwards moved to Newport, and we find Asbury in his home, baptizing his children.

In Madison county, lived Rev. Joseph Proctor. He
was not only a good preacher, but a gallant soldier and
a famous Indian fighter. He took part in almost every
expedition from this section against the Indians, and

is credited with the slaying of a noted Indian chief at Piqua, Ohio. He was with Captain Estill in that fierce battle with the Wyandottes, near Mt. Sterling, in which Captain Estill lost his life. A bullet from Proctor's rifle immediately laid low the Indian whose knife had been plunged into Estill's heart. He then carried the body of the brave Estill on his shoulders to his home nearly forty miles away. He lived to be a very old man, and died at Irvine, Ky., in 1844, and was buried there with military honors. "Proctor's Chapel," named in his honor, was built not far from Boonesboro, but later was rebuilt as "Providence," near to White Hall.

In this same county lived John Cook, R. Baker, and Charles Kavanaugh, all local preachers. William Burke says:

Charles Kavanaugh was a preacher of splendid talents and great usefulness. He was an able defender of the doctrines of the Methodist Church, and was highly respected by all denominations. There were several families of that connection. Williams Kavanaugh was raised in that neighborhood, and was a cousin of Charles .... Charles Kavanaugh, after having made full proof of his ministry in Kentucky, removed, in 1796 or 1797, to the neighborhood of Nashville, Tennessee, where I found him settled in 1798. He there commenced the practice of medicine, and was celebrated as a cancer doctor. Of his labors and usefulness in that country, and the manner in which he closed his life and labors, we hope some friend will furnish the account.

Rev. Manoah Lasley, the father of Rev. Thomas Lasley, the missionary to Louisiana, was the progenitor of a number of other Methodist preachers of that name. He settled on Green River, not far from Greensburg, and his house was a preaching place for that community, and his influence extended far and wide. In the Cumberland country, not far from Nashville, Rev. John McGee had located, and it was under his ministry that the Great Revival of 1799 and 1805 began.

Other local preachers had, by this time, come into Western Kentucky and Middle Tennessee, and we would that their names and a record of their services had been preserved so as to take their place in the pages of the early history of the Church in these sections. But "their works do follow them," and the memory of their good deeds will not be lost in the day of Judgment.

Quite a number of men who had spent some time in the itinerant field, but who had been compelled by failing health or family cares to drop back into the local ranks, had either remained in Kentucky or had come into the State as immigrants. Dropping out of the itinerancy did not mean that they ceased from their labors as ministers of the gospel. As far as health and opportunity would permit, these were constantly employed in preaching and ministering to the needy souls of the people. And it is interesting to note how a wise Providence distributed these men over the field. When John Sewell and John Ball retired to the local ranks, they made their homes in the Cumberland section of Middle Tennessee, and were abundantly useful in this part of the country. We have already mentioned that Barnabas McHenry and William Duzan found homes in Washington county and did a great work for the cause of Christ in all that county. Ignatius Pigman was one of three men who were elected and ordained deacons at the Christmas Conference in 1784. He located in 1788, came to Kentucky a few years later, and settled in Ohio county. The old Bethel Church, "built of logs in the form of an octagon," was the church to which he was attached.*

---

*The daughter of Ignatius Pigman married Stephen Stateler, and, if I mistake not, was the mother of Rev. Learner Blackman Stateler, the great pioneer of our Church in the State of Montana.

Jacob Lurton became a resident of Jefferson county, while James Ward resided in Oldham, not far away. Both these men were eminently useful.

Henry Ogburn was admitted on trial as early as 1779. After several years of hard work on eastern circuits, he came to Kentucky about 1795, and found a home near Port William, now Carrollton. His humble house was a home for the traveling preachers and a preaching place, and it was through Ogburn's labors that Methodism had its beginning in that part of the State.

Joseph Lillard located in Mercer county, where "Joseph's Chapel" still bears witness to the high esteem in which he was held. After leaving Bethel Academy, John Metcalf lived in Nicholasville, taught school and preached in all that part of the State. John Pace settled in Madison county, and "Pace's Chapel" was a center of gospel influence until within the memory of persons now living. John Ray located near Mt. Sterling and organized societies throughout that section. Williams Kavanaugh lived in Clark county and was a charter member of the Ebenezer church. Benjamin Lakin spent several years in Bourbon county, while Benjamin Northcutt, Jeremiah Lawson, James O'Cull, and Thomas Scott were in Fleming and Mason, where their work abides to this day. From this it will be seen that ex-itinerant preachers were scattered throughout the State and bore no small part in the triumphs of Methodism at this early day.

Quite a number of meeting houses had been built by this time. Most of them were small and inferior structures, but they in some measure met the needs of the people and gave permanence to the cause. There were many preaching places where the man of God could deliver his message, but most of them were in private houses. Sometimes a court house was used, or, when no other place was available, a barroom answered the purpose of a church. Often the services were held in the open air. On the Salt River circuit there were fifty-eight preaching places, and on the Lexington circuit there were twenty-six. The average was not less than thirty.

Most of these preaching places were in the country. Maysville had a small society prior to 1800, but Newport was not organized until 1811. Covington waited for the coming of Methodism until 1827. Valentine Cook was said to have visited Danville before 1800, and was the first Methodist preacher to preach there, but no Methodist church existed in that place until Henry McDaniel organized it in 1823. Harrodsburg was organized in 1828; Winchester in 1824; Mt. Sterling in 1825; Cynthiana later still. Frankfort had no church of any kind in 1810. After passing through the place on October 17th of that year, Bishop Asbury says in his Journal: "Came to low-seated Frankfort. Here are elegant accommodations provided for those who make the laws, and those who break them, but there is no house of God!" Perhaps there was an organization in Paris at an earlier date, but the foundation of the first Methodist church building there was laid in 1813. This same year the meeting house in Shelbyville was erected. A Methodist meeting house was built in Nicholasville in 1799.

The western part of the State was settled at a later date than the eastern, and naturally fewer church edifices were built there prior to 1800 than in the eastern section. Russellville, in Logan county, became a part of the old Cumberland circuit before this time, but there was no organization in the town until 1808. Hopkinsville, Henderson, Owensboro, Elizabethtown, and other places in what is now the Louisville Conference, were not then occupied. Louisville was among the first towns laid off in the State, but it was surrounded by marshes and swamps, and was exceedingly unhealthy until these were drained or filled in, and consequently the town had a slow growth. The first Methodist society there was organized in 1806. Mrs. Morrison, William Farquar, Thomas Biscourt, Messrs. Catlin and Mosely, and a few others constituted this first society. In 1809 a lot was secured on the north side of Market street, between 7th and 8th, and a small brick house, thirty-four by thirty-eight feet, was erected—the first church of any kind in the village.

Nearly all of these church buildings, whether in town or country, were of logs. At first, round, unhewn logs were used, and these often destitute of any sort of "chinking" to keep out the wind and rain. Often there was no chimney, and no provision for fire in winter. Services were held in these open fireless buildings when snow was on the ground. Later, the logs were nicely hewn and made comfortable by stopping cracks and by putting in huge fire-places. W. B. Landrum, in his "Life and Travels," describes a meeting house that stood in Clark county, as "a log building, with a dirt floor, and was sometimes used as a school house. It had a kind of temporary pulpit, with a few puncheons for the preacher to stand upon, and a couple of forks stuck in the ground with a cross piece for a hand board." "Ferguson's Chapel" was first built of round logs, with clap-board roof. "Some of the oldest inhabitants have a recollection of attending Divine service in this building, when they were so small that, becoming weary of the exercises, they would climb from the gallery through a crack in the wall, and then descend to the ground by means of a walnut sapling that grew thereby."

These buildings compared very favorably with the houses in which the people lived, and are not to be taken as evidences of want of interest in the house of God. Materials out of which to build, other than logs, was scarce in those days. The finest of oak and walnut and poplar timber abounded in the great forests, but there was no way to cut out framing and flooring except by whip-saws, operated by hand, and to get out enough, by this method, to build a frame structure was out of the question. As soon as there were more people to do the work, and as there were better facilities for securing materials, better houses of worship took the places of these crude buildings erected by the first settlers.| Nicely hewn logs, neatly "chinked" with lime mortar, splendidly adzed puncheon floors, windows, capacious fire-places, and backless seats,—made of split logs with legs fitted into auger holes on the under sides, —became the prevailing style of architecture for the houses of worship used by all the denominations. "Brick Chapel," erected in Shelby county, in 1804, was the first church of that material built by the Methodists in Kentucky, and the second of the kind built by any denomination.

Mention has already been made of the house built by Richard Masterson, about five miles Northwest of Lexington. Bishop Asbury speaks of this as "a very comfortable house." It was built of logs, and later was weather-boarded. It stood for more than a hundred years, and an electro of it is herewith presented. After the old house was torn down, the logs were acquired by First Church, Lexington, with the intention of reconstructing the building on the lot occupied by First Church, but this has never been done. While the Mastersons lived here, it was a favorite gathering place for the Methodists, but after their removal to Carroll county, the society was soon scattered and the building abandoned as a place of worship.

A log meeting house was built at an early day on the farm of John Durham—the exact date we do not know, but it was prior to 1800. This building was, about 1803, superceded by a more pretentious building in the same neighborhood, and was known as "Durham's Chapel," or, as it was afterwards painted white, as "The White Chapel." In 1858, a great revival was held in Perryville by Revs. J. C. C. Thompson, L. G. Hicks, and W. J. Snively, and a church was built at that place. This was less than three miles from The White Chapel, and the congregation here was disbanded, some going to Danville, but most of them merging with the congregation at Perryville. Perryville can be said to be the legitimate successor of "Durham's Chapel." A great camp meeting was held for years near the old Chapel, and was the birth-place of hundreds of souls. It was around this church that the Danville circuit was formed.

Ferguson's Chapel, mentioned above, was thought to have been the second house of worship built by the Methodists in Kentucky, and it is thought that the building was erected in 1792. It was the nucleus around which the old Salt River circuit was formed. The original log structure was replaced by a brick building in 1816, and this by a larger brick about 1844. This church flourished for a time, but in the development of the country, it was left off on a country road, and was about to die. In 1908, the old site was abandoned and a church built at Woodlawn, a short distance away.*

Another church in this section of the State was Thomas' Meeting house, six miles from Lebanon. Among the first members of this church were Owen Thomas and his wife. Jacob Young, while making his first round on his first circuit, in 1802, came to this church, and has left us an interesting account of his visit to Father Thomas'. He says:

My next appointment was at what is called Thomas' meeting house. I went to this place with fear and trembling, for I had heard many things of old father Thomas. He was very severe on the young preachers, often telling them, if they could do no better, they had better go home. I prayed much on my way thither. He met me at the door, and gave me a very cold reception. He was a large man, of rough features, stern countenance, and of great decision; withal, he was very rich, and felt his own importance. He sat down and looked at me as if he would examine my head and heart, and I felt very uneasy.

---

*In a letter to the writer, Rev. C. H. Greer, D. D., says: "This church stood on a point easily accessible while the country was open, but when the farmers fenced in all their land they left it with a big hill to go down and one to go up on both sides. After that, the congregation dwindled until it looked like the church would die. Fortunately, the old building, about that time, got in such a condition it looked like it would fall down, and something had to be done. As is nearly always the case, sentiment was strong to rebuild on the old site. . . . Woodlawn is the railroad station about three quarters of a mile from the site of the old church. The congregation was so run down that they thought they did not need a large church, and built one that has been too small from the day of its dedication. . . . C. M. Humphrey, John Humphrey, William Summers, (now in Missouri) and I have entered the ministry from that church. . . . Joseph Ferguson is buried in a small burying ground just down the hill from the old burying ground of the old brick church."

Mrs. Thomas entered the room with a smiling countenance, shook my hand, and gave me a hearty welcome. She was a fine figure, and reminded me of what I had read of Lady Huntington. Her mind was filled with good sense, and her heart overflowed with charity. The congregation soon assembled. As the day was cold, and there was no stove in the meeting house, they concluded to have the preaching in the house, which was large enough to accommodate them. I arose under a heavy cross, and went to a little stand. My Bible being in one pocket, and my hymn-book in another, I was not dependent on any one for books. My congregation was gay for those early days. The above named Wickliffe (Hon. Robert Wickliffe) sat before me. I read my hymn, they sang, and I kneeled down to pray. The clouds dispersed, and in the light of almighty God I saw light. I had studied my text well, and the Lord gave me great liberty. Old father Thomas wept freely, his brother shouted, and his wife praised God with a loud voice. Brother Thomas was never cross with me after that day. I had a pleasant night and a most delightful morning.

Still another church in this part of the State was at Level Woods, in Larue county. A society had been organized here in 1796, by Rev. John Baird, who, after traveling for several years in the East, had broken under the terrific strain, located, came to Kentucky, and settled in this neighborhood. He was soon instrumental in forming a class. He was a man of more than ordinary ability in the pulpit, and during the fifty years he lived in this part of the State, he was everywhere recognized as a saintly man and an able expounder of the Word of God. A meeting house was erected here, though we do not know exactly when it was built, or what kind of a structure it was.

Lewis' Meeting House stood not far from Bethel Academy. Doubtless it took its name from John Lewis, who gave the ground on which Bethel was built. The Conference met here in 1794. Not a trace of the building is left. It was in the Lexington circuit.

On the Danville circuit, William Burke mentions three log meeting houses that had been built as early as 1793—Proctor's Chapel, in Madison county; Garrett's meeting house, in Garrard; Shawnee Run, in Mercer, and Burke's Chapel, somewhere in Garrard county, near the Madison line, was built in 1795 or 1796. In our mention of Proctor's Chapel, in giving a brief sketch on Joseph Proctor, we stated that Providence church succeeded Proctor's Chapel and that it stood further south, and nearer Foxtown, or White Hall. This church was finally abandoned, the congregation, with that of Pace's Chapel, merging to form the church at Red House, which is a part of the College Hill circuit.

Mt. Olivet, on the Burgin circuit, stands nearest the site of Garrett's Chapel, and is doubtless the successor of this church. While pastor at Harrodsburg, in 1930-34, the writer tried to locate the old Shawnee Run meeting house, but could find no trace of it. There is now a strong Baptist church called Shawnee Run, but no one knew where the old Methodist chapel stood. Burke says it was not far from Harrodsburg, and Bishop Asbury, after holding a Conference at Bethel Academy, crossed the Kentucky river and preached at that church.

As early as April, 1798, the Treasurer's book of the Limestone circuit records the fact that a Quarterly Meeting was held at "Bracken Meeting House." This building was erected in Bracken county, not far from where Brooksville now stands. Another building was erected in this county the following year, and was known as "Dora's Meeting House," afterwards called "Mt. Zion," about three miles from the town of Augusta.

On Cassidy Creek, in Nicholas, in 1793, Richard Bird organized a society, and not long afterwards, a log meeting house was built. This house was burned, and was succeeded by another on a site not far away. The church still exists and has had a most remarkable history. It has been a great Methodist center, and it is said that nearly a hundred Methodist preachers have gone out from it. It was here that the writer, when a very small boy, united with the Church.

One of the historic churches in Kentucky Methodism is Grassy Lick, in Montgomery county, about six miles from Mt. Sterling. "A preaching place was established there before the Hinkstone circuit was formed in 1793, and the first church building was erected about 1800." James Wren gave the ground, and a hewed-log house, twenty-four by thirty-four, was built about 1800. This church was "on a beautiful hill or ridge," while the present building stands in a valley. "Among the first members at Grassy Lick, were the Wrens, Riggses, Sewells, Tauls, and Farrows." A great campground was located nearby, and the place contributed much to the cause of Christ in all that section. "From Grassy Lick there went out a salutary Methodist influence, which reached Mount Sterling, the O'Rear settlement, and other parts of the county. For a long time old father Spratt was almost the only member of our Church in Mount Sterling, when the revival power reached that place first in 1825, and some of the principal families were converted." Susan Taul, the grandmother of Rev. W. T. Poynter, long a member of the Kentucky Conference and President of Science Hill School, at Shelbyville, was perhaps the best known member of the Grassy Lick church. She was indeed a "mother in Israel," and her godly life was a benedic-

tion to all who knew her. It was from this church that
John Fisk, that gifted and zealous preacher, went into
the Conference in 1826. Bishop Kavanaugh received
his recommendations for license to preach from this
church. At the camp meeting held at that place, hundreds of souls were born into the kingdom of Christ.

About three miles from Cynthiana, on the road
from that place to Ruddles Mills, stood old Mount
Gerazim, where the Western Conference was held in
both 1803 and 1804.

Mount Gerazim, or Broadwell, is a historic church. It
was built about the beginning of the present (last) century.
The ground where it stands was given jointly by Richard Tim-
berlake and Samuel Broadwell, the former a Presbyterian, the
latter a Methodist. The first house was built of blue ash logs,
so nicely and smoothly hewed that not a trace of the scoring
could be seen. The logs were furnished by the neighbors; and
when they were all collected on the ground, one of the neighbors, because his set of logs was not as nice as some others,
hauled them away, and got out an entire new set, determined
to excel all the rest. This house was burnt about 1825—accidental—when the brick house now standing was erected. Two
Conferences were held here. This church, which was the great
center of Methodism for all of now interior Kentucky, was, at
this early period, in the old Hinkstone circuit, which circuit
was traveled by William Burke, Dr. Cloud, Littleton Fowler,
Samuel Parker, Learner Blackman, James Ward, William Pat-
terson, George Askins, H. B. Bascom, William Holman, Jonathan Stamper, etc.

More than a dozen camp meetings were held here. The
numbers attending were immense. At one of these camp meetings, Bascom and Stribling preached on different days from
the same text—being accidental; hence, quite a discussion
among the people which preached the greater sermon.

The church stood for many years as a great beacon-light,
long before there was any church at Cynthiana, Millersburg, or
Paris. Mount Gerazim, or Broadwell, is hallowed on account
of the great revivals of religion. Thousands of souls have been
converted on its consecrated grounds.—Redford, Vol. II. P. 398.

The Presbyterians still have a church called Broadwell, but the Methodist congregation was long since
absorbed by those of Cynthiana, Paris, Ruddles Mills,
and Millersburg.

One of the most noted gathering places of early
Methodism in this State was Ebenezer, six miles from
Winchester, on the road to Lexington. This was the
church of the Hindes, the Kavanaughs, the Martins,
and others of the leading families of this section. A
letter from Dr. W. T. Poynter to Dr. Redford says:

·The first Methodist society at Ebenezer was organized in
1797, and consisted of eight persons, as follows, viz., Dr. Thomas
Hinde, Mary Todd Hinde, Martha Hinde, Williams Kavanaugh, Hannah Kavanaugh, John Martin, Mr. Summers, and
Elizabeth Hieronymous. In the year of 1798, the first church
was built on the lands of John Martin and Dr. Thomas Hinde,
of logs; and in the year 1810, it being found too small for the
congregation, who attended, it was enlarged. Seven camp-
meetings were held in the neighborhood between 1820 and 1830,
and were largely attended—this being a great central point for
Methodism in those days. In the year 1826, the old log church
gave way to a neat brick church, which, in 1843, was replaced
by a still larger and more finished building, which was burned
in 1853; since which time the society there has been connected
with the church at Winchester. Ebenezer has sent forth from
its society thirteen preachers, among them Jonathan Stamper,
H. H. Kavanaugh, B. T. Kavanaugh, W. B Kavanaugh, and
William Askins. All the first preachers of the Connection have
at some time or another, preached at this point. Bishops
George, Bascom, McKendree, and Kavanaugh have all held forth
the word of life to the people there. Maffitt, in 1841, held a
meeting there, and received many into the church.

In addition to those preachers named by Dr. Poynter as having gone into the ministry from Ebenezer,
might be named Leroy Kavanaugh, Henry McDaniel,
(who organized the church at Danville) and Stephen
and Obadiah Harber, twin brothers, who served the

Church for many years, and left a most honorable family of that name in Madison county. In a letter to Dr. Redford, Dr. B. T. Kavanaugh says:

The measure of religious influence exerted by the society at Ebenezer is not to be confined to the number of her members, or the ministers she has sent out; but it is entitled to the credit of having given rise to other societies, and in greatly aiding such as had a previous existence. The church at Winchester, for example, was wholly constituted by members from Ebenezer. The church at Lexington received great aid from the camp-meetings held at or near Ebenezer. In 1819, the church at Lexington was very small, and worshipped in a little ill-shaped house, far out in the east end of the town, which was afterwards sold as a cabinet shop. In the fall of 1819 and 1820, the revival influence was carried from the camp-meetings at Ebenezer into Lexington, by those who attended it; and the society there thus received its first religious impulse toward a large and healthy growth. Previous to that time, there was not a young person in the society—none when I joined there. Old fathers Chipley, Chatton, Bryan, Gibbon, and a few others, were the fathers of the church. In 1820 and 1821, the revival continued, and a great many young people were brought into the Church.

After the burning of the building in 1853, the organization at Ebenezer was temporarily abandoned, but was soon revived, and a substantial brick edifice erected on the main road to Lexington, and for many years was a part of the Winchester charge. "Winchester and Ebenezer" was the way the appointment read in the Minutes, and the same minister served both congregations until about 1890, when the organization at Ebenezer was discontinued, the church torn down, and, at this writing, only a pile of brick-bats tells the story of the once prosperous society.

Among the leading families attached to Methodism in Kentucky prior to the time of which we write, mention has been made of several, such as the Clarks, Dur-

hams, and Eastlands ,of Boyle county; of Mrs. Harrod
and the Lettimores of Mercer; of the Lewises, Pryors,
and Metcalfes, of Jessamine; the Mastersons of Fayette; the Hindes, Martins, Kavanaughs, Scobees, and
Owens of Clark; the O'Rears, Wrens, Riggses, Sewells, Tauls, and Farrows, of Montgomery; the Stampers
and Harbers of Clark and Madison; the Hardins and
Wickliffs of Nelson, and of others in various places
over the State. Besides these, mention should be made
of Ilai Nunn, who was among the first Methodists to
arrive in Kentucky. He settled in the District in
1783, and it is stated that he attached himself to a
Methodist society before coming to the West. It is
probable that Francis Clark and John Durham preceded him, but he was certainly one of the first to arrive. He settled first near Lexington, but after two
years here,

he purchased a tract of land near Millersburg, which he improved, and which was widely known as 'Nunn's farm,' and on
which he established a camp-ground, which is still remembered
by all the old citizens of Bourbon county. His home, one of the
best in the neighborhood, was the home of Methodist preachers,
as well as those of other denominations who chose to call on
him—and for many years the only preaching place in the neighborhood. It was in the vicinity of his house that the Cane Ridge
meeting was held, in 1801, and at it occurred the most remarkable revival meeting ever held on this continent   (Quoted
from a letter to Dr. Redford from Rev. H. A. M. Henderson).

Ilai Nunn was the grand father of Rev. John P.
Durbin, D. D., one of the really great preachers of
America, and Dr. Durbin was greatly indebted to his
grand-father for his advice and influence. His mother,
the daughter of Mr. Nunn, was a woman of far more
than ordinary intelligence and character. William
Nunn, one of the most honored citizens of Millersburg,

was a son of Ilai Nunn. The splendid property in which he lived, is now the site of the Millersburg Military Institute. When a student in the old Kentucky Wesleyan College, which stood just across the street from the Nunn home, the widow of William Nunn was still living and was well known to the writer. She was a very brilliant woman, and was said to be able to converse fluently in as many as three different languages. By her first marriage, she was the mother of Rev. H. A. M. Henderson, D. D., a most brilliant preacher and lecturer, and for several years Superintendent of Public Instruction in Kentucky.

A brief sketch of Willis Green has already been given. He should be held in remembrance by the Methodist people of Kentucky. One of the first Methodists in the State, one of the promoters of Bethel Academy, a representative in the Legislature, and filling other offices of honor and trust, he was one of the most valuable laymen of his day. His descendants for many years blessed the Church in Boyle and Lincoln counties.

Major John Martin was another layman who, in those early times, wielded an influence for good in the Church. He was a native of Virginia, born in 1748. He was a Captain during the Revolutionary war. and was promoted to Major at the siege of Yorktown. He came to Kentucky in 1784, settled in Clark county, and for many years was one of the Judges of the Court of Quarter Sessions. He was the first sheriff of Clark county. At the time of his coming to Kentucky, he was an infidel. Notwithstanding their different sentiments regarding religion, he and Dr. Thomas Hinde became warm personal friends. One day while in conversation with Mrs. Hinde, she made a remark that sent deep conviction into his soul. He could not get rid of it, and after wrestling all night in an agony of prayer, the light of heaven shone around him, and he came out of the struggle a whole-souled disciple of the Lord. A complete change was made in his life, and one of his first acts after his conversion was to feed to the hogs a fine crop of peaches which he had intended to make into brandy! His house became a house of prayer, and he delighted to attend and take part in the great camp-meetings in this part of the State. He would take his whole family and encamp on the grounds. He was one of the charter members of old Ebenezer church, lived to a ripe old age, and died in the triumphs of the faith.

Reference has been made to Dr. Thomas Hinde. No family did more for early Methodism in this State than did his. Though born in England, and in the service of that country as a surgeon in the royal navy, Dr. Hinde was induced to resign his position and come to America about 1765. He had been trained in the branches of both medicine and surgery by the best instructors, and was well qualified for the practice of both. After coming to Virginia, he was married, on September 24, 1767, to Mary Todd Hubbard, the daughter of an English merchant. Soon after his marriage, Dr. Hinde removed to Hanover county, and became the family physician in the home of Patrick Henry.

Mrs. Hinde was a remarkable woman. She had been favored with the best educational advantages of her times, and her mind was well cultivated. With a pleasing manner and most kindly disposition, she brought cheer and sunshine wherever she went. For several years after marriage, she was a stranger to the joys of religion, and unfortunately, her husband, who was an avowed infidel, was no help to her religiously, but, being bitterly antagonistic to all religion, did everything in his power to hinder her even in her formal religious life.

However, Methodist preaching was introduced into that part of Virginia in which the Hindes lived, and a daughter was deeply convicted and soon after was converted. Through her conversations and her changed life, her mother was soon awakened, and under the preaching of the Methodists, was led into a happy religious experience. Dr. Hinde was greatly enraged. Though ordinarily the kindest of husbands, he peremptorily ordered his wife not to go to the Methodist meetings, and when she persisted, refused to let her have a horse to ride, so that she was compelled to walk. "He became persuaded that these people had set those persons thus affected crazy, and thus concluded that his wife and daughter were really deranged, and that without a proper remedy being immediately applied, the consequences would become very serious." So he at length put a blister on the neck of his wife, to bring her to her senses! Her grand-son, Bishop H. H. Kavanaugh, thus tells the story:

After the blister plaster was put on, she and her daughter went on to the meeting again. The next day the doctor asked her how her blister was coming on. 'Did the plaster draw well?' She said, 'I know nothing about the plaster.' He exclaimed, 'What, did you take it off?' She answered, 'No.' Of course he knew it was in bad condition. He stood astounded, until, she told me, he looked as if he were petrified, and doubted if he had the use of himself. She said she arose from her seat and purposely brushed by him, when he staggered and caught, showing the want of self-control, from the intensity of his feelings; for though he had thus treated his wife, he loved her with a warm devotion. Reflecting on this transaction, conviction seized on his mind, and troubled him for his sins. He dressed the blister as best he could and taking a seat by his wife, he said, 'I expect if you would join these people you would feel better.' With animation she exclaimed, 'Thank you, blister plaster! Thank you, blister plaster!' believing that her blister had accomplished that much for her.

The end of it was that the doctor was soundly converted and became one of the most devoted of Christians. He was a man of prayer. It is said that, around the farm he cultivated in Kentucky, you might often see little houses built of sticks of wood, and covered with bark, with a little door for entrance. His grandchildren, the Bishop among the rest, soon came to know these as "Grand Pa's Prayer Houses." His secret devotions could not remain secret. He prayed so loud his neighbors heard him, and his praying lead to the conversion of some of them. He was a great worker in camp-meetings and in revivals everywhere, and was much used of God in winning lost souls to the Savior. During the latter part of his life, religion was his constant theme. When very old his memory of recent events entirely failed him, but he never forgot the Lord Jesus Christ. Numerous anecdotes are told of him, illustrative of his deep religious fervor, but we have no room to cite them here. Sometime before his death he removed to Newport, Ky., and lived with his daughter, Mrs. Mary Taylor, and it is here that he died, aged ninety-two years.

The family of Dr. and Mrs. Hinde have greatly blessed the Church of Christ in Kentucky and elsewhere. One of their sons, Thomas S. Hinde, became a minister of note in the Methodist Church. His writings, under the pen name of "Theophilus Arminius," have added much to our knowledge of early Methodism in this State. One of their daughters married Rev. Leroy Cole, the founder of the Methodist church in

Cynthiana, and promoter of one of the greatest revivals that ever visited that part of Kentucky. He revived camp-meetings at a time when they had almost passed out of use in Methodism, and did much to spread the work of the Church in Harrison and adjoining counties. A sketch of his life and labors will be given in another place. Another daughter married Williams Kavanaugh, and was the mother of four Methodist preachers, viz., Bishop H. H. Kavanaugh, one of the most eloquent preachers Kentucky ever produced; Rev. Benjamin T. Kavanaugh, a truly great man; Rev. Leroy H. Kavanaugh, and Rev. Williams B. Kavanaugh, once the President of the Kentucky Conference. Of their grand-sons, Rev. Peter E. Kavanaugh was for many years a member of the Kentucky Conference. Rev. Hubbard H. Kavanaugh, Jr., was for a long period the beloved Chaplain of the State prison, at Frankfort. Rev. Edward L. Southgate, Sr., and Rev. Edward L. Southgate, Jr., were descendants of this worthy pair. Besides these an unusual number of their descendants have been useful members of the Church.

We regret that we have not àt hand sufficient information of the Hardins, the Humphreys, the Helms, the Hites, the Houstons, the Griffiths, the Hords, the Whitakers, the Becks, the Highlands, the Reeses, the Doras, and others, who, prior to 1800, located in Kentucky and invested their lives in the cause of Christ in this State. Their toils and sacrifices in behalf of Methodism have borne fruit during all the years. They laid the foundation stones; others have builded on them. A very great structure has taken form to the glory of God the Father and of His Son, Jesus Christ.

CHAPTER X.

While there was a slight increase in the colored membership in Kentucky and Cumberland between 1795 and 1800, there was a decrease in the white membership of 237. There was a spiritual dearth throughout the land. "Theophilus Arminius" is authority for the statement that "the most influential political characters at an early period in Kentucky were, in general, either *infidels* or *sceptics*. To their views they attempted to make all bend." Barton W. Stone says that "apathy in religious societies appeared everywhere to an alarming degree. Not only the power of religion had disappeared, but also the very form of it was waning fast away, and continued so until the beginning of the present (i. e., the nineteenth) century." While a gracious revival had followed the preaching of Haw and Ogden from 1787 to 1791, this tide of spiritual power had spent itself against the rocks of wickedness, infidelity and greed. A history of the West at that period will show a mad rush for the rich lands on the part of settlers, and a wild and conscienceless speculation on the part of adventurers that is almost without a parallel. There were a few revivals among the Methodists, but they were widely scattered and of meager results. The situation was truly alarming and brought great distress to those who remained in real fellowship with Christ.

A gracious revival sprang up in the Cumberland circuit, under the labors of Jacob Lurton, about 1795, and had extended across the State line into Logan county, Kentucky. This revival continued among the people for months, and, though confined to a limited section, was, perhaps, the beginning of the Great Revival which swept over the western country in 1799 to 1805. In the spring of 1799, John Page was appointed Presiding Elder of the Cumberland District, and the revival was carried forward by his effective ministry, and many were converted to God. Redford says: "If this remarkable revival (of 1801) did not owe its origin to the instrumentality of John Page, it was certainly promoted and extended through his pious labors and exertions."

John and William McGee, the former a Methodist local preacher and the latter a minister of the Presbyterian Church, had settled in Sumner county, Tennessee, in 1798. John McGee, the Methodist minister, is described as "below the medium size, but formed for activity and durability; a model of industry, energy, and economy; .... possessed a strong and vigorous intellect, clear perception, sound, discriminating judgment, and a mind well stored with varied, useful knowledge; was thoroughly versed in the scriptures, understood the doctrines and usages of his Church, and was well prepared to explain and defend them. His manner in the pulpit was mild, plain, and methodical; he never attempted embellishment, but, when fired by the divinity of his theme, frequently rose to the sublime, and carried his hearers with him to the mount to take a view of the heavenly Canaan, and his applications and exhortations were often overwhelming to the unconverted." William McGee was, at that time, pastor of a Presbyterian church in Sumner county. The brothers lived close together and labored together in greatest love and harmony. John McGee tells the story of the revival in the following letter to Rev. Thomas L. Douglass:

In the year 1799, we agreed to make a tour through the Barrens, toward Ohio, and concluded to attend a sacramental solemnity in the Rev. Mr. McGready's congregation, on Red River, on our way. When we came there, I was introduced by my brother, and received an invitation to address the congregation from the pulpit, and I know not that ever God favored me with more light and liberty than he did that day, while I endeavored to convince the people that they were sinners, and urged the necessity of repentance, and a change from nature to grace, and held up to their view the greatness, freeness, and fullness of salvation, which was in Christ Jesus, for lost, guilty, condemned sinners. My brother and the Rev. Mr. Hodge preached with much animation and liberty. The people felt the force of truth, and tears ran down their cheeks, but all was silent until Monday, the last day of the feast. Mr. Hodge gave a useful discourse; an intermission was given, and I was appointed to preach. While Mr. Hodge was preaching, a woman in the east end of the house got an uncommon blessing, broke through order, and shouted for some time, and then sat down in silence. At the close of the sermon, Messrs. Hodge, McGready, and Rankin went out of the house; my brother and myself sat still. The people seemed to have no disposition to leave their seats. My brother felt such power come on him, that he quit his seat and sat down on the floor of the pulpit, (I suppose, not knowing what he did). A power which caused me to tremble was upon me. There was a solemn weeping all over the house. Having a wish to preach, I strove against my feelings. At length I rose up and told the people I was appointed to preach, but there was a greater than I preaching, and exhorted them to let the Lord God omnipotent reign in their hearts, and to submit to him, and their souls should live. Many broke silence; the woman in the east end of the house shouted tremendously. I left the pulpit to go to her, and as I went along through the people, it was suggested to me; 'You know these people are much for order—they will not bear this confusion. Go back, and be quiet.' I turned to go back, and was near falling. The power of God was strong upon me; I turned again, and, losing sight of the fear of man, I went through the house, shouting and exhorting with all possible ecstacy and energy, and the floor was soon covered with the slain. Their screams for mercy pierced the heavens, and mercy came down. Some found forgiveness, and many went away from that meeting feeling unutterable agonies of soul for redemption in the blood of Jesus. This was the beginning of that glorious revival of religion in this country which was so great a blessing to thousands; and from this meeting camp-meetings took their rise. One man, for want of horses for all his family to ride and attend the meeting, fixed up his wagon, in which he took them and his provisions, and lived on the ground throughout the meeting. He had left his worldly cares behind him, and had nothing to do but attend on divine service.

The next popular meeting was on Muddy River, and this was a camp-meeting; a number of wagons loaded with people came together, and camped on the ground; and the Lord was present, and approved of their zeal by sealing pardon to about forty souls. The next camp-meeting was on the Ridge, where there was an increase of people, and carriages of different descriptions, and a great many preachers of the Presbyterian and Methodist orders, and some of the Baptist, but the latter were generally opposed to the work. Preaching commenced, and the people prayed, and the power of God attended. There was a great cry for mercy. The nights were truly awful; the camp ground was well illuminated; the people were differently exercised all over the ground—some exhorting, some shouting, some praying, and some crying for mercy, while others lay as dead men on the ground. Some of the spiritually wounded fled to the woods, and their groans could be heard all through the surrounding groves, as the groans of dying men. From thence many came into the camp, rejoicing and praising God for having found redemption in the blood of the Lamb. At this meeting it was computed that one hundred souls were converted from nature to grace. But perhaps the greatest meeting we ever witnessed in this country took place shortly after, on Desha's Creek, near Cumberland River. Many thousands of people attended. The mighty power and mercy of God were manifested. The people fell before the word, like corn before a storm of wind, and many rose from the dust with divine glory shining in their countenances, and gave glory to God in such strains as made the hearts of stubborn sinners tremble; and, after the first gust of praise they would break forth in volleys of exhortation. Amongst these were many small, home-bred boys, who spoke with the tongue, wisdom, and eloquence of the learned; and truly they were learned, for they were all taught of God, who had taken their feet out of the mire and clay, and put a new song in their mouths. Although there were converts of different ages under this work, it was remarkable that they were generally the children of praying parents.

This was in 1799. It is well to keep the dates well in mind. John Page was on the Cumberland circuit, and was one of the leaders in this great revival. Methodists and Presbyterians labored side by side. Denominational differences were forgotten in the supreme effort to reach and save the lost. The work went on through the year 1800, and news of it spread far and wide. William McKendree was appointed Presiding Elder of all this western territory in the fall of 1800, and soon visited the Cumberland region. Of course he was, after this, in the thick of it all. When he went on toward Central and Northern Kentucky in his round, he told the people everywhere of the wonderful things the Lord was doing in Middle Tennessee and Western Kentucky. As Bishop Pierce would say: "A clean-cut, sky-blue conversion will stir a soul under the ribs of death," and the news of this great work sent a thrill through the apathetic Church. A deep spiritual interest was awakened in all the denominations.

Barton W. Stone was pastor of the Presbyterian churches at Cane Ridge, Bourbon county, and Concord, Nicholas county, only eight or ten miles apart. He was lamenting the spiritual deadness prevailing there as elsewhere. He says:

Having heard of a remarkable religious excitement in the South of Kentucky, and in Tennessee, under the labors of James McGready and other Presbyterian ministers, I was very anxious to be among them; and, early in the spring of 1801, went there to attend a camp-meetnig. There, on the edge of a prairie in Logan county, Kentucky, the multitudes came together, and continued a number of days and nights encamped on the ground; during which time worship was carried on in some part of the encampment. The scene to me was new, and passing strange. It baffled description. Many, very many fell down, as men slain in battle, and continued for hours in an apparently breathless and motionless state—sometimes for a few moments reviving, and exhibiting symptoms of life by a deep groan, or piercing shriek, or by a prayer for mercy most fervently uttered. After lying thus for hours, they obtained deliverance. The gloomy cloud, which had covered their faces, seemed gradually and visibly to disappear, and hope in smiles brightened into joy—they would rise shouting deliverance, and then would address the surrounding multitude in language truly eloquent and impressive. With astonishment did I hear men, women, and children declaring the wonderful works of God, and the glorious mysteries of the gospel. Their appeals were solemn, heart-penetrating, bold and free. Under such addresses many others would fall down into the same state from which the speakers had just been delivered.

Two or three of my particular acquaintances from a distance were struck down. I sat patiently by one of them, whom I knew to be a careless sinner, for hours, and observed with critical attention everything that passed from the beginning to the end. I noticed the momentary reviving as from death—the humble confession of sins—the fervent prayer, and the ultimate deliverance—then the solemn thanks and praise to God—the affectionate exhortation to companions and to the people around, to repent and come to Jesus. I was astonished at the knowledge of gospel truth displayed in the address. The effect was that several sunk down into the same appearance of death. After attending to many such cases, my conviction was complete that it was a good work—the work of God; nor has my mind wavered since on the subject. Much did I then see, and much have I since seen, that I considered to be fanaticism; but this should not condemn the work. The Devil has always tried to ape the works of God, to bring them into disrepute. But that cannot be a Satanic work, which brings men to humble confession and forsaking of

OLD CANE RIDGE MEETING HOUSE

Built by the Presbyterians about 1796. In this House the Great Meeting of August, 1801 was begun, but was soon moved to the surrounding woods.

sin—to solemn prayer—fervent praise and thanksgiving and to sincere and affectionate exhortations to sinners to repent and go to Jesus the Savior.

This was in April or May, 1801. When Stone got back to his people in Bourbon county, he found them very eager to hear of the great work he had witnessed. We shall allow him to tell the story of what followed:

The meeting being closed, I returned with ardent spirits to my congregations. I reached my appointment at Cane Ridge on Lord's Day. Multitudes had collected, anxious to hear the news of the meeting I had attended in Logan. I ascended the pulpit, and gave a relation of what I had seen and heard; then opened my Bible and preached from these words: 'Go ye into all the world and preach the gospel to every creature. He that believeth and is baptized shall be saved, and he that believeth not shall be damned.' On the universality of the gospel, and faith as the condition of salvation, I principally dwelt, and urged the sinner to believe now, and be saved. I labored to remove their pleas and objections, nor was it labor in vain. The congregation was affected with awful solemnity, and many returned home weeping. Having left appointments to preach in the congregation within a few days, I hurried on to Concord to preach at night.

At our meeting at Concord, two little girls were struck down under the preaching of the word, and in every respect were exercised as those were in the south of Kentucky, as already described. Their adresses made deep impressions on the congregation. On the next day I returned to Cane Ridge, and attended my appointment at William Maxwell's. I soon heard of the good effects of the meeting on the Sunday before. Many were solemnly engaged in seeking salvation, and some had found the Lord, and were rejoicing in him. Among these last was my particular friend, Nathaniel Rogers, a man of first respectability and influence in the neighborhood. Just as I arrived at the gate, my friend Rogers and his lady came up; as soon as he saw me, he shouted aloud the praises of God. We hurried into each others embrace, he still praising the Lord aloud. The crowd left the house, and hurried to this novel scene. In less than twenty minutes, scores had fallen to the ground—pale-

ness, trembling, and anxiety appeared in all—some attempted
to fly from the scene panic stricken, but they either fell, or returned immediately to the crowd, as unable to get away. In
the midst of this exercise, an intelligent deist in the neighborhood, stepped up to me, and said, 'Mr. Stone, I always thought
before that you were an honest man; but now I am convinced
that you are deceiving the people.' I viewed him with pity, and
mildly spoke a few words to him—immediately he fell as a dead
man, and rose no more till he confessed the Savior. The meeting continued on that spot in the open air, till late at night, and
many found peace in the Lord.

The effects of this meeting through the country were like
fire in dry stubble driven by a strong wind. All felt its influence more or less. Soon after, we had a protracted meeting
at Concord. The whole country appeared to be in motion to
the place, and multitudes of all denominations attended. All
seemed heartily to unite in the work, and in Christian love.
Party spirit, abashed, shrunk away. To give a true description of this meeting cannot be done; it would border on the
marvelous. It continued five days and nights without ceasing.
Many, very many will through eternity remember it with
thanksgiving and praise.

Such are the accounts given by two of the men who
were chief promoters of the glorious work.

About this time the revival fires began to burn in
another section of Central Kentucky. This work was
independent of the work about Cane Ridge and Concord, and began in Clark county, under the ministry
of William Burke and Benjamin Lakin. Burke was
that year on the Hinkstone circuit. Owing to the immense territory to be covered in making his rounds
on the Western District, McKendree, the Presiding
Elder, could visit the various charges only once in six
months, and the preachers had to assist one another
in holding their Quarterly Meetings when the Presiding Elder was in some other part of the District.
Burke gives us the following account of the beginning
of the revival among the Methodists of this section:

The spring of 1801 the quarterly meetings in Kentucky were held without the presiding elder. The quarterly meeting for Hinkstone circuit was held early in June, at Owen's meeting-house, Four Mile Creek, commencing on Friday and breaking up on Monday morning. At this meeting was the first appearance of that astonishing revival to which we have alluded. Several professed to get religion, and many were under deep conviction for sin, and the meeting continued from Sunday morning till Monday morning with but little intermission. From thence Brother Lakin and myself proceeded in company, on Monday morning, to a Presbyterian sacrament, at Salem meeting-house, in the neighborhod of Col. John Martin's. The Rev. Mr. Lyle was pastor of that church. There had been during the occasion more than ordinary attention and seriousness manifested. I arrived on the ground before the first sermon was concluded, and during the interval they insisted on my preaching the next sermon; and, notwithstanding I was much fatigued from the labors of the quarterly meeting, I at length consented, and commenced about two o'clock, p. m. I took for my text, 'To you is the word of this salvation sent;' and before I concluded there was a great trembling among the dry bones. Great numbers fell to the ground and cried for mercy, old and young. Brother Lakin followed with one of his then powerful exhortations, and the work increased. The Presbyterian ministers stood astonished, not knowing what to make of such a tumult. Brother Lakin and myself proceeded to exhort and pray with them. Some obtained peace with God before the meeting broke up. This was the first appearance of the revival in the Presbyterian Church. From these two meetings the heavenly flame spread in every direction. Preachers and people, when they assembled for meeting, always expected the Lord to meet with them. Our next quarterly meeting was for the Lexington circuit, at Jesse Griffith's, Scott county. On Saturday we had some indications of a good work. On Saturday night we had preaching in different parts of the neighborhood, which at that time was the custom; so that every local preacher and exhorter was employed in the work. Success attended the meetings, and on Sunday morning they came in companies, singing and shouting on the road. Love-feast was opened on Sunday morning at eight o'clock, and such was the power and presence of God, that the doors were thrown open, and the work became general, and continued till Monday afternoon, during which time numbers experienced justification by faith in the name of Jesus Christ. The work spread now into the several circuits. Salt River and Shelby were visited, and Danville shared in the blessing; also the Presbyterian Church caught the fire. Congregations were universally waked up; McNamer's congregation on Cabin Creek; Barton Stone's at Cane Ridge; Reynolds, near Ruddell's Station and in Paris; Rev. Mr.| Lyle at Salem; Mr. Rankin at Walnut Hills; Mr. Blythe at Lexington and Woodford; and Rev. Mr. Walsh at Cane Run; and likewise in Madison county, under the ministry of Rev. M. Houston. The work extended to Ohio at Lower Springfield, Hamilton county; Rev. Mr. Thompson's congregation on Eagle Creek; Rev. Mr. Dunlavy's congregation, Adams county. The Methodist local preachers and exhorters, and the members generally, united with them in carrying on the work, for they were at home wherever God was pleased to manifest his power; and having had some experience in such a school, were able to teach others. The Presbyterian ministry saw the advantage of such auxiliaries, and were pressing in their invitations both for the traveling and local preachers, to attend their sacaments through the months of July and August.

This quotation, while slightly partisan in its tone, and containing a few slight errors, gives us a good idea of the beginning of the work among the Methodists of Central and Northern Kentucky. It should be emphasized that this great revival was not promoted by, nor confined to, any one denomination. While perhaps the Baptists were a little more shy of it than others, many of them worked side by side with Presbyterians and Methodists in the effort to reach and to save the lost. Denominational prejudices had been extremely bitter prior to this time, and had been a great hindrance to the cause of Christ. People were disgusted with the discussions over insignificant or else incomprehensible points of controversy, and were glad of an opportunity to lay these aside and join together in an effort to lead lost souls to Jesus. Among the workers in this revival it was difficult to distinguish Methodists from Baptists or Presbyterians—all were servants of God, working together to bring lost sinners to a knowledge of saving grace.

Undoubtedly the Methodists bore a conspicuous part in the work. Mention has already been made of a meeting held in Fleming county in 1800 by Revs. Northcutt and Allen, at which, under the preaching and exhortations of Mr. Northcutt, remarkable manifestations of power were witnessed. At the meeting at Concord, related in Barton W. Stone's account, Mr. Northcutt was invited to attend and assist. When he reached the grounds, out of deference to the prevailing denominational prejudice, it was thought best that he should not be known as a Methodist preacher. It was arranged that he should preach without an introduction, and under his sermon more than two hundred people fell as dead men. He was present at Cane Ridge, and at other meetings where there were wonderful displays of divine power under his preaching. Burke, Lakin, Page, and others were recognized leaders in the great work.

During the spring and summer of 1801, great meetings were held at Cabin Creek, in Lewis county; Indian Creek, in Harrison county, and in other places; but the greatest of all the meetings was that at Cane Ridge, in August of this year. As already stated, Barton W. Stone was pastor of this church at this time, and it is but fair that we let him tell us something of the mighty work at that meeting. He says:

This memorable meeting came on Thursday or Friday before the third Lord's Day in August, 1801. The roads were literally crowded with wagons, carriages, horsemen, and footmen, moving to the solemn camp. The sight was affecting. It was judged, by military men on the ground, that there were between twenty and thirty thousand collected. Four or five preachers were frequently speaking at the same time, in different parts of the encampment, without confusion. The Methodist and Baptist preachers aided in the work, and all appeared cordially united in it—of one mind and one soul, and the salvation of sinners seemed to be the great object of all. We all engaged in singing the same songs of praise—all united in prayer—all preached the same things—free salvation urged upon all by faith and repentance. A particular description of this meeting would fill a large volume; and then the half would not be told. The numbers converted will be known only in eternity. Many things transpired there which were so much like miracles, that if they were not, they had the same effect as miracles on infidels and unbelievers; for many of them by these were convinced that Jesus was the Christ, and bowed in submission to him. This meeting continued six or seven days and nights, and would have continued longer, but provisions for such a multitude failed in the neighborhood. To this meeting many had come from Ohio and other distant parts, who returned home and diffused the same spirit in their neighborhoods, and the same works followed. So low had religion sunk, and such carelessness universally had prevailed, that I have thought that nothing common could have arrested the attention of the world; therefore these uncommon agitations were sent for this purpose.

As William Burke was one of the most active workers in this great revival, we shall allow him also to tell us about it. He says:

The Rev. Barton W. Stone was pastor of the Church at Cane Ridge. I had been formerly acquainted with him when he traveled as a missionary in the Holston and Cumberland country, previous to his settling at Cane Ridge; and we agreed to have a united sacrament of the Presbyterians and Methodists at Cane Ridge meeting-house, in August. The meeting was published throughout the length and breadth of the country to commence on Friday. On the first day I arrived in the neighborhood; but it was a rainy day and I did not attend on the ground.

On Saturday morning I attended. On Friday and Friday night they held meeting in the meeting-house; and such was the power and presence of God on Friday night, that the meeting continued all night; and the next morning, Saturday, they repaired to a stand erected in the woods, the work still going on in the house, which continued there till Wednesday, without intermission. On Saturday the congregation was very numerous. The Presbyterians continued to occupy the stand during Saturday and Saturday night, whenever they could get a chance to be heard; but never invited any Methodist preacher to preach. On Sunday morning Mr. Stone, with some of the elders of the session, waited on me to have a conference on the subject of the approaching sacrament, which was to be administered in the afternoon. The object in calling on me was, that I should make from the stand a public declaration how the Methodists held certain doctrines, etc. I told them we preached every day, and that our doctrines were published to the world through the press. Come and hear; go and read; and if that was the condition on which we were to unite in the sacrament, 'Every man to his tent, O Israel;' for I should require of him to make a declaration of their belief on certain doctrines. He then replied that we had better drop the subject; that he was perfectly satisfied, but that some of his elders were not. I observed that they might do as they thought best; but the subject got out among the Methodists, and a number did not partake of the sacrament, as none of our preachers were invited to assist in administering.

There is a mistaken opinion with regard to this meeting. Some writers of late represent it as having been a camp-meeting. It is true there were a number of wagons and carriages, which remained on the ground night and day; but not a single tent was to be found, neither was any such thing as camp-meeting heard of at that time. Preaching in the woods was a common thing at popular meetings, as meeting-houses in the West were not sufficient to hold the large number of people that attended on such occasions. This was the case at Cane Ridge.

On Sunday morning, when I came on the ground, I was met by my friends, to know if I was going to preach for them that day. I told them I had not been invited; if I was, I should certainly do so. The morning passed off, but no invitation. Be-

tween ten and eleven I found a convenient place on the body
of a fallen tree, about fifteen feet from the ground, where I
fixed my stand in the open sun, with an umbrella fixed to a
long pole and held over my head by Brother Hugh Barnes. I
commenced reading a hymn with an audible voice, and by the
time we concluded singing and praying we had around us, standing on their feet, by fair calculation ten thousand people. I
gave out my text in the following words: 'For we must all
stand before the judgment seat of Christ;' and before I concluded my voice was not to be heard for the groans of the distressed and the shouts of triumph. Hundreds fell prostrate
to the ground, and the work continued on that spot till Wednesday afternoon. It was estimated by some that not less than
five hundred were at one time lying on the ground in the deepest
agonies of distress, and every few minutes rising in shouts of
triumph. Toward the evening I pitched the only tent on the
ground. Having been accustomed to traveling the wilderness,
I soon had a tent constructed out of poles and pawpaw bushes.
Here I remained Sunday night, and Monday and Monday night;
and during that time there was not a single moment's cessation, but the work went on, and old and young, men, women,
and children, were converted to God. It was estimated that on
Sunday and Sunday night there were twenty thousand people
on the ground. They had come far and near from all parts of
Kentucky; some from Tennessee, and from north of the Ohio
river; so that tidings of Cane Ridge meeting was carried to
almost every corner of the country, and the holy fire spread in
all directions.

Immediately after this meeting the last round of Quarterly
meetings commenced for that conference year, and they were
appointed for four days, to commence on Friday. The work
continued, and quarterly meetings were attended by thousands,
and generally continued night and day with but little intermission; and during the week, at appointments in different parts
of the country, we had to preach in groves to thousands of
people.

The number of souls converted at this great meeting was estimated at not fewer than five hundred,—
possibly many more—while many others who were
brought under deep conviction there, were converted

while on the way, or after reaching their homes. Rev. James B. Finley, D. D., was converted at Mays Lick, while returning to his home in Ohio. Thus the revival spread until its gracious influence reached almost every part of the United States. A mighty work was in progress on the eastern shore as well as in the West.

As Dr. Finley became one of the leading figures of American Methodism, and as he was one of those who were brought under the weird spell of the Cane Ridge revival, we think the reader will appreciate his account of the scenes as he saw them, and the feelings of one who was exercised under the strange influence that pervaded that great assembly. He says:

We arrived on the ground, and here a scene presented itself to my mind not only novel and unaccountable, but awful beyond description. A vast crowd, supposed by some to have amounted to twenty-five thousand, was collected together. The noise was like the roar of Niagara. The vast sea of human beings seemed to be agitated as if by a storm. I counted seven ministers, all preaching at one time, some on stumps, others in wagons, and one—the Rev. William Burke, now of Cincinnati—was standing on a tree which had, in falling, lodged against another. Some of the people were singing, others praying, some crying for mercy in the most piteous accents, while others were shouting most vociferously. While witnessing these scenes, a peculiarly strange sensation, such as I had never felt before, came over me. My heart beat tumultously, my knees trembled, my lip quivered, and I felt as though I must fall to the ground. A strange supernatural power seemed to pervade the entire mass of mind there collected. I became so weak and powerless that I found it necessary to sit down. Soon after, I left and went into the woods, and there strove to rally and man up my courage. I tried to philosophize in regard to these wonderful exhibitions, resolving them into mere sympathetic excitement—a kind of religious enthusiasm, inspired by songs and eloquent harangues. My pride was wounded, for I had supposed that my mental and phyiscal strength and vigor could most successfully resist these influences.

After some time I returned to the scene of excitement, the waves of which, if possible, had risen still higher. The same awfulness of feeling came over me. I stepped up on to a log, where I could have a better view of the surging sea of humanity. The scene that then presented itself to my mind was indescribable. At one time I saw at least five hundred swept down in a moment, as if a battery of a thousand guns had been opened upon them, and then immediately followed shrieks and shouts that rent the very heavens. My hair rose up on my head, my whole frame trembled, the blood ran cold in my veins, and I fled for the woods a second time, and wished that I had staid at home. While remaining here my feelings became intense and insupportable. A sense of suffocation and blindness seemed to come over me, and I thought I was going to die. There being a tavern about half a mile off, I concluded to go and get some brandy, and see if it would not strengthen my nerves. When I arrived there, I was disgusted with the sight that met my eyes. Here I saw about one hundred men engaged in drunken revelry, playing cards, trading horses, quarreling, and fighting. After some time I got to the bar, and took a dram and left, feeling that I was as near hell as I wished to be, either in this or the world to come. The brandy had no effect in allaying my feelings, but, if any thing, made me worse. Night at length came on, and I was afraid to see any of my companions. I cautiously avoided them, fearing lest they should discover something the matter with me. In this state I wandered about from place to place, in and around the encampment. At times it seemed as if all the sins I had ever committed in my life were vividly brought up in array before my terrified imagination, and under their awful pressure I felt that I must die if I did not get relief. . . . At night I went to a barn in the neighborhood, and creeping under the hay, spent a most dismal night. I resolved, in the morning, to start for home, for I felt that I was a ruined man.

He did leave for home, and got as far as Mays Lick, when his burden grew so heavy that he betook himself to earnest prayer, and was graciously saved. Not a great while afterwards, he entered the ministry, and took his place among the leading men of his day.

For years he was superintendent of our mission to the Indians in Northern Ohio.

The bodily agitations attending this great work were astonishing, though not new. Some of the forms of the exercises may have differed from those at other times and places, but one who is familiar with the history of revivals knows that most of these manifestations have appeared elsewhere and at other times. Under the preaching of John Wesley, men and women often fell as if shot with a gun, or pierced through with an arrow. In the great revival that swept over Virginia in 1787, to mention no other, hundreds of people fell to the ground and lay as if dead, until they revived with praises to God upon their lips. Elder Stone, in whose congregation at Cane Ridge, more of these exercises were seen than in any other place, has left us one of the best descriptions of them that we know, and we shall allow him to tell the reader about them. In his autobiography he says:

The bodily agitations or exercises, attending the excitement in the beginning of this century, were various, and called by various names;—as, the falling exercise,—the jerks,—the dancing exercise,—the barking exercise,—the laughing and singing exercise, etc. The falling exercise was very common among all classes, the saints and sinners of every age and of every grade, from the philosopher to the clown. The subject of this exercise would, generally, with a piercing scream, fall like a log on the floor, earth, or mud, and appear as dead. Of thousands of similar cases I will mention one. At a meeting, two gay young ladies, sisters, were standing together attending to the exercises and preaching at the time. Instantly they both fell, with a shriek of distress, and lay for more than an hour apparently in a lifeless state. Their mother, a pious Baptist, was in great distress, fearing they would not revive. At length they began to exhibit symptoms of life, by crying fervently for mercy, and then relapsed into the same death-like state, with an awful gloom on their countenances. After awhile, the gloom on the face of one was succeeded by a heavenly smile, and she cried out, 'Precious Jesus!' and rose up and spoke of the love of God —the preciousness of Jesus, and of the glory of the gospel, to the surrounding crowd, in language almost superhuman, and pathetically exhorted all to repentance. In a little while after, the other sister was similarly exercised. From that time they became remarkably pious members of the church.

The Jerks cannot be so easily described. Sometimes the subject of the jerks would be affected in some one member of the body, and sometimes the whole system. When the head alone was affected, it would be jerked backward and forward, or from side to side, so quickly that the features of the face could not be distinguished. When the whole system was affected, I had seen the person stand in one place, and jerk backward and forward in quick succession, the head nearly touching the floor behind and before. All classes, saints and sinners, the strong as well as the weak, were thus affected. I have inquired of those thus affected. They could not account for it; but some have told me that those were among the happiest seasons of their lives. I have seen wicked persons thus affected and all the time cursing the jerks, while they were thrown to the earth with violence. Though so awful to behold, I do not remember that any one of the thousands I have seen ever sustained an injury in body. This was as strange as the exercise itself.

The dancing exercise. This generally began with the jerks, and was peculiar to professors of religion. The subject, after jerking awhile, began to dance, and the jerks would cease. Such dancing was indeed heavenly to the spectators; there was nothing in it like levity, nor calculated to excite levity in the beholders. The smile of heaven shone on the countenance of the subject, and assimilated to angels appeared the whole person. Sometimes the motion was quick and sometimes slow. Thus they continued to move forward and backward in the same track or alley till nature seemed exhausted, and they would fall prostrate on the floor or earth, unless caught by those standing by.

While thus exercised, I have heard their solemn praises and prayers ascending to God.

Mr. Stone then goes on to describe the *barking*

exercise, which was nothing more than the involuntary sound made by the vocal organs of one who was affected with the jerks; and the *laughing exercise,* a loud, hearty laughter by persons who were deeply religious, but not mirthful, nor did it provoke mirth in those who heard it; and the *running exercise* which was nothing more than an attempt, on the part of persons feeling something of these bodily agitations, to run away, and thus escape them. Perhaps the most curious and unaccountable of all was the *singing exercise.* Mr. Stone says that "the subject, in a very happy state of mind, would sing most melodiously, not from the mouth or nose, but entirely from the chest, the sound issuing thence. Such music silenced everything, and attracted the attention of all. It was most heavenly. None could ever be tired of hearing it." No one seemed able to account for it.

It is not for the historian to turn scientist or philosopher—his mission is to state facts. In attempting to account for these remarkable phenomena, various theories have been advanced. Some thought them wrought by the Holy Spirit, in attestation of the fact that the work of the revival was of God. Mr. Stone thought that "so low had religion sunk, and such carelessness universally had prevailed, that nothing common could have arrested the attention of the world; therefore these uncommon agitations were sent for this purpose." Others thought they were brought on by the Devil, in order to discredit the work, and to divert the attention from the salvation of souls. Some thought that they were a sort of epidemic hysteria, purely natural in origin and sympathetically communicated from one to another. Elder Purviance in his account says: "I have no doubt many of my readers will pronounce it a delusion. Some of that day called it so; others called it the work of the devil, and some witchcraft." Others argued that it could not be the work of the devil when it lead men to repentance and to a genuine and abiding experience of saving grace. Many persons have made themselves ridiculous by their confident but unsatisfactory "explanations" of these strange agitations.

It is likely, when we consider all that were the subjects of these exercises, that there was an element of truth in all these theories. Certain it was that there was a great and glorious work accomplished in the saving of thousands of souls, in checking the prevalent tide of iniquity, and in turning the hearts of the people back to God. Equally certain is it that Satan used these strange manifestations to discredit the religion of Christ in the minds of many; and in a few years there was a reaction that greatly impeded the progress of the revival. That there was fanaticism mingled with the good work, all the sane participants in the meetings freely admitted. Persons began to seek after these extraordinary manifestations for their own sakes, mistaking the *signs* for the *thing signified*. They began to think that no one had religion unless exercised by some of these strange bodily agitations. Generally the Methodists, as in the days of Wesley, regarded these bodily exercises as merely incidental accompaniments to religious experiences, and they clearly distinguished between the experience and its incidental accompaniments. They attached but little importance to the exercises. The New Lights attached greater importance to these things than did other workers, and the "jerks," the "dancing" exercises, etc., lingered with them for many years. It cannot be denied that the reaction against the extremes of ignorant and excitable people did much to check the progress of the revival after the first few years.

It is the history of all revivals that they ebb and flow like the tides of the sea. This great tide of revival influence lasted until 1805 or 1806; possibly longer in some places. The results of the tide abide to this day. All the Churches received a large increase of members—the increase in the Methodist Church being a little more tardy in its appearance than others, because of the six months probation required before receiving persons into membership. Communities that were noted for drunkenness, profanity, and evil of every sort, became sober and peaceable and law abiding. Undoubtedly the revival brought in a new era in the history of the Church.

Of course a revival of such intensity could not be expected to continue indefinitely. If only natural causes operated to stay the tide, the weariness of the workers, the necessity of getting back to the ordinary business of life, and the want of unconverted persons to respond to their appeals—all these would naturally bring about a relaxation in the progress of such a work. But in addition to these things, the excesses to which excitable people were given, and the foolish things that characterized the acts and sayings of foolish people, naturally caused a reaction and a hardening against the revival.

CHAPTER XI.

NEW DENOMINATIONS

Out of this great revival at least two new denominations came into being, and another came into Kentucky for the first time. We refer to the Cumberland Presbyterian, the "Christian" ("New Light," or "Stoneite," or "Reform") under the leadership of Barton W. Stone, and the Shakers. Both of the new denominations came out of the Presbyterian Church, and represented a revolt against the High Calvinism of that day.

The doctrines preached in this great revival were distinctively Methodist doctrines, doctrines the Methodists had been preaching from the beginning of their existence. McFerrin, in his History of Methodism in Tennessee, speaking of the great work in the Cumberland country, says:

> The doctrines that were preached in the revival were Methodistic doctrines, distinctively so. Free salvation, full salvation, present salvation, justification by faith, the regeneration of the heart by the Holy Ghost, the knowledge of sins forgiven, or the witness of the Holy Spirit that the believer is born of God, the joy of religion which is the fruit of the Spirit, and that now (to-day) is the day of salvation; these doctrines, for more than ten years had been kept before the people. Ogden and Haw, Poythress and Lee, Massie and McHenry, Brooks and Burke, Wilkerson and Page, McGee and others, all through the settled portions of Tennessee and Southern Kentucky, proclaimed these doctrines by night and by day, and under their ministry already had thousands been converted.

While the two new denominations sprang out of

214

the Presbyterian Church, they originated in two different sections, and, due to differing circumstances, took entirely different directions—that in the Cumberland section resulting in the organization of the Cumberland Presbyterian Church, and that in Central Kentucky, under Stone and others, resulting in establishing the "Christian" Church. Yet both were a revolt from Calvinism, and in the beginning both preached the doctrines so familiar to Methodism. Stone gives these doctrines as follows:

The distinguished doctrine preached by us was, that God loved the world—the whole world, and sent his Son to save them, on condition that they believe in him—that the gospel was the means of salvation—but that this means would never be effectual to this end, until believed and obeyed by us—that God required us to believe in his Son, and had given us sufficient evidence in his Word to produce faith in us, if attended to by us —that sinners were capable of understanding and believing this testimony, and of acting upon it by coming to the Savior and obeying him, and from him obtaining salvation and the Holy Spirit. We urged upon the sinner to believe now, and receive salvation—that in vain they looked for the Spirit to be given them, while they remained in unbelief—they must believe before the Spirit or salvation would be given them—that God was as willing to save them now, as he ever was, or ever would be— that no previous qualification was required, or necessary in order to believe in Jesus, and come to him—that if they were sinners, this was their divine warrant to believe in him, and to come to him for salvation—that Jesus died for all, and all things were now ready. When we began first to preach these things, the people appeared as just awakened from the sleep of ages— they seemed to see for the first time that they were responsible beings, and that a refusal to use the means appointed, was a damning sin.

While a Methodist might not express it in these terms, and while fault might be found with some of the statements, yet one clearly sees that these doctrines were Arminian, and not Calvinistic.

The fellowship between the Methodists and Presbyterians during this great revival was beautiful and very sincere. They planned together, they held meetings together, they preached time about from the same pulpit, they prayed for, and instructed penitents at the same altar, and the tears and shouts of Methodists and Presbyterians were mingled in weeping over lost sinners and in rejoicing over the saved. In the Cumberland country, a *union* was formed, in which was set forth the terms upon which they labored together in the same cause. Their camp-meetings, their prayer meetings, their testimony meetings, were *union* meetings in that all participated freely, and an observer could not distinguish a Presbyterian from a Methodist. The Presbyterian forgot all about his doctrine of predestination and particular election, and offered salvation freely to all who would come to Christ. The Methodists relaxed their rigid regulations by which they excluded from their conferences and class-meetings all who were not Methodists, and freely invited their brethren of other Churches to join with them in these services. Burke says that

the Presbyterians appeared to have forgotten that they had any Confession of Faith or discipline, and the Methodists had laid aside their Discipline, and seemed to forget that they were bound to observe the rules contained therein, and as established from time to time by the General Conference. . . . The class meetings were free to all; the love feasts open to all; and they were mixed up in such confusion that it was impossible to tell to what Church or denomination they belonged. Jacob Young, who came to the Nashville circuit in the fall of 1806, says: I found the Presbyterian and Methodist churches were closely united. They had taken many of our efficient class-leaders and made them elders in their church, and their elders had been made class-leaders in the Methodist church. I could not tell who were Methodists and who Presbyterians.

In the Conference of 1802, several Presbyterian ministers sat with the Methodists in the Conference room—a new thing in Methodism—and Bishop Asbury, too sick to preach, had Revs. William Hodge and William McGee, Presbyterian ministers, to preach in his stead; and he says they did it "with great fervency and fidelity."

As the work grew, the demand for workers to carry on the work was great. The regularly ordained ministers could not visit all the communities where souls were appealing for the Good News of salvation to be preached unto them, nor could they care for the young converts who needed direction and training. The harvest truly was great, and the laborers few. The local preacher and the class-leader among the Methodists in large measure supplied this need; but among the Presbyterians the lack of workers was keenly felt. Moreover, a number of young men had been converted and felt called of God to preach. While they had not the advantages of a seminary training, some of them had marked ability, were full of zeal, and burning with the message of salvation to their fellows. Under these circumstances, the Cumberland Presbytery relaxed the rule concerning the training of ministers, and licensed several of these young men without the required course in the seminary. Nor did they require subscription to the teachings of the Confession of Faith in the matter of predestination and particular election. James Haw, who had joined O'Kelly in the Republican Methodist Church, applied for a place among the ministers of the Presbyterian Church, and was admitted without being required to subscribe to the Confession of Faith.

It is not surprising that these things scandalized the severely orthodox and regular elements of the Presbyterian Church. Not only did ministers of this kind stand aloof from the work, but they preached against it and set in motion means to correct what they thought a hurtful innovation. The Synod of Kentucky, to which the Cumberland Presbytery belonged, appointed a Commission to investigate matters within the Cumberland Presbytery and to discipline the too liberal ministers in that section. This commission labored faithfully to bring back those who had strayed from the beaten path, but they found the offenders unwilling to retrace their steps or to give over the gracious work in which they were engaged. The result was, that "some were censured, some were suspended, some retraced their steps, while others surrendered their credentials of ordination, and the rest were cut off from the Church." It was some time before the Cumberland Presbyterian Church was organized. This was not done until February, 1810. Peter Cartwright says that "they called a general meeting of all their licentiates. They met our Presiding Elder, J. Page, and a number of Methodist ministers at a quarterly meeting in Logan county, and proposed to join the Methodist Episcopal Church in a body; but our aged ministers declined this offer, and persuaded them to rise up and embody themselves together, and constitute a Church. They reluctantly yielded to this advice, and, in due time and form, constituted what they denominated the 'Cumberland Presbyterian Church.'" Whether this be exactly correct, we do not undertake to say—we only give the statement of Cartwright. If the statement has ever been questioned we are not aware of it.

Jacob Young, who was on the ground and had ample opportunity to know, informs us that

Jealousies began to operate in the Synod of Kentucky. They began to think and say that the Presbyterians were all turning Methodists, and, indeed, it looked a good deal like it. They preached and prayed like Methodists; shouted and sung like Methodists. They had licensed several young men to preach who had not a collegiate education. They had formed circuits like the Methodists; had their saddle-bags and great-coats mailed on behind, sweeping through the country like itinerant evangelists. The Tennessee Presbytery was a part and parcel of the Kentucky Synod, and when the Kentuckians heard these things, they sent a deputation of learned men to make a thorough investigation, authorizing them, if they found that the people had departed from the doctrine and discipline of the Presbyterian Church, and refused to return, to dissolve the Presbytery.

The committee came on and acted according to instructions. They ordered these licensed young men to desist from preaching. They refused. Several of the old theologians, such as Hodges, McGready and others, became alarmed, submitted to the authority of the Church, and returned to their old paths. But the young men, with old Billy McGee at their head, held on their way. Some of them were superior men, such as James Porter, and Thomas Cahoun; and they, after having spent two or three years in trying to reconcile the Kentucky Synod, and having found it a forlorn hope, withdrew from the Presbyterian Church, and constituted a Church and congregation of their own, called the Cumberland Presbyterian Church. They soon extended their influence far and wide, and as a body are a successful and holy people.

In doctrine, the Cumberland Presbyterians rejected that part of the Westminster Confession which teaches unconditional election and reprobation, but retained the doctrine of the final perseverance of the saints. In this they are clearly inconsistent. A man, while he is a sinner, is a free moral agent—can accept or reject the Savior, and his salvation or damnation depends upon the exercise of his power of choice; but when he is regenerated, he loses that power of choice and is unable to cast himself away! At all other points they are essentially Methodistic in their teachings, even allowing the candidate for baptism his choice of the mode by which the ordinance is to be administered. In government they are Presbyterial. The Church flourished for many years, gathered a large number of members, had many Sunday Schools, built colleges, and did a great work in the field of spiritual life and enterprise. But in 1906, the greater part of the Church effected a union with the Northern Presbyterian Church, which had so revised its Confession of Faith as to rid it of the most objectionable features of Calvinism. A small part of the Church, however, refused to go into the union, and still maintains a separate existence, though they are not very prosperous.

The disaffection in Central and Northern Kentucky and Southern Ohio, was largely under the leadership of Barton W. Stone. Born in Maryland, December 24, 1772, he was the son of John and Mary Warren Stone. His father dying when he was quite small, his mother moved to Pittsylvania county, Virginia, where Stone spent his boyhood amid rather primitive conditions in a backward community. He was educated chiefly at a Presbyterian academy in Guilford, N. C., was happily converted when in his nineteenth year, and felt his call to the ministry. His mother was a Methodist, and he was greatly impressed by the Methodist ministers. He, however, finally took orders in the Presbyterian Church. Having made considerable attainments in the languages, he was, for two years, professor of languages in the Methodist academy established by Hope Hull, at Washington, Georgia. Resigning this position, and receiving license to preach from the Presbytery, he was engaged for some time as an evangelist in North Carolina and Tennessee, and near the close of the year 1796, came to Kentucky and became pastor of the Presbyterian churches at Cane Ridge, Bourbon county, and Concord, in what is now Nicholas county. When the time for his ordination came, he was much troubled over the doctrine of the Trinity, as taught in the Confession of Faith, and over election, reprobation, and predestination as taught therein. Unable to accept such doctrines, he frankly told some of his brethren of his scruples, and they could not convince him that these doctrines were true. He says: "I went into Presbytery, and when the question was proposed, 'Do you receive and adopt the Confession of Faith as containing the system of doctrine taught in the Bible?' I answered aloud, so that all the congregation might hear, 'I do, as far as I see it consistent with the word of God.' No objection being made, I was ordained."

We have already quoted from Stone his account of his visit to Cumberland, his contact with the great work that was in progress there, and the great revivals that occurred at Concord and Cane Ridge under his ministry. In this mighty work, Stone was an incessant laborer, "preaching, singing, visiting and praying with the distressed." His lungs failed and became inflamed, and he was so troubled with violent cough and spitting of blood that he almost despaired of life. At a camp-meeting near Paris, for the first time the opposition from the regular and orthodox Presbyterian preachers became open and decided. They "labored hard to Calvinize the people, and to regulate them according to their standards of propriety." These held tenaciously to the teachings of the Confession of Faith, and vigorously inveighed against the doctrines that had been preached in the great revival. Stone says:

There were at this time five preachers in the Presbyterian connection, who were in the same strain of preaching, and whose doctrine was different from that taught in the Confession of Faith of that body. Their names were, Richard McNemar, John Thompson, John Dunlavy, Robert Marshall, and myself; the three former lived in Ohio, the two latter in Kentucky. David Purviance was then a candidate for the ministry, and was of the same faith.

In order to stamp out the "heresy" and to restore the "order" of the Church, the Presbytery of Springfield, Ohio, brought charges against McNemar, and his case was handed on to the Synod of Kentucky, of which the Presbytery of Springfield was then a part. A majority of the Synod were hostile to the teaching of these evangelical brethren, and they clearly saw what their fate would be; so they withdrew from the jurisdiction of the Synod, and organized themselves into what they called "the Springfield Presbytery." At the end of a year, they were dissatisfied with this arrangement, and drew up and published that peculiar document, "The Last Will and Testament of the Springfield Presbytery." While they were banded together as a Presbytery, they "went forward preaching and constituting churches." But at the end of the year they disbanded the Presbytery, and soon after took to themselves the name "The Christian Church," discarded all creeds and Confessions of Faith, and professed to take the Bible as their sole guide in all matters of faith and practice.

The withdrawal of these brethren from the Synod did not prevent that body from issuing against them a sentence of suspension, and committees were immediately sent to their congregations, declaring their pulpits vacant. Great confusion resulted. These men had their following. Many in their churches had been converted and built up under their ministry, and when they withdrew from the Synod, these members—often whole churches—went with them. Under the conditions existing at the time, the principles adopted by these brethren made a very strong appeal to the people. Denominational prejudices had been extreme and bitter, and the people were heartily sick if these bickerings. During the great revival, the various denominations had laid aside their differences, and labored together in greatest harmony for the salvation of souls. Many of the young converts could not tell under whose ministry they had been lead to Christ, whether it was a Methodist or Baptist or Presbyterian—what difference did it make? "Why could not all take the Bible as their guide and come together in one Church, and work together as one people in the common cause of winning souls to Christ? And what name so appropriate for the united followers of Christ as the name *Christian?*"

Persons who reasoned in this way did not stop to think that, while all accepted the Bible as their only rule of faith and practice, there would be, of necessity, various *interpretations* of this Bible; that all our teachings must be based upon our *interpretations*, and that these interpretations might be so diverse that it might be infinitely better for those of like minds to gather themselves together in groups, under appropriate names, or denominations. So these neophytes, with much enthusiasm undertook to fuse all Christians into one body. But of course the well-meant movement resulted only in creating another denomination. Small minds can never understand how others can fail to see just as they see, or how the views of others can be just as sacred to them as their own views are to themselves.

As stated in a previous chapter, the followers of

O'Kelly, at the insistence of Rice Haggard, changed their name from Republican Methodists to "Christians." Rice Haggard and his brother David, came to Kentucky and cast their lot with Stone. It was Rice Haggard who influenced Stone and his followers to adopt this name. Stone says: "Under the name of Springfield Presbytery we went forward preaching, and constituting churches; but we had not worn our name more than one year before we saw it savored of a party spirit. With the man-made creeds we threw it overboard, and took the name *Christian*—the name given to the disciples by divine appointment (sic) first at Antioch. We published a pamphlet on this name, written by elder Rice Haggard, who had lately united with us."

There is always danger when one breaks away from previous standards of thinking. The pendulum, loosed from one extreme, is apt to swing to the other. The attention of Stone and some of his followers (not all) was called to the subject of baptism. They soon showed their complete rupture with the Presbyterian faith by repudiating infant baptism and adopting exclusive immersion as the mode. In this they departed from their own principle of taking the Bible as the only guide, by demanding that all others accept their interpretation of the Bible on this point! No one among them having been immersed, they, like the Baptists before them, immersed one another, and thus joined the ranks of exclusive immersionists.*

---

*Stone says: There were no elders among us who had been immersed. . . . The preachers baptized one another.—Page 61

Drawing largely from all churches the followers of Stone increased rapidly, and became popularly known as "New Lights," "Reformers," "Stoneites," etc. They established many organizations throughout Central and Northern Kentucky and Southern Ohio. Stone was considered unorthodox on the doctrine of the Trinity and several other points, while among his followers there was great variety of beliefs. We shall have occasion to refer to them at a later period in our history, and so dismiss them for the present.

Mention has been made in a former chapter of the extravagances and fanaticism that attended the great revival. It was not unnatural that such should be the case. Many persons who were totally ignorant of the teachings of the Scriptures were brought under the power of God. That they had experienced a change of heart and purpose was unquestioned. But being ignorant of the teachings of the Scriptures, yet filled with a mighty enthusiasm, they readily responded to all sorts of errors, and ran into all sorts of excesses. There are always persons ready to take advantage of such conditions in order to propagate strange and unwarranted notions. The bodily agitations were so many and so much a part of the great work, that excitable persons ran into ridiculous extremes with regard to them. They confounded these merely incidental attendants with religion itself, and thought that the agitations were the measure of one's religious experience. It has been commented upon by many writers that the Methodists were less affected by these things than were others. They were accustomed to shouting, and for persons to fall to the ground under the strong presentation of the truth, was not a new thing with them.

While there were some new forms of the phyiscal exercises, and while they were on a larger scale than had ever been known before, the Methodist leaders were men of poise and discretion, and they held steadily to the essentials, making but little of the merely incidental.

But taking advantage of the excited state of the people in general, three Shaker missionaries from New York—Bates, Meachum, and Young—made their appearance in Kentucky, began to preach their mysteries, and to urge the excited people on to greater excitement still. Ann Lee, the founder of this peculiar sect, taught that Christ had come to the world once, in the form of a man, and that he would return again in the form of a woman; that he had so appeared to her, and had so identified himself with her, that she was the embodiment of the Christ; that she and her followers received revelations from him, which superceded the revelations of the Holy Scriptures; that they had the gift of tongues, and could work miracles; that they were commissioned to establish the heavenly state here on earth, and that Christ was about to appear in his own persons to rule the saints and dispose of his enemies. Stone tells us that the missionaries who appeared in Kentucky and Ohio were eminently qualified for their mission. "Their appearance was prepossessing—their dress was plain and neat—they were grave and unassuming at first in their manners—very intelligent and ready in the Scriptures, and of great boldness in their faith." They began by approving the work that had been done in the revival; said it was all right as far as it had gone, but that it had not gone far enough; that they had been sent to teach the way of the Lord more perfectly, and held out the promise of perfect holiness to all who would accept of their way. They denounced matrimony as a sin, and urged husbands to abandon their wives, and wives to forsake their husbands. They established a communal colony at Mount Pleasant, or "Shakertown," in Mercer county, and a similar colony in Logan. Also a colony in Ohio and one in Indiana. These colonies flourished for a while. They bought large tracts of land around their villages, erected handsome and substantial buildings, established quite a number of industries, held all property in common, were industrious, economical, peaceable, and, in their way, very religious. In their worship they were highly emotional, made much of bodily agitations, shouting, clapping of hands, dancing, trembling, etc. Undoubtedy there were some most excellent people among them, and they were uniformly quiet, charitable, kindly, and strictly moral. The name "Shakers" was given them on account of their bodily exercises during their worship, but their real designation was "The United Society of Believers in Christ's Second Appearing." They are now almost extinct. Both their colonies in Kentucky long since passed out of existence and their property is now in the hands of others.

Strange as it may seem, the Shakers made great inroads upon the members of the "Christian" Church. Three of the preachers associated with Stone, and who came out of the Presbyterian Church with him, joined the Shakers. Matthew Houston, Richard McNemar, and John Dunlavy, forsook the married state, and for a time were quite prominent as preachers in the new sect. Only Houston continued with the Shakers through life. Stone says that John Dunlavy died in Indiana, "raving in desperation for his folly in forsaking the truth for an old woman's fables. Richard McNemar was, before his death, excluded by the Shakers from their society, in a miserable, penniless condition, as I was informed by good authority. The reason for his exclusion I never heard particularly; but from what was heard, it appears that he was convinced of his error. The Shakers had a revelation given them to remove him from their village, and take him to Lebanon, in Ohio, and to set him down in the streets, and leave him there in his old age, without friends or money. Soon after he died." Two others of Stone's associates, Robert Marshall and John Thompson, returned to the Presbyterian Church, and became quite active in opposing the movement lead by Stone.

These extravagances and these unlooked-for new movements must not be allowed to discredit the great revival at the beginning of the nineteenth century. That a very great work was done cannot be doubted The changed lives of many thousands, the establishing of new congregations, the quickening of the Churches into new life and zeal, the lifting of the moral tone of society, the lessening of crime and immorality in general —all these things bear testimony to the fact that the work was of God, and that a mighty good was done by these wonderful meetings. We doubt if history furnishes an instance of any great religious reform that has not been attended by emotional execesses of some kind. Satan, with his "lying wonders," is always ready to deceive and mislead the unwary, and to stir up opposers of the work of God. His Sanballats and his Tobiahs are ever at hand.

CHAPTER XII.

When the General Conference met in Baltimore, on May 6, 1800, it was evident that the Episcopacy must be strengthened by the election of another Bishop. During the quadrennium, Bishop Coke had spent most of his time in Europe, leaving to Asbury the administration of the affairs of the Church in America. Asbury's health was very poor. He was a great sufferer. He could, at this time, travel only in a carriage, and then must have with him a traveling companion, to assist him in and out of the carriage, and to care for him almost as an infant. His life was very uncertain. On the 12th of May, Richard Whatcoat was elected a Bishop of the Methodist Episcopal Church, and given equal authority with Bishop Asbury. Whatcoat had been ordained both deacon and elder by Wesley and sent over with Coke in 1784. He was born in the parish of Quinton, Glousershire, England, February 23, 1736. "At the age of twenty-one, 'he became a hearer of the Methodists,' and on the 3rd day of September, 1758, he was converted to God, and on the 28th of March, 1761, he professed sanctification." He was admitted into the British Conference in 1769, served important charges in England and Ireland until 1784, when he volunteered to come to America. He was present at the Christmas Conference at which the Methodist Episcopal Church in America was organized, and, with the exception of about four years, was

229

a Presiding Elder until his election to the office of
Bishop. He was a most godly man, abundant in labors, and uniformly successful as a winner of souls.
He accompanied Bishop Asbury to Kentucky in 1790,
when the first Conference was held at Masterson's Station, and was here twice after his election to the Episcopacy. He came to the Conference of October, 1800,
and again to the Conference held at Anthony Houston's,
in Scott county, in 1805.

Bishop Asbury esteemed Whatcoat very highly. He
speaks of him as "a man of solid parts, a self-sacrific-
ing man of God. Whoever heard him speak an idle
word? When was guile found in his mouth?" He was
thirty-eight years in the ministry—sixteen in England, Wales, and Ireland, and twenty-two years in
America; twelve years as Presiding Elder, four years
in cities, or traveling with Bishop Asbury, and six
years in the Superintendency. Asbury adds: "A man
so uniformly good I have not known in Europe or
America." Bishop Whatcoat died at Dover, in the
State of Delaware, on the 5th of July, 1806. His remains were buried under the altar of the Wesley
church, at Dover. He had been much afflicted during
the later years of his life, and suffered great pain before passing away.

The General Conference of 1800 was remarkable
for the great spiritual interest that attended it. The
preachers were burning with revival fire, preached
with great power, and more than a hundred souls were
converted during the session. The preachers attending
the General Conference had their hearts rekindled by
the glow of this gracious work, and went back to their
homes to spread the flames in every part of the Church.

While the General Conference of 1796 had created the "Western Conference, for the States of Kentucky and Tennessee," the Conference in the West was not known by that name until 1802. This Western Conference had, up to 1800, been meeting in the spring; but now it was changed to the fall; and, as before stated, two Conferences were held for this section this year. At the spring Conference, Asbury planned to bring a new set of preachers to this Western field, and made only a list of temporary appointments. But failing to get the new workers, the temporary appointments were continued until the fall session at Bethel Academy, October 6, 1800. Both Asbury and Whatcoat were there. They brought with them from a District in Virginia the greatest man ever brought into this western field—William McKendree—and placed him as Presiding Elder over the whole Western Conference, embracing Kentucky, Eastern and Middle Tennessee, a part of Southwestern Virginia, and Ohio.

Never was a more felicitous appointment made than was the selection of this devoted servant of Jesus to the Western work. His deep piety and fervent zeal; his intimate knowledge of the doctrines and discipline of the Church; his remarkable capacity to govern, and to infuse into the preachers his own spirit; his almost morbid love of order, and his methodical manner of conducting business; his wonderful astuteness and quickness of apprehension, combined with a grave and yet most prepossessing personal appearance; and his wonderful power of illustrating whatever he sought to teach—all concurred to mark him as preeminently the man for the people and the country. God seems to have raised him up for this position; and while thousands have already blessed God for it, future generations of Methodists in the West and South will look back with gratitude to his influence in building up and extending the work of God in this wide field of his operations. How much Methodism owes to him for its success in this region, can never be known until the light of eternity shall reveal it.

William McKendree was a Virginian, born in King William county, July 6, 1757. His family were "a plain, industrious, and moral family, without pretensions to fame or extraordinary talents; yet, even in the 'Old Dominion,' holding a reputable position for intelligence, integrity, and honorable estimation." His father removed from King William county, and finally settled in Greenville county, on the southern border of the State, where William McKendree came to manhood. He was a soldier in the Revolutionary war, and was at the battle of Yorktown. He was a moral youth, and had many struggles with his conscience, which told him he was not right with God. He was converted during the great revival in Virginia in 1787, under the ministry of John Easter. He says:

Not long after I had confidence in my acceptance with God, Mr. Gibson preached us a sermon on sanctification, and I felt its weight. When Mr. Easter came, he enforced the same doctrine. This led me more minutely to examine the emotions of my heart. I found remaining corruption—embraced the doctrine of sanctification, and diligently sought the blessing it holds forth. The more I sought the blessing of sanctification, the more I felt the need of it—and the more important did the blessing appear. In its pursuit, my soul grew in grace and in the faith that overcomes the world. But there was an aching void which made me cry. 'Tis worse than death my God to love, And not my God alone.' One morning I walked into the field, and while I was musing, such an overwhelming power of the Divine Being overshadowed me, as I never experienced before. Unable to stand, I sank to the ground, more than filled with transport. My cup ran over, and I shouted aloud.

He was received on trial in the Conference in 1788, and for twelve years filled important stations and districts in Virginia. By hard study and systematic reading he became a good scholar and a great preacher. For a short time, he was lead astray by O'Kelly, but such a man could not be held in such a movement after he learned the facts. He was too just to condemn without good cause, and his mind was too judicial to be controlled by impulse or prejudice. He was soon reconciled to Bishop Asbury, and became the strongest exponent of the very system against which O'Kelly had inveighed. He did more to clarify Methodist law and to establish Methodist government than any other man. He was to his Church what John Marshall was to the American Government.

When placed in charge of the great field here in the West, he took up his work with great vigor and efficiency. Jacob Young, than whom there are few more capable of estimating such things, says of him:

McKendree had been but a few months on the ground till he understood perfectly his field of labor—moving, day and night, visiting families, organizing societies, and holding quarterly conferences. It was his constant practice to travel from thirty to fifty miles in a day, and preach at night. All classes of people flocked to hear him—statesmen, lawyers, doctors, and theologians of all denominations clustered around him, saying, as they returned home, 'Did you ever hear the like before?' Some indeed, were so captivated, that they would say, 'Never man spake like this man.' He saw that the harvest was truly great and the laborers few. Early in the morning and late in the evening, with streaming eyes he prayed to God, with hands and heart uplifted, that he would send forth more laborers into the harvest. He was actively engaged in forming new circuits, and calling out local preachers to fill them. Whenever he found a young man of piety and native talent, he led him out into the Lord's vineyard; and, large as his district was, it soon became too small for him. He extended his labors to every part of south-western Virginia, then crossing the Ohio river, he carried the holy war into the State of Ohio; and there he formed new charges and called out young men.

Nor did he stop here. It was not long until he was visiting Indiana, Illinois, and Missouri, as well as covering the States of Kentucky and Tennessee. It was a great day for Methodism in the West when McKendree was made Presiding Elder over this great field.

This second Conference in 1800 lasted but two days. Whatcoat and McKendree did the preaching, though on the last day, Asbury, feeble as he was, gave "a long, temperate talk," on the text, "Now the just shall live by faith; but if any man draw back, my soul shall have pleasure in him. But we are not of them who draw back unto perdition; but of them that believe to the saving of the soul." William Burke was elected secretary—"the first secretary of an Annual Conference in America." William Marsh and Benjamin Young were admitted on trial. Lewis Hunt, Thomas Allin, and Jeremiah Lawson were readmitted; though Allin, after being ordained a deacon, was located again at this session. Besides the two Bishops and McKendree, the only members of the Conference present were Burke, Sale, Harriman, and Lakin. Several local preachers were elected to deacons orders; the deficiencies in the salaries of the preachers were noted, and the time and place for the next session were fixed. This, with the list of appointments, is about all that the Minutes of the session contain.*

---

*Separate Minutes for the Western Conference were kept from 1800 on, and Dr. W. W. Sweet, in his book, "The Rise of Methodism in the West," has published these Minutes exactly as they appear in the manuscript journal. He has thus rendered a great service to the Church, and from now on we will be able to draw more help from these Minutes. We gladly acknowledge our indebtedness to Dr. Sweet.

The appointments are as follows:

Kentucky District, William McKendree, Presiding Elder.
Scioto and Miami—Henry Smith.
Limestone—Benjamin Lakin.
Hinkstone and Lexington—William Burke, Thomas Wilkerson, Lewis Hunt.
Danville—Hezekiah Harriman.
Salt River and Shelby—John Sale, William Marsh.
Cumberland—John Page, Benjamin Young.
Green—Samuel Douthet, Ezekiel Burdine.
Holstein and Russell—James Hunter.
New River—John Watson.

The number of members in all these circuits, as given in the General Minutes, is 3,183 whites, and 243 colored. It will be noticed that the Conference embraces not only all of Kentucky and Tennessee, but includes three circuits which lay partly in Virginia, and one in Ohio.

Of the men who labored in Kentucky this year, we have already made mention of all except Lewis Hunt and William Marsh. Lewis Hunt was born in Virginia, but his parents had removed to Kentucky and settled in Fleming county. "He was a tall, slender young man, with a depressed cheek. He possessed great zeal, and exerted himself beyond his natural strength. He was a very humble, sociable man, whose labors in the ministry were greatly blessed." He was a young man of great promise, but a feeble constitution could not stand the strain of itinerant work. Admitted in 1798, his health permitted him to serve only irregularly. He was, for a time, on the New River circuit, in Virginia, but health failing, he returned to his home. He was then for a time on the Miami circuit, in Ohio, but here, too, he found himself unable to continue long in the work. He spent a few months on the Salt River circuit, then was for a time with Burke and Wilkerson at Lexington, where his labors were confined almost wholly to the town. He was compelled to give up before the Conference year closed.*

He went to his father's in Fleming county, where he soon sank, a victim of tuberculosis. Thus passed a most lovable and popular young man.

The name of William Marsh appears this year as the colleague of John Sale on the Salt River and Shelby circuit, and in 1801, he was on the Danville circuit. His name then disappears, and we know nothing more about him.

1801. The year between the Conferences of 1800 and 1801, was notable for the very unusual spiritual interest that prevailed throughout Kentucky. The Great Revival was at its height. When the Conference of 1801 met at Ebenezer, in East Tennessee, on October 1st, it was but a few weeks after the meeting at Cane Ridge, and Methodist preachers throughout the State were in the midst of the mighty work of which this meeting was only a part. They could not leave their charges to go to the Conference. Only McKendree and Thomas Wilkerson were there from Kentucky. Asbury says: "Our brethren in Kentucky did not attend: they pleaded the greatness of the work of God." While Burke was not present, his name is attached to the Minutes of the Conference *as Secretary*. We suppose he was again elected to this place, but some one acted in his stead.

---

*Burke says that Wilkerson did not come on from Baltimore until the spring of 1801. So while Hunt was preaching in Lexington, Burke was taking care of the country appointments of the combined Hinkstone and Lexington circuits.

But one person was this year admitted on trial—
John Adam Grenade. When his name was presented,
the following very frank statement is made in the
Minutes: "It is the Judgment of the Conference, that
he has a certain hardness and stubbornness in his temper, which has produced, some improper Conclusions;
but as he has given some hopeful assurance, that in
future, he will be more teachable, and as his piety, and
zeal, is not doubted, the Conference, is of opinion that
he be admitted, after receiving a Special Council from
the Bishop." We are not responsible for either the
spelling or punctuation in this statement, but it gives
us an example of the straight-forward and candid way
in which these fathers dealt with the applicants for
admission on trial. Grenade was an eccentric but an
able man. Inasmuch as he was not assigned to labor in
Kentucky this year, we will wait until he makes his
appearance in this field before giving a sketch of his
life.

Poor Francis Poythress is mentioned in a tender
minute which shows the affection in which he was held
by his brethren.

The minute, which has already been quoted, reads:
"Whereas, Francis Poythress appears to be incapable
of taking a station, it is agreed to by the Conference
that his name shall stand on the Minutes among the
elders; and that he shall have a proportionate claim on
the Conference for his support." His mind unbalanced, tortured by hallucinations the most distressing,
the poor old man who had served the Church in Kentucky so long and so well, was in retirement at his
sister's, in Jessamine county, but his brethren esteemed
him and were anxious that he should not suffer want.

The Conference this year was divided into two Districts, the Kentucky and the Holston. McKendree is again Presiding Elder of the Kentucky District, and John Watson of the Holston. It seems that no statistics reached this Conference, and the same number of members is given as last year. It will be noticed, that Natchez, in the Mississippi Territory is added to the Western Conference, and Tobias Gibson is again assigned to that mission. We shall not atempt to follow the appointments in the Holston District, as that lies outside the scope of our History. The appointments to the Kentucky District are as follows:

William McKendree, Presiding Elder.
Natchez—Tobias Gibson.
Scioto and Miami—Benjamin Young, Elisha W. Bowman.
Limestone—Henry Smith, Lewis Hunt.
Hinkstone—Benjamin Lakin.
Lexington—William Burke, Lewis Garrett.
Danville—John Sale, William Marsh.
Salt River—Hezekiah Harriman.
Shelby—Gabriel Woodfield.
Cumberland—John Page, Thomas Wilkerson.

Of the men who were assigned for the first time to work in the Kentucky District, we have Benjamin Young and Elisha W. Bowman. Benjamin Young had been admitted in 1800, and served the Cumberland circuit. This year he is sent to Scioto and Miami circuit, in Ohio. At the next Conference he was ordained both deacon and elder, in view of his being sent as a missionary to Illinois. During the year in Illinois, he was charged with some indiscretions, and though, according to the statement of his brother, Jacob Young, his repentance was deep and bitter, he was expelled from the Conference. Afterwards, McKendree found him in Illinois in a back-slidden state, and under Mc-

Kendree's ministry, he was reclaimed and his parchments restored. Asbury thought his expulsion was unjust, but the brethren in those days were very rigid in their discipline. We do not know what the charge against him was, nor do we have any information as to his end.

Elisha Bowman's entrance into the Conference is not noted in the Minutes, but inasmuch as his name appears in the list of appointments, we presume he entered this year. He was sent with Benjamin Young to the Scioto and Miami circuit. In 1802, this circuit was divided and Bowman was continued on the Miami, or Western end of it. He then spent two years on the New River and French Broad circuits, in the Holston country, and in 1805, volunteered to go to New Orleans as a missionary. It will be remembered that only two years before Louisiana had passed into the hands of the United States, and Methodism was eager to establish itself in that part of our possessions. Bowman made the dangerous trip on horseback, through "the wilderness," first to the Mississippi Territory, then on to New Orleans, and was the first Protestant minister to preach the gospel in that city. He found but few Americans in the city, and he says that a majority of those he found "may truly be called the beasts of men." What few respectable families he found were Episcopalians, and they were about as much opposed to the coming of Methodism as were the more numerous Catholics. He tried hard to get a foothold in New Orleans, but his funds were so meager it was impossible to pay the rent of a house in which to preach, or to stay until a way opened. So, late in December, he "shook off the dirt from his feet against this ungodly city of Orleans." He then made a trip over rivers and bayous and lakes and through swamps to the Opelousas country, far to the northwest of New Orleans. He found the people mostly French, and a few Americans as ignorant of the nature of salvation as the untaught Indians. He returned to Kentucky in the fall of 1807, with his once robust constitution completely shattered by the hardships through which he had passed during his two years in Louisiana. He was granted a superannuate relation, and though he tried to take up his work as a traveling preacher again, his health was too greatly impaired, and he was compelled to locate. He studied medicine, and practiced for several years in Clay county, then removed to Estill, where he spent the remaining years of his life. As a local preacher, he preached as often as he was able and was eminently useful in this sphere. His house was a preaching place when there was no church building in the neighborhood. He attained eminence as a physician, and was a very able preacher. He was born in Virginia, but his parents came to Madison county, Kentucky, when he was only a child. He was converted early in life, and was licensed to preach at the age of sixteen. He died at his home in Estill county, October 3, 1845.

In speaking of the meeting houses erected in Kentucky prior to 1800, we mentioned, in a previous chapter, Garrett's Meeting-House, in Garrard county, and there gave a brief notice of Lewis Garrett. Though admitted into the Conference in 1794, his field of labor had been in East Tennessee, Virginia, and North Carolina until this year, 1801, when he returns to Kentucky and is assigned to Lexington circuit as the colleague of William Burke. Born in Pennsylvania. his parents removed while he was yet a child, first to Virginia, then started to Kentucky. His father died before reaching this State. His mother, with eight children, came on and settled in Garrard county, in what is known as the Forks of Dix River. Here, under the most trying circumstances of poverty and danger, Lewis Garrett spent his boyhood. Converted while yet in his youth, he entered the ministry and was admitted on trial in 1794. After this year on the Lexington circuit, he served Danville one year, sharing, during this time, in the revival then in progress, and in 1803, was made Presiding Elder of the Cumberland District. His health was already impaired, and the hardships incident to traveling a District that reached from Natchez to Illinois, was too great even for his rugged constitution; so in 1805 he asked for and received a location. He was readmitted several years later, was Presiding Elder of the Nashville District, and became one of the leading ministers of the Tennessee Conference. In connection with John Newland Maffitt, he established *The Western Methodist,* a popular weekly journal, which advocated the claims of the Methodist Episcopal Church. It was the fore-runner of the old *Southwestern Christian Advocate,* then of *The* (Nashville) *Christian Advocate.* He was also Agent for the Book Depository established in Nashville, and this was the fore-runner of the Methodist Publishing House at that place. He wrote for The Western Methodist a series of articles under the title, "Recollections of the West," afterwards published in book form, from which many of the facts concerning early Methodism in the West are drawn. After his location in 1836, he removed to Mississippi, near Vernon, where he died, April 28, 1857.

Mr. Garrett is described as one who in person was, "rather under-size; slender, but well formed. His face was finely chiseled, and his features were indicative of strength and sprightliness of intellect. His eye was a dark brown, and very piercing; his voice was full and mellow, his accent and articulation superior, his manner very deliberate, and his sermons at times overpowering. Indeed, he was an extraordinary man, and accomplished much for the Church."

1802. In the Conference of 1801, when the question, "Where shall the next Conference be held?" was called, the answer was,

The arguments in favor of Cumberland, and which carried the Conference, were advanced by John Page, and are as follows, 1st, The union, and friendly state of affairs, between the Methodists and Presbyterians, 2nd, There never was a Conference held there. Conference was voted to Cumberland, by a majority of two-thirds. It is the opinion of this Conference, that there should be three permanent places for holding Conference, in the Western District, viz., Bethel in Kentucky, Bethel in Cumberland, and Ebenezer on Nolechucky.

The Conference of 1802, met at Bethel Chapel (better known as Strother's Meeting-House), October 1st.* Bishop Asbury was there, "but so afflicted with rheumatic affection that he could not walk; yet he traveled thus far West, attended to the business of the Confer-

---

*Strother's meeting house was in Sumner county, Tenn., about eight miles northwest of Gallatin. The old building was put to various uses, until 1934, when it was removed to Nashville and rebuilt on the grounds of Scarritt Bible and Training School, where it is preserved as "The Cradle of Tennessee Methodism."

ence, and preached while he had to be carried to and from his horse and to the house of business and worship." (Garrett.) Six men were received on trial, viz., Jacob Young, William Crutchfield, Ralph Lotspeich, Jesse Walker, James Gwin, and Levin Edney. Of these, Walker, Gwin and Edney were married, and their services, to begin "after a few weeks," were pledged for this year, and were to be continued, "provided circumstances will permit."

The following were ordained deacons: Jesse Walker, Samuel Mason, Manoah Lasley, Moses Floyd, Elliott Jones, Benjamin Whitson, John Jarratt, and Henry Jones. Elliott Jones was a local preacher in Pulaski county, Kentucky, and Manoah Lasley lived on Green River, in the bounds of the present Louisville Conference.

The Conference again very tenderly considered the case of Francis Poythress, and though the brethren thought it best "for the safety of the connection, that his name shall be left off of the General Minutes," at the same time they expressed a tender concern for his support and welfare, resolved that his name should stand on their Journal, and that he should be entitled to a claim on the Western Conference for his support. The following year, however, it was stated that he was able to support himself, and that he did not expect or wish that the Conference should contribute to his support.

A Committee, consisting of William McKendree, William Burke, Lewis Garrett, and Samuel Douthet, was appointed "to wait on the next Assembly, at Frankfort, in Kentucky, to attend to the business of Bethel Academy, in sd State, and that they are instructed to act upon their own judgment, and do the best they can." Burke informs us that, on his way to his new appointment on Limestone circuit, he performed that duty, which was to "obtain an act of incorporation for Bethel Academy." Just what was done by the Legislature at this time we have not been able to learn. That the institution was established and incorporated in 1798, by an act of the Legislature, we know, for a copy of the Articles of Incorporation is in the author's hands. These Articles may have been amended in 1802, or some other change in the status of the Academy may have required a new charter.

The Conference was growing. Three Districts appear in the appointments this year—Holston, Kentucky, and Cumberland. As no part of the Holston District lapped over into Kentucky, we leave it out of consideration. The greater part of the Cumberland District was in this State, and Ohio was, at this time so closely connected with Kentucky Methodism that we follow the appointments there for a few years longer. The appointments for the Kentucky and Cumberland Districts are as follows:

Kentucky District, William McKendree, Presiding Elder.
Limestone—William Burke.
Miami—Elisha W. Bowman.
Scioto—John Sale, Stephen Timmons.
Hinkstone—Hezekiah Harriman.
Lexington—Samuel Douthet.
Danville—Lewis Garrett, William Crutchfield.
Salt River and Shelby—Benjamin Lakin, Ralph Lotspeitch.

Cumberland District—John Page, Presiding Elder.
Nashville—Thomas Wilkerson, Levin Edney.
Red River—Jesse Walker.
Barren—James Gwinn, Jacob Young.
Natchez—Moses Floyd, Tobias Gibson.

The men who this year made their appearance in the Kentucky field for the first time, were Samuel Douthet, William Crutchfield, and Ralph Lotspeich.

Samuel Douthet and his brother James were both Methodist preachers. They were the sons of John Douthet, of North Carolina. Samuel Douthet was admitted on trial in 1797, and traveled Saluda, Little Pedee, and Anson circuits in South Carolna, the Washington circuit in Georgia, the Green and Holston circuits in East Tennessee. This year he is transferred to Kentucky, and placed in charge of Lexington circuit. He spent but one year in Kentucky, then went back to East Tennessee, and located in 1804. He was said to be "a hortatory and pathetic preacher."

William Crutchfield, was this year the colleague of Lewis Garrett on the Danville charge. An "amiable, eloquent, and gifted" young man, who in 1803, served the Wayne circuit, in what is now the Louisville Conference, and was sent to Nashville in 1804. Here his health failed and he located. We do not know what became of him.

Ralph Lotspeich was of German parentage, but was born in Culpepper county, Virginia, and removed with his father to Tennessee. Here he was licensed to preach, and entered the traveling connection this year. He was appointed to Salt River and Shelby circuit, with that splendid man, Benjamin Lakin. The next year he was sent to the Red River circuit, which lay along the line between Tennessee and Kentucky. In 1804, he was on the Barren circuit, and this ended his labors in Kentucky. For two years thereafter he was in East Tennessee, and six years in Ohio. He continued to preach until within a few weeks of the time of his death. It is said that his intellectual endowments were small, but that by close application and ardent devotion to his calling, he became a very useful minister. Experimental and practical religion was his constant theme, and everywhere he went he was the instrument of saving souls—much better than great talents and a barren ministry. He was said to be a "weeping prophet." On the day of his death he was asked how he was. He replied, "I can only say I am sure of heaven; not a doubt or cloud has appeared since my sickness began." His last words were: "Tell my old friends all is well, all is well."

The name of Stephen Timmons appears in the list as the colleague of John Sale on the Scioto circuit. He was located by the Conference of 1803.

Moses Floyd was this year sent to Mississippi to aid Tobias Gibson in the gracious work that had been begun in that State. Jones, the historian of Mississippi Methodism, says: "Mr. Floyd was a young man of medium size, rather spare, fair complexion, high forehead, mild and benevolent countenance, soft and agreeable manners, rather feeble voice in preaching, but his style of delivery was pleasant, and his sermons were clear, logical, and scriptural. The writer never saw him the least boisterous in the pulpit, though there was often so much earnestness and sympathy in his pulpit labors that the people were constrained to feel that he was deeply interested in their salvation. . . . His habitual pale face and failing strength soon told that the burden was more than he could bear." He married a Miss Griffing, out of one of the most prominent Methodist families in Mississippi, located, studied medicine, practiced this profession, and taught school. He finally died in the State of Louisiana. He was recognized as a good and useful man.

As a result of the great revival, the work in western Kentucky had entered upon a period of almost unparalleled enlargement. The old Cumberland circuit had hitherto embraced all that part of Tennessee around Nashville, about Gallatin and Fountain Head, down the Cumberland to Clarksville, and reached across into Kentucky, including Logan and perhaps some of the adjoining counties. This year the Cumberland circuit disappears from the appointments, and the Nashville and Red River circuits take its place. That section of Kentucky, known as "The Barrens," lying between Green River and the Cumberland settlements, was rapidly filling with settlers, and a new circuit was planned to cover this part of the State.

On the Nashville circuit, that good and great man, Thomas Wilkerson, was appointed preacher in charge, with Levin Edney as his colleague. A sketch of Wilkerson has already been given. Edney was continued on the Nashville circuit in 1803, and his name then disappears from the Minutes. Dr. McFerrin tells us that he "settled some twelve or fifteen miles west of Nashville, on the Harpeth river, where he lived to an advanced age." Eccentric in his manners, but a good and faithful man.

The three names now to be introduced were names of extraordinary men. Jesse Walker was one of the most remarkable men of all Methodism. Little is known of his early life. He first appears upon the scene as a local preacher living in Davidson county, Tennessee. He was admitted on trial this year, and sent to form the new Red River circuit. He is described as a plain, unlettered man, but an intrepid, laborious, persevering, and useful preacher. "He formed the Red River circuit, which embraced what is now Logan county, in Kentucky; Robertson, Montgomery, Dickson, and Stewart, in Tennessee—added many to the Church, and labored with great success." The next year he formed the Livingston circuit, near the mouth of the Cumberland, and his work was blessed with a most gracious revival, out of which came James Axley and Peter Cartwright, two of the noted preachers of early Methodism.

Walker was one of our greatest missionaries. We can do no better than to copy here Dr. Redford's sketch of this wonderful man.

Jesse Walker was admitted this year into the Western Conference, on trial. His first appointment was to the Red River circuit, which had previously been embraced in the Cumberland, and lay partly in Kentucky. In 1803, he was appointed to the Livingston, and in 1804 and 1805, to the Hartford. His labors on the Hartford closed his labors in Kentucky. From this period, as long as he was able to travel and preach, he occupied the most dangerous and difficult posts on the frontier. In 1806, his circuit was the Illinois, embracing all of what is now that flourishing State, where he could find a community that would hear the gospel. In 1807, he was sent to the Missouri circuit, to occupy the country embraced in that vast territory. On the following year he was returned to the Illinois circuit; in 1809 and 1810, to Cape Girardeau; and in 1811, we find him again in Illinois, prosecuting with apostolic zeal his high and holy calling. In 1812, he was placed in charge of the Illinois District—then included in the Tennessee Conference, and embracing the Missouri, Coldwater, Maramack, Cape Girardeau, New Madrid, and Illinois circuits—where he remained four years. In 1816, we find him in the Missouri Conference, in charge of the Missouri District, over which he presided for three years. In 1819 and 1820, his appointments are: Jesse Walker, missionary, investing him with authority to extend his labors to the farthest borders of civilization, and to plant the standard of the cross on its very verge.

In 1821, he is appointed missionary to St. Louis, and in 1822 he was Conference Missionary to the State of Missouri.

In 1823, his appointment reads: 'Jesse Walker, missionary to the Missouri Conference, whose attention is particularly directed to the Indians within the bounds of said Conference;' and in 1824: 'Jesse Walker, missionary to the settlements between the Illinois and the Mississippi Rivers, and to the Indians in the vicinity of Fort Clark.' In 1825, he is in the Illinois Conference, and missionary to the Pottawatomie Indians. In 1826 and 1827, his appointment is to the Pottawatomie Mission; and in 1828, to the Peoria, and in 1829, to the Fox River Mission, and the following year, he is Presiding Elder on Mission District, embracing five separate charges, and also missionary to Deplain. His appointment for 1832 is to the Chicago District, and missionary to Chicago, and the following year to the Chicago Mission. This was his last charge. From the Conference of 1834 until his death, he sustained a superannuate relation. Amongst the preachers of his day, for sacrifice, labor, and suffering Jesse Walker stands without a peer."

It was by such heroic labors and sacrifices that Methodism was planted in this western country. The story of the life of Jesse Walker puts those of us to shame who have undertaken so little for the Savior. At the risk of being thought too lengthy in our sketch of this holy man, we cannot refrain from inserting here the following portrait from the pen of Rev. A. L. P. Green, D. D., of the Tennessee Conference:

The Rev. Jesse Walker was a character perfectly unique; he had no duplicate. He was to the Church what Daniel Boone was to the early settler—always first, always ahead of everybody else, preceding all others long enough to be the pilot of the new-comer. Brother Walker is found first in Davidson county, Tennessee. He lived in about three miles from the then village of Nashville; and was at that time a man of family, poor, and to a considerable extent without education. He was admitted on trial in 1802, and appointed to the Red River circuit. But the Minutes, in his case, are no guide, from the fact that he was sent by the Bishop and Presiding Elders in every direction where new work was to be cut out. His natural vigor was almost superhuman. He did not seem to require food and rest as

other men; no day's journey was long enough to tire him; no
fare too poor for him to live upon; to him, in traveling roads and
paths were useless things—he blazed his own course; no way
was too bad for him to travel—if his horse could not carry him,
he led him, and when his horse could not follow, he would leave
him, and take it on foot; and if night and a cabin did not come
together, he would pass the night alone in the wilderness, which
with him was no uncommon occurrence. Looking up the frontier settler was his chief delight; and he found his way through
hill and brake as by instinct—he was never lost; and, as Bishop
McKendree once said of him, in addressing an Annual Conference, he never complained; and as the Church moved West and
North, it seemed to bear Walker before it. Every time you
would hear from him, he was still further on; and when the
settlements of the white man seemed to take shape and form,
he was next heard of among the Indian tribes of the Northwest.

In 1807, he was sent to Missouri, and at once bent his way to
St. Louis, which was at that time as destitute of true piety as
any point in America. On reaching the town, he passed through
it in various directions in search of a Methodist, but found no
one who could inform him where such a character could be
found. At length he passed out, and was making his way into
the country beyond; but when he had gone quite out of the
town, he drew up his horse, and looked back upon the place for
a few minutes, and at length said, in the name of that Savior
who said to his disciples, 'Go ye into all the world, and preach
the gospel to every creature,' 'I will not give you up; I will
try again.' So he turned about, rode again into the town, and
renewed his inquiry. At length he was told that there was a
man down on Front Street who was a Methodist. Taking the
name and directions, he went in search of his man, whom he soon
found. Calling him brother, telling his own name and business,
he asked such countenance and cooperation as the circumstances
of the case required. The man gave him the wink, and beckoned
him into a back room, several persons being present; and said
to him about as follows: 'Look here: I was a Methodist where
I came from, but it is not generally known here, and I do not
wish it to be. You cannot do anything in this town, and it is
useless to try.' Brother Walker soon after learned that the

man was keeping what would be called in these days a "doggery,' and could not be relied on in Church matters. He went at once to a public house, and put up. He made inquiry where he could rent a room. An old shell of a house was soon found and rented, and in a few days Walker had set up house-keeping on a scale of economy which would astonish the present generation, and took measures to have preaching in his own room; so that his little establishment was kitchen, chamber, diningroom, parlor, and meeting-house; and, gloomy as the prospects were, he soon gathered together a little handful of serious, welldisposed persons, some three or four of whom had been members of the Church before. But not much could be done, for the want of a house of worship. He could not rent a suitable building, and would not have been able to pay for one if it could have been found. At length he was told by an individual that he would give him timber to build him a church, but it was across the Mississippi, on the Illinois shore, growing in the forest. But notwithstanding, light began to break upon the mind of Walker. Next, he had the offer of a lot to build upon. So his plan was at once laid. He hired a man to aid him, took his tools, cheese and crackers, crossed over the river, and went to work, cutting, hewing, and sawing, and in a few months, had his frame and plank all gotten out; his plank was put in a kiln to dry, and by the time he had put up his frame, the plank was sufficiently seasoned to work. The result was, that at the end of the year he reported to Conference a church in St. Louis—house, congregation, and all—the labor of his own hands. Such was Jesse Walker.

After his superannuation, Walker retired to his own little home, in Cook county, Illinois, where he died October 5, 1835.

James Gwin lived in Sumner county, Tennessee, in full view of where the Louisville and Nashville Railroad now runs, and not far from the Kentucky line. He came to Tennessee as early as 1791, and built a cabin in the wilderness, about ten feet square. It was not long until he was visited by Rev. Barnabas McHenry, who was sent to the Cumberland circuit about that time. Gwin was a gallant soldier, and took part in a number of battles with the Indians. He was among the men who took part in the famous Nickajack expedition, which ended the Indian wars in this section, and has left a very interesting account of that expedition. He was known as "Colonel Gwin." He was a brave man, one who never feared danger, or quailed in the presence of a foe. He was a great favorite of Gen. Andrew Jackson, and was his chief chaplain in the New Orleans expedition. He was at the battle of New Orleans, and his tender care of the sick, his attendance upon the disabled, and his bearing and ability as a minister so won the soldiers that it is said he had unbounded influence over these companions in peril and hardship. "He so completely won the Commander-in-chief, that when he came into office as President of the United States, he conferred appointments on his sons, and would have promoted the aged minister himself, only he had a higher office than could be conferred by any earthly power." One of his sons was United States Marshal of Mississippi, and another was in the United States Senate. McFerrin tells us, (History of Methodism in Tennessee), that in person he

was commanding, being more than six feet in height, and in his later years he weighed over two hundred pounds. His features were large and symmetrical, and his voice unsurpassed for strength and sweetness; he was inferior to few in the power of song. Alone, in singing one hymn, he would move a multitude. His early educational opportunties were limited, but he was a great student of nature, and had wonderful fluency of speech. His sermons were not remarkable for order or symmetry, nor did they show much familiarity with the classics or scholarly divinity; but he was well-versed in the Scriptures, and had studied the human heart; hence, his discourses were direct, and oftentimes eloquent and powerful. He was gifted in prayer and exhortation, and won many souls to the cross. Said a young minister, who was his colleague in Nashville, while Mr. Gwin was pastor there, "Brother Gwin, how is it that you are ever prepared to preach? You seem to be seldom in your study, and scarcely ever read." "O my son," replied Mr. Gwin, "You do not understand it; you preachers of your class have to read and study books to master your subjects, but I know what the books are made of before they are printed."

Mr. Gwin gave most of his ministry to Tennessee, as pastor of the Nashville, Red River, and Fountain Head circuits, and of the city of Nashville, and as Presiding Elder of the Cumberland and Caney Fork Districts. He was a delegate to the General Conference of 1828. In 1838, his children having moved South, he was left without an appointment and permitted to spend his time in Mississippi and Louisiana. He was for a short while a member of the Mississippi Conference, stationed at Vicksburg, where he died in 1841. His last words were, "I die in peace. I have unshaken confidence in my Maker, and trust, without doubt, in Jesus Christ."

At the Conference of 1802, Mr. Gwin and Jacob Young were assigned the task of carving out a new circuit in the Barrens of Kentucky, but upon consultation, they agreed that the territory was too large to be included in one circuit, and it was decided that they divide the work, Mr. Gwin taking the west end, and Young the east. At the end of the year he reported the Barren Circuit, with 224 members. In his work this year he was greatly aided by the Rev. Richard Pope, a local preacher who, a short while before, had emigrated from Virginia, and had already organized two or three small societies.

Buck Creek church, in what is now Allen county, was the principal society of the circuit. Redford says that one of the first societies formed by Mr. Gwin, in

Barren county, was in the house of Winn Malone, who, in 1788, had removed from Virginia and settled nine miles north of Glasgow, on the Greensburg road. Mrs. Malone had become a Methodist in Brunswick county, Virginia, and their home in Kentucky was a preaching place for more than thirty years.*

Four sons became Methodist itinerants.

The first, Benjamin, died in great peace, in Indianapolis, Indiana, in 1856. Green Malone, after having filled many important positions in the Church, breathed his last in great triumph, near Eufaula, Alabama, in the autumn of 1860. Isaac Malone resides in Muhlenberg county, Kentucky, where he preaches as his health permits, having been compelled to retire from the itinerant work in consequence of physical disability. Thomas R. Malone, the youngest of the four brothers, resides with his son, Rev. Joseph S. Malone, of the Louisville Conference—at present (1868) the pastor of the Methodist Church in Russellville—and is confined with a rheumatic affection, from which he has suffered through long years, exhibiting that patience which Christianity alone can bestow.—Redford.

Jacob Young, who took the eastern end of the proposed new circuit, was equally successful in establishing preaching places in that part of the State now embraced in Green, Adair, Casey, Pulaski, Wayne, Clinton, and Cumberland counties. He began his work at Manoah Lasley's, on Green river, and found a helpful friend in this excellent local preacher. He was young and inexperienced, and found himself at great loss to know how to form a circuit in that vast wilderness. "I preached on Sabbath day in Father Lasley's house, and set off on Monday, on my great and import-

---

*Preaching was continued in the house of Winn Malone until 1835, when Concord Church was built.—From a letter to Dr. Redford from Rev. Joseph S. Malone, of the Louisville Conference and a grand-son of Winn Malone.

ant enterprise. I concluded to travel five miles, as nearly as I could guess, then stop, reconnoiter the neighborhood, and find some kind person who would let me preach in his log-cabin, and so on until I had performed the entire round." He pursued this plan until he had formed a very large circuit, had many very interesting experiences, held quite a number of successful revivals, called the circuit "Wayne," after General Anthony Wayne, and took into the Church three hundred and one members.

Jacob Young has left an Autobiography which is invaluable to the student of Methodism of that period. From it we learn that he was born on the frontier, in Alleghany county, Pennsylvania; that he came with his father to Kentucky when a young man, and they found a home in Henry county, not far from New Castle. The social life of the community into which they came was rough and very ungodly. It was not long however, until the Methodist preachers, Henry Smith, John Page, and Lewis Hunt, came into the neighborhood and established a preaching place in the home of a good man named Hugh O. Cull. Young was brought under conviction, sought and found the Savior, and entered the ministry. He traveled for a few months under appointment of the Presiding Elder, and was admitted on trial in 1802. The Minutes for 1803, give his appointment as "Wilderness," but he explains that he served the Clinch circuit, in the Holston country, this year. The Wilderness circuit was to have been formed later in the year, but for some reason was never formed. It was expected to center in the vicinity of Barboursville, or Pineville, and extend through part of the mountains of Kentucky. He served in succession the Holston circuit in Tennessee; the Marietta, in Ohio; the

Limestone, in Kentucky; the Nashville, in Middle Tenness; then to the Mississipi District; then back to Ohio, where he spent the remaining years of his life, mainly as Presiding Elder. He was a man of no ordinary ability, and took his place among the leaders of Methodism in the West.

The Church during this year was growing rapidly. Revivals were the order of the day. New territory was being occupied, and the migrations of the people were closely followed. Under the aggressive leadership of McKendree, on the Kentucky District, and of John Page on the Cumberland, there had been a notable increase in membership—Redford says the increase was five hundred and eighty-four, though he is counting but a part of the Western Conference.

1803. The Conference for 1803, was held at Mount Gerazim, Harrison county, Kentucky. This was in the country. Indeed, every Conference in the West was held in the country until 1807, when it met in the village of Chillicothe, Ohio. Towns during this period were small. There was not much upon which to build a town in those days. Stores were few and small, and trade was meager. So far removed from the older settlements, with such limited means of transportation, and with so little money in circulation, neither barter nor sale was possible beyond a very limited extent. The people produced and manufactured in their homes nearly everything they used. They carded and spun their own wool and cotton, wove their own cloth, and made their own clothing. The spinning wheel and the loom were indispensable in the home. The wild life of the forests supplied the meat for their tables, while garden and field yielded the other staple foods. Maple trees and sorghum patches furnished the sweets used

by the family, and one preacher testifies that he did not
smell coffee in ten years! There was but little induce-
ment to live in town, and the wealth of the country was
in the rural sections. It was much easier for a body of
people to find entertainment in the country than in
the towns.

Again, the business of the Conference was small.
There were no Sunday Schools, no Young People's organizations, no general missionary enterprises, no publishing interests to be supervised by the Conferences,
almost no educational institutions, and the whole ma-
chinery of the Church was very simple. Beyond the
examination of the characters of the preachers, admit-
ting candidates for the itinerant service, ordaining
those who were eligible to deacon's or elder's orders,
there was but little to claim the attention of the Conference except to preach the gospel to those who gathered upon such occasions. But the business was en-
larging constantly as the Minutes will show.

Camp-meetings by this time were firmly established
as a means of reaching and saving souls. They were
used by all the denominations. Meeting-houses were
not numerous and were too small to accommodate the
people. A place would be selected near a large spring,
where there was plenty of shade, a stand and rude pulpit would be erected, a brush arbor would be constructed, logs arranged in a semi-circle, or puncheons
served to seat the people. The women were gathered on
one side and the men on the other—they were not allowed to sit together. Camp fires were built around
the place of worship to light the ground at night, with
a few tallow candles or grease lamps about the speakers' stand. The people came on horse-back, in wagons,
or on sleds, though many would walk for miles to at-

tend the camp-meeting. Each family carried provisions sufficient for several days encampment, erected tents, or constructed for themselves rude arbors under which to sleep. Several of these camp meetings would be held in each charge during the summer. The people came by the thousands, and many were led to Christ in the four or five days devoted to the meeting. Bishop Asbury thanked God that, in one year soon after this time, there would be as many as four or five hundred of these camp-meetings held throughout the Church.

Those were the days of orators and of great preaching. Circumstances had much to do in bringing about the wonderful effects produced. Bishop Foster says of these wonderful times:

The country was new. The age was uncritical. The pulpit was the great throne of power. The pen and printed page were less in use. The people were eager to hear. Impassioned speech thrilled and swayed the expectant assemblies who rushed for miles to hear the famous orator. There was eloquence in the air. All the circumstances conspired to kindle enthusiasm. It was inevitable that, standing in the focus of such forces, the speaker should be at his best. The effect was inchoate before he began. Hungry of combustion, the assembly took fire at the first spark. On the eager flame, the orator himself more impassioned, rose and soared to the sublimest heights of inspired eloquence. The effect was often magical. It is impossible for this generation to conceive of it. The waves of feeling that rushed over the assembly were as visible as the effect of the storm on ocean or forest. Hundreds would rise to their feet under unconscious impulse, lean forward, press toward the speaker, weeping, sobbing, or shouting, under the thrilling appeal. Many times numbers fell like the slain in battle. Under Durbin and Bascom I have repeatedly witnessed all these effects myself. It would not accord with the truth to say there are not as great men now living; but the times make it impossible that any should produce such visible signs of emotion as attended these mighty and glorious men.

There was much prayer and testimony and personal work during one of these meetings. People were there for a holy purpose, and devoted themselves unreservedly to the attainment of this purpose. Nearly every great spiritual awakening is attended by a revival of song. It was so in the days of Wesley, and it was so in the days of the Great Revival in the West. What Charles Wesley was to the revival in England, John Adam Grenade and Caleb Jarvis Taylor were, though in less degree, to this greatest of American revivals. All these circumstances, plus the mighty power of God, account for the wonderful work wrought in these early days.

The Conference of 1803 formed another District in the Western Conference, and established several new circuits. The Ohio District was formed, with the Muskingum, Hockhocking and Guyandotte circuits added to the Scioto and Miami, with William Burke as Presiding Elder. In the Kentucky District, the Salt River and Shelby becomes two circuits instead of one. In the Cumberland District, the Wayne, Livingston, and Illinois circuits are added. The first *station* in the Western Conference appears this year—"Lexington-town," with Thomas Wilkerson as pastor. Though the Minutes do not state the fact, it is known that John Page located this year. Adjet McGuire, William Pattison, Anthony Houston, Joseph Oglesby, Abraham Amos, John McClure, Fletcher Sullivan, and John Johnson were admitted on trial. If the Minutes of our present-day Conferences were as frank in giving the facts concerning those admitted on trial as were the Minutes of this Conference, we fear there would be fewer applicants for admission. "Queston 1. Who are admitted on trial? Answer. William Pattison. A man of but little education and small abilities, but is said to be pious, and useful, and came well recommended." "Joseph Oglesby, A man of tolerable gifts." "Abraham Amos, of small gifts, and illiterate; but was useful and much esteemed in his neighborhood." Nor can we commend the liberties taken with the laws of the Church in the matter of receiving candidates. Of Abraham Amos it is said: "He was admitted as a local speaker at the last Quarterly Meeting in Lexington Circuit, but at that time was not proposed to them as having any intention to travel, after which he attended several Quarterly Meetings, with the Elder, and was thought to be useful; the Conference admitted him into the traveling connection upon the judgment of some of the traveling preachers, who think he would have been recommended, if an application had been made." John McClure brought no recommendation from the Quarterly Conference. "It was thought to be the fault of the Presiding Elder, and therefore he was received upon the persuasion, that he could have obtained a recommendation, if application had been made." Beside the young men received on trial, the Minutes mention the fact that Learner Blackman and Louther Taylor had been transferred from the Philadelphia to the Western Conference. Blackman was assigned to the Lexington circuit, and Taylor to the Limestone.

Adjet McGuire had traveled the Limestone circuit during the preceding year under the Presiding Elder, and was this year placed in charge of the Salt River circuit. After serving this and the Danville, Licking, and Mad River, and the Salt River a second time, he located in 1808.

The labors of William Pattison were in the States of Ohio, Mississippi, and Tennessee, until 1811, when he came back to Kentucky and served the Shelby and Lexington circuits, and located in 1813.

Anthony Houston, admitted this year and sent to Barren circuit, was said to have been remarkably useful on this circuit. After a year each on the New River circuit, in Virginia; Holston, in Tennessee; Scioto, in Ohio; Wachita and Claiborne in Mississippi, he returned to Kentucky and served the Limestone and Fleming circuits. He located in 1810, and having studied medicine, he practiced this profession in Flemingsburg for many years. He lost his wife, and all his children but two, in a single week, by cholera. Jonathan Stamper says, "Dr. Houston was a man of more than ordinary preaching talents. He was fond of investigation, and often went into such fine-spun metaphysical disquisitions as to be sometimes suspected of heterodoxy; but he always insisted that he was a Methodist of the Wesleyan School." He was the son of Anthony Houston, of Scott county, Kentucky. He died of apoplexy.

Joseph Oglesby, admitted this year and sent to Miami, in Ohio, was a man who gave many years to the work of the ministry and accomplished great things for the Church. He deserves an extended notice, but as his labors in Kentucky did not begun until 1808, we shall wait until then to give a more adequate sketch of this excellent man.

The work in the Mississippi Territory was not growing in the number of members. The health of Tobias Gibson was rapidly failing, and he was not able to take care of the opportunities that were springing up on every hand. Though quite feeble, Gibson determined to visit the Conference at Mount Gerazim and beg for help. He made the trip on horse-back from Natchez, and though hardly able to stand, made an impassioned plea for assistance. Two men were sent to his help—Hezekiah Harriman and Abraham Amos. We have already given a sketch of Hezekiah Harriman. Amos remained but one year in Mississippi and was then transferred to Ohio, where he labored on the Miami and Mad River circuit, then on the Guyandotte. He was then brought back to Kentucky, where he served Licking in 1806, and Livingston in 1807. In 1808, his charge is "Missouri," and in 1809, "Illinois." No wonder he was broken down and ready for a location at the end of this year!

Fletcher Sullivan remained in the work but two years—on the Shelby circuit in 1803, and on the Nashville in 1804. His name then disappears from the Conference roll.

John McClure, who brought no recommendation from his Quarterly Conference, but was received on trial notwithstanding, was sent to the Limestone circuit. The next year to Wayne, which closed his labors in Kentucky. After two years on the Clinch and Powell's Valley, and one on the Cumberland, he was sent to Mississippi, and was for two years Presiding Elder of the Mississippi District. Another year was given to Flint circuit, in the Nashville District, after which the inevitable location was received.

Three men for the first time enter the western field this year, though they have been in the service of the Church for some time before. Louther Taylor spent this year on the Limestone circuit, the only year he spent in Kentucky. His first year was in Delaware and Maryland; then two years in the Holston District.

After his service on the Limestone charge, he was sent to Ohio for two years, and located at the end of that time. Beyond this brief record from the General Minutes we know but little of the man or his success in the work.

John Adam Grenade, already mentioned in this chapter, was this year assigned to the Hinkstone circuit, and gave but one year to this State. He had been admitted in 1807 and served the Green circuit, in East Tennessee. The following year he was on Holston, and at the end of his year on Hinkstone, his health was gone and he asked for a location.

In many respects, John Adam Grenade was a very remarkable man. Highly emotional, very intense, decidedly poetic in temperament, yet sincere, pious, and exceedingly zealous, he claimed more popular attention than any man of his day. A native of North Carolina, he removed to Tennessee about 1798. He had professed religion before leaving North Carolina, and felt strongly the call to preach; but refusing to obey the call, he lost his experience and lapsed into a most distressing state. He imagined that he had committed the sin against the Holy Spirit, and firmly believed that his destiny was sealed for eternity. In greatest distress of mind, he wandered in the woods and over the mountains, bewailing his lost condition. Because of this extreme agony and his very unusual actions, he was called the "wild man," and people thought he had become deranged. All the time he was pouring forth in verse the laments of his wretched soul. Finally, after more than two years spent in this condition, while attending a meeting held by Rev. William Lambuth (great-grandfather of Bishop W. R. Lambuth) and Rev. John Rankin, a Presbyterian, he was most wonderfully reclaimed. He at once began to exhort the people to repent of their sins, and his exhortations were attended by most marvelous results. Sinners fell on every hand, crying for mercy. Many were converted and brought into the Church.

It was not long until he was licensed to preach. His zeal and passion for souls knew no bounds. He went into bar-rooms and balls—anywhere he could find unsaved men and women, and warned them to flee the wrath to come. He was wonderfully gifted in speech, and his sermons were delivered with telling effect. Revivals sprang up in all his charges, and at his regular services many were brought to Christ. Such strenuous and constant efforts soon wore out the physical frame, and at the end of three years he was compelled to cease work as an itinerant. Having studied medicine under Dr. Hinde, after his location, he returned to Wilson county, Tennessee, where he married, practiced medicine with much success, and preached whenever he was able. During the great revival in the West, he wrote some of the most stirring hymns that were used in those remarkable services. He and Rev. Caleb Jarvis Taylor were the principal song writers of that wonderful religious movement. Each had his gift, and a study of their writings reveals the marked difference in the mental and spiritual conceptions of the two men.

One of the best loved and most useful men ever brought into Kentucky was Learner Blackman, who was stationed this year on the Lexington circuit. He spent but one year in Kentucky before going to Mississippi, but he will return to Kentucky and we shall meet with him frequently during the next few years. We shall defer our account of him until his return to this State.

The quadrennium closing with the Conference year 1803-4, was one of great progress. In 1800, there was but one District, covering all of Kentucky and Tennessee and parts of Virginia and Ohio; at the close of the quadrennium there were four Districts in this territory. In 1800, there were nine circuits; in four years these had increased to twenty-six. In 1800, there was one Presiding Elder and fifteen itinerant preachers; in four years these had grown to four Presiding Elders and thirty-three preachers. The membership had reached 9,082 whites and 513 colored. Besides these things, the spirituality of this whole field was much higher than at the beginning; revivals were sweeping over every State touched by the Conference, and a splendid set of young preachers had been raised up to carry forward the work. Taken all in all, it was a most wonderful quadrennium.

CHAPTER XIII.

FROM 1804 TO 1808

The General Conference which met at Baltimore, May 7, 1804, while making a good many minor changes in the Discipline, enacted but two measures which we think should be noticed here. The first was the Time Limit—a restriction upon the Bishop, forbidding him to appoint a preacher for more than two years successively to the same appointment. Hitherto this matter was entirely in the discretion of the Bishops, though there was but little disposition on their part to keep men in the same charges for an undue length of time; they more frequently changed them at the end of six months. In a few instances in the cities men had remained for three years, and this enactment served to check a tendency that was becoming evident. It is said that the measure pleased Mr. Asbury very much. He is quoted as saying at a later date, "I said nothing in Conference; but Frank told Asbury, that will save you some trouble; besides, it will guard against locality, and the preachers have done it themselves; but let them take care not to throw in too many exceptions." The exceptions they had thrown in were those of Presiding Elders, supernumeraries and superannuates, and the agents of the Book Concern. In those days the preacher was an evangelist rather than a pastor. The local preacher and the class leader did much of the work that is now done by the pastor, such as visiting the sick, conducting funerals, and caring for the spiritual culture of the members.

The other measure was that concerning the troublesome question of slavery. This question was a Banquo's Ghost in every General Conference until 1844. The Church, in the South as well as in the North, always regarded slavery as an evil, and proclaimed its dislike of the evil in no uncertain terms. This General Conference ordered that the first question in the Discipline concerning slavery: "What shall be done for the extirpation of the evil of slavery?" should be answered in a way that placed both ministers and laymen under severe restrictions in the matter of owning, buying or selling slaves. Many persons in the sensitive South, were thereby alienated from the Methodist Church. Later on we shall thoroughly discuss this matter as the occasion of the division of the Church, and shall refrain from its discussion until we reach that period. We here merely emphasize the fact that the continual agitation of this question did awaken prejudice and opposition on the part of many, and closed the doors of the Church against us in many wealthy homes. Our interest in the spiritual welfare of the slaves, however, grew with the passing years, and our missions to the negroes in the South were the pride of Methodism in that early day. Some of our very best men gave themselves without reserve to the work of evangelizing and organizing into churches the negro slaves of the South. The large number of colored church members gathered by us attests the genuineness of our interest and the success of our endeavors.

At this General Conference of 1804, a motion was made to do away with the Presiding Eldership. The motion provoked a long discussion, but was voted down by a large majority.

Methodism in the West began the quadrennium of 1804—1808 under most favorable conditions. William McKendree was the acknowledged leader of the forces. He was still on the Kentucky District. Lewis Garrett, a most worthy co-laborer, was assigned to the Cumberland District, while William Burke was in charge of the newly-formed District in Ohio. Several veterans remained in important charges, while a long list of strong young men had come out of the great revival to take their places in the growing ranks. Fifty new men were received on trial in the Western Conference during the quadrennium. The revival was still in progress, though confusion in some sections, and wild fanaticism in others had slowed down the work. According to the testimony of all, however, Methodism, with its splendid leadership and its most excellent organization, was not greatly troubled by these things. Peter Cartwright says:

"In this great revival the Methodists kept moderately balanced; for we had excellent preachers to steer the ship or guide the flock. But some of our members ran wild, and indulged in some extravagances that were hard to control . . . The Methodist preachers generally preached against this extravagant wildness. I did it uniformly in my little ministrations, and some times gave great offense; but I feared no consequences when I felt my awful responsibility to God."

1804. The Conference of 1804, was held at Mount Gerazim, as was that of 1803. Bishop Asbury was sick and could not get there. William McKendree was elected President, and admirably performed all the duties of a Bishop, except those of ordination. Eighteen young men were received on trial, viz., William Ellington, Samuel Parker, Joshua Oglesby, William Thompson, Abdel Coleman, William Houston, Richard Browning, Peter Cartwright, Joseph Williams, Miles Harper, Ed-

mond Wilcox, Joshua Barnes, James Axley, Joshua
Riggin, Thomas Lasley, Caleb W. Cloud, Benjamin
Edge, and Obed Noland. Of these, Obed Noland left his
charge during his first year, married and went home.
Abdel Coleman and Joshua Barnes remained in the
traveling connection but one year. Coleman was on the
Hinkstone circuit, and Barnes on the Livingston. Of
Barnes the Minutes say, "being a married man, and
somewhat encumbered, he desisted from traveling."
Edmond Wilcox served the Lexington circuit with
John Sale, but was discontinued at the end of the year.
The Minutes state that "he behaved so very impru-
dently, that the Conference resolved to expunge his
name from the Minutes." Yet, in 1807, he was readmitted, serving two years on the Maramack and
Fleming circuits, then located. He was a half brother
of Peter Cartwright.

Joshua Riggin and William Thompson traveled but
two years. After traveling the Limestone and Miami
circuits, Riggin came up before the Conference at the
end of his two years of probation. We presume we are
far enough away from the event to give, just as we
find it in the Minutes, a rather curious and amusing
note with reference to his case. We are not responsible
for either the spelling, or the form of expression, but
give the note just as it appears in the Minutes:

Joshua Riggin, haveing road out his probation, stands accused by John Whitaker of haveing acted contrary to the char-
ecter of a minester and a Christian, in a case between said
Riggin and said Whitaker's daughter Nancy. Said J. Whitaker,
states by letter that J. Riggin promised his daughter Nancy
marriage, but failed to comply with his promise, and said J.
Whitaker, failing to produce the necessary documents, the Conference did not determine against said J. Riggin. Motion,
Shall J. Riggin be admitted into full Connection? Not agreed.

Motion, Shall J. Riggin remain on trial? Not agreed. Motion, Shall J. Riggin be readmitted on trial? Not agreed. The reason why Joshua Riggin is rejected from the travilling connection, is that the Conference judge he wants preaching abilities.

Mention has already been made of William J. Thompson, as the co-worker with Francis Clark and John Durham in establishing the first societies in Kentucky. In 1800, he was ordained a local deacon, and during nine months of 1803, he had traveled the Danville circuit under the Presiding Elder. He is now admitted on trial and for two years is assigned to the Danville circuit. He then located, "from the particular situation of his family concerns." Afterwards he removed to Ohio, joined the Ohio Conference, and did faithful work until 1831, when he again located.

William Ellington was a native of Georgia, and gave but one year to work in Kentucky, and that was in 1805, when he was assigned to the Wayne circuit. After two years in Ohio, he located.

Richard Browning came recommended from the Barren circuit, and served Roaring River, Hinkstone, Clinch, Natchez, and two years on the Cumberland circuit, locating in 1810.

Joseph Williams spent but one year in Kentucky. He was on the Hinkstone circuit in 1806, and was located in 1809, having served most of the time in Ohio.

Joshua Oglesby was recommended for admisison by the Quarterly Conference of the Danville circuit, was admitted, and during the five years of his service, gave one year to Barren, one to Hinkstone, and one to Fleming circuit. He located in 1809.

Few men have made a finer record in the Confer-

ence than did Samuel Parker. He was born in New
Jersey, September 10, 1773, came to Kentucky from
Pennsylvania about 1800, and located at New Castle,
where he had a cabinet-maker's shop. He was a man
of fine mind and of much information. He was deeply
pious, and enjoyed the love and confidence of all who
knew him. "I never knew a man," said one of his
neighbors, "who doubted Sam. Parker's religion." He
was a class leader, a counselor, and an adviser in all
that community. He had a wonderful gift of song.
Not only did he possess a voice of great sweetness, but
he had cultivated it to a high degree, and many were
attracted to the house of God to hear him sing. He
was quite diffident, and hesitated long before yielding
to the insistent call of the Spirit to enter the ministry. But he finally yielded, and was admitted at this
Conference of 1804, and was appointed successively to
the Hinkstone, Lexington, Limestone, and Miami circuits. Not only was he remarkable for his gift of
song, but J. B. Finley pronounces him one of the finest
speakers he ever heard. "He had an eloquence and
power in the pulpit that were irresistible, and wherever he went wondering and weeping audiences crowded to hear him." He was wonderfully successful in
winning souls on the circuits he filled, and at the end
of four years, he was ordained an elder and immediately appointed Presiding Elder of the Indiana District. This District embraced the whole of Indiana,
Illinois and Missouri. This wide reach of country was
but sparcely settled, and great stretches of prairie and
swamp and forest lay between the settlements he must
visit. But the faithful messenger of the Cross was not
deterred by these difficulties. As far as the daring
pioneer had wandered, there did Parker seek him out

in order to preach to him the gospel of Jesus Christ. No cabin was too wretched for him to visit; no swamp so dismal, or prairie so broad as to prevent his crossing. Often he slept on the open plain or in the dark woods, exposed to wild beasts and savage men. For four years he endured such hardness as a good soldier of Christ, never once thinking that his talents were wasted in this wilderness or that he ought to have a better appointment! He was in quest of souls, and, like his Master, he was willing to go anywhere to find the sheep that were lost. When he began his work on this District, there were in all its bounds only three hundred and eighty-two members. At the end of four years there were upward of two thousand, the District had been divided into two, and more laborers were called into the field.

At the close of his term on this District, he was sent to the Deer Creek circuit in Ohio, the next year to the Miami District. After one year here he was placed on the Kentucky District where he served for four years. During this time he was married to Miss Alethia Tilton, the daughter of Rev. Richard Tilton, an honored and useful local preacher in the bounds of the Limestone circuit. At the Conference of 1819, Parker's health was much impaired. The exposure, the unremitting labors he had performed, and the privations of the life he had lived had told heavily upon his none-too-robust constitution. Nevertheless, an insistent call came from Mississippi for a man to lead the work in that part of the Church, and it seemed that of all the men in sight, Parker's qualifications best fitted him for the place. He did not hesitate to offer himself for that trying position. He was appointed Presiding Elder of the Mississippi District. Some hoped that the milder climate would be beneficial, but the country was not healthful, and the heat was too protracted for one in his condition. Tuberculosis had fastened itself upon him and he rapidly sank under it. After he and his young wife reached Mississippi, he was unable to do any work on the District and died, in great peace, December 6th, 1819.

We deeply regret that our space will not permit a more adequate sketch of this good man. There are many things about him that would be interesting to the reader, but we must not trespass further upon the limits set for us. Sweet-spirited, patient, lovable, useful, the great singer, the eloquent preacher, the devoted servant of God, he literally gave himself a "sacrifice, holy, acceptable unto God, which he deemed only a reasonable service." His funeral was conducted by William Winans, and his remains sleep near the town of Washington, Mississippi.

William Houston was the son of Anthony Houston, Sr., of Scott county, Ky., and a brother of Rev. Anthony Houston, Jr. Though born in Virginia, he came to Kentucky with his father at an early date. We do not know when or under whom he was led to Christ, but he entered the Conference this year and was appointed to the Holston circuit. In 1805 he served the Livingston, in Western Kentucky, and in 1806 the Limestone circuit. This ended his labors in Kentucky, but he continued to travel in Tennessee, Virginia, Mississippi, Maryland, and Ohio until 1817, when he located.

No name connected with the early history of Methodism in Kentucky is more familiar than that of Peter Cartwright. He was one of the most unique characters ever in the Methodist ministry. The unusual characteristics of the man—his wit, his abounding good humor, his bluntness, his pugnacity, his daring—these things have lingered in the traditions of those early days and have obscured the memory of the more sterling qualities of this old hero of the cross. It is not generally known that he was a Presiding Elder for fifty years; that he was a delegate to thirteen General Conferences; that the degree of D. D. was conferred upon him; that he was a member of the Illinois Legislature; and that he was Abraham Lincoln's opponent in a race for Congress. That he was of the rough-and-ready type of the pioneer preacher; that he did and said things which today would be considered outlandish and unbecoming in a minister of the gospel; that he fought his way through opposition when it was necessary, is all true. Too often these eccentricities which in fact belonged only to a few, have been taken as characteristic of all the pioneer preachers. Nothing is farther from the truth. Among those early pioneers there were gentlemen of the highest order, men who in culture and information were the equals of any men of their day. Schools were few, and the best of them are now laughed at by our modern educators. Yet there are some who think that because men did not attend these poor schools, they were illiterate men. Very few lawyers or doctors or ministers of that day were trained in these schools. Wilson Lee, Barnabas McHenry, Thomas Wilkerson, Tobias Gibson, William Burke, William McKendree, Learner Blackman. Samuel Parker, and many others, were men who could move in any society and instruct any class of men

Peter Cartwright has left an Autobiography, which, if it could be transferred to these pages would be interesting reading throughout. But of course only a brief sketch can be given here.

Born in Amherst county, Virginia, September 1, 1785; his father came to Kentucky when Peter was a small boy, and settled for a while in Lincoln county. Later, he moved to Logan county, where Peter grew up, a sturdy youth, and, according to his own estimate, desperately wicked. Says he: "I was naturally a wild, wicked boy, and delighted in horse-racing, card-playing, and dancing. . . . My father gave me a young race-horse, which well nigh proved my everlasting ruin; and he bought me a pack of cards, and I was a very successful young gambler."

It was in 1801, while the great revival was sweeping over the land, that he was brought under deep conviction for sin. He was happily converted not long after, while attending a sacramental meeting not far from his father's house, in which John Page and other Methodist preachers assisted the Presbyterians. He joined the Church under Page at the little Ebenezer church, in Logan county, in June, 1801. He at once became very active in prayer-meetings and in exhorting sinners to be saved. Without any solicitation on his part, and very much to his surprise, Jesse Walker, the preacher in charge, gave him license to exhort. He never was licensed to preach! This permit to exhort was the only license he received from the Church until he was ordained a deacon!

His father having removed to Livingston county, in which at that time there was no Methodist Church, Walker insisted that he go through the county, gather together what scattered Methodists he could find, and form a circuit by the time of the next Conference. Though only eighteen years of age, he left school and set about this work, received seventy into society, organized them into classes, and reported the Livingston circuit ready for a preacher to be sent them the following year. Among those received by him was James Axley, who became one of the most noted of the preachers of that day.

Young as he was, he yielded to the importunities of the Presiding Elder, Lewis Garrett, and consented to travel the Red River circuit in 1803. But at the end of one quarter, the preacher on the Wayne circuit was taken sick, and he was transferred to that field and put in charge, with young Thomas Lasley as a helper. Here he had quite a number of gracious revivals, took many into the Church, and had many interesting experiences. It was here that he had his first encounter with the Baptists. At a place called Stockton Valley, there was an old, dilapidated and abandoned Baptist church. In making his round of the circuit, Cartwright was called on to preach a funeral at this old church. He did so, and quite a revival broke out as a result of his preaching. There were twenty-three very clear and sound conversions. Being only nineteen and very young in the ministry, and unacquainted with the proselyting ways of some other denominations, he did not then open the doors of the Church, but told his young converts that he would do so at his next appointment. In the meantime, he left them some copies of the Methodist Discipline, telling them to read and inform themselves, and if they liked our rules and doctrines, they could then join the Church. In a few days after he left, three Baptist preachers sent appointments for the following Sunday! They all three preached and "as their custom was, they all opened with the cry of 'Water, water; you must follow your Lord down into the water.'"

Cartwright says: "They then appointed what they called a union meeting there, to commence the following Friday and hold over Sabbath, and although I have lived long and studied hard, I have never to this day found out what a Baptist means by a union meeting."

The few Methodists in the neighborhood took the alarm, and dispatched a messenger for Cartwright to return at once. When the meeting began, Cartwright was on the ground, determined, if possible, to save his young converts to the Methodist Church. The Baptist preachers preached, each one stressing the necessity of immersion, then opened the doors of the Church, insisting that persons give in their experiences and be baptized. After much entreaty, one of Cartwright's young converts arose, gave in his experience, and claimed Cartwright as the instrument, under God, of his conversion. Then followed another, and another, until every one of the twenty-three had given an experience, each one claiming Cartwright as the man who lead him or her to Christ. Cartwright says: "Their experiences were pronounced good, and the right hand of fellowship was freely given, and there was great joy in the camp, but it was death in the pot for me. I thought I could not bear up under it . . . . About the time they were done giving the right hand of fellowship and rejoicing over my stolen children, a thought struck my mind very forcibly to give in my experience, and act as though I intended to join the Baptist Church. It may be that I can yet save them. I rose up, and gave in my experience; they gave me the right hand of fellowship, and then there was grea^ rejoicing over the Methodist preacher boy."

A great crowd gathered on the creek bank to see the

converts immersed. All were lined up ready to be taken into the water. A song was sung, a prayer offered, and an exhortation given, then they were called upon to come forward. Says Cartwright:

I knew all the time that it was all important to my success that I should present myself first. Accordingly, I stepped forward and said, 'Brother M———,' —who was the preacher and administrator—'I wish to join the Baptist Church if I can come in with a good conscience. I have been baptized, and my conscience is perfectly satisfied with it, and I cannot submit to be re-baptized. Can I come into your Church on these terms?'

The position I occupied startled the preacher.

'When were you baptized?' he asked.

'Years gone by,' I replied.

'But how was it done? Who baptized you?' was the next inquiry.

'One of the best preachers the Lord ever made.'

'Was it done by sprinkling?'

'Yes, sir.'

'That is no baptism at all.'

I replied, 'The Scriptures say that baptism is not the putting away the filth of the flesh, but the answer of a good conscience, and my conscience is perfectly satisfied with my baptism, and your conscience has nothing to do with it.'

'Well,' said he, 'it is contrary to our faith and order to let you come into the Baptist Church in that way. We can not do it.'

'Brother M———,' said I, 'your faith and order must be wrong. The Church has heard my experience, and pronounced it good; and you believe that I am a Christian, and cannot fall away so as to be finally lost. What am I to do? Are you going to keep me out of the Church, bleating around the walls, like a lost sheep in a gang by myself? Brother M———, you must receive me into the Church. I have fully made up my mind to join you on these terms; now, will you let me into the Church?'

Our preacher by this time had evidently lost his patience, and he very sharply bid me stand away, and not detain others. It was an intensely thrilling moment with me. I cast a look around on the crowd, and saw they were enlisted in my favor.

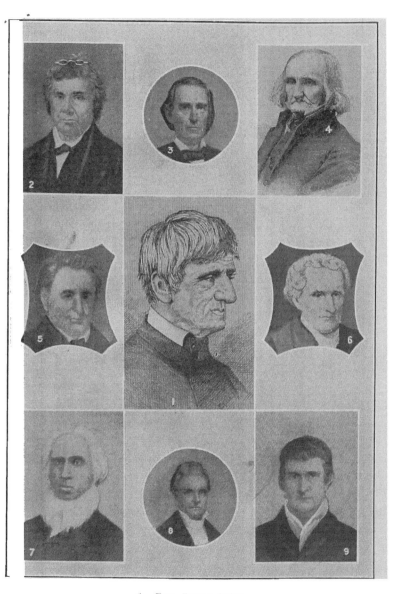

1.   Rev. James Axley

2. Rev. Peter Cartwright, D. D.
3. Rev. B. M. Drake
4. Rev. Elisha Bowman
5. Rev. J. B. Finley

6. Rev. John Collins
7. Rev. Andrew Monroe
8. Rev. William McMahon
9. Rev. William Wians

I cast a wistful eye on the young converts; their eyes met mine most sympathetically, and many of them were weeping, they seemed so deeply affected. They all involuntarily seemed to move toward me, and their looks plainly spoke in my favor. It was an awful moment. O, how I felt! who can describe my feelings?

I stepped aside. Brother S—— stood next to the preacher, dressed ready for baptism; his wife was also dressed, and leaning on her husband's arm. Brother S—— said:

'Brother M——, are you going to reject Brother Cartwright, and not receive him into the Church?'

'I cannot receive him,' said Brother M——.

'Well,' said Brother S——, 'if Brother Cartwright, who has been the means, in the hand of God, of my conversion, and the saving of so many precious souls, can not come into the Church, I can not, and will not join it.' 'Nor I,' said his wife; 'Nor I,' 'Nor I;' and thus it went around until every one of my twenty-three young converts filed off, and gathered around me. 'That's right, brethren,' said I, 'stand by me, and don't leave me; the Lord will bring all right!

But Cartwright was not yet done with the matter. From the creek, they repaired to the old log church, where the three Baptists preached. Cartwright came in for a round of abuse, and was compared to the Pharisees of old, who would neither enter the kingdom themselves nor suffer others to enter. They stated that in all probability these souls he had hindered would be lost, and if so, their damnation would be laid to him. But inasmuch as they had already pronounced all of them good Christians, and as they taught that, if once saved, they could never be lost, Cartwright was not greatly alarmed over such a possibility. Then came the communion. When the table was prepared and the communicants were invited to come forward, Cartwright took his place among them, followed by all of his twenty-three converts. Of course they were passed by, and the elements were not given them. When they got round, Cartwright arose and asked for the bread and wine for himself and his converts. This the preacher peremptorily refused. Cartwright said: "My brethren, you, after hearing our experience, pronounced us Christians; and you say a Christian can never be lost; and our Savior pronounced a solemn woe on those that offend one of his little ones; now do, therefore, give us the bread and wine!" This brought a sharp reproof from the preachers, but won for Cartwright the complete sympathy of the people. Only such a character as Cartwright could have attempted and carried through such an adventurous scheme. It may well be doubted if the Lord had anything to do with such measures, but Cartwright proceeded to organize a Methodist Church on the spot, took in every one of his twenty-three converts, and reported a society of seventy members there at the end of the year!

Cartwright is described by Mrs. Johnson, in her very interesting Life of her husband, the Rev. John Johnson, as being "short, thick, heavy set, with a large and short neck, coarse and rough in his manners, and anything else than grave." After preaching with power, and praying as few other men could pray, he "would have a dozen or twenty persons, frequently some of them the roughest in the congregation, all indulging in uproarous laughter at his jests, before he was ten feet from the pulpit. He had an indescribable 'te-he-he' in laughing, which was expressive of infinite merriment, and irresistibly contagious." But she credits him with having a tender heart and being very affectionate in his family. She had seen him weep like a babe when compelled to leave his wife or a child sick and go to his appointment. "And when he came home from his round of quarterly meetings, it was not an hour before he got up a romp with the children. Upstairs and down they went, overturning chairs and whatever else was in the way, sometimes one of the children, or Cartwright himself, falling heavily upon the floor; and the whole performance, accompanied by a grand chorus of shouts and screams, and the clatter of many feet, made such an uproar as was truly alarming." At the end of his first year in the Conference, the Minutes state that "Peter Cartwright stood reproved before the Conference for some of his conduct, but promising amendment, he was continued on trial." When he came to be received into full connection at the end of his second year, the Minute reads: "Peter Cartwright, elected with the proviso, that the president give him a caution to be more serious. The president proceeded to give him the caution."

This is one side of Peter Cartwright's character. There is another side, which the reader must see if he would properly estimate the man. Cartwright was endowed with a liberal supply of common sense. He was absolutely fearless. With a strength of body rarely equalled, and with courage that never quailed before any foe, such a man was needed in order to cope with the rowdies and desperadoes of this wild western country. Bands of these conscienceless young men, filled with liquor and urged on by those whose gains were endangered by the success of religion, would have broken up the camp-meetings and other services if they had not been held in check by the strong arms of these fearless men of God. Cartwright was a powerful preacher, and a most effective leader of men. He was always ready to banish and drive away strange doctrines, or to bear aloft the banner of Christ in the face of any foe. Being received on trial at this Conference of 1804, he was sent to the Salt River circuit. The following year he served the Scioto, and then the Muskingum, the Barren, the Livingston, and the Christian circuits. We shall meet with him often as we proceed with this narrative, and will, for the present, postpone any further consideration of this remarkable man.

The name of James Axley is commonly associated with that of Peter Cartwright. A raw youth, "truly a child of nature," and utterly unacquainted with either the conveniences or conventions of polite society, Cartwright had found him in the bounds of the Livingston circuit, while he (Cartwright) was hunting up the scattered Methodists in that region and forming the circuit. Axley had been converted sometime before, but was taken into the Church by Cartwright. He felt a call to preach, received license, and was recommended for admission on trial in the Western Conference by a Quarterly Conference held at the home of Isham Browder, August 17, 1804. When he came before the Conference for admission, the Minutes read: "Has been converted about two years, has traveled some months, was received as a man of undoubted piety, but small gifts, and came recommended by the Quarterly Conference of the Livingston circuit." Yet he became one of the greatest preachers of his day!

It is said that he was a native of North Carolina. He was endowed with a great mind, was a hard student, became thoroughly posted on the doctrines of Christianity, and was a profound expositor of holy Scriptures. Mrs. Johnson, who knew him well, describes him as "a young man .... exceedingly grave in his demeanor. He was large, rather tall, slightly inclined to a rotund appearance, quite handsome; and every word and gesture was slow, and replete with dignity." He possessed a wonderful voice. Rev. D. R. McAnally, D. D., than whom Methodism has furnished few greater editors or better judges of such matters, says of him:

Few men, perhaps, ever had a finer voice, and never yet have I met with one who could control it better. So completely was it under his command, that the manner in which something was said often affected the hearer more than the thing itself. He was a natural orator, after the best models—those which nature forms. To those who never personally knew him, and have been accustomed to regard him only as a sour, querulous old man, it may sound strangely, but even at the risk of exciting a smile of contempt, I venture the expression, that his was the best specimen of true oratory to which it has ever been my privilege to listen—and I have attentively listened to a large portion of the celebrated speakers of this country. I have listented to popular orators among our statesmen, to distinguished pleaders at the bar, and to preachers who were followed and eagerly heard by enraptured thousands; but the superior of James Axley, in all that constitutes genuine oratory and true eloquence, I have not heard. His power over the masses was beyond that of any other man I have ever known. He often seemed to move and sway them at will; and with hundreds upon hundreds closely crowding around him, I have witnessed the whole mass thrown into an irrepressible burst of laughter at something he had said, or rather the manner in which he had said it, and two minutes thereafter I have looked in vain for one unmoved among the whole—perhaps not one dry eye to be seen.

There was much of oddity and drollery in both the matter and manner of his addresses. There was never another like him. His absolute originality and his independence of others were marked characteristics. There was an inflexible adherence to what he thought was right, regardless of what others might think; yet there was with it all a humility and kindliness that carried the conviction that he was simply following his own conscience and not intending merely to oppose. He was absolutely fearless in preaching and reproving evil-doers. He had a sermon which he sometimes preached which became known as "Axley's Abominations"—these abominations being slavery, whiskey, tobacco, Masonry, and fashions. Dr. McAnally tells of hearing him preach a sermon against these things at a camp-meeting near Athens, Tenn. The auditorium was arranged to seat from two thousand to twenty-five hundred people, and the seats were packed, and from a thousand to fifteen hundred were standing or sitting on improvised seats around the auditorium.

When he commenced preaching, every idler about the camps or ground, together with all the better-disposed people, gathered as closely around as convenient. As he progressed, these pressed nearer. Those standing crowded those on the seats, and they rose to their feet, and still closer and closer the crowd pressed together. I was seated by the side of the pulpit, facing the congregation, and had a fair opportunity of witnessing the effect of the sermon upon the mass of listeners. They crowded and crowded from every direction toward the speaker. Those nearest stood on the ground; immediately behind, many were standing on the seats; others, still farther off, had actually climbed the posts of the shed, and were seated on the stays and girders; while beyond them again many had mounted the high fence that enclosed the encampment, a line of which ran near by; and a few, Zaccheus-like, climbed the trees and rested among the branches—all attentive to the sermon. The scene thus presented, and the alternation of feeling, as expressed in the countenances of the hearers—now smiling, now weeping freely, now bursting into irrepressible laughter, then the whole encampment resounding with groans, sobs and cries—all combined to present what 'no tongue can tell, nor pencil paint.'

And this sermon was three hours long!

Many striking incidents and ludicrous anecdotes are told of Axley which can not be repeated here. Our space forbids. Notwithstanding his eccentricities, he was by all recognized as a great and saintly man. Most of his ministry was given to Tennessee, though Western Kentucky, Ohio, Indiana, and Louisiana shared the benefit. He was never in what is now the Kentucky Conference, though we claim an interest in him in common with other Methodists of the State. When he was admitted on trial in 1804, he was sent to the Red River circuit, lying partly in Kentucky and partly in Tennessee. He then spent a year on the Hockhocking circuit, in Ohio, then to French Broad, in North Carolina, then to Opelousas, Louisiana, then back to Tennessee. In 1811 he was placed on the Wabash District in Kentucky and Indiana, and continued in the Presiding Eldership practically all the rest of his itinerant life. In 1822, his rugged body worn down by great hardships and continuous labors, he located, settled on a farm near Athens, Tennessee, where he lived and served as a local preacher, until called to his eternal reward. A writer in *The Home Circle* says: "Taking James Axley 'all in all, I shall never look upon his like again.' "

Few, if any, Conferences have ever received into their membership as many remarkable men as did this Conference of 1804. Nearly all of them were products of the great revival of that period. A man who deserves a place alongside of these of whom we have just spoken was Miles Harper. A native of Virginia, he was born November 4, 1784. He had been converted about four years and had traveled under the Presiding Elder for several months before he was received on trial. His first appointment was to the Red River circuit. The second was to Lexington, but before he had been there very long, his Presiding Elder removed him to the Limestone circuit as assist Jacob Young on that charge. Young says of him:

Harper was the most useful Methodist preacher I ever knew. Before he had gone once round, his praise was in all the churches. As I followed him round, I could hear sinners crying for mercy at all his appointments, and the young people flocking to join the Church. Harper was an excellent preacher and excelled in exhortation. He was one of the sweet singers of Israel. His lungs appeared never to tire. He had an elastic body, and his whole soul appeared to be in the work of God. Our first revival was at Limestone (Maysville). It commenced the first time brother Harper preached there, and continued through the Conference year.

They reported a net increase of more than three hundred members that year. The same success followed his labors on Roaring River and Clinch circuits in Tennessee. In 1808, he was made Presiding Elder of the Cumberland District, embracing all Western Kentucky and Western Tennessee. In 1809 he went to Mississippi, where practically all the remainder of his life was spent. Jones, in his History of Methodism in Mississippi, says:

He was a man of medium size, compactly built, well-proportioned, of attractive personal appearance, and capable of great endurance. He was a natural orator, which gift he greatly improved by cultivation and experience. His voice was round, full, clear and distinct, and unusually pathetic. He was thoroughly Methodistic in doctrine and discipline. In the discharge of his ministerial duties, he was bold and intrepid. Describing a scene at a camp-meeting where Harper preached, Jones says, "About the middle of his discourse, persons in various parts of the vast audience began to rise to their feet, one after another, until nearly the whole congregation was standing; then followed a gradual pressing inward, until by the time he was done most of his hearers were on their feet and as near him as they could get. This is a sample of the overpowering eloquence with which he sometimes preached, and the divine unction that attended his ministry.

After he had spent several years in Mississippi, some trouble arose between Harper and some other ministers over a matter which was small in its beginning, but grew as the days went by. Charges were brought against him, and he was expelled from the ministry and Church. This expulsion was considered by many to be very unjust. He persistently asserted his innoncence of any intentional wrong-doing, and insisted that he could not acknowledge wrong when he had committed none. Consequently he remained for several years out of the Church. But he retained the confidence of many, and was finally taken back into the Church without "confession and evidence of repentance;" was re-licensed to preach, and his credentials restored. Bishop McKendree was his fast friend, and visited him for a week or more sometime before his death. He had married a very intelligent lady, out of one of the best families in Mississippi, and reared a most interesting family of children. For some time he was a very useful local preacher, and died in the full assurance of faith.

Another name to be added to this galaxy is that of Thomas Lasley. He came of a family of Methodist preachers. His father and an uncle, and two of his own sons and a grand-son shared with him the labors of the ministry, and other members of the family were actively engaged in the Master's work. Born in Virginia, he came with his father to Kentucky in 1795, and settled on Green River, near where Greensburg now stands. He was converted in 1802, the year that Jacob Young was organizing the Wayne circuit, though perhaps not directly under his ministry. Licensed to preach, he traveled the Wayne circuit with Peter Cartwright during the early part of 1804, and was admitted on trial in the Conference in October of that year. His first appointment was Nollichuckie, East Tennessee. At the next session of the Western Conference in 1805, a call was made for volunteers to go to the hard field of Mississippi and Louisiana, and together with Elisha W. Bowman, Caleb W. Cloud, and William Pattison, he volunteered for that service. He has left a brief but very interesting account of the horseback journey of these four men, with Learner Blackman, the Presiding Elder, from Kentucky to the settlements about Natchez. They were thirteen days making the trip through the wilderness, the last two days without anything to eat. Arriving at the settlements, Bowman left them and went on to New Orleans, while Lasley labored on the Natchez circuit this year. After leaving New Orleans, Bowman had, through almost incredible hardships, visited the Opelousas country and had loosely drawn up a plan for a circuit. To this new field Lasley was sent the second year of his stay in the South. The difficulties and dangers through which he passed were amazing, and his simple, and very modest account of them reads like a work of wild fiction. An instance is given in his unpretentious narrative of his experiences of this year. In going to his field of labor, it was necessary to cross a dismal and dangerous swamp, sixty miles in width. He says:

Coming to a slough in which the mud appeared very deep, I dreaded the attempt to pass, but seeing no way of avoiding it, I plunged into it, and my horse sinking under me, was unable to extricate himself from the mud. I immediately alighted, and took my saddle-bags on my arm. My horse, thus unencumbered, made a powerful struggle and released himself, and soon gained the opposite side. Wending my way onward, and thankful to Providence for the difficulty overcome, I arrived at a large, deep, muddy creek, which I supposed to be about sixty or seventy feet wide, where, ever and anon, the alligators rising to the surface of the water, rendered the prospect still more gloomy. Summoning all the fortitude I possessed, and committing myself to the care of God. I fastened my saddle-bags to my shoulder, and plunged into the stream. Reaching the opposite shore, I found the mud deep and the bank steep, and felt confident that my horse could not rise with me. Hence I sprung from him and gained the bank, which my horse endeavoring to ascend, his hind feet sunk in the mud, and he fell back again into the water. Recovering again, he made the second effort, at which time I threw my weight on the bridle, and he reached the bank, pitching forward and falling with one of his fore legs doubled under him in such a manner as to cripple himself. Not being able to put his foot to the ground by several inches, I was apprehensive that he had slipped his shoulder, and of course would not be able to travel from that place. My condition was the subject of reflection—far from home, a stranger in a strange land, in the very midst of a very ugly swamp, no human help to afford relief, while the poor animal stood trembling under the agony of pain. For a few moments I almost despaired, but throwing myself on my knees before God, I committed my cause into his hands, and prayed most earnestly that he would heal my horse and bless me with courage. Feeling within myself that he had heard my prayer, I arose from my knees and found my horse perfectly sound, and immediately recommenced my journey, rejoicing in the Lord.

Mr. Lasley was a man of prayer and wonderful faith. The author of the History of Methodism in Mississippi, tells us that Lasley made a visit to Mississippi on business, when an old man. Mrs. Jones was very sick. On being informed of it, Mr. Lasley said that, in obedience to the Scriptures, they would go to prayer in her behalf. He says the prayer was a most wonderful plea for the recovery of the sick woman. Upon rising from their knees, Lasley calmly assured him that his wife would get well, which she did in a few days.

People of this generation have but little conception of the sufferings and privations of the men who first preached the gospel in the goodly land we now occupy. Lasley this year endured what it would seem impossible for human kind to endure, and, so far as we have been able to find, received absolutely nothing for it! He never in all his ministry received more than sixty dollars for a year's labor and that only once. At the end of this year in Louisiana, he says, "My resources for support were all exhausted, my clothing literally worn out, and I was compelled to go." He reported a circuit formed, with forty members. One of the societies he organized was in the home of Mr. Bowie, whose son gave his name to the Bowie knife.

Returning to Kentucky at the end of two years in this mission field, he was sent to the Red River circuit, lying partly in Kentucky and partly in Tennessee. Recovering in a measure his impaired health, he was ready, in 1808, for another mission field, and was sent to Letart Falls, on the Ohio river, an entirely new field. At the end of the year he reported one hundred members. In 1809, he was selected to travel with Bishop McKendree. In 1810, he was appointed to Danville circuit where he remained for two years. During the first year he was married to Miss Susan Nelson, a sister of Revs. Thomas and William Nelson, of the Kentucky Conference. He located in 1812, and though he re-entered the Conference and did some work at a later period, his energies were used up, and he could do but little more. As late as 1835, he was re-admitted into the Kentucky Conference, and served the Greensburg District with great acceptability for two years, but was then compelled to give up active work. He was useful as a local preacher and a constant benedic-

tion to the community in which he lived.   His last
days were spent on a well-cultivated farm near Greensburg.

Caleb Wesley Cloud was a native of Delaware, born
February 11, 1782.   He came into the Western Conference from Ohio.   After one year on the Scioto circuit,
he volunteered to go to Mississippi, where he spent
two years on the Wilkinson and Natchez circuits. Returning to the older settlements, he was one year on
Holston, then in 1808 was on the Lexington circuit.   In
1809, the town of Lexington was, for the second time,
separated from the circuit, and Dr. Cloud was appointed to the station.   But again the station was abandoned and the church at Lexington thrown back into
the Lexington circuit, and Dr. Cloud was once more
appointed to that circuit.   In 1811, he located and settled in Lexington where he engaged in the practice of
medicine.   Becoming dissatisfied with some feature
of the Methodist Episcopal Church, he withdrew from
it in 1812, and built a neat brick church of his own on
Main Street.   But his congregation was small and
steadily dwindled away.   Two years before his death
he returned to the Methodist Episcopal Church.

Benjamin Edge was also received in 1804.   When
and where he was born we do not know.   He came from
Ohio, where for several months he had traveled the
Miami circuit under the appointment from the Presiding Elder.   The Minutes say that he "is esteemed
for his undoubted piety, but of contracted abilities, accompanied with some peculiarities." Jacob Young, who
was in his company for several days, speaks of him as
"a curious, eccentric man."   Yet he seems to have been
quite successful in his work and to have rendered very
acceptable service during a ministry of several years.

At the Conference this year, the western end of the Limestone circuit was cut off, and out of it the Licking circuit was formed. Benjamin Edge organized the circuit, with Newport the principal preaching place. He reported 178 members at the end of the year. He was then transferred to the western part of the Conference and served Roaring River and Hartford, each one year. He served again in Tennessee and gave one year to the hard work in Mississippi. Jones says that, of the preachers who labored there that year, "Benjamin Edge, on some accounts, made the most lasting impression. He was somewhat eccentric and very earnest in his work, and such was his zeal and power in the pulpit that one compared him to a strong man knocking down green corn-stalks with a handspike!" One year he traveled with Bishop McKendree. Later he was transferred to the Virginia Conference, where after six years of effective labor, he was superannuated. He died, in the city of Norfolk, February 10, 1836.

Two men appear in the list of Kentucky appointments this year who are worthy of notice. Asa Shinn had traveled the Red Stone, Shenango, Hockhocking, and Guyandotte circuits before coming to Kentucky and being assigned to the Wayne cricuit. In 1805 he was on the Salt River circuit, then went back toward the East. He was a man of deep piety, and very zealous in the cause of Christ. His two years in Kentucky were marked with success. He began his career in the ministry with very little education, but, like so many other preachers of his day, applied himself to the study of the best books, and became one of the strong men of the American pulpit. He became the leader of the movement which ultimated in the establishment of the

Methodist Protestant Church in 1830, and we will have occasion to refer to him when we reach that period of our history. That he was a good man is not doubted by any, though many think he made a grievous mistake in promoting that movement.

George Askins also came to Kentucky this year, and gave five years to the work in this State. He had been in the Conference four years, traveling in Ohio and West Virginia. An Irishman by birth, a man of small stature, a cripple, one of his legs being withered up to his hip; yet Jonathan Stamper says that, "notwithstanding this bodily infirmity, he was full of sprit, and a stranger to fear. No threats could deter him from speaking his sentiments, no matter who might hear them, and he would reprove sin wherever or by whomsoever committed. In doing this he often gave offense, and on two or three occasions suffered personal injury." While in Kentucky he served successively the Limestone, Hinkstone, Lexington, Danville, and Shelby circuits. Soon after leaving this State, he was transferred to the Baltimore Conference where he spent the remainder of his days. He died February 28, 1816, triumphing over death and rejoicing in the expectation of resting with Jesus his Savior. He requested friends to sing, "O glorious hope of perfect love," and among his last words were, "Holiness is the way to heaven." "O what a beautiful prospect lies before me!"

Learner Blackman went this year from Lexington to Natchez and began his splendid work of organizing and extending the work in that Territory. Burke remained on the Ohio District, where there was a net gain of more than five hundred members. Samuel Douthitt, John A. Grenade, and Moses Floyd, located, and Benjamin Young was excluded from the Conference. In the whole of the Western Conference there was a gain of nearly thirteen hundred members. The Licking circuit, in what is now the Kentucky Conference, was formed, and the work greatly extended in every part of the field. Redford calls attention to the fact that several churches were organized this year in Ohio and Breckinridge counties. He quotes from a letter written him by Rev. H. C. McQuown, saying: "The first church organized in Ohio county was at Goshen, two miles south of Hartford, in the year 1804. Very shortly after this, in the same year, another church was organized at Bethel, seven miles north-east of Hartford. Next, and about the same time, in the same year, No Creek church was organized." McQuown credits this good work mainly to Rev. Thomas Taylor, a local preacher, "a man of more than ordinary ability and decisive character. . . . Associated with him was Ludwick Davis, also a man of good preaching ability; and Joshua Barnes, of ordinary talents." A great revival was experienced in this part of the State that year.

Redford also mentions the fact that Jesse Walker came into Breckinridge county this year and organized a society at Thomas Stith's on the road from Hardinsburg to Louisville, consisting of thirteen members, viz., Thomas and Rhoda Stith, William and Nancy Stith, Richard and Betsey Stith, Matthew Sanders, Mrs. Jordan and her two daughters, (Lucy and Katy), Little Dick Stith and wife, and Betsey Hardaway. "A few years afterwards, Stith's Meeting-House, a log church, was built, at an obscure point, four miles west of Big Spring. The first camp-meeting in this county was held on Sugar-tree Run, sixty years ago, (1807), under the supervision of John Craig." (Rev. H. C. Settle). Katy Jordan became the wife of Rev. W. F. King, and after his death was married to Rev. Pleasant Alverson, both members of the Kentucky Conference.

1805. Redford says that "The Western Conference for 1805 was held at Griffith's, in Scott county, Kentucky, commencing October 2nd." The Minutes of the Western Conference say it was held "at Anthony Houston's, Scott county, Kentucky." Jacob Young, who was present, confirms the Minutes, telling us that the Conference "was held in a large stone house belonging to old Anthony Houston. He had two sons preachers, William and Anthony." Jesse Griffith lived in the same neighborhood, but the evidence is conclusive that the Conference was held at Houston's. This was only a few miles from Mount Gerazim, where the Conference had been held the two preceding years. Both Bishops Asbury and Whatcoat were present, and both were in poor health. Both were greatly afflicted, and Whatcoat died a few months later.

Not very much was done in this Conference that requires our notice. While the Minutes state that "the Conference proceeded to nominate Jacob Watson Secretary," the Minutes are signed by William Burke, as secretary, and no explanation is given and no mention of the election of Burke occurs.

The ordination at this Conference of Jesse Head as a local deacon is an event that should not be passed without notice. It is a well-known fact that Jesse Head officiated in the marriage of Thomas Lincoln and Nancy Hanks, the parents of Abraham Lincoln. Several years ago, when partisan writers were trying to

disparage Lincoln in every way possible, it was asserted that his parents were never married, that Jesse
Head was a fictitious person, and as no such man
ever lived, he could not have joined the parents
of Lincoln in holy wedlock. Such a statement was
utterly false, and could have originated only in the
disordered brain of a bitter partisan who was willing
to resort to anything in order to besmirch the character of the great man who guided the destinies of the
nation through the perilous days of the Civil War.
Jesse Head was, at the time of the marriage of Thomas
Lincoln and Nancy Hanks, an ordained local minister
of the Methodist Episcopal Church, living at Springfield, Kentucky. He later moved to Harrodsburg, Ky.,
where he was one of the most prominent citizens of
that city. He was President of the first Bank established in Harrodsburg; edited a paper in that town;
was a member of the city council; died there, and is
buried in the cemetery at that place. The citizens of
Harrodsburg have erected a neat marker at his grave.
Bishop McKendree was a guest in his home during a
stay at the famous Harrodsburg Springs; a grand-son,
Rev. E. B. Head, was for years a member of the Kentucky Conference, and numerous other descendants are
still living in Harrodsburg and in other parts of Kentucky.

This year a District is formed in Mississippi. This
was a hard field. The country was low and far from
healthful and the men who went there from higher
and more northern latitudes suffered much on account
of the climate. Under Spanish rule, which had ended
only a few years before, Catholicism was dominant and
Protestant worship was not allowed. The few Protest-
ants who lived in the Territory were compelled to hide

their Bibles or have them burned. Catholicism was still the dominant faith, and while open persecution was not now tolerated, the preachers who went there must face a most persistent opposition. These and many other difficulties discouraged the missionaries sent to this new country, and most of them remained but a short while. The progress of the work was slow.

Since the preceding Conference, Tobias Gibson, the founder and pillar of the infant church there, had gone from the toils and sufferings of earth to his glorious rest and reward in heaven. Moses Floyd had married and determined to locate. Hezekiah Harriman was dangerously ill with protracted sickness at Adam Tooley's, in the vicinity of Natchez; and in case of his recovery—which at that time was very doubtful—he intended to leave the country. Abraham Amos, for some cause not known to the writer, had left the country not to return. The reports showed a considerable decrease in the white membership of the Church, notwithstanding some valuable acquisitions by immigration."—(Jones).

At the Conference of 1804, Learner Blackman was sent to Natchez. Jones says of him: "He bid fair to make an itinerant minister of the primitive Methodist stamp. He was not content to make his regular rounds on his circuit, or simply to take charge of this or that Society. He was a progressive man; not satisfied with what he had in hand, but determined to gain all he could—to go into the regions beyond, and lead as many lost sinners to the Savior as possible." Speaking further of him, Jones says:

After being in the country a few months, Mr. Blackman had so ingratiated himself into the favor of the people that he was accepted as a worthy successor of the sainted Gibson. He had no eccentricities, no sharp points to unnecessarily irritate and offend either those within or without the Church; there was nothing repulsive in his personal appearance, words or actions, either in or out of the pulpit. He was more than ordinarily well balanced in all respects; genial in spirit, dignified without stiffness, a fluent conversationalist without levity, he could associate without embarrassment with the high officials of the Territory and with the most refined, intelligent, and elevated classes of society, and at the same time make himself so agreeable in the cabins of the poor and less cultivated, and even with the negro slaves, that he was everywhere hailed as a friend and benefactor, intent on doing them good without any mixture of evil. . . . Mr. Blackman was in no respect a negative character. Under his judicious management and regular and faithful labors, both in and out of the pulpit, the prospects of the Church grew brighter everywhere. Church edifices were built, camp grounds located and successfully occupied, new settlements were visited and plans projected to supply them at no distant day with regular preaching.

After planning large things for the Church in Mississippi Blackman came eight hundred miles on horseback to this Conference at Houston's. He had planned that the old Natchez circuit should be divided into three —Natchez, Claiborne, and Wilkinson—and that New Orleans and other parts of Louisiana should be entered. He needed help, and plead for men to occupy this needy field. As we have already seen, Elisha W. Bowman, Thomas Hellums, and at least two others, consented to go with him to Mississippi, and with Blackman directing the forces as Presiding Elder, the work in this Territory entered upon a new era.

William McKendree was transferred from the Kentucky District, where he had labored for five years, and put in charge of the Cumberland District, while William Burke was brought from Ohio back to Kentucky to take McKendree's place on the Kentucky District. New circuits appear in both Ohio and Holston, while the Hartford circuit is cut out of the Livingston, in the Cumberland District.

Joshua Barnes and Obed Noland cease from traveling, and Edmond Wilcox is dropped from the list. Lewis Garrett, William Crutchfield, and Joab Watson located.

Eleven persons were received on trial, viz., George Christopher Light, William Hitt, Zadok B. Thackston, Thomas Hellums, John Thompson, Charles R. Matheny, Samuel Sellers, David Young, Henry Fisher, Moses Ashworth and William Vermillion. Of these, Charles R. Matheny was sent to Illinois circuit, but his name disappears from the Minutes after one year. William Vermiillion never did any labor in Kentucky, but served four years in Ohio and Tennessee. John Thompson, after a year on the Mad River circuit, in Ohio, and one on Hinkstone, in Kentucky, was discontinued in 1807. William Hitt served Powell's Valley, in East Tennessee, one year, and Danville one year, after which his name disappears. Moses Ashworth was assigned to Salt River in 1805, to Wayne in 1806, to Silver Creek, in Indiana, in 1807, to Holston in 1808, and located in 1809. He was afterwards re-admitted to the Tennessee Conference, but located again after one year. Henry Fisher was colleague of William Ellington on the Wayne circuit for this year, but was unable to travel longer. The name of George C. Light is an honored name in Kentucky Methodism. He was admitted this year, and served for two years on the Clinch circuit, in East Tennessee, and for one year in the Baltimore Conference. He then married and located, and continued in the local relation until 1821, when he again united with the Conference and entered upon a brilliant career. We shall wait until this later period before presenting an account of his useful life.

Zadok B. Thackston was admitted this year, and appointed to Nashville circuit. The following year his appointment was Red River, partly in Kentucky; in 1809, to Barren, and on account of health failure, he located in 1810. He was afterwards re-admitted, and for fifty years his name was familiar to the Methodists of Kentucky. A character sketch will be given when we come to the time of his re-admission.

Thomas Hellums was born in Green county, Tennessee, June 5, 1781. He was converted when about eighteen years of age, admitted on trial in 1805, and assigned to the Red River circuit. He traveled successively the Whitewater circuit (in Indiana), Shelby, Natchez, Nashville, Tennessee Valley, Cumberland, and Licking, and in 1813, was compelled to locate. "His uniform piety, his fervent zeal, and his commanding talents as a preacher, together with his tragic end, at once awaken our anxiety." After locating, he taught school for awhile, but his feeble health forced him to give up this employment. Having previously studied law, he practiced at the bar, but because he thought it embarrassed his ministerial and Christian standing he gave up this also. He labored as a local preacher for a time, but his mind gave way, and he was partially insane. He preached often, without the least sign of derangement, investigating and presenting his subjects with clearness and force. But as soon as he was out of the pulpit, he became fearful of his best friends, imagining that they wanted to kill him. He would sometimes go so far as to draw weapons of defense, and threaten them if they approached them. He was at length persuaded to go with some friends to Arkansas to attend a camp-meeting. On Sunday he preached a most lucid and powerful sermon, but immediately afterwards became violently insane. He exhibited great fear of those about him, and drew a great knife as if to defend himself; then got his horse and left the camp ground, heading out upon a vast prairie. He was never heard of again! It was thought that he was murdered!

Samuel Sellers, who was admitted this year, spent the first four years of his ministry in Kentucky, on the Limestone, Hartford and Danville circuits—his second and fourth on Hartford. In 1809 he was on the Claiborne circuit, in Mississippi, then back to Kentucky where he served the Barren circuit. In 1812 he went back to Mississippi, and for four years presided over the Mississippi District. He was highly esteemed, and for two or three sessions of the Mississippi Conference, when no Bishop was present, he presided over that body. He located in 1818.

For more than fifty years David Young gave himself without reserve to the ministry in this western world. A Virginian by birth, carefully reared by pious Presbyterian parents, he had a great fondness for study, and, at the age of twenty-one, was at the head of a grammar school in Tennessee. He came into a conscious experience of saving grace in 1803. At once he began to exhort and to call sinners to repentance. As many as one hundred and fifty were converted as the result of his efforts before he received license to exhort. He was admitted on trial in 1805, and sent to Salt River, but was soon changed by the Presiding Elder to Wayne. The following year he was on the Livingston circuit and this closed his ministry in Kentucky. After one year at Nashville, he served the Whitewater circuit in Indiana, then went to Ohio, where he spent the remainder of his long life. For years he presided over Districts. For fifty-three years he was a member of an Annual Conference, and six times a member of a General Conference.

In person, Mr. Young was tall, straight, and well-proportioned; in movement, easy, dignified, and graceful. . . . His manners were those of a finished Southern gentleman of the old school. . . . As an orator, according to the united testimony of those who knew him in his palmiest days, he had few equals. In style, he was clear, logical, and chaste—when roused, grand and overwhelming. He was always equal to the occasion. His voice was musical, his enunciation distinct, and, as a reader of the Holy Scriptures and the Communion service, I have never met in our own, or a sister Church, his equal.—Rev. James B. Finley.

1806. Ohio, Indiana, Illinois, and Missouri had, by this time, been opened to settlers, and there was a great rush to get possession of the cheap lands they offered. Many families left Kentucky and Tennessee for these new territories, and the Church felt the effect of the exodus. Nevertheless, there was a net gain of nearly twelve hundred members in the Western Conference reported at the Conference of 1806. Nine hundred and eighty-five of these were in Kentucky.

The Western Conference this year met at Ebenezer, in East Tennessee, September 15th. Bishop Asbury was present. He says in his Journal, "There are fourteen hundred added within the bounds of this Conference. Of the fifty-five preachers stationed, all were pleased. The brethren were in want, and could not provide clothes for themselves, so I parted with my watch, my coat, and my shirt." Wonderful old man!

Bishop Whatcoat had died on July 5th. No more saintly man has ever graced the Episcopacy than he. Though afflicted with a very painful affection of his kidneys, he traveled through the Conference as long as he was able to ride in a carriage, then was taken to a friend's in Dover, Delaware, where he died and was buried under the pulpit of Wesley Church at that place.

At this Conference at Ebenezer, Bishop Asbury was requested to preach a funeral sermon, which he did, using John 1:47-50 as his text.

After his return to England, Bishop Coke had married—the first Methodist Bishop to take unto himself a wife. The lady whom he married was a woman "of a large fortune, of deep piety, and of an ardent devotion to the cause of God." At this Conference a letter from Coke, addressed to the various American Conferences, was read, proposing to become a resident of America on condition that the continent be divided into two parts, one of which to be under his superintendency, the other under the superintendency of Bishop Asbury. The Conference ordered a reply sent Bishop Coke, adverse to making any such division. The superintendence must be *general*, not diocesan.

The following minute is self-explanatory, and we think very few of our people know that any such matter was ever proposed in our Conferences:

Bishop Asbury proceeded to read the letter addressed from the New York to the New England and succeeding Conferences, respecting the propriety of delegating a Conference to meet in Baltimore, on the 4th of July, 1807, for the express purpose of electing a Superintendent or Superintendents of the Methodist Episcopal Church in America. The Conference proceeded to adopt the method of the New York Conference. Resolved, by a unanimous vote, that a delegation shall take place. The Conference proceeded to elect by ballot the following members: William McKendree, Thomas Wilkerson, John Sale, Benjamin Lakin, Thomas Milligan, Jacob Young and William Burke.

George Askin and Jesse Walker were elected as alternates, to attend in case any of those elected as principals could not go. The death of Bishop Whatcoat and the precarious health of Bishop Asbury seemed to make it necessary to provide against the Church being left without a Bishop. We suppose the proposition was not adopted by all the Conferences, as the special session was never held.

William Thompson—the co-laborer with Francis Clark—Moses Black, James Quinn, and Louther Taylor were located.

The following were received on trial: James King, Milton Ladd, Hector Sandford, Frederick Hood, John Tarver, Abbott Goddard, Hezekiah Shaw, John Collins, John Travis, John Crane, and Joseph Bennett. In this connection we find the following interesting minute: "Benjamin Wofford came from South Carolina, as a licensed local preacher, into the bounds of the Western Annual Conference, and was employed by the Presiding Elder of the Cumberland District, to ride Hartford circuit, and from the Quarterly Conference of said circuit obtained a proper recommendation. The Annual Conference think proper to admit him upon condition that he provide, as soon as may be, for the emancipation of his two slaves, now in South Carolina." A letter was addressed to him on the subject, and, as no appointment was given him, we presume the condition was not met. Afterwards, Rev. Benjamin Wofford gave $100,000.00 to found Wofford College, at Spartanburg, South Carolina.*

*The following letter from Dr. Henry M. Snyder, President of Wofford College, gives additional information concerning Benjamin Wofford:

Dear Bro. Arnold: I have your letter of March 7th. In reply I write to say that your item from the minutes of the old Western Conference, which met, as I recall it, at Ebenezer, in east Tennessee, is correct. I believe you will note that after Wm. McKendree read in open Conference a letter addressed to Benjamin Wofford about his freeing his negroes, the name of Benjamin Wofford

Of those admitted on trial, John Tarver, the first applicant for admission from Mississippi, was sent to Claiborne circuit, in that Territory, and his name appears no more. Frederick Hood was appointed to Salt River this year, and to Guyandotte the year following, and was discontinued at the end of two years. James King was sent to Hockhocking, in Ohio, then to Wayne in 1807, to Limestone in 1808, and to Saltville, in the Holston country in 1809. He located in 1810. Milton Ladd was a man of some ability, and served successively the Scioto, the Licking, the Tennessee Valley, and the Lexington circuits, then was transferred to the Virginia Conference, but located the following year. The first assignment of Hector Sandford was to Limestone, which ended his labors in Kentucky. After two years in Ohio and one in Indiana, he too located. Abbott Goddard was recommended by the Quarterly Conference of Limestone circuit. Six or seven miles east of Flemingsburg, stands Goddard Chapel, which community was then in the Limestone charge, and we are of opinion that it was named for him or for some of

disappears from the minutes of the Western Conference. He came back to South Carolina and served the Enoree circuit in this State for a few years, but proceeded to acquire more lands and more negroes until when he died he left a fortune of more than $100,000.00. He bequeathed to his wife $30,000.00, to missions, $4,000.00, and to relatives smaller gifts. He had no children. I have seen the statement made that this gift of $100,000.00 to found the College was the largest single gift made up to that time to the cause of education in the United States. I have never tried to verify this statement. At any rate, it was an extraordinary thing for a local Methodist preacher to do in 1850. Yes, this is our own Benjamin Wofford, and I have often wondered what might have happened to him and to South Carolina Methodism had he been accepted with his negroes in the Western Conference.

his family. He gave but two years to work in Kentucky, serving Barren in 1806, and Licking in 1809. The rest of his time was spent in Ohio, except one year in Powell's Valley, in Tennessee. He was on the supernumerary and superannuated lists for several years in the Ohio Conference, and finally located in 1822. He is said to have been one of the most powerful exhorters of his day. Hezekiah Shaw was for five years an itinerant, but never in Kentucky. Joseph Bennett served the Danville, Scioto, Barren, and Guyandotte circuits, then his name disappears without explanation.

John Collins, who was admitted this year, spent only a part of one year in Kentucky, and that was on the Limestone circuit in 1812. He was no ordinary man. He was born in New Jersey, November 1, 1769. Awakened to a sense of his need of salvation by a severe affliction, he was converted in October, 1794, and was licensed to preach soon afterwards. He was the means of securing the conversion of nearly all his father's family, then of nearly all of his wife's family, one of whom was her brother, the greatly beloved Learner Blackman. Mr. Collins was very active and very useful as a local preacher in New Jersey, preaching with great power and unction. Learner Blackman, speaking of a sermon he heard him preach while in New Jersey, says: "To all human appearance, he could not have manifested more zeal, and spoken with more earnestness, if he had stood in sight of a dissolving universe. The people seemed appalled, as if thunderstruck, and I can not compare his preaching to anything that seems to answer the description, except thunder rolling through the concave, accompanied with repeated flashes of lightning, that causes a constant glare."

Mr. Collins came to Ohio in 1804, and settled in Clermont county. Admitted into the itinerancy in 1806, he was six years in Ohio before his appointment to the Limestone circuit. He served this circuit but a part of the year and located at the ensuing Conference, but in 1817 he is again in the ranks, and is appointed Presiding Elder of the Scioto District. He filled some of the most important appointments in the Ohio Conference until 1836, when he was superannuated. He died in Maysville, Ky., August 21, 1845. He was the grand-father of our Bishop Collins Denny.

To John Travis "belongs the distinguished honor of being the first to carry beyond the Father of Waters the tidings of a Redeemer's love." Admitted this year, he was sent to the newly-created circuit, "Missouri." The population of that territory was then small, but constantly increasing by a flood of emigrants from the older States. To these Travis preached the gospel, and at the end of the year reported two circuits formed— the Missouri and the Maramack. The following year he was sent to the Wilkinson circuit, in Mississippi, then, successively to Roaring River, in Tennessee, Green River, in Kentucky, (two years), Livingston, Dover, and Holston. Worn down by excessive labors, he located in 1814, and practiced medicine for a number of years. A good man, always devoted to his Church, useful in his community, and was granted a most triumphant death, on the 11th of November, 1852.

John Crane was a saintly man. Born in 1787, in Eaton's Station, two miles below Nashville, he was the son of Rev. Lewis Crane, who was one of the first converts among the Methodists in the Cumberland country. Jacob Young says that John was converted when eight years old. He had lived in the midst of a revival eight years before he started to preach. I have seen him stand on some eminence, before he was nine years old, with five or six thousand people round him, and exhort for two hours. He carried the spirit of revival wherever he went. His race as an itinerant was short, but successful. He turned many to righteousness, and was a burning and a shining light in the Church, and is doubtless a star in the kingdom of glory.

He was nineteen when he entered the Conference. He served Holston, in Tennessee: Deer Creek, in Ohio; Cold Water, in Indiana; Missouri circuit, in Missouri; Green River, in Kentucky; and Duck River, in Tennessee. He continued to travel and preach till the end, or near the end, of January, or about the 1st of February, 1811, when he ceased from overmuch fatigue and a very severe cold, which terminated in an inflammation of the lungs; and about the 14th of February, death sounded the retreat. He died at the house of Mr. Mitchell, on Duck River, with much confidence in the Lord.

John Clingan was admitted by the Baltimore Conference this year and sent to the Guyandotte circuit. He was in Kentucky but one year, serving the Licking circuit in 1808. He labored in Ohio until 1813, when he located.

Sela Paine was also admitted by the Baltimore Conference this year. He served the Wayne circuit for two years, 1807 and 1808, gave two years to Indiana, two to Mississippi and three to the Holston country before locating in 1815.

1807. The Western Conference for 1807 was held at Chillicothe, Ohio, the first Methodist Conference ever held in that State. Bishop Asbury was present, and William Burke is again the Secretary.

John Thompson was discontinued; William Hitt ceased to travel; and John Meek and Thomas Wilkerson were located.

The following were received on trial: From Holston District, John Henninger; from Cumberland District, John Craig, William Lewis, Thomas Kirkman, Edmond Wilcox and Jedidiah McMim; from Ohio District, Jacob Turman and William Mitchell; from Kentucky District, Josiah Crawford, Thomas Stillwell, Mynus Layton, and Henry Mallery—twelve in all. James Blair and Francis McCormack also applied for admission, but the Conference thought best not to receive them. Francis McCormack was a local preacher who had moved from Bourbon county, Kentucky, and built his cabin near Milford, on the Little Miami River. It was in this house that the first Methodist Society in Ohio was formed. The minute states that he was so situated that he could not travel any other circuit than the one in which he lived, and for that reason the Conference thought best not to admit him.

Of those admitted, William Mitchell and Jedidiah McMin never rendered any service in this State. Josiah Crawford, Thomas Stillwell, and Mynus Layton served in Kentucky but one year each. Mynus Layton was on the Limestone circuit in 1807, and his name appears no more in the list of appointments. Thomas Stillwell was sent this year to Livingston, but after this his field of labor was chiefly in Tennessee. Josiah Crawford traveled the Shelby circuit this year, then Silver Creek, in Indiana, afterwards going to the Holston country in East Tennessee. Edmond Wilcox, the half brother of Peter Cartwright, had been admitted in 1804, but was discontinued at the end of one year. This year he was again admitted and sent to Maramack, in Missouri. The following year he was on the Fleming circuit, after which he located. While Thomas Kirkman was admitted on trial this year, his name does not appear in the list of appointments. In 1808, he is on the Livingston circuit. In 1809, the minute reads: "Considering his local situation, his bodily debility, and want of attention to his circuit," he was discontinued. William Lewis served Hartford, Dixon and Henderson circuits, then located in 1810. Henry Mallery came recommended by the Quarterly Conference of the Hinkstone circuit, and served in succession the Lexington, Shelby, Lexington, (a second time), and Hinkstone circuits. He located in 1811.

John Craig was said to be "plain, eccentric, and faithful," with "talents moderate." He was on Hartford twice, in 1807 and in 1809, and 1818 he was on Christian circuit. He lived until 1840, serving the Church in Tennessee.

Jacob Turman was admitted this year, and sent to the Limestone circuit with William Houston and Mynus Layton. In 1808, he was on Hartford, then in 1812 on Christian, which closed his labors in this State. He located in 1814.

Of the class admitted in 1807, John Henninger remained in service for the longest time, and was, perhaps, the most efficient. He was assigned in 1807 to Carter's Valley, in Tennessee, and the following year to Danville, which was his only service in this State. After two years in Louisiana and Mississippi, he came back to Tennessee, where the remainder of life was spent. He was Presiding Elder of the French Broad and Washington Districts, in what is now the Holston Conference; agent for the Holston College, and pastor in Knoxville. He is characterized as a man of "fervent piety, expansive intellect, and burning eloquence." His life was most useful and his death very triumphant. He died in December, 1838.

The name of John Hays appears this year in connection with the Lexington circuit. He was from the Baltimore Conference, and was admitted in 1802. In 1806 he came west, and served the Hockhocking circuit in Ohio. After one year at Lexington, he located, and we know nothing further concerning him.

The reader must bear in mind that more than a century and a quarter has passed since these men began their labors as itinerant preachers. Most of them were humble but faithful men, who wrought well during the time they were in the service, but when they were gone they were soon forgotten. All we know of some of them we glean from the meager records of the Minutes of the Conferences in which they served. Most of them located after a few years of service, and as the Conference Minutes contain memoirs of only those who were members at the time of death, those who located are left without even this memorial of their character and labors.

While a motion was made in the General Conference of 1800 to provide for a delegated General Conference, the motion was "negatived," and such delegated General Conference was not provided for until 1808. Nevertheless, the Western Conference this year anticipated the matter by electing seven of its members to represent them in the General Conference the following year, and made at least a tentative provision for the payment of their expenses. The delegates elected were William McKendree, William Burke, James Ward, Benjamin Lakin, Learner Blackman, Thomas Milligan and John Sale. In 1804, but four members of the Western Conference were present at Baltimore, and one of them was declared ineligible, not having traveled for four full years. By a unanimous vote, this Conference approved a memorial from the New York Conference asking for a delegated body.

The net increase of members in the Western Conference in 1807 was 2,147. Of this increase Kentucky furnished 1,494. The total membership of the Western Conference had grown to 15,202 white, and 795 colored members. Of these the Kentucky District had the largest number of any of the Districts—4095 white, and 324 colored. The Cumberland District lay mostly in Kentucky, the Barren, Wayne, Livingston and Hartford circuits, with 1665 white and 56 colored members, lying entirely in this State, while the Red River circuit embraced a considerable portion of the State. Thus it will be seen that this State had in 1808 about 6,000 members.

CHAPTER XIV

Two notable things were done by the General Conference of 1808—a plan for a Delegated General Conference was adopted, and William McKendree was elected to the office of Bishop.

From the organization of the Church up to this time, the General Conference had been a body in which all the preachers were members who had traveled a given length of time and could get to the seat of the Conference. But as the work enlarged and the distance to the seat of the Conference was increased, it was inevitable that those Conferences that were far removed from the place of meeting would have but few members present, while the Conferences near at hand would have large representations. Thus the control of the affairs of the Church would be in the hands of two or three Conferences. The preachers attending from the Baltimore and Philadelphia Conferences in 1808 constituted almost half of the total number present. Five of the seven Annual Conferences had given their approval to the plan of a delegated body. Acting upon a memorial from New York, a committee of fourteen, two from each Conference, was appointed to consider the matter, and this Committee reported a plan for a delegated body. When put to a vote the plan was defeated, largely by the votes of the two overshadowing Conferences. This created such dissatisfaction that, later in the session, the measure was again taken up and adopted. As a result, future General

Conferences, acting under Restrictive Rules as laid down in the Discipline, have been composed of delegates chosen by the various Annual Conferences, according to a fixed ratio.

Bishop Whatcoat was dead. Bishop Coke was in Europe, and had never been of much assistance in supervising the affairs of the American Church. He was a man of large affairs, and the service he was rendering to the British Conference was so important that they requested that he be permitted to remain in England, which request was granted. Bishop Asbury was so worn down by the heavy duties of his office that his life was very uncertain. His rheumatic affection was so severe that he could "neither stand, nor sit, nor walk," but had to be carried about like a little child. On several occasions he preached to the people lying in his bed. It was imperative that some one be selected to share with him the superintendence of the Church.

William McKendree, the acknowledged leader in the West, had gone up with other members of the Western Conference. In the East he was little known. Some of the leading men had never heard of him. He had been for eight years in the wild regions of the West, and went to the General Conference clothed in the rough garb of a backwoodsman—the only clothes he had. But on Sunday morning he was appointed to preach in Light Street Church, in the city of Baltimore, and Dr. Nathan Bangs, the future historian of American Methodism, says that when he saw the plain man, "clothed in very coarse and homely garments, which he had worn in the woods of the West," he was filled with misgivings as to the wisdom of putting forward such a man on such an occasion. As McKendree proceeded, however, these feelings of distrust gave way to amazement. Describing the sermon, he says that, when the climax was reached, "the congregation was instantly overwhelmed with a shower of divine grace from the upper world. At first, sudden shrieks, as of persons in distress, were heard in different parts of the house, then shouts of praise, and in every direction sobs and groans. The eyes of the people overflowed with tears, while many were prostrate upon the floor or lay helpless on the seats." The effect of the sermon was so great that at once the members of the General Conference said, "This is the man we want for Bishop!" The next day, when the election came on, McKendree, on the first ballot, received ninety-five out of one hundred and twenty-eight votes, and on the 17th day of May, 1808, was ordained to the office which he filled with such signal ability and with such general satisfaction to the Church. For twenty-seven years he went in and out among the Conferences, leading the forces and molding the government of the Church as no other man has done. We shall have much to say about Bishop McKendree as we progress with the history of Kentucky Methodism.

Of course the questions of slavery and the Presiding Eldership were prominent in the considerations of the General Conference of 1808. In the matter of slavery, finding it impossible to adopt any rule that would be satisfactory throughout the Church, it was ordered that "each annual Conference be authorized to form their own regulations relative to buying and selling slaves." Perhaps this was the best that could be done under the circumstances, but it was a dangerous policy to say the least. The Presiding Elder question entered largely into the matter of a delegated General

Conference. There was a strong contingent in the body who favored abolishing the office altogether, or else having the Annual Conference elect its Presiding Elders instead of their appointment by the Bishop. When the Committee of Fourteen brought in its report providing for a delegated body, acting under specified Restrictive Rules, it was recognized that the adoption of the Rules would place with the Bishops the right to appoint the Presiding Elders. This led some to vote against the whole plan, and, in part, accounts for the defeat of the plan when first presented. But the motion to elect the Presiding Elders by the Annual Conference was made and voted down by a large majority, after which the plan for a delegated General Conference was adopted.

1808. The session of the Western Conference of 1808 was held at Liberty Hill, in Middle Tennessee. Both Bishops Asbury and McKendree were present. Asbury says: "Our Conference was a camp-meeting, where the preachers ate and slept in tents. We sat six hours a day, stationed eighty-three preachers, and all was peace. On Friday the sacrament was administered, and we hope there were souls converted, and strengthened, and sanctified. We made a regulation respecting slavery," etc.

At this Conference it was ordered that $33.50 then in the hands of the former trustees of the Charity Fund, should be placed in the hands of William Burke, "for the use and benefit of the trustees of Bethel Academy"—showing that the Church was still in possession of the property in which this school was taught, though it is probable that the money was to be used in repairs on the building and not for the expense of a school.

The Conference was deeply concerned over the deficiencies in the support of the preachers. The meager amount of $80 was allowed to each, an equal amount to the wife of each married preacher, and a small sum for each child under fourteen years of age. Peter Cartwright says:

These were hard times in these western wilds; many, very many, pious and useful preachers were literally starved into location. I do not mean that they were starved for want of food; for although it was rough, yet the preachers generally got enough to eat. But they did not generally receive in a whole year money enough to get them a suit of clothes; and if people, and preachers too, had not dressed in home-spun clothing, and the good sisters had not made and presented their preachers with clothing, they generally must retire from itinerant life, and go to work and clothe themselves. Money was very scarce in the country at this early day, but some of the best men God ever made breasted the storms, endured poverty, and triumphantly planted Methodism in this Western world. . . . Indeed, such was our poverty that the Discipline was a perfectly dead letter on the subject of house rent, table expenses, and a dividend to children; and although I had acted as one of the stewards of the Conference for years, these rules in the Discipline were never acted upon, or any allowance made (for children), till 1813, when Bishop Asbury, knowing our poverty and sufferings in the West, had begged from door to door in the older Conferences, and came on and distributed ten dollars to each child of a traveling preacher under fourteen years of age.

At this Conference the Committee on Finance found that, after distributing the amounts received from the Book Concern, the Chartered Fund, and a donation from the Ohio District, the salaries of the preachers were over $2,500 short. Out of their deep poverty, they took a collection for the most needy brethren amounting to $69.50.

That great old veteran, William Burke, was granted a supernumerary relation this year, the first opportunity to get any rest for sixteen years. But he did not rest. His name appears as one of the preachers on the Hinkstone circuit, and for several years longer he was very laborious in building up the Church.

The work was expanding in every direction. In 1807 there were five Districts in the Western Conference; this year there are seven. The Indiana District, including both Illinois and Missouri, was formed, and Samuel Parker placed in charge. The Ohio District was divided, and the Miami and the Muskingum took its place, with John Sale and James Quinn presiding over them. New circuits appear in almost every District. In Holston, Watauga and Tennessee Valley appear for the first time. In the Kentucky, Green River and Fleming; in the Miami, Cincinnati and White Oak; in the Muskingum, West Wheeling, Marietta, Little Kanawha, and Leading Creek. While William Ellington, Joseph Hays, Adjet McGuire, and James Davison located, Thomas Trower, from the Virginia Conference, was received into full connection; James Quinn and Moses Black are readmitted; and seventeen men are admitted on trial. We shall not tax the reader with sketches of any except those who were appointed to work in Kentucky. Of these, David Hardesty, who was appointed to the Danville circuit with John Henninger, remained but one year in the service. His name then disappears. William E. Elgin labored but one year in Kentucky. He was appointed to Lexington with Caleb W. Cloud, after which he went to Tennessee, where he served the Clinch, Nashville, Tennessee Valley, Lebanon, and Caney Fork circuits, located, and later in life united with the Methodist Protestant Church. For several years he had been Secretary of the Tennessee Conference. He was a good and useful man.

Richard Richards was three years in Kentucky, giving his first two years to Green River and Hinkstone, then after a year at Carter's Valley, he was on Barren circuit one year; then at Vincennes, in Indiana, then at Knoxville, Tennessee. He located at the end of this year, and, we are sorry to say, took to drink. For many years he was out of the ministry and Church. He wrecked his fortune, ruined his reputation, and doubtless brought himself to an untimely grave. In his last days, "amid the bitterest tears of repentance and keenest pangs of remorse," he tried, at least, to cast himself upon the mercy of the Lord.

John Lewis remained in the work four years, laboring on Barren, Duck River, Henderson, and Red River and Goose Creek circuits. He located in 1812. A gifted speaker, but quite eccentric. He lived many years in Tennessee.

Eli Truitt was a worthy and useful man. After serving Hinkstone, Limestone and Fleming, and Lexington circuits, he located in 1811. He was readmitted in 1815, labored on the Brush Creek and Scioto charges, in Ohio, then again located and engaged in mercantile business. But his heart was in the ministry. Again joining the Conference, he was sent to Michigan as a missionary to the Indians. Later he was pastor at Portsmouth, Ohio, and died, "leaving his testimony that it is no vain thing to serve God."

After two years on Hinkstone and Wayne circuits, the name of John Watson disappears until 1819, when he is again admitted, and serves successively the Salt River, Danville, Barren, Somerset, Fleming, and Hinkstone circuits. During the Conference year 1824-5, charges were brought against him, and he was expelled from the ministry and Church. Recognizing the justice of the verdict against him, it is said that he took no appeal and made no protest, but having settled in Hart county, was regular in his attendance upon the services of the Church, and, to the end, was deeply devoted to its interests. In 1840, he was invited by the pastor to again unite with the Church, which he did; enjoyed the confidence and respect of the community in which he lived, and died in hope of eternal life. While a false step may debar a man from leadership, he still has access to God's mercy and can walk in a straight path before the Lord.

A man who gave the Conference a good deal of trouble was James Blair. Redford mentions him as one who was admitted this year, but the Minutes are not clear upon this point. In the Minutes of 1807 we find the following: "James Blair came properly recommended from the Quarterly Meeting Conference of Scioto circuit, but the Conference are of opinion that, owing to his instability and frequent backslidings, and having but lately been restored to morality and the Church, they judge it improper to admit him." This year, 1808, the Minutes read: "James Blair came properly recommended from the Quarterly Meeting Conference of Limestone circuit, and after the Conference had taken his case under mature deliberation, they think best to leave the Presiding Elder at liberty to employ him if it be found that his circumstances will admit of it." He was employed, and his name appears in connection with the Hinkstone circuit, but there is no mention of his ever having been received. In 1809 nothing was stated against him and he was sent to Salt River. The following year, charges were brought against him, and the committee recommended that he be reprimanded before the Conference by the Bishop.

Nevertheless, he was admitted into full connection and elected to deacon's orders. In 1811 he was "suspended from all official services in our Church." In 1814 he was "restored to all the privileges of a local deacon" by the Ohio Conference; then in 1820 he was readmitted, and sent to the Hinkstone circuit. At the next Conference charges were again preferred against him and he was expelled from the ministry and Church. To say the least, it is unwise to hold in a Conference a man who has such a knack at getting into trouble.

Of those admitted this year, the man who became most prominent and served the Church in the largest way was Wm. Winans. He was born in Western Pennsylvania, November 3, 1788. His mother was a widow and poor, and the son worked in the iron foundries in the neighborhood in order to make a support for the family. With a vicious environment, it is not to be wondered at that he fell into wickedness. But his mother's home was a home of the Methodist preachers, and through their influence he was early brought under conviction for sin. At the age of sixteen, he removed with the family to Ohio, and here at the age of nineteen, he was converted, and soon after was appointed a class-leader and was given license to exhort. In August, 1808, he was licensed to preach, and was admitted on trial at the Conference held in October. He was assigned to the Limestone circuit with James King. He remained in Kentucky but one year, then was sent to Vincennes, Indiana, and after a year there, volunteered for service in Mississippi and Louisiana, where he spent the remainder of his life. While at Vincennes he was closely associated with the Governor of the Territory, Gen. William Henry Harrison. The Church in this new country grew under his ministry, and success attended him everywhere he labored.

Appointed to Mississippi, he made the trip through the wilderness on horseback, and, after counsel with the Presiding Elder, went on to New Orleans, to take up again the work in that wicked city. Here he hired a house, in which he preached, and taught a small school to get a support while laying the foundations of Methodism in that place. At the end of the year there was reported from "Orleans Territory" a membership of forty-three. He then returned to Mississippi, and for many years filled the leading appointments in that Conference, and was the acknowledged leader in the work of the Church in that State. One has said of him:

He never sought inglorious ease; he never grew weary of well-doing; he never became selfish and worldly. With persevering and undaunted spirit he labored on. The generation that witnessed his coming, and most of his colleagues, went down to the grave; and still his enthusiasm, and energy, and masculine intellect survived, and his spirit glowed like some eternal flame upon the altar of a ruined temple. Often have I seen him, on his tours of circuit duty, scarcely able to sit in the saddle, dragging himself to the pulpit, preach for two hours with surpassing power and unction, and then fall down, faint and exhausted, his handkerchief stained with blood; and for days thereafter motionless, hovering, as it were, between life and death. Thirty years ago, and at intervals since, he was thought to be in a rapid decline. He was afflicted with hemorrhages, bronchitis, derangement of the vital organs, and general debility; and physicians prohibited the excitement of the pulpit. But he would preach, he felt called of God to preach.

In his memoir it is said that "he was a man of inflexible firmness, of untiring industry, of earnest piety, of vigorous intellect, of mighty faith in God—dignified, social, pure." A volume of his sermons was published, and he wrote his autobiography. He was a member of every General Conference for thirty years, and usually lead his delegation. His debate with Orange Scott in the General Conference of 1836, gave him a great reputation throughout the Church. In the General Conference of 1844, when the case of Bishop Andrew was under discussion, he was one of the leading speakers in behalf of the South, and the carefulness of his analysis and the keenness of his logic were hardly equalled during that debate. Stevens, in his History of Methodism, is quoted as saying that Winans possessed

a mind of astonishing power, comprehensive, all-grasping, reaching down to the foundations and around the whole circuit of its positions—not touching subjects, but seizing them as with the claws of an eagle. He threw himself on his opponent as an anaconda on its prey, circling and crushing it. It was a rare curiosity to critical observers to witness this rude, forbidding-looking man exhibiting in debate such a contrast of intellectual and physical traits. His style was excellent, showing an acquaintance with the standard models, and his scientific allusions proved him well-read in general knowledge. (History of the M. E. Church, Vol. IV, ppg 411, 412).

Twice was the degree of D. D. conferred upon him —by the Baton Rouge College, of Lousiana, and by Randolph-Macon, of Virginia. In 1815, he was married to Miss Martha DuBose, "a woman of great worth, of earnest piety, and sincere devotion to the cause of God." After great suffering, he died, August 31, 1857.

1809. On September 30, 1809, the Western Conference began its session in Cincinnati. Both Bishops Asbury and McKendree were present, but Bishop Asbury was in the chair only the first day. He was shifting the burden to the stronger shoulders of Mc-

Kendree. McKendree alone signed the Minutes as President. On his way to the Conference, Bishop Asbury had spent nearly a month in Ohio, preaching at various places. He comments on the great number of camp-meetings held in the Western Conference that year—Muskingum District, four; Miami, seventeen; Scioto, four, etc. The camp-meeting was a favorite method of reaching the people in that day. Asbury also visited his friend, ex-Governor Tiffin, at Chillicothe. He makes this characteristic entry in his Journal: "But these long talks about land and politics suit me not; I take but little interest in either subject. O Lord, give me souls, and keep me holy!" He was indeed a man of one work.

Two or three quite interesting things occurred at this Conference. Judge Thomas Scott, who labored in Kentucky in 1794-5, and who, after studying law, had removed to Chillicothe, Ohio, continued as a local preacher for many years at that place. At this Conference he presented an appeal from the decision of the Quarterly Conference of the Deek Creek circuit, where he had been charged with misconduct, and expelled from the Church. It was brought out in the appeal that the misconduct of which he was accused was, "that he attended a barbecue in the town of Chillicothe on the 4th of July!" For want of complete information, or some other informality, the matter was sent back to the Quarterly Conference, with a very conciliatory letter, urging that it be settled amicably in that court. Inasmuch as the records make no further mention of the case, and as he continued as a minister, we presume the matter was amicably adjusted.

In the examination of the character of the elders, it seems that some question was raised as to the orthodoxy of some of the brethren. McKendree, who was in the chair, thought that a committee should be appointed "to examine into doctrines," and report to the Conference. The Committee appointed consisted of Bishop McKendree, Learner Blackman, Samuel Parker, and William Burke. Certainly no objection could be offered to such a committee. Their report constitutes the only *official* pronouncement by a Methodist body on the moral status of infants of which we have any knowledge. It is as follows:

It is the opinion of your committee

I. That original sin is corruption of the nature whereby man is far gone from original righteousness, and of his own nature inclined to evil and that continually.

II. That the Savior of the world tasted death for every man; that all (infants not excepted) are benefitted by atonement; that as they were not lost in Adam by a voluntary act of theirs, so neither is a voluntary act of theirs necessary to their salvation.

III. As to the manner of qualifying infants for heaven, we pretend not to know, nor are we able to say how nearly, or how remotely the justification of an infant and that of an adult are connected, or how to get out of one into the other, with, or without, sin; to us these knotty questions do not appear to be revealed; and your committee humbly confesseth we have no intuitive knowledge of these things, for we have forgotten, if we ever knew, where or how our moral agency or accountability took place; nor do we know how it was with ourselves (much less every child that cometh into the world), a minute or an hour before or after this accountability took place; therefore to attempt an explanation is, in our opinion, to undertake what can not be performed. It is an attempt to be wise above what is written.

Hence we conclude that the proper way to preach the gospel is

I. To preach the fall of man as it is held forth in the Scriptures and illustrated in Mr. Fletcher's unequalled Appeal.

II. To set forth the atonement in its full Scriptural extent

as we believe Messrs. Wesley and Fletcher have done. And
when circumstances make it necessary to apply these grand doctrines to the case of infants, proceed to show that men are to
be judged by revelation of a righteous judgment, and will stand
acquitted or condemned according to their words, works, and
deeds done in the body; and that the law does not take cogniz-
ance of the words, works and deeds of infants, and so lay the
foundation of their acquittal, and leave them and their qualifications for heaven in the hands of a merciful Reedemer, and
where the Scriptures leave them, and so keep out of the field
of conjecture, which frequently leads to dissension, disputa-
tion, and schism.

But when we apply these grand truths to men as we are
taught by the gospel to do, we should authoritatively demand
repentance, faith and holiness in all their relative branches,
with their inseparable and proper fruits; the Gospel being our
standard.

The Minute states that "no amendment was offered, neither was there any opposition. The question
was called for, and it passed with only few exceptions."
Whether or not this pronouncement will be aceptable
to the reader it is not for us to say; but we think the
advice is good that we leave these knotty questions out
of our ministry as far as possible.

The Kentucky District was divided this year, and
became the Kentucky and Green River Districts.

The Conference this year suffered considerable
losses. Elisha W. Bowman, after more than ten years
of almost incredible hardships, was placed on the
superannuate list. Thomas Kirkman and Horatio
Barnes were discontinued, and Thomas Milligan, Nathan Barnes, Moses Ashworth, William Vermillion,
Thomas Church, Joseph Oglesby, Edmond Wilcox, John
Oglesby, and Joseph Williams, located.

Of the thirteen men admitted on trial, four of them
were assigned work in Kentucky. Samuel West was

appointed to Shelby circuit. The next year he was on the Cumberland, then until 1816, he was in Ohio. In 1816 he was stationed on the Limestone charge, but went back to Ohio the next year and spent the remainder of his life in that State. He served important charges in the Ohio Conference, and at one time was Presiding Elder of the Scioto District.

Samuel Hellums came to the Conference recommended from the Nollichuckie circuit. He was admitted and sent to Hinkstone. He afterwards served the Clinch, Fleming, Little Miami, Little Sandy, and Danville circuits, but was compelled to locate in 1815. He was later readmitted and gave two years to Hinkstone and Little Sandy, but his health was too badly shattered to continue longer, so he took a superannuate relation. He was said to be a most excellent man.

Henry McDaniel was recommended by the Quarterly Conference of the Hinkstone circuit. He lived in Clark county, and as a boy, had grown reckless and wicked. He is said to have been "an unpromising youth, ignorant and unlettered, and his manners of the most uncouth and rustic order." But in a revival at old Ebenezer church, he was converted, and his conversion brought an entire change in his character. Giving evidence of ability, if developed, Rev. Williams Kavanaugh, then teaching a school in Clark county, took interest in him and gave him a start in the matter of getting an education. He was admitted on trial at this Conference and continued for thirty years, one of the most respected and useful of our men. He spent five years on Salt River, Hinkstone, Limestone, Danville, and Shelby circuits, and was then compelled to retire from active service for three years. In 1817 he was on Limestone circuit, then after another year's rest, was sent to Georgetown, "to change with Nathaniel Harris," at Lexington station. While at Georgetown, the place was visited by a gracious revival, the first that ever crowned the efforts of the Methodist ministry in that place. Sixty were added to the Church. In 1820, he was assigned to Lexington and Georgetown. In 1821 to Louisville, then to Danville, where he organized the Methodist Church. Here his health completely failed him and he retired permanently from active service. Later in life, he removed to Illinois, where he died in great peace.

Charles Holliday was recommended from the Licking circuit. He was born in Baltimore, November 23, 1771. His parents were Presbyterians and he was educated with reference to the ministry in that Church. Before reaching manhood, however, he lost his parents and abandoned the purpose of entering the ministry. Having married a pious woman, they united with the Methodist Episcopal Church. It is not known when he was converted, but he was licensed to preach in 1797. After being a local preacher for twelve years, he was admitted on trial this year and his first appointment was to the Danville circuit. The following year he was sent to Lexington, and owing to the failure of the health of his two colleagues, he was left to care for the entire circuit. In 1812 he was on Salt River circuit, and in 1813 was appointed Presiding Elder of the Salt River District. From that time until 1825, Mr. Holliday was in District work, serving the Salt River, Cumberland, and Green River Districts. He had fine executive ability and was peculiarly fitted for this work. He was able in the pulpit, kind and considerate of the men under him, and a general favorite.

In 1825, he was transferred to Illinois, and appointed to the Wabash District. In 1828 he was elected by the General Conference as Book Agent in charge of the Book Concern at Cincinnati. He remained in this position for eight years. At the expiration of his second quadrennium as Agent for the Book Concern, he returned to Illinois, where he rendered several years of excellent service as pastor and Presiding Elder. His useful life came to an end about 1850. There have been few men who were more useful and more beloved.

A man was admitted at this Conference who never served in Kentucky, but who is worthy of mention in these pages. We refer to James B. Finley. We have already quoted from his account of the great meeting at Cane Ridge in 1801, and mentioned his conversion while on his way home from that meeting. A few years before this meeting, his father, then a Presbyterian minister, came to Kentucky, settled at Cane Ridge, and became pastor of the Presbyterian Church at that place and at Concord, in Nicholas county. He also taught a select school, in which quite a number of young men were trained who afterwards became prominent of the affairs of both Church and State. So Finley's youth was spent in Kentucky, and he was converted in this State. After his admission into the Conference he rose rapidly, and became the superintendent of our first mission—that to the Indians. His book on "Wyandotte Missions" is of thrilling interest, and his Autobiography is a mine of information concerning the early times in the West. His "Sketches of Methodism in the West," contains more history of the men and the struggles endured in founding Methodism in this western country than any other work within our knowledge. Finally, it was he who offered the substitute resolution upon which the General Conference of

1844 acted, which action precipitated the division of American Methodism. His having spent a part of his youth in Kentucky, his having been converted here, the information he has given us, and the fact that he was the warm personal friend of many of our leading preachers, entitles him to a place upon the pages of our History.

1810. The place selected for the session of the Conference in 1810, was the Brick Chapel, in Shelby county, Kentucky. This was the first brick church building erected by the Methodists in the State, nearly all the rest being built of logs. It was located in a rich country community, and we have no doubt the people of that neighborhood bountifully provided for all the physical wants of their visitors.

But little was done that challenges the attention of the historian. Most of the work of the Conference was in the nature of routine. John Bowman and Daniel McElyea were discontinued. Jedidiah McMin, James King, Hector Sandford, Anthony Houston, Zadock B. Thackson and Richard Browning located. John McClure, who had worn himself out in Mississippi, was placed on the superannuate list. For the first time in the history of the Conference a set of Rules was drafted for the government of the body. Twenty-six new men were admitted on trial. Of these, seven were assigned work in Kentucky, viz., Baker Wrather, James G. Leach, Nathan Pullum, Samuel S. Griffin, Matthew Nelson, Caleb J. Taylor, and Marcus Lindsey. The number of Districts remained the same as last year, but several new circuits are added. In the Cumberland District, Richland, Goose Creek, and Cash Creek are new circuits, while Vincennes is transferred from the Indiana District to the Cumberland. In the Kentucky District, the Sandy River appears for the first time. In Mississippi, Natchez and Washington are made a station, while Amite and Rapids are newly formed circuits. In Ohio six new circuits are added: Union, Enon, Pickaway, and Delaware, in the Miami, and Tuscarawas and Detroit in the Muskingum District.

Of the men admitted and assigned to work in Kentucky, Baker Wrather was sent to Danville, and served but one year in this State. He then went to Tennessee, and after traveling Cash River, Abingdon, Dover and Nashville, was expelled from the Conference, on the ground that he had sold a slave, who was to go South, thus separating man and wife.

Samuel S. Griffin and Nathan Pullum traveled but one year, Griffin on Limestone and Pullum on Wayne circuit.

Matthew Nelson came recommended from the Danville circuit, traveled four years, all of them in Kentucky, then located. The charges served by him were Limestone, Hinkstone, Salt River and Jefferson.

James G. Leach was a good man, but very eccentric. He brought a recommendation from the Lexington circuit. He was sent to Licking, but stayed only until the second quarterly Conference when he left his charge of his own accord. He was admitted again in 1815, and traveled Salt River, Shelby, Breckinridge, Jefferson, Mount Sterling, and Fleming circuits, locating in 1822; settled in Carlisle, where he practiced medicine for a number of years; finally moved to Jefferson county, where he died, February 19, 1866. Doutbless his eccentricities stood in the way of his success as a preacher, but his religious character and his devotion to the Church could not be questioned.

We have already given a brief notice of Caleb Jarvis Taylor. "His praise was upon every lip. Distinguished for his refined manners, his masterly intellect, his great zeal, and his uncompromising devotion to the Church, he was welcomed wherever he went. Such was Caleb Jarvis Taylor." (Redford). Born in Maryland in 1753, an Irishman by descent, he was trained up under Roman Catholic influences. With a good English education, he left home and taught school. When about thirty-eight years of age, he married and came to Kentucky, locating about one mile from Washington, Mason county. He had been converted and had united with the Methodist Episcopal Church before coming to Kentucky. Receiving license to preach, he labored with great zeal and earnestness throughout the northern part of the State. In 1792, he organized the Mt. Gilead society, three miles out from Paris, in the home of Daniel Matheny. He was very actively engaged in the work of the great revival in 1799-1803, and being gifted as a song writer, he wrote many of the popular hymns that were used in that wonderful work. He rivaled John Adam Grenade as a songwriter during that remarkable visitation of the Holy Spirit.

Being admitted on trial this year, Mr. Taylor is assigned to the Fleming circuit, contiguous to the charge in which he lived. The following year he was assigned to Limestone, which embraced his own home. Gracious revivals crowned his efforts on these charges. In 1812, he located and removed to Campbell county, afterwards traveling the Licking and other circuits under appointment of the Presiding Elder. He was one of those local preachers who, driven out of the itinerancy by the necessity of providing for their families, were ever at work in every place they could reach.

The present generation of Methodists in the Kentucky Conference, who knew and loved the late Rev. W. F. Taylor, D. D., will recall that he was the grand-son of Caleb Jarvis Taylor.

Marcus Lindsey was one of the strong men of Methodism. Born of Protestant parents in Ireland, December 26, 1787, he came to Kentucky with his parents when about ten years of age. He grew up on a farm located about seven miles from Newport, on the road to Falmouth. He had educational advantages beyond those of most young men of the day. He studied law with the intention of practicing at the bar, but when his legal studies were about completed, he was awakened to a sense of his need of a Savior, and converted under the ministry of the Methodist preachers. Feeling called to preach, he was licensed, and in this year, 1810, sought admission to the Western Conference. His first appointment was to Hartford circuit, in what is now the Louisville Conference. In 1811, he was sent to Sandy River, one of the hardest fields in all the Conference. This country "was a sort of neutral ground between Kentucky and Virginia, and its deep glens, and mountain gorges, and dense, unbroken forests, made it the home of a daring, reckless race of individuals, and the horse-thief, and gambler, and counterfeiter, have often sought refuge in its dark defiles from the pursuit of justice." After this year and another year on the Little Sandy circuit, he was sent to Ohio, first to the Union circuit, then to Marietta. It was while preaching on the Marietta charge that he was instrumental in the conversion of that remarkable colored man, John Stewart, who, under God, led Methodism to its first mission to the Indians. Stewart was a drunken wretch, suffering from delirium tremens, and had started to the Ohio river to drown himself. His way lead him by the place where Lindsey was holding a meeting. Hearing the sound of the preacher's voice, he stopped to listen. Lindsey was telling of God's willingness to save the vilest sinners who would come to him, and the message found the heart of the wretched man. He returned to his place, fell upon his knees, plead for mercy and found it. He immediately joined the Church, and Lindsey gave him instruction in the way of the Lord. He had some education, was a fine singer, and the conviction fastened upon him that he must preach the gospel. For three nights in succession he had a dream or vision, in which he heard a voice bidding him go to the Indian nations to the northwest and tell them about Christ the Savior. So strong was the impression that this was his duty, that he started, not knowing where he was going, but following the voice he had heard in the dream. He finally came among the Wyandottes, and through an interpreter, he began preaching to them. Some were converted, and thus began the Methodist mission to the Wyandottes.

Soon after this, Lindsey came back to Kentucky and was a Presiding Elder on three or four Districts for a period of sixteen years. In the fall of 1832 he was stationed at Shelbyville and Brick Chapel. He entered zealously upon this work, though his family remained in Washington county on a farm which he owned. The awful scourge of cholera, which made its appearance in 1832, broke out with greater violence in 1833, and Lindsey, hearing that it was raging in the neighborhood of his home, left Shelbyville and went to care for his stricken neighbors. He became a victim of the dreadful disease. He had a presenti-

ment that he would be a victim, and in February before
his death in July, he is said to have written on an in-
side door of his family room, "I shall die with cholera
in the summer or fall of 1833." He died July 27th.,
and was buried in a grove near Thomas' Meeting-
house. Redford says of him:

His person commanding, his manners prepossessing, his
voice strong, full, and musical, and familiar with all the doctrines of the word of God, he wielded a mighty influence for
good wherever he went, and he went almost everywhere throughout Kentucky. The labors of his noble life were spent principally on large and extensive Districts for which he was well
qualified. . . . The loss of Mr. Lindsey was deeply felt by the
Church in Kentucky; for a great man had fallen in Israel, in
the prime of life, and in the midst of his usefulness. . . . In
height he was fully six feet, of herculean frame, and weighing
over two hundred pounds. His hair was black, his complexion
dark, with high forehead and brilliant black eyes. His nose
was very large, and his mouth delicately formed. He was a
member of every General Conference from the time he was
eligible until his death.

His hands and arms were badly deformed from
birth, but his intellectual powers were great. He was
a strong doctrinal preacher, and had no superior as an
administrator. His daughter, Mrs. Catharine H. Wilson, gave the money with which to found "Lindsey
Wilson School," at Columbia, Ky., in honor of his
grand-son, Lindsey Wilson, and Marcus Lindsey Memorial church, in Louisville, is named in his honor.

Another very remarkable man received his first
appointment in Kentucky this year. John Johnson had
been received on trial in 1808, and had given two years
to the Hockhocking and White Oak circuits in Ohio.
This year he is sent to the Sandy River circuit in
eastern Kentucky. There are few instances on record

where such an unpromising youth entered the ministry, and yet developed into such a strong and valuable man. He was born in Virginia. His father died when he was only a few weeks old, leaving his mother in destitute circumstances. The struggles of the family to secure a living were indeed pathetic. For some reason, the mother determined to emigrate to Tennessee. With all their belongings in a cart, drawn by a yoke of oxen, the family made the long trip of 600 miles to their new home in Sumner county, to begin anew the struggle for existence. John had no educational advantages, and was not able to read or write when he reached manhood. Determined to learn, he resorted to the cabin of an old negro man, who taught him the alphabet—all the old negro knew. Then came the effort to learn to read. He would often sit until after midnight, with no other light than the open fire, trying to "spell out" the words of hymns that he had learned "by heart." With dogged determination, he finally was able to read a little in the New Testament and to copy a few old song ballads, written by some of his friends.

His mother was a very pious woman, and her children were brought up around a family altar. A series of prayer-meetings were started in the neighborhood, and John was brought under conviction, and was soon after gloriously converted. He at once began to exhort others to repent and be saved, and almost before he was aware of it, he was the recognized leader in a gracious neighborhood revival. Jacob Young, then on the Cumberland circuit, received him into the Church, gave him license to exhort, and after six months he was appointed a helper on the circuit.

By most persistent efforts he made steady progress in his studies, and by October, 1808, he was an applicant for admission on trial in the Western Conference, sitting at Liberty Hill. While still a very ignorant youth, his piety, his earnestness, and his determination carried him through and he was admitted on trial. He went at once to his appointment in Ohio, and began a ministry that was successful beyond that of most of his fellows. His personal appearance at this time was grotesque, but did not hinder him from mastering the best literature of the day and preaching with great power and effect. Without following him in his steady rise in the Conference, or noting his improvement in all that belongs to a successful ministry, it is enough to say that, in 1818, he was appointed pastor of Nashville Station. Later, he was stationed in Louisville, was one year pastor of the church at Maysville, and when Valentine Cook died, Mr. Johnson was selected to preach his funeral sermon before the Kentucky Conference. Later still, Mr. Johnson located, removed to Mount Vernon, Illinois, where he remained until his death, April 9, 1858. This is a very imperfect sketch of a most remarkable man. If our readers could secure a copy of the book, "Recollections of the Rev. John Johnson," written by his wife, they would find it very interesting indeed.

1811. The last session of the old Western Conference met in Cincinnati, October 1, 1811. The Market Place was used by the Conference as the place of meeting. Both Bishops were present, though Bishop Asbury was in the chair but once, and McKendree alone signed the Minutes. However, Bishop Asbury examined the class to be admitted into full connection, and had much to do in making the appointments. William Burke, after acting as Secretary for eleven years, was

wearing down, and Learner Blackman was elected secretary in his stead. One hundred preachers were stationed, but Bishop Asbury states that they lacked twenty-two to properly fill the various charges. Ten Districts appear in the Minutes instead of eight—the
Nashville and Wabash appearing for the first time.
Quite a number of new circuits were formed. An increase in the membership of approximately 3,600 was
reported. William Young, because of illness, was placed on the superannuate list, and Eli Truitt, Hezekiah
Shaw, Thomas Trower, Henry Mallory, and Saul Hinkle were located.

A disvision of the Conference was anticipated, and
it was decided that in case of such a division, the
"lower Conference" next year would meet at Fountain
Head, Tennessee, while the "upper Conference" would
meet at Chillicothe, Ohio. In the plan adopted for a
delegated General Conference, each Annual Conference was to decide for itself whether its delegates
should be chosen by *seniority*, or be *elected* by vote of
the body. The Western Conference decided that its
delegates should be *elected*, by ballot. Under the rule
adopted, they were entitled to thirteen delegates, and
the following were elected: Samuel Parker, David
Young, John Sale, James Quinn, Learner Blackman, F.
Stier, John Collins, James Ward, Benjamin Lakin,
James Axley, William Pattison, Isaac Quinn, and William Houston. James Ward declined to serve, and
Thomas Stillwell was elected in his place.

Of the twenty-three persons admitted on trial, sev-
en were assigned to work in Kentucky, viz., John Caliman, Jonathan Stamper, Charles Bonwell, Benjamin
Rhoton, Thomas D. Porter, William Hart, and Shad-
rack B. A. Carter.

Mr. Carter was assigned to Somerset circuit, created this year, embracing territory that hitherto had been embraced by Wayne and Danville charges. He remained in the Conference but one year. John Caliman also remained but one year, serving Danville with Thomas Lasley. Charles Bonwell labored on Jefferson circuit, but his name appears no more on the list.

William Hart is said to have been a most useful man. He received two appointments in Kentucky, being sent to the Henderson circuit in 1811, and to Jefferson in 1817, remaining there for two years. In the mean time he was in Missouri and Tennessee. Like so many others whose zeal outran their strength, his health failed and he was compelled to locate in 1819.

Thomas D. Porter was a man of ability. He came into the Conference from the Nollichuckie circuit and was this year appointed to Licking, where splendid revivals blessed his efforts and a large increase of members was reported. He subsequently traveled Lexington, Cumberland, Jefferson, again the Lexington, then the Salt River circuit. In all these fields of labor he was eminently successful in winning souls. In 1818, he was appointed Presiding Elder of the Tennessee District, with some of the most able men of the Church under him. After three years on this District, he went as so many others had gone—health failed, and he was compelled to locate. He died in Texas, of yellow fever.

Dr. Benjamin Wroton was a North Carolinian—born May 12, 1792. He was converted at the age of fifteen, while at secret prayer. He came to the Western Conference in 1811 from French Broad circuit, which was then in the Holston District. He served in succession the Hinkstone, Limestone, Fleming, Licking, and Danville circuits. In 1815, he was married to

Miss Martha Jeffries, after which he located, and began the practice of medicine, receiving his diploma from Transylvania University. For many years he had a large and profitable practice in Versailles, Ky., where he lived as a local preacher and physician. It is said that he was a man of unquestioned piety, possessed a sound mind, vivid imagination, and much more than an ordinary range of vision. His sermons were characterized by clearness and classical finish. His life was a benediction and his death a triumph. The end came on February 26, 1863.

The subject of our next sketch can not be dismissed with a few words. Greatly beloved, a man of the people, a revivalist of much power, a writer of ability, a polemic of great force and clearness, a leader wherever he went, Jonathan Stamper was one of the most influential men ever admitted into the Western Conference. His mother was one of the first converts under the preaching of James Haw and Benjamin Ogden. Their home was in Madison county, afterwards in Clark, and the son was born April 27, 1791. He grew up under religious influences, but was not converted until he was nineteen. He has left an account of his religious experience, in which he tells of the profound conviction and deep anguish of soul through which he passed, bordering on despair. This, after about three months, was followed by a glorious passing from darkness into light—a conversion that was ever after a sheet-anchor to his faith. It occurred at a camp-meeting where the power of God was manifested in the conversion of many souls.

Out of the fullness of his heart he began at once to tell to sinners the preciousness of a Savior's love. He became a preacher in 1810, and was appointed by the

Presiding Elder to assist the preacher in charge on the Fleming circuit. After six months here, the health of Eli Truitt having failed, he was transferred to the Lexington circuit to take Truitt's place. Charles Holliday was the senior preacher. Several revivals attended the labors of these two men, though it was at the beginning of the War of 1812, and a time of great excitement in Kentucky. "The treachery of the British Government, and the cruelties of the savages, were themes of conversation in all circles, producing an ex· citement among the people which tended greatly to destroy all religious influences, and create a sad state of morals throughout the country." War fever was at its height. Young men in every part of the State were offering themselves to fight. Stamper enlisted as a chaplain, and left Lexington with the regiment on September 1, 1812. It is said that he preached to the men whenever there was an opportunity, and left "upon hundreds of minds an impression in favor of religion."

He returned from the army in time to take up his work on the Big Sandy circuit the first of December. In the Home Circle, a magazine published by the M. E. Church, South, in the fifties, Mr. Stamper contributed more than thirty articles under the title, "Autumn Leaves, or Memories of an Old Man." In these papers he has given much information concerning affairs as he saw them, including many of his personal experiences.

Mr. Stamper had splendid success on the Licking and Limestone circuits, which he served in 1813 and 1814. In 1815, in order to care for his aged parents, he located, but re-entered the Conference in 1817, having traveled under the Presiding Elder in 1816 the

Lexington circuit, which was contiguous to his home.
The Lexington circuit was very large, including all the
eastern half of Harrison county, with a part of Bourbon, as well as Fayette, Jessamine, Woodford, Franklin and Scott. He tells us of a great camp-meeting,
held this year at White's Meeting-house in Harrison
county, with most interesting results. Says he:

The town of Cynthiana had long withstood the gospel. Although repeated efforts had been made by all denominations
of Christians, no one of them had ever been able to gain a
foothold in the place, which at this time was given up to pleasure and dissipation. The people felt themselves secure in their
sins, and, like Gallio of old, 'cared for none of these things.'

On Sunday night of the camp-meeting, there was an immense concourse of people present, and the altar became so
crowded that the mourners were likely to be trampled upon.
Brother Thomas Hinde was there, and assisted very much in
carrying on the meeting. He said to me: 'If you will go up on
the green above the seats, fix benches for the mourners, and
form a ring of old members to guard them from the crowd, I
will take them up from the stand.' The arrangement was made,
and, when I gave him the signal, he came with the mourners,
some fifty in number. As they entered the ring, the power of
God fell upon the assembly in a most extraordinary manner.
Just at this moment, a band of thirty young men, who had come
from town with the avowed purpose of breaking up the meeting, made their appearance. They marched in rank and file,
their captain being armed with a bottle of whiskey. As they
advanced to the mourners' circle, the power of the Holy Spirit
met them, and they fell like men in battle; some in their tracks,
others after running a little distance; but not one escaped. In
twenty minutes the work had become so general over the encampment, that it was impossible to tell where the most good
was being done.

I have never before or since witnessed so great a display of
divine power. It seemed as if there was almost a visible man-
ifestation of the Holy Spirit; and the most reckless sinners
turned pale and trembled while they felt its awful presence.
The work continued all night without abatement. Scores were

converted; not less than two hundred persons were seen crying for mercy. The camp broke up on Tuesday; the people carried the sacred fire which had been kindled there into their respective neighborhoods. A meeting was commenced immediately in Cynthiana, under the direction of Father Cole, which continued until largely over one hundred were added to the Church in that hitherto wicked place.

This revival pervaded the neighborhoods of Mount Gerazim, Ruddle's Mills, Pleasant Green, Millersburg, Whitaker's Settlement, and many other places. In the space of six weeks, not less than twelve hundred persons professed religion. The work was deep and genuine, comparatively few falling back. Hundreds who are now in heaven were converted at that time, and a dozen ministers were brought out among the fruits of this mighty visitation.

After two more years, one on the Hinkstone, the other on Brush Creek, in Ohio, Mr. Stamper was made Presiding Elder of Muskingum District. In 1820 he was a member of the General Conference. In the fall of this year, he was brought back to Kentucky and placed on the Salt River District, then in 1822 the Augusta District, and for years he continued to fill prominent places and to be the acknowledged leader of the Conference. We shall have occasion to refer to him frequently hereafter, and will then tell more of his life and influence upon Kentucky Methodism.

Several men who had been admitted on trial previous to 1811, came to Kentucky this year for the first time, but no one of them gave more than three years to work in this State. John Phipps was this year on Wayne circuit, and 1815 on Green River. He spent one year in Mississippi and one in Tennessee.

James Dixon, an Irishman by birth, a man of splendid ability, was this year on Green River circuit, but for the most part, his ministry covered charges in Illinois, Ohio, Mississippi and Tennessee. After preaching for several years, he was afflicted with a form of amnesia, forgetting everything he ever knew. After a long illness, he regained consciousness, began learning his letters again, and in part regained what had passed out of his mind. He afterwards became insane, and died in an asylum at Nashville.

Francis Travis spent two years in Ohio, one in Tennessee, and two in Kentucky before locating in 1814. He was this year on Hartford, and in 1813 on the Livingston circuit.

Thomas Nelson was seven years an itinerant, spending this year on Madison circuit, 1813 on Danville, and 1815 on Hinkstone. He was a brother of Matthew Nelson, whom we have already noticed.

William Pattison was admitted in 1803. He gave only this year to Kentucky on the Shelby circuit. The rest of his ministry was in Ohio and Mississippi.

Joseph Oglesby, though born in Virginia, was brought up in Jefferson county, Ky. Converted at eighteen, he joined the Conference in 1803. In 1806 he was on Shelby circuit, this year on Salt River, and in 1812 on Fleming. His ministry reached the States of Ohio, West Virginia, Indiana, Illinois, and Tennessee, as well as Kentucky. He was a man of fine preaching ability, but broke down and was compelled to locate. He went to Indiana, where for many years he was very popular and rendered splendid service. He died at the home of his son, in Louisville, March 20, 1852.

CHAPTER XV.

A RETROSPECT

We have now reached the last year of the old Western Conference and it will be profitable to review the work done during this period of twelve years. The Western Conference was remarkable in many ways. In extent, it reached from Detroit, Michigan, to New Orleans, Louisiana; from French Broad, in North Carolina, to beyond St. Louis, Missouri. It included all or parts of twelve States—Kentucky, Tennessee, North Carolina, Virginia, West Virginia, Ohio, Michigan, Indiana, Illinois, Missouri, Mississippi and Louisiana. It is difficult for those of this day to conceive of the task of traveling this vast area. The method of travel was horseback. When Conference was ended, the brethren, who had brought their belongings to Conference with them in their saddle-bags, embraced each other and started out upon their perilous journeys. Mrs. Johnson, in her Recollections of her husband, says: "It was usual for ministers to take their families—especially if they were small ones—to Conference, in order that they might go immediately on to their work; as some, if they had to go back after their families, would have to travel several hundred miles."

In 1800, there were, in the Western Conference, one District and nine circuits; at the Conference of 1811, there were ten Districts and seventy-one circuits. In 1800, there were in all fifteen preachers; in 1811, one hundred and two preachers received appointments, and the Presiding Elders were expected to find twenty-two local preachers to supplement the work of the itinerants. In 1800, the General Minutes give the number of white members in the Western Conference as 3,183; colored members, 243. In 1811, the white members have increased to 29,093, and the colored to 1,648.

Kentucky's part of this increase was as follows: The one District in 1800 was called the Kentucky District, and William McKendree was the Presiding Elder. In 1811, the Kentucky circuits made up two entire Districts (except the Silver Creek circuit, in Indiana), and by far the greater part of two others. The four circuits—Hinkstone and Lexington, Danville, Limestone, and Salt River—had grown to twenty-one, while the white membership had increased from 1,626, to 12,265, and the colored membership from 115 to 894.

As already stated, the membership was largely in the rural sections. Methodism was slow in occupying the towns. In 1811 small churches existed in Lexington, Louisville, Nichólasville, Versailles, Shelbyville, Newport, Maysville, Flemingsburg, Hartford and Russellville, but there were none at Danville, Harrodsburg, Frankfort, Gorgetown, Covington, Cynthiana, Paris, Winchester, Mount Sterling, Richmond, Hopkinsville, or Henderson. There was no church of any kind at Frankfort. What was then called "Old Kentucky," was settled several years before the western part of the State, and the Church in the older section was ahead of the newer in members and material equipment. Later, with less opposition confronting it, the western portion made the more rapid progress.

The war with Great Britain was raging in 1812, and the country was in a state of excitement and confusion. As is always the case in time of war, the moral and religious interests of the country suffered from the general demoralization. Many of the men who were most active in religious work were with the colors. The restraints of the law were slackened, and wickedness of every sort flourished. War always turns loose the worst that is in men. But for this, Methodism in Kentucky was in position to do a more aggressive and effective work than ever. The country had been mapped and divided up into circuits and Districts so that almost every part was visited by Methodist preachers. Church buildings were being erected; many local preachers had come into the State; a splendid force of class-leaders and zealous laymen had been raised up; and the great fight with Calvinism had given Methodism favor with the people, who were attracted by the doctrines which represented God as a Being with heart big enough for all the world and a Christ who died that salvation might be sincerely offered to all men. The more rational teachings concerning God's goodness and Man's responsibility appealed to the intelligence of the people and gained for our preachers an access to the minds and hearts of their hearers.

The Organization of the Cumberland Presbyterian Church affected the work of Methodism in the western part of the State to some extent. This organization took place in February, 1810. More serious in its effects upon Methodism was the work of Barton W. Stone in Central Kentucky. He and those associated with him were Arminian in their teachings; and those holding to Arminian principles were thus divided. Their slogan was the union of all Christians upon the Bible, and their zeal for the "Reformation" was intense. These things made a strong popular appeal and drew many after them.

We have already mentioned a number of local preachers who were very helpful in establishing the Church in certain parts of the State. Many others had settled in the new country and were equally helpful. It is to be regretted that we know so little about some of these good men. When Jacob Young, in 1802, was forming the Wayne circuit, he found four or five local preachers who had preceded him into the new territory he visited. These men preached to the people as they had opportunity, formed classes, visited the sick, buried the dead, opened their homes to the itinerant when he came, and were often angels of mercy in their respective neighborhoods. But no records were kept of their labors and in many instances even their names have been lost to the present generation. But they are written in the Lamb's Book of Life, and will be known in the last day!

Among those whose names have come down to us, that of Thomas Taylor, of Ohio county, deserves special mention. He was a Virginian by birth. His parents were members of the Church of England. At the age of twelve years he became a member of the Methodist Church, and was afterwards one of its most popular and influential local preachers. He removed to Kentucky in 1802, and settled in the Green River country. The traveling preachers had not yet come into that section, and he ranged over Henderson, Hopkins, Muhlenburg, Butler, Grayson, Hardin, Larue, Hancock, Daviess, and McLean counties, preaching wherever there was an opening for him, rebuking sin, defending the Scriptures against the attacks of infidelity, and winning souls to Christ. "To no one man is Ohio county so much indebted for the moral and religious influence they now enjoy, as to Thomas Taylor." When more than seventy years of age, and when the issues that lead to the organization of the Methodist Protestant Church were so much in the thought of our people, he united with the new organization, but lived to serve in it only two years, when death ended his life of usefulness. His wife remained strongly attached to the old Church. He was a good man and served his generation well.

When James Gwinn formed the Barren circuit in 1802, he found in that section Richard Pope, a local preacher who had come from Virginia some time before. Pope had already formed several societies in Barren county. He had been a traveling preacher in Virginia, serving the Hanover and Bedford circuits. "Plain, pointed, energetic," he was abundant in labors, and left a lasting impress upon the part of the State in which he lived. He gave a son to the Methodist ministry—the Rev. Solomon Pope, for years a member of the Kentucky Conference.

Rev. John Pirtle settled in Washington county at an early date. He was an eloquent preacher, a most valuable citizen, and accomplished great good among the people in that part of the State.

Philip Kennerly came to Kentucky in 1807 and settled in Logan county. He was a native of Augusta county, Virginia, was converted at an early age and soon after was licensed to preach. After serving in the local ranks for nearly twenty years, he joined the Baltimore Conference in 1804, but after two years in the itinerancy, he located and came West. It was in his home, about ten miles north of Russellville, Ky., that Kennerly's Chapel was organized in 1807 or 1808. The society consisted at first of Philip and Jane Kennerly, John Hanner and his wife, and John Groves and his wife. A log meeting-house was built in 1811. Mr. Kennerly was re-admitted in the Kentucky Conference in 1821, and appointed to Christian circuit, but died on the 5th of October following his admission, being the second member of this Conference to enter upon his heavenly reward.

Ignatius Pigman, who was elected a deacon at the Christmas Conference in 1784, and served as an itinerant about Baltimore and in Virginia for several years, came to Kentucky and settled in the Green River country. We have but little information concerning him after coming to this State. Jesse Thomas is mentioned also as a local preacher.

In the bounds of what is now the Kentucky Conference, the number of local preachers of this period is larger than in the western section. Among them, none held a more honorable place than did George Strother, of Trimble county. Born in Culpepper county, Virginia, he came to Kentucky in 1796, settled first in Bourbon county, not far from Paris, then removed to Trimble county, where he built one of the first flouring mills in that part of the State. "Strother's Mill" became known far and near and drew custom from farms many miles away.

George Strother was present at the great revival at Cane Ridge in 1801, and has left a vivid account of the work as witnessed by him. While he was brought under deep conviction at this meeting, he was not converted until 1803, after his removal to Trimble county. This event took place in his own home while listening to a local preacher expound the Word. He at once erected a family altar; was soon made a class-leader, then licensed to exhort. He was licensed to preach in 1812. In building his house in 1811, he prepared a room large enough to accommodate the congregations who might attend the regular preaching services of the circuit, and for a long time it was one of the preaching places in that section.

His biographer says that "George Strother was the apostle of Methodism in that part of Kentucky where he resided." He knew and loved the doctrines of his Church and faithfully preached them to the people. He preached more funerals and married more couples than any man in Northern Kentucky. "His appearance in the pulpit was commanding, his eye black and piercing, his voice mellow and deep. His action was simple, yet with the grace of unstudied nature. He impressed you with his clear, strong, scriptural presentations of the gospel truth." He held the respect and love of all who knew him. He was closely related to Sarah Dabney Strother, the mother of Gen. Zachary Taylor. They both lived in the home of his grandfather, Capt. John Strother, and were educated in the same private school. He was a warm personal friend of General Taylor, and upon one occasion while visiting him, he was asked to baptize the children of the household, which he did. One of these children was Sarah Knox Taylor, who became the wife of Jefferson Davis. Three of his sons were Methodist preachers. His oldest son, Rev. Jeremiah Strother, was for many years a member of the Kentucky Conference. His grand-son, Rev. J. P. Strother, and his great-grand-son, Rev. W. B. Strother, are now members of this body; while his grand-daughter is the wife of the writer, and his great-grand-daughter, Miss Katharine Arnold, is a deaconess under the Woman's Council of the M. E. Church, South.

In this same county of Trimble lived the Rev. Henry Brenton. He came to Kentucky from Pennsylvania about 1800. His widowed mother was a member of the Methodist Church before coming to this State, and it was largely through her influence that Methodism was established in the county of her adoption. Her son organized the first society in Trimble county, known for many years as Mount Tabor.

It was Benjamin Whitson who was preaching in the home of George Strother when the latter was converted. Whitson came from one of the Carolinas to Trimble county at an early date. "Blessed with a superior intellect, and with an energy that was untiring, to which was added a holy life, he failed not to avail himself of every opportunity that was afforded to persuade the people to turn to God." Several of the early societies in Kentucky were formed by him before he removed to Indiana, finding a home a few miles below Madison. Amos Chitwood, another local preacher of Trimble county, removed to Indiana and was a neighbor of Mr. Whitson.

In the adjoining county of Henry, lived Elijah Sutton, a local preacher of piety and usefulness. He came from Pennsylvania to Kentucky about 1793. Shortly after his conversion he united with the Methodists at a society at Meek's Station, two miles from Newcastle. Later he removed to a home nearer Newcastle, and identified himself with a society which had been organized in the home of William Galbraith. For several years the meetings of the Mt. Gilead congregation were held in Father Sutton's home. Three of his sons became Methodist preachers.

Elijah Sparks was both local preacher and lawyer, and a man of no mean ability. Jacob Young mentions him as living in the bounds of the Salt River circuit in 1802, but in 1805, Bishop Asbury finds him at Newport, and baptizes two of his children.

Charles Sherman lived in the bounds of the Salt River circuit. His life and ministry were a benediction to the people in that early day. Reuben Medley and Eli Hobbs were local preachers in Nelson county, in or near the town of Chaplin. Medley was said to have been a very superior preacher, and Hobbs the *best man* that ever lived at Chaplin. The ministry of these men meant much to that section of the State. Reuben Medley was the father of Rev. John F. Medley, who took such a prominent place in the Western Virginia Conference.

In the bounds of the Hinkstone circuit lived John Vice, Absalom Hunt, David Anderson, and John Evans, all local preachers whose influence and labors aided in establishing the Church in that circuit. Besides those mentioned in a former chapter, Henry Robertson, Robert Miller and William Rogers were in the local ranks in the Fleming circuit; Michael Rouse in the Licking; Reuben Hunt, Jonathan Kidwell, and Jesse Griffith in the Lexington; Elliott and Henry Jones in Wayne; Samuel Harvey in Henderson; and others whose names have not come to the knowledge of the writer, blessed the communities in which they lived by their godly walk and earnest ministry.

Besides these local preachers, quite a number of excellent families came into the State between 1800 and 1812, who gave to Methodism solidity and strength, and added much to its respectability and standing among the moral and religious forces of the State.

We have in a previous chapter made mention of a number of such families who came into Kentucky prior to 1800. In mentioning a few of those who came later, it is with the distinct understanding that the list is by no means complete. Besides those that may be named, there are others just as worthy of mention, whose names are not at our command, or who, by reason of a faulty memory, are not recalled at the time of writing. It is a matter of deep regret to us to overlook any of the excellent people who aided in making Methodism in Kentucky, though it is impossible to avoid it.

We have already mentioned Winn Malone, of Barren county, who gave four sons to the Methodist ministry. Anthony Thompson, of Daviess county, was the father of three preachers of note. Reuben Wallace was the father of Rev. Thomas Wallace, of the St. Louis Conference. He settled near Campbellsville, Taylor county, where he remained until 1833, when he removed to Independence, Mo. Albrittain Drake, a North Carolinian, settled in Muhlenburg county, opened his house as a place of worship, and a society was there formed which became a center of Methodism in that section of the State. He was the father of Rev. Benjamin M. Drake, who became one of the recognized leaders of the Church in Mississippi.

In the bonds of what is now the Kentucky Conference, the Landrums, the Owenses, and the Scobees should be had in lasting remembrance. They were citizens of Clark county and were staunch supporters of Methodism. In Madison county, the Paces, the Powells, the Harbers, the Ballards, and the Bennetts bore a conspicuous part in building the kingdom of God in that county. The Robertsons, the Fitches, the Plummers, and the Dickeys were among the loyal Methodists in Fleming. In Mason, the Reeses, the Duffs, the Ingrams, the Kirks, the Armstrongs, and others equally worthy, contributed much to the establishment of the Church of the Wesleys. In Scott county were the Griffiths, the Houstons, and the Tomlinsons. But time would fail me to mention all the families who loved God and Methodism in those early days of the century.

A number of interesting incidents connected with the work of Methodism during this period might be mentioned as illustrative of the providence of God and of the labors of His workmen in this great Western field. One of these incidents is related by Jonathan Stamper in connection with the work of Charles Holliday, while serving the Lexington circuit. This circuit was very large, extending over into Harrison county. Says Mr. Stamper:

One neighborhood, in the hills of Beaver Creek in Harrison county, was famous for its zeal and religious fervor. Three or four local preachers among them were distinguished for their energy and perseverance in the cause of God; and the history of their conversion is so singular, that I make no apology for introducing it here. They, with some others who had long been companions in wickedness, and engaged in every kind of sport and folly, were collected together to spend the Christmas holidays. It was proposed that, in derision, they should hold a Methodist meeting, and one of the number was singled out to preach. He got up, and gave out for his hymn,

> Old Grimes is dead, that good old soul,
> We ne'er shall see him more, etc.

and they joined in singing it, after which all knelt down to pray. That over, the preacher took his text in the almanac, and commenced his sermon by telling them they were all a pack of ungodly sinners, and if they did not repent, they would all go to hell! After a little, a wonderful excitement seized him; a torrent of awful warnings flowed from his lips, as if the spirit of some powerful preacher was using him against his will as a mouth-piece. Strange to relate, he became powerfully convicted under his own preaching, and started to run, but fell at the door. His audience, greatly alarmed, attempted to make

their escape, but fell beside their preacher. All joined now
in genuine cries for mercy, and every one of them obtained a
sense of pardon before they left the spot.

Mr. Stamper gives the names of the men thus
strangely brought to Christ—Waggoner, Giddings,
Mullens, and two brothers Monigal. One of them had
been known as "The Blue Lick Devil," but after their
conversion they remained faithful until death, and
labored zealously for the promotion of the cause of
Christ. A gracious revival in that neighborhood followed this strange incident, and for many years the
community was noted for piety and good citizenship.

It was during this first decade of the century that
the controversy between the Methodists and Baptists
over baptism began in earnest. Burke debated with
Shelton, and McKendree, Page and others threw themselves into the conflict until a peace was conquered.

When Jacob Young and Samuel Parker were young
preachers, a revival of considerable extent occurred in
Henry and Gallatin counties, in which the Baptists,
with others, were quite active. Young and Parker were
zealous in the promotion of this work. Two Baptist
preachers came into the neighborhood, said they had
come to visit the county generally, and begged the
young brethren to go with them. This they did, and
the most friendly relations existed between the workers. One day when the service was held in a Methodist
meeting-house, Brother Ashur, one of the Baptist brethren, got up to preach. He stood and for a long while
looked over the congregation, then said, "I believe we
are nearly all Baptists today. . . . . As for Brothers
Parker and Young, I want them to be Baptists. I hope
they will come forward, give in their experience, and
be baptized, that they may be useful to the people."

Parker and Young very promptly declined to be proselyted, but a long and bitter controversy followed.

The Baptists then began to try to make proselytes throughout both counties. They preached hardly anything else but baptism by immersion. Our elder (McKendree) came round to hold his quarterly meeting at the mouth of Kentucky river. On Sabbath he preached a sermon on baptism. There were a great many Baptists in the congregation; among others a very respectable old lady by the name of C————, who became so deeply affected that you could hear her breathe all over the house. The friends had to carry her out, else she would have fallen on the floor. An aged man rose up and addressed the preacher in the following words, 'Sir, you have preached lies to-day, and I can prove it by the word of God.' The elder replied, very mildly, 'You had better take your seat and be still.'— Young, Autobiography, ppg. 78-81.

In the end, McKendree and a Baptist preacher named Kelly had a public debate on the subject of baptism; the pastor, John Sale, took up the matter and preached on the subject all over the Salt River circuit, and conquered a peace.

A little later, when John Johnson was stationed at Nashville, a Baptist minister named V————, from northern Kentucky, came to Franklin, Tennessee, about twenty miles from Nashville, and made a terrific assault upon the Methodist Church. "The Baptists actually thought he was going to wipe Methodism out of existence in Middle Tennessee." He then came to Nashville, and there opened his guns upon the Methodists.

He preached at night, and defied any man to dispute or controvert a single statement he had made. Mr. Johnson arose and disputed several of them. This led to a debate. V———— was pompous and defiant. The rules and questions were soon agreed upon, and it was expected that the debate would continue a week or more. V———— spoke in the morning on the appointed day, and then took a conspicuous seat, and pompously drew out his paper and pencil to take notes. He grew exceedingly restless during Mr. Johnson's reply, but still wore a look of confidence. In the afternoon, V——— spoke again, and Mr. Johnson replied. Next day V——— was not present, and upon inquiry it was found that he had left town. In a day or two Mr. Johnson got a note from Clarksville, stating that V——— was holding a series of meetings there, and making violent assaults upon the Methodist Episcopal Church. He set out at once, and reached Clarksville about nightfall. Of course he was present at V———'s meeting. The redoubtable debater presented his points, defied the world to dispute or controvert a single one of them, and wound up by saying that he had recently been attacked by a Methodist preacher at Nashville—he had forgotten his name—and he had literally sponged him out, and could sponge out any preacher in the Methodist Episcopal Church. To his unspeakable dismay, as soon as he had announced his appointment for the next night, Mr. Johnson arose in the congregation and meekly said: 'I will reply to what the gentleman has just been saying, if the friends will meet me at the Methodist Church tomorrow at 11 o'clock.' Mr. V——— was dumbfounded, but durst not now retreat. With the best grace he could, he stammered out . . . that he would be pleased to hear what the gentleman had to say. He took care, however, not to be present at Mr. Johnson's appointment, though it seemed that everybody else was present for the house was crowded to overflowing. V——— preached the following night, and left town very early the next morning.

In about a week, Mr. Johnson got a letter saying that V——— was at Hopkinsville, and requesting him to come at once and defend the Methodist Church from the terrific assaults being made upon it. He set out at once, and on the second night was in V———'s congregation, though unseen by V———. As usual, V——— threw out his pompous challenge, and to his consternation, Johnson arose and announced he would reply at the Methodist Church at 11 o'clock the next day. When the hour arrived, the house was jammed to its utmost capacity. For *five hours* John-

son poured forth a stream of "solid logic and hot shot."
It was said that not one person left the house during
this time, except V———, who slipped out. When
they looked for him he was gone, and was never seen
in that section again!

Another incident illustrative of this denominational
warfare shall close this chapter. This time the conflict
was not over baptism, but over the teachings of Calvinism. It is related by Jonathan Stamper, and occurred
at Shelbyville, soon after he had removed his family to
that place. He was Presiding Elder of the Salt River
District, and tells the story in his "Autumn Leaves."

"After becoming acquainted with the state of things in this
vicinity, I determined to preach a series of sermons on the
points of difference between the Methodists and the Calvinists.
The cause of my determination was simply this: The Methodists had been completely down-trodden by Calvinistic preachers,
who made a point of assailing our doctrines and usages in almost every sermon. Our people had become disheartened, and
were rather disposed to bow down and submit to this petty tyr-
anny, without resistance or defense. Such a state of things
did not at all comport with my ideas of justice or duty. One
Presbyterian and two Baptist preachers, all famed for talent,
had occupied the ground. These three men seemed to have arrived at the conclusion that the Methodists would tamely submit to be mauled and ridiculed at their pleasure.

"I commenced my series and crowds came to hear. The
above-mentioned ministers attended, to take notes and make
large threats; but I continued my course, regardless of all that
was said. At the close of one of my sermons, the following
notice was handed me:

"Mr Stamper: Please publish to your congregation that on
this day four weeks, Rev. Silas Toncray will preach in the Baptist church, in reply to the discourses delivered by you against
the doctrines of grace, commonly called Calvinism."

"I announced the notice, with the following remarks: 'I do
not consider this the best or fairest way of conducting this matter. Mr. Toncray and Mr. Waller have heard my arguments.

Those arguments are now fresh in the minds of the people, and if a reply is intended, this is the time for it. Mr. Toncray is welcome to the use of my pulpit, and I am the more anxious to hear him this evening, because it will be out of my power to attend at the time specified in the notice. I claim it as a right that I shall be present to defend myself.'

" 'We feel disposed,' said Mr. Waller, 'to make our own arrangements in our own way.'

" 'I hope, then,' replied I, 'that you will have candor enough to make the appointment at a time when I can be there!'

" 'That,' said he, 'is your own lookout; we shall not hinder you from being present.'

" 'Still,' I insisted, 'as you say you will not hinder me, I hope you will so arrange the time that I can be with you.'

"The answer was, 'We feel disposed to follow our own course in this matter, and it is our opinion that no one has a right to dictate either when or where the reply shall be made.'

"I rejoined that I did not dispute their right or power to do so, but hoped that the congregation would claim the right to look upon them as cowards, seeking to skulk from a fair investigation of the points under discussion. To this Toncray very quickly replied, that he was not afraid to meet me anywhere upon these points. 'Then,' said I, 'act like a man, and give me a chance to defend myself.'

"This brought them to a stand; and seeing that if they did not meet me fairly, their cause would suffer, they, after counseling together for a moment, begged to be excused on that evening, adding that they would be ready at any other time.

" 'Will tomorrow at ten o'clock do?' I asked. They answered in the affirmative, and I then announced to the people that Mr. Toncray would reply to my discourses in that house at the hour agreed upon.

"The appointment flew as if on the wings of the wind. As early as nine o'clock in the morning, the people were seen coming in every direction, anxious to witness the contest. Toncray and Waller were a little late; but when they came, I met and conducted them to the pulpit with all the politeness at my command. When we were seated Mr. Toncray turned to me and asked,

" 'What course are you going to pursue?'

" 'I think that is clear from what passed yesterday. I understand that you are to answer my discourses, confuting my arguments if you can, and that I have the liberty of replying when you are done.'

" 'I do not understand it so. My understanding is, that the matter will end with my remarks. I object to your replying, and you shall not do it.'

" 'But I will.'

" 'You shall not.'

" 'I will.'

" 'You shall not; and if you persist, I will not say one word.'

" 'You can do as you please. If you will not preach, I will. This congregation shall not be disappointed; and just as certainly as you occupy the pulpit, I claim the right of replying.'

"Brother Corwine, who was sitting in the stand with us, turned to me and said, 'Stick to it, Brother Stamper; it is your right, and you must not relinquish it under any circumstances.'

"After a few moments' pause, Mr. Waller said to his discomfeited friend, 'Don't back out; you can prevent his replying.'

" 'How?'

" 'Do you take the stand, and occupy it all day; you can keep him out that way, if in no other.'

"Toncray took his advice, refraining from beginning as long as he could, and then talked five hours and a half!

"I felt insulted by this attempt to take advantage of me, and when he got through, arose and told the congregation the whole affair from beginning to end. There was not time for me to say much, but I noticed a few of the gentleman's arguments then, and pledged myself for a full answer subsequently. I assured Mr. Toncray that he should be duly notified of time and place, and furthermore promised that I would not treat him as he had treated me on this occasion.

"One of his strong points, which I noticed, was the case of Judas Iscariot. Toncray affirmed that this man was a devil from the beginning, being appointed by our Lord in view of the part he should act. In connection with this, he remarked that the eternal purpose of God in the redemption of the world could never have been accomplished without a traitor; that Judas was predestined to that part, and did what God had determined he should do. In answer to this I said: 'If Judas fulfilled the commission assigned him by the Almighty, he was a good and faithful servant, and was certainly approved of his Master for his obedience. It would be a reflection upon the divine integrity

to suppose that he would be assigned a special work, and then
sent to hell for doing it. Furthermore, if one traitor was necessary in making up the twelve apostles in the commencement
of the gospel ministry, it is not unreasonable to conclude that
God yet has need of traitors in the same ratio; if they were
necessary in carrying out the gospel ministry in the apostolic
age, they are equally so in carrying out that ministry in all
ages. If the clergy has to lie under this censure, I do not see
why this community has not the right to say that Mr. Toncray
is a Judas as well as to say it of any other minister. If they
should charge him with this, he would have no right to complain, but should content himself to be hanged, and go to his
own place, seeing that he had accomplished the end for which
he was born. Judas and Mr. Toncray would have one thing in
common to console them in hell, if the doctrine you have heard
today be true; and that is, that they were both damned, not for
doing their own will, but for doing the will of God!'

"It was between five and six o'clock when the services closed,
after my announcement that on the next Sunday week I would
reply more fully to Mr. Toncray.

"The ball was now fairly in motion. The people were waked
up, and began to think and read for themselves. Methodism
from this hour held up its head in that region, its advocates being greatly increased and emboldened. Our Calvinistic friends
felt somewhat disconcerted, and complained that we should have
the impudence to attack the doctrines of the Reformation as
taught by Calvin, Beza, and others; but we held on our course
steadily, saying but little, and hoping and praying for the
triumph of truth.

"Mr. Cameron, the pastor of the Presbyterian Church, was
a Scotchman by birth and education—a generous-hearted man,
but uncommonly impulsive in his temper, over which neither
he nor his friends had any control. Being a strong Calvinist,
of the old school, he felt a concern for the safety of his favorite
scheme, and thought it incumbent on him to come to the help
of his Baptist friends. When the day came for my reply, Mr.
Cameron dismissed the congregation at what was called the
Mud Meeting-house, a few miles in the country, came to town
under whip and spur, and reached the church just as I arose to
commence. He pressed through the crowd, took a seat, and prepared to take notes.

"I took up the subject that day in regular order, from the

doctrine of decrees down to the final and unconditional perseverance of the saints, and occupied about three hours in its investigation.   After getting through the arguments against Calvinism, I proceeded to lay down the plain articles of Calvinism and Methodism in their undress, side by side, telling the congregation that they might inspect them at their leisure, and make what comparisons and deductions they chose.

"I read the first two articles agreed to by the Synod of Dort. My old friend Cameron could contain himself no longer, and rising to his feet, shouted out, in his broad Scotch dialect:

" 'Stop, Mr. Stomper! Stop, Mr. Stomper! I do not want this large congregation to go away and believe that we hold such damnable doctrines.   Mr. Stomper has dressed Calvinism in rags, and set the dogs after it!'

"At this, Philip Taylor, who was a magistrate as well as a local preacher, arose and commanded order, telling Mr. Cameron that he was disturbing the peace of the congregation. I urged Mr. Taylor to sit down, and turning to Mr. Cameron, assured him that he should have full liberty to say what he chose, without fear of being considered a disturber. This softened him into kindly thanking me for the courtesy shown, and I immediately asked him whether I had read the articles aright.

" 'Yes,' he answered, 'but they need explanation, and that you have not given.'

" 'I think an article of religion which has been signed by a grave synod, ought to be so definite as to render explanation unnecessary.'

" 'Well, Mr. Stomper, after all you have said, we do not differ so widely. You tell us that we must believe in order to justification, and I tell you that he that believeth on the Lord Jesus shall be saved.'

" 'Yes, Mr. Cameron, but your doctrines carry some horrible consequences after them from which ours are happily freed.'

" 'None that I can conceive,' was his reply.

" 'Will you permit me,' I said, 'to ask you two or three plain questions?'

" 'Yes, sir; and I will answer them. If I had a glass of water and my Bible, I would show beyond contradiction that Mr. Stomper is wrong.'

"Some one handed him a glass of water; and after he had drunk, I asked the following question:

" 'Do you believe that God has made it possible for all men

to be saved?'

" 'Certainly I do.'

" 'Do you believe that Jesus Christ purchased redemption for all men?'

" 'No; I do not believe any such thing.'

" 'Will you please to tell me, and this congregation, how those may be saved for whom Christ did not die, and for whom he procured no redemption?'

"The old gentleman, at once seeing the dilemma into which he had fallen, flew into a perfect rage, and declared that he was not bound to answer any such question. His Presbyterian brethren ran to him and begged him for God's sake to be silent, or he would injure the cause and ruin himself. But he cried out at the top of his voice, 'Let me alone! I will say what I please!' and so he made his way to the door, followed by his beseeching brethren, while the congregation was in a paroxism of laughter at his violence. Hundreds followed him from the church to the public square, where he lectured half an hour before his friends could quiet him.

"I finished the reading of the articles, and called on Messrs. Toncray and Waller for a reply, but they declined making any.

"Mr. Cameron published that he would answer my sermon on the ensuing Sabbath in the Presbyterian church. I wrote him a note, requesting the privilege of being there to defend the doctrines of Methodism; but he said to the messenger, 'Tell Mr. Stomper I consider him a gentleman—he treated me as such; but tell him I have such a devilish temper, I can't bear it, and he must excuse me for not granting his request.'

"It was circulated about that I had been denied the privilege of hearing him, and the leading members of the Presbyterian Church determined to stay away, so that he had only about twenty persons in the house. Thus the controversy ended between Mr. Cameron and myself. We were on the most friendly terms to the day of his death, and I always respected him for his honesty and simplicity of character. His impulsiveness almost amounted to a disease, but he was perfectly ingenuous and without malice; so that if he flew into a pet with me, it was soon over, and he was kind as ever.

> "A lamb that bore anger as a flint bears fire;
> When much inflamed, it shows a hasty spark, and
> straight is cold again."

CHAPTER XVI.

FROM 1812 TO 1816

The first Delegated General Conference met in the city of New York, May 1, 1812. The Western Conference was represented in that body by Learner Blackman, Benjamin Lakin, James Quinn, Frederick Stier, John Sale, William Pattison, Isaac Quinn, William Houston, John Collins, Samuel Parker, James Axley, David Young, and Thomas Stillwell.

The extent of territory embraced in the Western Conference made its division imperative. As we have seen, the ten Districts of this Conference covered all, or parts of twelve States, and it was impossible for one Conference to serve this vast territory efficiently. The General Conference divided it into two Conferences, viz., the Ohio and the Tennessee. The Ohio Conference was to be composed of the Miami and Muskingum Districts in Ohio, and of the Kentucky and Salt River Districts in Kentucky. To this was added a large slice of Pennsylvania and Western New York, which had hitherto belonged to the Baltimore Conference. The Tennessee Conference was to be composed of the Holston, Nashville, Cumberland, Wabash, and Illnois Districts, including all of Tennessee, Indiana, Illinois, and Missouri, a small part of North Carolina and all western Kentucky. The Mississippi District also remained attached to the Tennessee Conference, though the Bishops were given authority to make another Conference out of it if they thought proper to do so.

This division was an exceedingly unfortunate one

for Kentucky Methodism. The line of division ran roughly from the mouth of Salt River, across the State in a southerly direction to the Tennessee State line, putting the Danville, Salt River and Jefferson circuits (including Louisville) in the Ohio Conference. All of Kentucky west of that line was in the Tennessee Conference. This made the two parts of Methodism in Kentucky mere minorities in the Conferences with which they were placed—mere adjuncts to them. There were more than twice as many members in the State of Ohio as there were in that part of Kentucky embraced by the Ohio Conference and the same was true of Tennessee and western Kentucky. Unity of action was not possible on the part of Kentucky Methodists, and no enterprise looking to the advancement of the Church in this State was projected during the eight years this arrangement lasted! During these eight years the Ohio Conference was held in Kentucky but once—in Louisville in 1816—while the Tennessee Conference met in this State only twice. The center of gravity had shifted to other States, and very naturally the interests of Methodism in those States were paramount.

The Ohio Conference of 1812 met at Chillicothe, Oct. 1st. At this Conference Elijah McDaniel, Presley Morris and John Dew were admitted on trial and sent to charges in Kentucky. McDaniel spent but one year in the Conference, and that on the Jefferson circuit. Presley Morris, who was recommended from Madison circuit, was his colleague. In 1814 he was on the Fleming circuit, but his name then disappears from the Minutes until 1825, when he was re-admitted and traveled two years. John Dew spent three years in Kentucky, on the Salt River, Jefferson and Madison circuits. He came recommended from the Fleming circuit, and was a man of admirable character and of considerable ability. After serving for some time in Virginia, Tennessee and Missouri, he located, but in 1836, he was readmitted in the Illinois Conference, and appointed President of McKendree College. He died September 5, 1840.

Of men who had been previously admitted, but were sent to Kentucky for the first time, were John Collins, Daniel Fraley, John Cord, and William McMahon. Of John Collins we have already spoken in Chapter XIII. He remained on the Limestone circuit only a part of this year, when his domestic affairs compelled him to return to Ohio. William McMahon was removed from the Hinkstone circuit to fill out the year. Mr. Collins located at the succeeding Conference.

Daniel Fraley had traveled for two years, and was assigned this year to the Madison circuit. In 1813, he was on the Salt River circuit, after which his labors were confined to Ohio.

John Cord was admitted in 1811 and sent to Missouri. This year he is on the Cumberland circuit, after which he traveled no more in Kentucky. The circuit he traveled this year was not the old Cumberland circuit around Nashville, but another circuit of the same name, lying further up the Cumberland river and mostly in Kentucky. The old Cumberland District was also superceded by other Districts, and the "Cumberland District" which we shall meet in the future, was a new District lying almost altogether in Kentucky.

One of the strongest men admitted into the Western Conference was William McMahon. He was admitted in 1811, when the Conference met at Cincinnati, and served the Silver Creek circuit, in Indiana. This year he was assigned to the Hinkstone circuit, in Kentucky, and remained in this State four years, serving the Hinkstone, Lexington, Shelby and Jefferson, and Fleming circuits. His greatest service to the Church was performed in the Tennessee and Memphis Conferences, where, until he reached a very old age, he was among the greatest of the Church's leaders. While in Kentucky he was very successful, and many souls were converted under his ministry. He was versatile, could adapt himself to any grade of social life, and was the beloved leader in every community in which he labored. It is said that, in his day, he was almost without a peer in the pulpit.

His administrative talents have never been surpassed—not even by our most able Bishops. At Quarterly Conferences he conducted business with accuracy and dispatch. When difficulties arose—as they often did—his quick eye at once discovered the path of egress, and his guiding hand pointed to a safe issue. . . . At camp-meetings he was the presiding genius. He was at once the legislative and executive power. His rules to preserve order were wisely selected, firmly and prudently declared, and rigidly executed. No disorder was allowed, even in the earliest times, and among the most uncultivated people. . . . He was the ruling spirit among all classes, and with all people. Social, dignified, witty, full of anecdote, he was the delight of every circle, and the life of every company. . . . Few men ever possessed greater versatility of genuis. He was logical, lucid, illustrative, argumentative, observative, narrative, solemn, satirical, and hortatory. Below the medium height, compactly and stoutly built, with a large, round head, a very low, broad forehead, from which the hair was kept combed smoothly back, and beneath which shone out eyes of piercing power, he at once commanded the respect of all who heard him. The ignorant negro, the savage Indian, the wild hunter, the adventurous pioneer, and the man of high attainments, were alike awed into respect in his presence. (Rev. R. H. Rivers).

Kentucky was fortunate in having the ministry of such a man. Perhaps no man ever commanded the in-

fluence in the Memphis Conference that was commanded by William McMahon. It was he who organized the
first Methodist society in Georgetown, Ky.

The Tennessee Conference which met this year at
Fountain Head, received several young men on trial,
and sent into the work in Kentucky John Allen, James
Porter, Thomas Nixon, Benjamin Malone, and John
Bowman. Allen was sent to the Hartford circuit, but
died during the year. James Porter gave eleven years
to the itinerant ministry, one in Illinois, five in Tennessee, and five in Kentucky. This year, he was on the
Wayne circuit. Afterwards he served Somerset, Hartford, Fleming, then Wayne again, then located at his
own request. Thomas Nixon traveled the Somerset
charge this year, after which he went to Mississippi.

Entering upon the work this year, Benjamin Malone, son of Winn Malone, of Barren county, and one
of the four brothers who entered the Methodist ministry, traveled successively the Green River, Hartford,
Christian, Lebanon, Wayne, and Lexington circuits.
A useful man, who located in 1824, only because of failure of his health.

John Bowman served the Breckinridge circuit this
year, but his ministerial life was spent chiefly in the
Holston Conference.

John Manley had been admitted in 1809, laboring
until this year in Ohio and Tennessee. He was assigned to Livingston, then located in 1813. Samuel
King was in Tennessee two years before coming to
Kentucky. He was this year on Barren circuit, but he
also located in 1813. Joseph Foulkes had been on the
Elk circuit in Tennessee in 1811. This year he labored
on the Henderson, and the following year on Hartford
circuit. He then located, moved to Illinois, tried to take

up the itinerant work two or three times, but broken health compelled him to desist. He finally came back to Kentucky and found a home near Kennerly Chapel, in Logan county. His preaching ability was said to be above the ordinary, and in the local ranks he labored much and was abundantly useful.

The second war with Great Britain was raging at this time. War-time conditions very seriously affected the Church. Besides taking away many of its members to the battle fields—and many of these never came back—and besides that moral lapse so general at such times, the financial conditions of the country were deplorable. Jacob Young says:

We began to feel the effects of hard times. War between the United States and Great Britain was progressing. Provisions of all kinds were very high. Flour in some parts of the district was sixteen dollars per barrel, and other provisions in proportion. The more money the people gained, the less disposed they felt to pay quarterage. At times we felt discouraged, and some thought of retiring from the work, but their courage revived again, their wives were zealous for the good cause, and exhorted their husbands to weather the storm. Winter months came on—snow fell deep, weather extremely cold—sometimes we had not much to eat, and suffered greatly at night for bedclothes.

Those who had supplies were much given to extortion from their poorer neighbors. Some sold corn at two dollars per bushel, and Young tells of one man—a Methodist, too,—who sold his neighbors flour, taking their notes, to be paid in rye, after harvest—twenty-six bushels of rye for a barrel of flour. When he received the rye, he turned it into whiskey, making three gallons to the bushel, took the whiskey to the army and sold it at three dollars per gallon, in this way getting more than two hundred dollars a barrel for his flour! A money-madness seized the people, and a mania for wild speculation prevailed. Of course this led to bankruptcy in a short while, and the Church suffered by reason of it.

It was in this year, 1812, that Peter Cartwright began his very remarkable career as Presiding Elder. He was appointed to the Wabash District, which, though it took its name from the river dividing Indiana from Illinois, lay mostly in Kentucky. He was for fifty years a Presiding Elder. There may have been others who served in this office for as long a period, but we know of none other. At the end of this long service, a great jubilee was held at Lincoln, Illinois, commemorative of the event. A most interesting volume containing the addresses and letters, made and read on that occasion, was published under the title, "Fifty Years a Presiding Elder." Concerning his first appointment to this office, Cartwright says in his Autobiography:

I told Bishop Asbury that I deliberately believed that I ought not to be appointed Presiding Elder, for I was not qualified for the office; but he told me there was no appeal from his judgment. At the end of six months I wrote to him, begging a release from the post he had assigned me; but when he returned an answer, he said I must abide his judgment, and stand in my lot to the end of the time. I continued accordingly in the service, but the most of the year was gloomy to me, feeling that I had not the first qualification for the office of Presiding Elder. Perhaps I never spent a more gloomy and sad year than this in all my itinerant life; and from that day to this I can safely say the Presiding Elder's office had no special charms for me; and I will remark that I have often wondered at the aspirations of many, very many Methodist preachers for the office of Presiding Elder; and have frequently said, if I were a Bishop, that such aspirants should always go without office under my administration. I look upon this disposition as the outcropping of fallen and unsanctified human nature, and whenever this spirit, in a large degree, gets into a preacher, he seldom ever does much good afterward.

1813. The Ohio Conference met in 1813 at Steubenville, Ohio, on the first day of September. Both the Bishops were present. Ten young men were received on trial, but only one of these was sent to Kentucky. Jacob Hooper was sent to Shelby Circuit as the colleague of Henry McDaniel, but the next year he returned to Ohio.

Three men who had been previously received, were appointed to charges in Kentucky. John Somerville served the Hinkstone circuit, but returned north the following year. Daniel D. Davisson was his colleague, and James McMahon, gifted and eloquent, was on Madison circuit, but neither of them remained in Kentucky.

From the Tennessee Conference, which was held this year at Rees's Chapel, Tennessee, Kentucky received but one of the fifteen admitted on trial. John Schrader traveled the Henderson circuit, but remained in this State only one year. He continued in the itinerancy until 1821, laboring in hard fields, and proving himself useful, but was compelled to locate in the year mentioned. Of those who received appointments in Kentucky for the first time, Isaac Lindsey was appointed to Somerset. Returning to Tennessee, he located in 1816, and settled on the Cumberland river, some twenty miles above Nashville. Supposed to have money in his possession, he was murdered five or six years later, by a man named Carroll. Carroll was apprehended and hung for the crime. Samuel H. Thompson, said to have been one of the most incessant workers of his day, and who, prior to this year, had labored in Ohio and East Tennessee, served the Christian circuit. He then went to Illinois, where he served with great success and usefulness until 1841, when he died. He was a strong man and became an acknowledged leader among his brethren.

Samuel Brown was admitted into the Tennessee Conference in 1812 and traveled the Red River circuit. This year he was sent to Green River, then to Barren circuit. He located in 1815, studied medicine and practiced at Brandenburg until May, 1840, when death ended the career of a most excellent and useful man.

Claiborne Duvall's father emigrated from Virginia in 1794, and settled in Danville. Five years later he removed to Green county, and here, in 1811, the son sought and found salvation under the ministry of Thomas Lasley. Admitted in 1812, after serving the Roaring River charge, in Tennessee, he was sent this year to Barren circuit, then to Henderson, then to Christian. While on the Henderson circuit, he was instrumental in planting Methodism in Union county. He located in 1816, and the Church lost the services of a man who was eminently fitted to do great good in the traveling connection.

The winter of 1813-14 was severe. Jacob Young says, "The people were so much taken up with war and politics, that they lost their zeal in the cause of God. I suffered more with cold this winter than ever before. Sometimes I would have to pay fifty cents for a peck of oats to feed my weary horse, and I have paid as high as four dollars for getting my horse shod. I was often entirely out of money, but some one always took compassion on me and supplied my wants." An epidemic, called the "Cold Plague," broke out in the army camps, and swept through the whole Mississippi

Valley, carrying thousands to their graves. The doctors did not know how to treat it and their standard remedy of bleeding seemed only to hasten the death of the victim. Under these unfavorable conditions a decrease in membership was reported at the end of the Conference year.

1814. The little town of Cincinnati was growing, and was a favorite meeting-place for the Conferences. The Western Conference had met there in 1809 and again in 1811, and again this year the Ohio Conference held its session in the growing town. Bishop Asbury was present, but was too feeble to preside. Bishop McKendree had been thrown from a horse and badly crippled, so much so that he did not reach the seat of the Conference until near its close. He was very lame, but as soon as he reached the city, he took charge of affairs, which seem to have gone badly before his arrival. John Sale had been appointed to preside, but there are intimations that he was unable to guide the Conference very well.

Among those admitted on trial, were George Anderson, Russell Bigelow, and William Adams. These received their appointments in Kentucky. George Anderson was sent to Fleming circuit, but his name disappears from the Minutes after this year. Russell Bigelow was sent to Hinkstone circuit, but this was his only charge in this State. He was a great preacher. For twenty years he labored on circuits, stations and Districts in Ohio, and everywhere he charmed the people with his mighty reasoning and his almost matchless eloquence. Speaking of a sermon he preached in Chillienthe, the man who was pastor at the time says:

I have heard McKendree, George, Roberts, Bascom, Durbin, Simpson, and many others, preach great and powerful sermons, but never did I hear preaching attended with such divine power as Bigelow's. . . . He entered into his subject with all his heart. He chained the attention of all his audience. He proved his propositions by the clearest and most forcible reasoning. The judgment of his hearers was entirely convinced before he dismissed the theme. But along with this forcible reasoning there was the deepest feeling. His words penetrated the hearts of sinners, producing deepest conviction for sin, and they fired the hearts of Christians with heavenly joy. He is described by Mrs. L. L. Hamline, wife of the Bishop of that name, as follows: I wish you could have heard our backwoods orator. . . . A man of low, irregular figure—brown and sunburnt complexion —a mouth considerably toward one side of his face—of extremely rustic attire, and a manner as unpolished as his person. But disposition to smile would have given way to veneration for God's gifted messenger; then, perchance, your tears would have coursed in rapid succession at his pathetic appeals in behalf of the Man of Sorrows—the sinner's Friend; then you would have been overwhelmed by the weight of argument brought to bear upon the truths of the gospel; and, finally, you would have retired quite transformed in all the desires and purposes of your heart.

Russell Bigelow is recognized as one of the really great pulpit orators of Methodism, and good in character as he was fine in speech.

Among those admitted at this Conference, the man who meant most to Kentucky Methodism was William Adams. His ministry was given wholly to this State. When the Kentucky Conference held its first session in 1821, he was its first secretary, and retained that position for thirteen years. He was born in Virginia in 1785. He was a nephew of William Watters, the first native American traveling preacher. His father, Simon Adams, came to Kentucky in 1786 or 1787, and located near Lexington. Simon Adams and Benjamin Ogden were soldiers together in the Revolutionary war, and when Ogden came as a missionary to Kentucky, one of his preaching places was the home of Simon Adams. William Adams was converted early in life, and was this year admitted on trial in the traveling connection. He traveled the Salt River, Jefferson (three years), Danville and Madison, Franklin, Shelby, and Lexington circuits. In 1822 he was appointed Presiding Elder, and with the exception of one year, when he was stationed at Lexington, he continued in that office until his death, of typhus fever, August 5, 1835. Bishop Bascom said of him:

He had naturally a strong mind, and it was well stored with valuable information. To no mean pretensions to scholarship, especially as it regards English literature, he added an admirable store of theological attainments; and few men have appeared upon the same theater, whose every-day performances, throughout the year, ranked higher than those of William Adams. Although seldom overpowering in the pulpit, he was always lucid, strong, and convincing. His manner was singularly suasive and impressive. His moral and religious worth was universally known and appreciated among those who enjoyed his acquaintance. Grave and serious in manner, he was at the same time cheerful and amiable. Studious and laborious in his habits, he was always social and accessible. He lived beloved, and died regretted, by all who knew him well, and especially by those who knew his value as a member, and for many years the Secretary, of the Kentucky Conference.

His last message to the preachers of the Conference was, "Tell the preachers to live to God—to live to God alone." He died at the home of his son-in-law, Rev. William Gunn, in Shelby county, not far from Shelbyville. His death was triumphant. The words, "Glory! Glory to God!" were among the last upon his lips.

Of the men previously received, and sent to Kentucky for the first time, William Dixon, Oliver Carver, and John G. Cicil each traveled in Kentucky but

one year—the first on the Hinkstone, the second on
the Big Sandy, and the third on the Lexington circuit.
Robert C. Hatton was a man of good ability and was
eminently useful. He traveled this year on the Cumberland circuit, then went back to Ohio. In 1831, he withdrew from the Methodist Episcopal Church, and united
with the Methodist Protestant Church, but later came
back to the Church of his youth, and died a member of
the Tennessee Conference, in 1866—a man greatly beloved by the people whom he served.

Leroy Cole was one of the early preachers of American Methodism. Born in Virginia, June 5, 1749, he
was converted, united with the Methodists, and was admitted into the traveling ministry in 1777. At that
time there were only thirty-six traveling preachers in
America, and fewer than seven thousand members. His
first appointment was to the Tar River circuit, in
North Carolina, and he traveled through the period of
the Revolutionary War. During this period, prejudices against the Methodists were bitter and unreasonable, and Cole was a victim of this violent prejudice. He was arraigned on charges, and, upon the testimony of his persecutors, he was expelled from the
ministry and the Church. In less than a year, however,
the Conference was convinced of his entire innocence,
and asked him to return to the Church, which he did.
He was at once put in charge of a District. He was one
of the twelve men elected and ordained elders by the
Christmas Confrence of 1784. After a few more
years of hard service, he located. He came to
Kentucky in 1808. Having married a daughter of
the famous Dr. Hinde, he settled in Clark county, at no
great distance from his father-in-law, and was eminently useful as a local preacher until this year, 1814,

when he was re-admitted into the Conference and appointed to the Licking circuit. After two years on this circuit, he was superannuated, and, we think, made his home near Cynthiana until death, which occurred in 1830. It was he who organized the first Methodist church in that place. We have already given an account of the great camp-meeting held in Harrison county, not far from Cynthiana, which resulted in a great awakening and ingathering into the Church. "Father Cole," as he was affectionately called, was the prime mover in that camp-meeting and as soon as it was over, he began a meeting in Cynthiana, which resulted in the saving of many souls. About four hundred in this place and in the vicinity around, were added to the Church, and the revival spread in every direction. Jonathan Stamper states that in six weeks something like twelve hundred professed conversion. Father Cole was a great believer in camp-meetings, and was the main cause of their revival after they had become unpopular, following the extravagances of the revival at the beginning of the century. It should be borne in mind that Leroy Cole was, by marriage, an uncle of Bishop Kavanaugh.

Francis Landrum was one of the family of Landrums who settled in Clark county, Ky., and were such loyal supporters of Methodism in that section. He was born in Virginia in 1789, and was converted and licensed to preach in that State. He came to Kentucky in 1810, and was admitted into the Western Conference in 1811. His first work in Kentucky was this year on the Big and Little Sandy circuit, one of the roughest and most mountainous parts of the State. His ministry, from this time until his death, was given to Kentucky, with the exception of one year on the White

Oak circuit, in Ohio. His last appointment was to the Jefferson circuit, but he died at Augusta, Kentucky, in the fall of 1834. Dr. Bascom preached his funeral, and he was buried in the lot surrounding the old Methodist church in that town. During the course of his ministry, he received about five thousand persons into the Methodist Church.

Bishop Asbury had been accustomed to look after every detail of the Annual Conferences, watching and guiding them like a father watching and guiding his little children. But, too sick to be in the Conference room, and the Conference, with John Sale as President, going forward with the business, the old man saw that the American Methodists were now capable of taking care of themselves, and he makes this entry in his Journal: "One thing I remark—our Conferences are out of their infancy; their rulers can now be called from among themselves." He had been a *father* from the beginning, but he is fast hastening to the end of his pilgrimage. After the Conference, he pulled himself together and started to western Kentucky to be present at the Tennessee Conference, which met at Kennerly's Chapel, September 29th. Only one of the new recruits in the Tennessee Conference was stationed in Kentucky this year, viz., George McNelly.

George McNelly was the son of William McNelly, one of the first fruits of the Methodist missionaries in the Cumberland country—a good man, and a useful exhorter in his community. George McNelly, being admitted this year, was assigned to Hartford circuit, with W. F. King as his colleague. His ministry was mostly in the western part of the State, the only charge he served in central Kentucky being Danville and Harrodsburg, in 1836. For three years he was Secretary of the Conference and three times was elected a delegate to the General Conference. In 1837, he was agent for Augusta College. By all accounts he was a devoted servant of God and the Church.

Several men appeared in Kentucky from this Conference who had hitherto served in other portions of the Church. Jesse Hale was appointed to Livingstor this year, then went to Missouri and Illinois, where he spent several years in useful labors. Thomas Bailey traveled the Wayne circuit this year and Somerset the next, then located. Haman Bailey gave only this year to Kentucky, serving the Green River charge. Nicholas Norwood was assigned to Somerset this year, then returned to East Tennessee, where, in 1819, complaints were brought against him and he was left without appointment. William F. King, who was colleague to George McNelly on the Livingston circuit, traveled six years and was a faithful minister of Jesus Christ.

1815. Bishop Thomas Coke died May 2, 1814, while enroute to India, to establish a mission in that far-off land. He died and was buried at sea, somewhere in the Indian ocean. His heart was ever burning for the extension of the kingdom of God. During the last years of Mr. Wesley's life, when the great founder of Methodism was old and his strength was failing, Coke assisted him very much by traveling extensively throughout England, Ireland, Scotland, and Wales, preaching and superintending the interests of the Societies. After Wesley's death, he went at once from America to England, and was of such value in directing the affairs of Methodism that the British brethren wrote the American Methodists, requesting that they allow Coke to remain in England and assist in carrying forward the great work begun by the Wesleys. This request was granted, and most of his time between 1792 and 1814 was spent in England, though he made frequent visits to America. He established the Methodist mission in the West Indies, and was successful in starting a mission among the French. He was very anxious to begin mission work among the Indians and among the Germans in America. Having inherited a considerable fortune and having married a woman of wealth whose money was placed at the disposal of her husband to be used in the Lord's work, he bore his own expenses in all his travels.

He proposed to the Wesleyan Conference that he would go personally as a missionary to the East Indies. The Conference objected on account of the expense, but he offered to bear the entire expense himself, to the amount of $30,000; and selecting some six missionaries he embarked with them. . . . A few days before the company expected to land, having retired to rest, feeling a little unwell, he was found in the morning dead in his room. No man in Methodism except Mr. Wesley did more for the extension of the work throughout the world than did Dr. Coke.

Asbury and Coke could not always agree, but Asbury held Coke in highest esteem. He regarded him, next to Wesley, as the greatest man of his century. Asbury was growing more and more feeble. He realized that the end was not far off. Nevertheless, he started out, in the fall of 1815, upon another round of Conferences. The Rev. John Wesley Bond had for sometime been his traveling companion, and he cared for the old Bishop as if he had been a child. He lifted him in and out of his carriage, and carried him to a chair or platform, from which the Bishop preached or presided over a Conference. It was not his age, but his toils that wore him down to this helpless condition. He was

only seventy. Many men at that age are physically
strong, but the incessant labors, the long journeys,
the exposures, the hard fare, together with asthma
and rheumatism, had worn out his body and brought
him near his end. He well knew that his life's work
was about done, and seriously began to shift the bur-
dens to the shoulders of McKendree. He had a long
talk with McKendree about the division of the work
in the West into five Annual Conferences, and other
matters. He had resigned the presidency of the Conferences to his younger colleague, but still insisted
on making the appointments. Jacob Young, who was
one of the Presiding Elders of the Ohio Conference,
tells us that the Elders assisted him a great deal, that
he made the appointments with great care, and prayed
much before he would allow the name of any preacher
written down. When he reached Lebanon, the seat of
the Ohio Conference this year, he was, on Sunday, prevailed upon to preach a funeral sermon of Bishop
Coke, and though not able to walk or stand, he preached
the sermon sitting in his carriage, in the market-place,
to a very large congregation.

At this Conference of 1815, several things occurred
worthy of note. Among them, Jonathan Stamper located for a time in order to care for his aged parents,
and his efficient services were lost to the itinerancy
for a while.

The Minutes state that "William Burke *continued*
superannuated." The very imperfect Minutes of the
preceding year make no mention of it, but it is evident
that he retired in 1814. For twenty-one years he had
been in the forefront of every battle of Western Methodism. He was one of the ablest and most devoted of
the pioneers. Making the rounds of circuits larger

than any of the Districts we have now; traveling Districts which reached into several States; diligent in warding off false doctrines and in defending the faith; holding great camp-meetings; pioneering work in parts of the country where no other preacher had been, he at last felt the wear of these extensive labors, and asked for less burdensome work. He was assigned to Cincinnati, in 1811, and was the first stationed preached in that city. After his retirement, he was appointed judge of the county and served in that capacity for some time. He was then appointed Post Master of Cincinnati, and through successive administrations, served for twenty-eight years. He was a leading citizen of the city, as well as a devout and powerful preacher of the gospel. His voice had grown husky, his bodily strength was impaired, but he continued in a superannuate relation to do much in promoting the Master's cause.

Unfortunately, a difficulty of some kind arose between him and his Presiding Elder. The matter was said to have been trifling, but Burke was charged with treating the Elder with contempt, and largely through mismanagement of the case, he was suspended from the ministry for one year. He took the sentence meekly and submitted to it until the expiration of the time. Then, thinking he had met the requirements of the law, he took his seat in the next session of the Conference, supposing the matter ended. But in some unexplained way, the case was brought up again. John Sale was presiding at the time, and seems not to have handled the case correctly. Any how, it got into a legal tangle, and finally resulted in Burke's expulsion from the ministry and Church. He took an appeal to the General Conference, but this body could give him no relief. He refused to make acknowledgment for things of which he felt himself innocent, and for twenty years or more he lived out of the Methodist Episcopal Church. Every account we have seen agrees that the Conference was more in the wrong than Burke. In the meantime, he organized an independent church, usually spoken of as "Judge Burke's church," in which he preached and did mission work. For a time he was connected with the movement which resulted in the organization of the Methodist Protestant Church, but did not join that body. He was finally restored to membership in the Methodist Episcopal Church, and when the Church was divided in 1845, he cast his lot with the M. E. Church, South, and brought his whole congregation with him. This was the occasion of our having "Soule Chapel" in Cincinnati, of which we shall have more to say hereafter. The following extract from "Pictures of Early Methodism in Ohio," will give the reader an idea of the esteem in which he was held:

William Burke was born in Loudon county, Virginia, January 13, 1770. He was converted at the age of twenty-one, and almost immediately began to exhort, and soon after to preach, even without a license. He showed himself a man of ability from the very first. In argument he had few equals; in doctrine he was incorrupt; in character blameless; and he knew how to reach the consciences and the hearts of his hearers. Wherever he labored he built up the Church. Many were the fruits of his ministry. He traveled large circuits and still larger districts, and the work prospered in his hands. As already intimated, he was the preacher in Cincinnati in 1811. The only church which the Methodists then owned was a small stone edifice erected where Wesley Chapel now stands, on the north side of fifth street, near Broadway. It long went by the name of "the Stone Church." Here he preached three times every Sunday and on Wednesday night. While stationed at this church his voice failed, and became raucous and hollow; so that at the end of the year he had to take a supernumerary relation. He never resumed active work in the ministry, though he often preached, and in his later years he was a superannuate in the Southern Branch of Methodism. He died December 4, 1855, and his remains are interred in the Wesleyan cemetery at Cumminsville. A small headstone in front of the public vault marks the grave where he lies buried.

Of the thirteen preachers admitted at this session of the Ohio Conference, John P. Kent, Othniel Talbot, Andrew Monroe, Absalom Hunt, and John Tevis were sent to Kentucky. Kent and Talbot served but one year in the State, Kent returning to Ohio, and Talbot being discontinued at the end of the year.

Andrew Monroe was beginning a career which was destined to bless the Church for more than half a century. The first nine years of his ministry were spent in Kentucky, first on the Cumberland circuit, then on the Jefferson, Franklin, Fountain Head, and Bowling Green. He was stationed at Hopkinsville one year, and at Maysville two years. His last appointment in Kentucky was to the Augusta District. He was transferred in 1824 to Missouri, and stationed in St. Louis. For many years he labored in that State, and was indeed a Father to Missouri Methodism. Throughout his life he was eminently useful as a minister of the gospel; many were the seals of his ministry, and he was greatly beloved in whatever field he served. He kept a Journal which is frequently mentioned by Dr. Redford, but this writer has not been able to find a trace of it. He was one of the outstanding men developed by Methodism during the nineteenth century.

Absalom Hunt was a Virginian. He came to Kentucky when a youth, and settled in Fleming county, not far from Hillsboro. Here he was licensed to preach, and until after he had passed the meridian of life, served the Church as a local preacher. For sometime he lived in Bath county, but in 1815 he joined the Conference and was sent to Madison circuit; then to Lexington, then to Hinkstone, Limestone, Mount Sterling, and Fleming. In 1823 he was placed on the superannuate list, but in 1828, his health somewhat improved, he was appointed to Liberty circuit, and then, as supernumerary, his name is connected with Paris, Lexington, and Hinkstone.

In a sketch of him written by Rev. T. N. Ralston, D. D., he is described as

a tall, large framed, stately figure, erect and majestic in attitude; his visage long, with features large and masculine; skin dark, eyes dark and solemnly impressive; a long, flowing suit of coal-black hair, straight and neatly combed, falling all around upon his shoulders; his person genteelly clad in a suit of black cloth—the coat made in the old-fashioned, round-breasted, Methodist style, with the skirt reaching nearly to the floor; vest long, and rounded off at the corners; cravat white, perfectly smoothe in front, and buckled on at the back of the neck. . . . He was a natural orator. He had none of the accomplishments of scholarship. To be able to read tolerably well, and to write legibly, was the extent of his education. He knew nothing even of the grammar of his mother tongue, and made some awkward blunders in the pronunciation of words, as well as frequent violations of syntax. Yet all these were soon forgotten amid the commanding and overpowering influences of his good sense, profound knowledge of human nature, deep acquaintance with the Scriptures, clear and evangelical views of the plan of salvation, connected with his deeply earnest, tender, and ardent feelings, and the peculiar solemnity of his appearance, voice, and manner. . . . He was one of the most useful and soul-stirring preachers I ever knew. I have heard hundreds more polished and accomplished speakers, but as a natural orator, it is my deliberate opinion, that I never heard the equal of the subject of this sketch.

John Tevis was born in Baltimore county, Maryland, January 6, 1792. He was converted after coming to Kentucky, and after reaching his manhood. Licensed to preach, he traveled under the Presiding Elder for a few months, then was admitted into the Conference in 1815. His first appointment was to the Lexington circuit, then the Salt River charge. After three years on the Zanesville and Columbus circuits, in Ohio, he was transferred to the Tennessee Conference and appointed to the Holston District, on which he remained for four years. Under his leadership, it is said that four thousand souls were converted and added to the Methodist Church during those four years. In 1824 he returned to Kentucky and was assigned to Louisville Station. He then went to Shelbyville and Brick Chapel for two years, after which he became a supernumerary.

Having married Miss Julia Hieronymus, they opened "Science Hill Female Academy" in 1825, and the remainder of his days were spent in Shelbyville. Science Hill Academy was the first school for girls founded in the West. Eternity alone will tell the story of its service to the womanhood of the country, especially of the South. For many years he and his accomplished wife invested themselves in training and fitting young women for the part they were to play in life, and literally thousands of homes have been blessed by their labors.

Brother Tevis was a man of the highest type. One who knew him well testifies that he never heard him speak an unkind word, or indulge an ungenerous sentiment. Everybody believed in him. "A sterling Christian gentleman, a strong preacher, in every relation of life perfectly reliable, the amount of good which he did will never be known until God comes to pass his final judgment upon the acts of men." "He was a Bible Christian; this gave him a clear map of the way to heaven. Full salvation, by simple faith in the atonement, formed the theme on which he loved to dwell. He saw, in the strong light of faith, Christ present, able and willing to save unto the uttermost." He died in Shelbyville, January 26, 1861.

Mrs. Julia A. Tevis was a most remarkable woman. She was the main factor in Science Hill School, and after her husband's death, carried on the school for many years, and made it one of the most celebrated institutions in America. Young ladies from every part of the United States, but especially from the South, gathered in its halls and enjoyed the excellent training received from the very superior woman at its head. Her book, "Sixty Years in a School Room," is a marvelous record of the work of a consecrated teacher. Science Hill continued under the management of Mrs. Tevis until 1879 when the school was sold to Rev. W. T. Poynter, D. D., who presided over its affairs until his death in 1896. It has ever since been under the able management of Mrs. Poynter and her daughters.

The Ohio Conference this year sent into Kentucky three men who had been received on trial the year before—Sadosa Bacon, Jabez Bowman, and William Hunt. Bacon served with William Adams on the Jefferson circuit, and spent three years in this State. Bowman and Hunt were sent to Shelby circuit. Bowman remained in Kentucky three years, but Hunt returned to Ohio, and in 1819, charges were brought against him and he was expelled.

Leaving the seat of the Ohio Conference, Bishop Asbury came on through Kentucky to the Tennessee Conference at Bethlehem Meeting-house, near Lebanon, Tenn. It was his last visit to this State. On the first day of October, he preached in the court-house at

Georgetown from the text, "To you is the word of this salvation sent." He proceeded to Lexington, where he preached the last sermon he ever delivered in Kentucky, using Zeph. 3:12, 13 as his text. Upon reaching the Tennessee Conference, he was so feeble that he had to resign all the work of the Conference to McKendree. He says:

My eyes fail. I will resign the stations to Bishop McKendree: I will take away my feet. It is my fifty-fifth year in the ministry, and forty-fifth year of labor in America. My mind enjoys great peace and divine consolations. My health is better, which may be because of my being less deeply interested in the business of the Conference. But whether health, life, or death, good is the will of the Lord; I will trust him; yea, and will praise him; he is the strength of my heart and my portion forever—Glory! glory! glory!"

Thus gracefully did the Grand Old Man remove his hand from guiding the affairs of the Conferences. It was the last Conference he ever attended.*

---

*The following incident, occurring at this session, and related by Mrs. Johnson in her Recollections of her husband, will be of interest to our readers:

On the last day of the Conference, we came by to have our child baptized. The church was out of town; and the Bishop, that the Conference might not be disturbed, went with us a little distance into the grove, accompanied by a man who brought a horn-cup of water. This cup, I may say to my younger readers, was of a kind generally carried by travelers in those days, because not easily broken, and was made of a piece of cow's horn about five inches long, the smaller end being stopped by a securely tacked plug of wood.

We went to a large log, and the Bishop, pointing to it, said, in his inimitable deep and solemn tones, 'Sit down there, sister, and sit all the time.' I wished to name the child for my father, Thomas Brookes. The old man's stern features relaxed slightly for an instant, as he said, 'I'd call him Thomas Coke;' but, without further hesitation, he gave him the name of 'Thomas Br-rokes,' trilling the r and sounding the double as a single o.

From this Conference but one new man came into Kentucky—John Smith. He traveled Hartford circuit, but spent only one year in this State.

Jesse Cunnyingham was received on trial in 1811. He was in Kentucky but one year, laboring on the Wayne circuit. His ministerial life was given to the Holston country, where he was greatly beloved because of his gentle Christian character and the splendid work he did among the people.

William C. Stribling was this year on the Henderson circuit. He had been in the work for two years, in Tennessee and Missouri, but from this time until his location in 1827, he remained in Kentucky. He then removed to Illinois where he lived for many years. It is said that he was a strong preacher, but quite eccentric. We may have occasion to notice him again.

On the 7th of June, 1815, occurred one of the most tragic events to be recorded in this history. Learner Blackman was drowned in the Ohio river, at the foot of Main Street, Cincinnati. His brother-in-law, Rev. John Collins, lived in Ohio, and he and his wife had made a visit to him and Mrs. Collins, who was Mr. Blackman's sister. While returning to his charge in Western Kentucky, they reached Cincinnati, and spent the Sabbath. Here Mr. Blackman preached, and on Tuesday morning they resumed their journey. Boarding a ferry boat to cross the river, the ferryman hoisted a sail in order to facilitate the crossing. Mr. Blackman's horses took fright, plunged into the river, dragging Mr. Blackman with them. Before help could reach him, he was drowned! The body was recovered, and

---

He baptized by a triple affusion on the child's forehead as he lay in my lap, pouring at the name of each person in the trinity.

buried in the little burying ground in the rear of Wesley Chapel. Thus ended the career of one of the most useful, and most beloved men who ever preached the gospel in the Great West.

The quadrennium we have just traversed was a hard period for the work of God. The demoralization of the war with England; the depression in financial affairs which succeeded the inflation of war times; the madness with which people plunged into speculation during the flush period, and the desperate straits to which they were brought when this period was over—all these things were against the progress of the kingdom. While advancement was made in some directions, the Church hardly held its own during these four years.

CHAPTER XVII.

FROM 1816 TO 1820

On his way from Kentucky to the Tennessee Conference in October, 1815, Bishop Asbury, as his custom was, stopped at many of the homes along the way, prayed with and exhorted the people, and gave away a number of copies of the New Testament. From the Tennessee Conference, he proceeded by slow stages, into Georgia and South Carolina, where he spent part of the winter, going from place to place and preaching as his strength would permit. Knowing that his race was run, he deliberately set his house in order, made his will, leaving his horses, his books and manuscripts to Bishop McKendree, and to the Book Concern he left the proceeds of a few small legacies he had received. He wrote a Valedictory Address to Bishop McKendree, in which he set forth his views upon various matters. He started north early in the new year, hoping to reach Baltimore and be present at the General Conference in May, but death overtook him before reaching that place. On March 24th, he was in Richmond, Va., and there, sitting in his chair, he preached his last sermon. He went on toward Baltimore, traveling slowly, and on Friday reached the home of his old friend, George Arnold, about twenty miles south of Fredericksburg, Va., and there, on Sunday, March 31, 1816, he breathed his last. He was buried in the family burying ground at the Arnold home. But a few weeks later, the General Conference had his remains removed to Baltimore and deposited in a vault under the pulpit of the Eutaw Street Church. Later, the remains were again removed and buried in the beautiful Mount Olivet cemetery, in the city of Baltimore. We once stood by the grave of this truly apostolic man and were thrilled as we recalled the wonderful service that he rendered. Next to Wesley, Methodism has never had a greater man. More than any other, he gave to American Methodism its organization and its discipline, and infused into it a spirit of evangelism that has enabled it to carry the gospel message into every part of our broad land and to win millions to Christ.

At the General Conference which met in Baltimore, May 1, 1816, Enoch George and Robert Richford Roberts were elected Bishops. Bishop George was born in Lancaster county, Va., about 1767; received his first religious impressions under the preaching of Devereux Jarratt, the evangelical minister of the Church of England; was converted under John Easter; received on trial, 1790; made Presiding Elder, 1796; served the Potomac, Baltimore, and Georgetown Districts; was elected Bishop in 1816; died at Staunton, Va., August 23, 1828. "He was a man of deep piety, of great simplicity of manners, a pathetic, powerful, and successful preacher, greatly beloved in life, and very extensively lamented in death." (Simpson).

Bishop Roberts was "eminently a good man, full of faith and the Holy Ghost. He was a man of more than ordinary intellectual power, had been a careful reader, was a clear and forcible speaker, and often quite eloquent. As a Bishop he was kind and conciliating, yet firm and decided. His simplicity of manner, his great plainness, and his abundant labors greatly endeared him to the Church." He was present and presided over more Conferences in Kentucky than any other man ever did. He was born in Maryland, August 2, 1778. Was received into the Baltimore Conference in 1802; served charges in Baltimore, Alexandria, Georgetown and Philadelphia; lived on a farm, first in Pennsylvania, then in Indiana. Even while carrying forward his work as a Bishop he lived on his farm in a log cabin. He died March 26, 1843.

This General Conference transferred the Salt River District from the Ohio to the Tennessee Conference, thus making quite a change in the work in Kentucky, placing everything west of the Kentucky river in the Tennessee Conference. The Ohio Conference for this year met in Louisville—then outside its own bounds. Louisville was, at that time, but a small town, and bears the distinction of being the first town in the State in which an Annual Conference was held. Hitherto the sessions had been held at Masterson's, Bethel, Lewis's, Mount Gerazim, Houston's, the Brick Chapel, and Kennerly's—all of them in the country.

At this session of the Ohio Conference, four of the fourteen new men were sent to Kentucky, viz., John Linville, Samuel Demint, Samuel Baker and William Holman. John Linville was assigned to Big and Little Sandy, but at the end of the year for some cause was discontinued. Samuel Baker spent two years in Kentucky, on Hinkstone and Newport circuits, but most of his work was in Ohio.

Samuel Demint was a product of the Big Sandy region. It was here that he was brought up, here he was converted, and here was his first field of labor. Later he served Guyandotte, Newport, Fleming, and

Lexington circuits. His death occurred after the Kentucky Conference had been authorized in 1820, but prior to its first session in 1821. He was the first member of this Conference to be called from labor to reward. He was said to have been a useful, godly man.

Few men have done more for Kentucky Methodism than William Holman. He was born in Shelby county, Kentucky, April 20, 1790. His parents were pioneers. At an early date they removed to the Indiana Territory, where they were exposed to all the dangers of Indian warfare. At the age of eighteen, William Holman held a captain's commission in a company of citizen-soldiers, enlisted for the defense of the border upon which they lived. In his twentieth year he married Miss Ruah Meek, whom he credited with introducing him to the Methodists and leading him into the experience of salvation. His first service as a minister was as a helper on the White Water circuit in Indiana. Admitted on trial in 1816, he was sent to the Limestone circuit. This circuit was gathered around Maysville, then a small town, with a Methodist society of sixty members, most of them very poor. John Armstrong was the only man of means among them. They worshipped in a small frame building. Washington was a part of the circuit, though at that time there was no organization of white people, but a well organized society of colored people, with about ninety members. He then served the Fleming circuit for two years, then Hinkstone, then Newport. After this he was sent to Frankfort, the capitol of the State, where as yet no Methodist church had been organized. He succeeded in organizing a class, and in building a small house of worship. From Frankfort he went to Danville and

Harrodsburg, where he was quite successful in building up the cause of Christ. During the first year of his ministry at Danville, the church was greatly strengthened by a revival of great sweep and power. At Harrodsburg there was no Methodist church until the spring of 1828, when Mr. Holman organized with Christopher Chinn, Sarah Chinn, John L. Smedley, Nancy Brown, Elias Passmore, Elizabeth Passmore, and Margaret Tadlock as charter members. "From Danville and Harrodsburg, we follow him to Lexington, Russellville, Mt. Sterling, where he was alike successful, either in organizing societies, or imparting especial vigor and vitality to those established."

In 1833, he was appointed to Old Fourth Street Church, Louisville; subsequently organized what was called the Upper Station; succeeded in building the Brook Street Church, now transferred to Broadway—a change becoming a necessity, which he endorsed very fully and cheerfully. Brother Holman spent from 1833 to the close of his ministry—except two years—in the city of Louisville—serving all the churches, either as pastor or Presiding Elder. During this time his heart became greatly enlisted in behalf of the boatmen, and he succeeded in erecting a Bethel, to which he devoted principally the later years of his life, and that he regarded the most important and productive field in which his ministry had ever been engaged. (Rev. J. H. Linn, D. D.)

During the Civil War, though he had been a slaveholder,* his sympathies were strongly with the United States Government, and believing that the M. E. Church was more nearly correct in its attitude toward

---

*In a letter to The Central Methodist in 1897, Rev. J. W. Cunningham states that at the session of the Kentucky Conference in 1844, some one made a political poll of the Conference. William Holman was the only Democrat in it. All the rest, nearly 150 of them, were Whigs.

this great conflict, he united with that Church. Friends
of his say that he later saw his mistake, and acknowledged it, and at his special request was buried from the
Broadway M. E. Church, South, his funeral being conducted by the pastor of that Church. He said he wanted
to die among his own people. "There is little doubt
that Mr. Holman solemnized more marriages, baptized
more children, visited more sick, attended more funerals, than any minister that ever lived in Kentucky.
. . . . But he will be remembered because he adorned,
by his walk and conversation, the doctrines he
preached." He died in great peace, August 1, 1867.

Others who came to Kentucky from the Ohio Conference this year were Samuel Chenowith, James Simmons, and William Cunningham. The last named was
sent to Fleming circuit, but after one year; returned to
Ohio, and was expelled from that Conference in 1825.

James Simmons traveled four years; was on the
Licking circuit this year, and on the Shelby circuit in
1818. Samuel Chenowith was admitted in 1815, and
this year came to Kentucky and traveled the Lexington circuit. After a year in Ohio, he came back to Kentucky, and was two years at Mount Sterling, but located at his own request in 1820.

The Tennessee Conference was held at Franklin,
Tennessee, October 23, 1816. Of the eleven preachers
admitted, Clinton Tucker, William Allison, and Benjamin Ogden received appointments in Kentucky. The
only station filled by Mr. Tucker in Kentucky was the
Wayne circuit. Two more years he spent in Tennessee,
then located in 1819.

William Allison was seven years in the itinerancy.
Beginning his labors this year on Hartford circuit, he
traveled successively Jefferson, Henderson, Hartford,

and Breckinridge, then the Henderson and Hartford circuits again. His name then disappears from the Minutes, but he seems to have located and to have lived in the bounds of Hartford circuit, which he had served at three different times.

Benjamin Ogden was re-admitted this year. The reader will not need to be reminded that James Haw and Benjamin Ogden were the first Methodist missionaries sent into Kentucky. This was in 1786. In 1787 he formed the Cumberland circuit, then returned to Virginia. At the end of three years Ogden located. Redford tells us that he "was attacked with disease of the lungs, from which he had suffered while in Tennessee," and that he was so completely prostrated that his life was despaired of, and on this account he was compelled to retire from active work. As already stated, before leaving Kentucky, James Haw had married him to Miss Nancy Puckett, of Mercer county, which no doubt had something to do with his return to this State.

For a time Ogden was connected with the O'Kelly movement. It seems that, after the recovery of his health, he backslid, and for several years lived out of any Church. After he was reclaimed in the camp meeting on the Breckinridge circuit in 1813, he joined the Church again, and was soon re-licensed to preach. He was re-admitted at this Conference of 1816, and was appointed to the Henderson circuit. But before the year expired he found himself unable to undergo the strain of the itinerant work, and again retired to the local ranks. In 1824, he is again in the number of preachers in the Kentucky Conference, and for three years does effective work on Tennessee Mission, the Christian, and the Yellow Banks circuits. He is then superannuated, and remains in that relation until November 20, 1834, when, at the residence of his son, near Princeton, Ky., he breathed his last. Redford says:

A Christian of the highest type, his last moments were full of calmness and peace. Calling his family to his bedside, he affectionately embraced them, and exhorted them to persevere in the way of holiness, until they should experience 'the breadth, and length, and depth, and height of the love of Christ;' and imparting to each his dying blessing, in the full enjoyment of his mental faculties, and in perfect assurance of eternal life, he fell asleep in Jesus.

He lies buried near Princeton, Kentucky. A monument has been erected at his grave, and the new church built in Princeton in recent years is called "The Benjamin Ogden Memorial."

John Bloome, who had been admitted in 1815, this year traveled the Breckinridge circuit, but located at the following Conference.

Upon the roll of membership of the Tenessee Conference in 1816, was entered a name which is immortal in the annals of Methodism—Henry Bidleman Bascom. He had been received into the Ohio Conference in 1813, but was transferred this year to the Tennessee Conference, and appointed to the Danville circuit. He was the son of Alpheus and Hannah Houk Bascom, and was born in the town of Hancock, on the east bank of the East Branch of the Delaware river, in the State of New Jersey, May 27, 1796. He had the advantage of tolerably good schools until he was twelve years old, but was never a pupil in any school after that time. In 1810, when about fifteen years of age, he was converted and soon after united with the Church under Rev. Loring Grant. He began exhorting almost as soon as he was converted, and although only fifteen, the people were amazed at the fluency and pointedness with which he poured forth the truth. In 1812, or when he was sixteen, his father removed his family to Kentucky, and stopped for a time in, or near, Maysville. He remained here but a short while, then crossed the river into Ohio and found a home about five miles from Maysville, on the road to Ripley. Feeling the urge to preach the gospel, Bascom split rails to get money with which to buy a horse, saddle and saddle-bags. In February, 1813, he was licensed to preach, and under the Presiding Elder, traveled the Brush Creek circuit until the Ohio Conference met that fall. He was then received on trial and sent to the Deer Creek circuit as helper to Rev. Alexander Cummins. He was diligent, pious, and made rapid progress in all that pertains to the ministry, though severely criticised because of his *flowery* style. These criticisms deeply wounded him. He kept a diary this year, and his biographer says: "I have never seen any other diary, in print or manuscript, that contains so much of severe self-scrutiny, or so much of devout supplication as this of Bascom, written in his eighteenth year.*

---

*Before he was licensed to preach, Bascom, young as he was, was made a class leader. Rev. Maxwell P. Gaddis, who was brought up in the same neighborhood in which the Bascoms lived, quotes the statement of Samuel Fitch, that "the late Bishop Bascom was the most faithful and devoted class-leader he had ever known. Often when Eagle Creek was running full of water during the winter season, this young exhorter, Henry B. Bascom, would strip off a part of his clothes and wade the swollen stream, holding them above his head, rather than disappoint those who were anxiously awaiting his arrival.

When he came up to Conference in 1814, there were many ungenerous criticisms of the young man. He was quite handsome, his form was almost perfect, he looked very neat in even the plainest clothing, and he neither looked like a Methodist preacher, nor was he like one in his manner and movement. He had been very diligent in all his labors, and very painstaking in administering discipline. No fault could be found with his service or conduct; but

such a man—a youth of eighteen summers, of elegant person, apparel and address, after whom the learned, and wealthy, and fashionable were running, and with whom he was becoming an idol, was not the man to get on without some difficulties among the Methodists and Methodist preachers of pikestaff plainness of that day, and on the still sparcely settled frontier. Accordingly on going to Conference, though he had made some fast friends, he met with coldness from many from whom he looked for cordiality and encouragement. This he felt acutely, for his sensibility was expisite.—(Hinkle's Life of Bascom).

It is difficult for an ordinary person to understand a really great mind. Bascom was a genius, and was beyond the comprehension of many of those with whom he had to do. They said, "he is proud,"—"ambitious and aspiring"—"a clerical fop." Some said "He gets his sermons from books, and memorizes them;" but nobody could find the books! Others thought he would soon quit the ministry and take up the law, but they little knew the depth of his sincerity or the strength of his religious conviction. So, after debate, he was continued on trial, but sent to the roughest, hardest circuit in the Conference with the avowed purpose of curing him or getting rid of him! Many predicted that within a year he would "turn lawyer or take the gown." But Bascom went to the Guyandotte circuit, braved its dangers and endured its hardships, traveled three thousand miles, preached four hundred times, and received in all a salary of twelve dollars and ten cents!

At the ensuing Conference he was eligible for deacon's orders and admission into full connection. Yet, when his case came up, he was refused admission, and held on probation another year. He had labored faithfully; there was no charge of neglect of duty; no crime or heresy was urged against him; but the majority thought that "his dress, his gait, his general unmethod, ist-preacher-like appearance afforded strong indications that he would never make an humble itinerant preacher." This year he was sent to the Mad River circuit, on the border of the Indian country. Troy, Piqua, Springfield, Urbana, and several Indian towns were embraced in this circuit. He served it faithfully and well. At the Conference of 1816, the opposition to his reception was even stronger than ever, solely on the ground of his personal appearance and of his supposed pride. His fame as an orator was spreading everywhere, and this was taken as an indication of pride and presumption. The matter of his reception into the Conference was debated long, and it was evident that he would not be received. Bishop McKendree finally said: "Brethren, if you have no use for that boy in your Conference, admit, and elect him, (to deacon's orders), and I'll take him out of your way, and take care of him." It was accordingly done, and Bascom was transferred to the Tennessee Conference. He was assigned to the Danville circuit, and made Harrodsburg his headquarters during the year. The following year he was reappointed to this circuit, though Madison circuit was added to it, thus forming a field of labor extending from Harrodsburg on the west to the Three Forks of the Kentucky river on the east. But as the name and work of Henry B. Bascom will appear so often in this narrative, we will not pursue this sketch further at this time. This will serve as an introduction to America's greatest pulpit orator, and one of the greatest ecclesiastical statesmen of modern times. Perhaps Southern Methodism owes more to Bascom than it does to any other man.

1817. The Ohio Conference met at Zanesville, September 3, 1817. Bishops McKendree and Roberts were present. Twelve persons were admitted on trial. Of these, George Atkins, Thomas Lowry, John P. Taylor, and Richard Corwine were sent to Kentucky.

George Atkins was appointed to Lexington circuit, but remained in the Conference only this year. Thomas Lowry served on the Big and Little Sandy this year, but he was discontinued in 1819. John P. Taylor was in Kentucky two years, serving the Limestone and Fleming circuits, then returning to Ohio.

Richard Corwine was a Kentuckian, and gave his life to the ministry in his native State. He was born in Mason county, August 29, 1789. His parents being religious, he received his first religious impressions at the family altar. When twenty years of age, he was converted and united with the Church, but was not licensed to preach until 1817. Received on trial this year, he was assigned to Hinkstone circuit as the colaborer of Jonathan Stamper and with Benjamin Lakin as supernumerary. During a ministry of more than twenty years, he served Hinkstone, Lexington, Madison, Goose Creek, Shelby, Danville, Hopkinsville, Red River, Fleming, and Mount Sterling circuits; Louisville and Shelbyville and Brick Chapel stations, and Augusta, Hopkinsville, and Louisville Districts.

While he did not take rank in the pulpit as one of the first preachers in the Conference, yet his talents were above mediocrity, and he was always acceptable to the Church as a minister of the gospel. He never preached what the world styles great sermons, but he never failed to interest and instruct. His was not the flood of impassioned eloquence that overlaps its banks and carries everything before it; but it was the gentle stream that rolled smoothly on within the limits assigned it, equally sure to reach its destination, bearing upon its placid bosom the hopes of the world. Loved by the Church, and respected by all who knew him, Richard Corwine was a blessing to every community in which he lived and labored."—(Redford).

He died most triumphantly, at the home of Rev. James G. Leach, in Jefferson county, February 12, 1843.

Simon Peter had traveled the Columbus, Ohio, circuit in 1816, and entered Kentucky in 1817, as the colleague of William Holman, on the Fleming circuit. From that time until 1828, he continued to labor in this State, then located, and in 1832, removed to Illinois, where he succeeded Peter Cartwright on the Sangamon District. He was afterwards on the Lebanon District, and pastor of Alton Station. In 1837, the General Minutes contain the sad information that he was expelled from the connection, but give no clue to the charge against him.

From among the five preachers admitted into the Tennessee Conference this year, John Devar and George W. Taylor received their appointments in Kentucky. With Benjamin Malone, John Devar was sent to Christian circuit, and after one year in East Tennessee, we find him, in 1819, on Fountain Head, a large part of which was in Kentucky. In 1820, he served Green River circuit, and in 1821 and 1822 was Presiding Elder of the French Broad District. He located in 1823.

The itinerant labors of George W. Taylor began on the Barren circuit this year. It has been said of him that he was "a great and a good man." W. B. Landrum pronounces him, "one of the greatest divines Kentucky ever produced." Appointed to the Columbia District in 1823, he continued to preside over Districts most of the time until 1849, when, for a time, he was compelled to superannuate. During the period of his active ministry, he traveled the Cumberland, Rockcastle, Greensburg, Harrodsburg, Bowling Green, and Hardinsburg Districts. "But few men in the Conference wielded so great an influence as he. In the community in which he was brought up, and in which he lived, no preacher was so much beloved. His popularity never waned— the changes of time did not impair it."—(Redford).

"Plain in his dress, and artless in his manner in the pulpit, his style simple, and his sermons replete with the teachings of Jesus, his ministry was invested with an importance and authority that carried conviction to the hearts of thousands. We never heard him preach an inferior sermon." His ministry was confined mostly to country districts, but the confidence he inspired and the influence he wielded throughout Methodism in Kentucky have been enjoyed by few other men. After a year's rest he returned to active work and was stationed at Columbia for two years. Worn out by his arduous labors, he again superannuated in 1852, and retained this relation until his death in 1866. On Sunday, January 21, 1866, while performing the evening chores about his home, his failure to return to his house at the expected time excited the anxiety of his wife, who, upon looking for him, found him lying in the snow, dead! His remains lie buried on the farm which he owned, not far from Columbia, Kentucky, and the simple head-stone bears the inscription: "George W. Taylor, Born Nov. 13, 1790; Died, Jan. 21, 1866. For more than fifty years a faithful minister of the gospel of Christ."

Of those sent from the Tennessee Conference into Kentucky for the first time, appear the names of John Hutchison, Nace Overall, Timothy Carpenter, Benjamin Peebles, and Lewis Garrett. John Hutchison traveled but one year. Nace Overall was but one year in Kentucky; Benjamin Peebles two years; and Timothy Carpenter, three years. The Lewis Garrett mentioned here was not the Lewis Garrett who entered the itinerancy in 1794, and of whom we have already made mention, but was a nephew of his, bearing the same name. Lewis Garrett, Jr., was admitted on trial in 1816. He was appointed to the Dixon charge that year, and this year is assigned to the Cumberland circuit, mostly in Kentucky. In 1820 he was sent, with Hezekiah Holland, as a missionary "to that part of Jackson's Purchase embraced in the States of Kentucky and Tennessee." He was afterwards Presiding Elder of the Forked Deer District, then went to Arkansas, where he was for years an honored member of the Little Rock Conference.

At the session of the Ohio Conference this year, James McMahon, John Collins, Jonathan Stamper and Francis Landrum, were re-admitted into the traveling connection. All of them had located temporarily, but now they come back into active service. We have already mentioned the fact of their location, but this will explain the appearance of their names in the list of appointments in the future. Henry McDaniel, who had been on the superannuate list, reported ready for service again. William Burke, in the quaint language

1. Bishop Thomas Coke

2. Bishop Richard Whatcoat
3. Bishop Enoch George
4. Bishop Robert R. Roberts

5. Rev. William Burke
6. Rev. Jacob Young
7. Rev. Jonathan Stamper

of the Minutes, still *"enjoys* a superannuate relation."

From these same Minutes it appears that several of the brethren had become members of the "Society of Free Masons," which, in the eyes of the Conference, was wrong. At the previous session, resolutions had been passed expressing disapproval of such membership, but at this session other resolutions were passed, and an address issued to the ministry and membership of the Conference, sharply voicing their disapprobation, on the ground that such membership was unfavorable to piety, and brought persons into too intimate fellowship with ungodly men! At a later Conference, Moses M. Hinkle was admonished from the Chair for joining the order. If these fathers were correct in their estimate of the spiritual results of membership in this and other fraternities, we fear there has been a great spiritual declension in these latter days!

1818. The year 1818 is rather remarkable for the number of preachers admitted on trial. There were nineteen admitted in each of the Ohio and Tennessee Conferences. This gain was offset to some extent by losses from locations—which at this time were very frequent,—and by superannuations. The increase in membership was gratifying—very nearly three thousand during the year. Extensive revivals had blessed the Church throughout the two Conferences, and there was need for an incrase in the working forces.

It was during this Conference year that what is known as "Jackson's Purchase" was negotiated and ratified, thus opening to us both the responsibility and privilege of sending missionaries into that field. By the terms of this purchase, the Chickasaw Indians ceded to the United States all that part of Kentucky and Tennessee, lying west of the Tennessee river, and

Methodism must needs follow the stream of settlers who found homes in this new territory.

Several new churches and new circuits were organized this year. Walter Griffith, pastor of the Limestone circuit, extended his labor so as to occupy Augusta, a growing town on the banks of the Ohio river, and destined to become the seat of our next denominational school. A great revival in the Fountain Head circuit, under the ministry of Andrew Monroe, resulted in the organization of a church at Bowling Green, where no society of any denomination had been formed prior to this time. Louisville was made a station this year, with the eloquent Bascom in charge. Hitherto the Hinkstone circuit embraced all the territory of Clark, Montgomery, Bath, Nicholas, and Bourbon counties, but this year the Mount Sterling circuit is carved out of it and appears in the Minutes for the first time. The Newport circuit is also created out of a part of the old Licking circuit, and included Newport, Covington, Burlington, and other places. Many camp meetings had been held, and at these there had been wonderful displays of divine power.

The Ohio Conference met at Steubenville, August 7th. All three of the Bishops were present. The plan of dividing the territory into Episcopal Districts was not adopted until several years later, and each of the Bishops felt it incumbent upon him to attend every Annual Conference. Of the nineteen preachers admitted, three were sent to Kentucky, viz., Hezekiah Holland, Josiah Whitaker, and Joseph D. Farrow.

Hezekiah Holland traveled but four years before locating, serving the Big and Little Sandy, the Mt. Sterling, the Dover (in Tennessee), and the Limestone circuits.

Dr. Redford pronounces Josiah Whitaker "one of the most laborious preachers" he ever knew. This very eccentric, yet very useful, man was a Marylander by birth—born in Baltimore county, November 30, 1779. He came with his father to Kentucky in 1792, and they settled in Bourbon county. The next year he joined the Methodist Church as a seeker, and was converted soon after while engaged in secret prayer. In 1799, he was married to Miss Susan Honey, of Bourbon county, who was indeed a heroine for the sake of the cause of Christ. It was sometime after his conversion that Mr. Whitaker took up the work of the ministry. He was licensed in 1813, and admitted into the Conference in 1818. He had traveled the Licking circuit under the Presiding Elder for several months before he was admitted, but the first two years of his service in the Conference were spent on this circuit. In the meantime, he had located his large family at what is now Oddville, Harrison county, and refused to move them. He went wherever he was sent by the Conference, no matter how far away from his home, but his family did not move. He was very much opposed to Freemasonry, and when a name was presented for admission into the Conference, he was careful to inquire whether or not the candidate was a Mason, refusing to vote for the admission of any man who belonged to that order. "He attracted no ordinary attention by the severity with which he preached against the peculiar views held by the Baptist Church, and the dangerous dogmas of Campbellism. Ready in his delivery, and well fortified with anecdotes illustrative of every position he either defended or opposed, he was an able champion for the truth, while he dealt the most withering sarcasm on every system that came under his censure."—(Redford).

Defending himself on the Conference floor against certain criticisms to which he had been subjected, he has given the best resume of his work we have seen. He said:

In the work of four-and-twenty years, I have lost no day from my work for want of health; and from any circumstance, I have not lost a round on any circuit of all my work, whether I have been sent where money grew, or not. For the first fourteen years of my travels, I did not get fifty dollars for each year, in quarterage, and the first four years, not ten dollars for each year—and my wife and ten children at home, doing the best they could. They kept circuit preaching twenty years in their dwelling-house, and they had eight camp meetings in sight of their house. Four years I traveled on the south side of Kentucky river, which threw me forty-five miles from my family, and caused the riding in the four years of fourteen thousand miles. During all this period, my family never said, "Do not go to your work." Wet or dry, cold or hot, high waters, deep mud, or ice, if I had an appointment they expected me to fill it. Even when my house was burned down, with almost all that was in it, and my family encamped around the ruins, trying to build a dwelling to shelter in, they still said, "Go on; for the honor of a preacher," they would say, "it will not do to stay away from your work. We will do the best we can, and you will feel better, and there will be some way provided for us." Who of the Conference ever made a motion to help my family in this distress? Perhaps, if it had been a Freemason's family, the case would have been thought of—but they had help from above. I have used no dose of medicine in my life, neither has my wife in her life; neither has either of us used tobacco in any way. I have not gone to bed for fatigue, sleep, or sickness, in twenty years; nor have I lost twelve appointments in twenty-four years. During this time I have tried to banish and drive away all erroneous and strange doctrine, that I have thought contrary to God's word, as our rule directs in our ordination vows. I have been in the habit of lecturing from four to five, and up to seven hours at a time; and in the year 1841, I lectured nine times to average five hours each, and yet my lungs are very strong. I can sing strong and clear after one of my lectures, all the while. With all my plainness and severity in doctrine, I have added to the Methodist Episcopal Church about five thousand members.

. . . . I have never been sent to any work because I asked for it in particular . . . . No, sir! I go to every work, far or near, and will do all the work that you give me. But I will not move Suky Honey; (He always called his wife by her maiden name) she cannot float. Who of you ever gave Suky Honey any money for her support? No, sir, I ask no favors; for I have ridden twenty-four years, and have never been superannuated, supernumerated, located, stationated, nor Presiding Elderated. But I repeat it, Suky Honey can't float!"

A few years ago, while the writer was visiting in the home where Brother Whitaker lived, we were shown his old beaver hat, his cane, his well-worn Bible, and a great bundle of sermon notes and papers of various kinds drawn up in his own hand-writing. Among these papers we found a number of contracts he had entered into with janitors of churches he had served, clearly specifying the labors they were to perform, the amount of remuneration they were to receive, and the time when they were to receive it. And he held them strictly to their contract, and held himself obligated to see that they were paid on time!

Another thing we learned was that, notwithstanding his own family was so large, he reared ten or more orphan children. There were no orphanages in those days, but when a child in the neighborhood was bereft of father or mother and had no place to go, Brother Whitaker would take the child and care for it, binding himself legally to send the child to school, and to give a girl her clothing, a bed and bedding, and to give a boy a suit of clothes, and a horse, saddle and bridle, when twenty-one. We visited the grave in which he was buried on his own land, not far from the house in which he lived so long. He died August 21, 1850.*

*Josiah Whitaker was the great-grandfather of Prof. D. W. Batson, so long President of Kentucky Wesleyan College, and the great-great-grandfather of Rev. H. W. Whitaker, D. D. of the Kentucky Conference.

After an itinerant service of nine years, ranging over a large part of Kentucky and West Virginia, Joseph D. Farrow located and made his home in Mason county. The charges he served were Mt. Sterling, Little Sandy, Limestone, Salt River, Licking, Big Kanawha, Lexington, Fleming, and Limestone a second time. He located in 1827.

Alexander Cummins was sent to Kentucky this year and appointed Presiding Elder of the Kentucky District, on which he remained for three years. A Virginian by birth, converted in his twenty-first year, he had been admitted on trial in the Western Conference in 1809, and with but one year of intermission, labored until 1823, when death brought him rest. As a preacher, "he was regular, zealous, acceptable and useful. His language was good, his sermons, in general, pointed and weighty. His talents were not the most brilliant, but his greatness consisted in variety and goodness; and such was his zeal, variety, and usefulness, that but few, if any, were more popular." (From Funeral sermon by Russell Bigelow).

Walter Griffith, while a native of Maryland, came to Scott county, Kentucky. He joined the Western Conference in 1810. Prior to this he had served the Shelby circuit under the Presiding Elder, but after being admitted into the Conference his work was in Ohio until 1818. He was appointed this year to Limestone, but after one year, was taken back to Ohio and placed on the Miami District. Two years on this District completely broke him down. Superannuated in the fall of 1821, he lived only to the 27th of the following June, when he passed from earth to that heaven to which he had guided many souls. A bright, good, and useful man.

From the Tennessee Conference this year, Isaac E. Holt and Joshua Boucher came to Kentucky, the former to the Danville circuit and the latter to Henderson. At the end of the year, Holt, on account of family concerns, asked to be discontinued. Joshua Boucher, after traveling the Henderson circuit, was sent next year to Limestone, then went back to Tennessee where for many years he ranked high among his brethren and was greatly beloved and honored.

We have already given a lengthy sketch of Barnabas McHenry. The reader may recall that in Chapter IV we told of his location after a brief but brilliant ministry, and of his taking up his residence at Springfield, Kentucky. This year he was re-admitted into the Conference and assigned to the Salt River District, on which he remained two years. He was then assigned to Bardstown and Springfield station, but at the end of the year he was compelled to retire again. His name was placed on the list of superannuates, and he retained this relation until he fell a victim of cholera in 1833. No man of his day had a finer record of splendid service, or was more greatly missed when he went away.

Edward Ashley traveled in Western Kentucky five years—three of these years, 1818, 1821 and 1823, on the Livingston circuit. His name does not appear in the list of appointments in 1819, but in 1820 he was assigned to Henderson, and in 1822 to Greenville. He was placed on the superannuate list in 1824, and located in 1827.

1819. The year 1819 records the death, in Mississippi, of one of Kentucky's most beloved men, Samuel Parker. We have already told the story of this splendid man. His ability as a preacher, as a master of song, as an administrator of the Church's affairs, placed him in the very first rank of workers of his day. His zeal knew no bounds. He literally wore himself out in the work of the Lord. He was spoken of as "The Star of the West." Tuberculosis had laid its cold hand upon him before he was drafted for the work in Mississippi, yet he was not only willing, but eager, to go into this hard field and carry on the work there. But he was not able to do any work after reaching Mississippi, and on the 20th of December, death sealed his hallowed lips.

This year also marks the beginning of Missions by the Methodists of America. Of course the whole movement was, in a sense, a missionary enterprise. New ground was being occupied continually, and the migrations of the people toward the West were closely followed by the Methodist preachers. Bishop Asbury was very diligent in raising funds to aid in establishing the work in the new communities. The evangelization of the slaves had been undertaken years before, and by this time the Church had a negro membership of near forty thousand. But this year, definite mission work was begun among the Wyandotte Indians of Ohio. Mention has already been made of the conversion of the Mulatto, John Stewart, and of his strange call to preach to the Indians of northern Ohio. At the session of the Ohio Conference, held this year at Cincinnati, "the Conference determined that a Missionary be sent to the northern Indians, and that James Montgomery, a local preacher, be employed." Montgomery consented to go, and the mission was placed under the direction of the Presiding Elder of the Lebanon District and the preachers of the Mad River circuit. John Strange, Moses Crume, and John Sale were appointed a committee to raise funds with which to pay Montgomery a salary of $200, and were authorized to employ John Stewart as an assistant. This was the beginning of organized missionary work in American Methodism.

The Ohio Conference this year assigned to charges in Kentucky five men whom it admitted on trial, viz., Nathaniel Harris, John R. Keach, Isaac Collard, David D. Dyche, and John Kinney.

The reader may recall that, in Chapter V, we made mention of Nathaniel Harris as one of the first, and one of the ablest, of the local preachers that came to Kentucky. After Bethel Academy had closed as a church school, he conducted a private school in the building for several years. His talents as a preacher were such that his services were in great demand, and he preached in all the towns and counties for many miles around his home. This year he was admitted on trial in the Conference and sent to Lexington station. Lexington was then the largest town in the State, and twice before, by special arrangement, had been a station, and this year it was again set off from the Lexington circuit. According to the Minutes, Harris was to exchange in six months with Henry McDaniel, who was stationed at Georgetown. In 1820, Harris was assigned to Lexington circuit, with Samuel Demint and Edward Stevenson as assistants. In 1821, he was stationed at Danville and Frankfort, and in 1822 on Paris circuit. He then located and took up his residence at Versailles, where he remained until death. Able, useful, spiritual, and greatly beloved by all who knew him.

John R. Keach served Hinkstone circuit in 1819, and in 1820 was assigned to Mt. Sterling, but during the year the unfortunate breaking of a blood-vessel almost ended his life, and compelled his superannuation at the ensuing Conference. With a good English education and with good talents as a preacher, he was acceptable and useful. He continued a superannuate until February, 1826, when he died.

Isaac Collard lived to be "the oldest man and member of the Kentucky Conference." Rev. J. W. Cunningham, in a letter to the St. Louis Christian Advocate, says that "he was born in New York City, was baptized by Joseph Pilmore, one of the first two missionaries sent by Mr. Wesley to America; joined the Church, August 15, 1810, at the age of sixteen years, in old John Street, New York, the first Methodist Chapel built in America. He worked, when a boy, at sail-making, in New York, and made sails, awnings, and bottoms for the berths for the first steamboat that Robert Fulton successfully ran up the Hudson River, before he obtained his patent. He came to Cincinnati in 1811, when it was a town of a few thousand inhabitants, and joined the old Stone Church, now Wesley Chapel, on Fifth Street—the only Methodist Church then in Cincinnati. Father Collard was licensed to preach in July, 1818, by the Quarterly Conference of old Stone Church." He was appointed this year, 1819, to Limestone circuit, and until 1848, traveled various circuits and Districts in the bounds of the present Kentucky, Louisville and Western Virginia Conferences. He was superannuated in 1848, and for many years lived in Cynthiana, loved and honored by all who knew him. He died in 1875.

David D. Dyche was above the ordinary as a preacher, and a man after whom parents named their children! Admitted this year, he was sent to Lexington, then to Guyandotte, Jefferson, Newport, and Hinkstone circuits. Broken in health, he was on the superannuate list for two years, then resumed his labors at Mt. Sterling and Frankfort. Transferred to Ohio in 1830, he served at Lebanon, Dayton and Piqua; located 1833, and died in great triumph, September 11, 1837.

John W. Kinney traveled five years in Kentucky, on John's Creek, Fleming, Licking, Franklin, and Fountain Head circuits; was transferred to the Ohio Conference in 1824, and after several years in that Conference, located and went to Texas, where he was very efficient as a local preacher. His wife was a daughter of Barnabas McHenry.

Zachariah Connell had been received in 1818, and traveled, without intermission, until December, 1863, when he expired. His only appointment in Kentucky was the Fleming circuit, which he traveled in 1819.

For two years in succession—1818 and 1819—the Tennessee Conference met in Nashville. The power and influence of H. B. Bascom was growing apace. He had come to this Conference in 1816, and for two years had been assigned to the Danville circuit. During this time his sermons had attracted much attention, and, young as he was, he was looked upon as one of the great orators in the American pulpit. It was during this time that he met Henry Clay, and a friendship sprang up between them that lasted as long as Bascom lived. Clay regarded him even then as one of the greatest *natural* orators he ever heard. At the session of the Conference in 1817, at Franklin, Tennessee, when only a little more than twenty-one years of age, he had preached with such power that people were amazed. A lady who heard him thus describes this sermon:

He was the most remarkable man I ever knew. He could not, I think, preach an indifferent, or even a medium sermon. Some, to be sure, objected to his ornate style, but to him it was perfectly natural. Had I then heard any one make this objection, I should probably have said, "As well might you command the sun not to gild the clouds of evening as to forbid Bascom, when warmed with his subject, to clothe his burning thoughts with those brilliant gems that flash out so gloriously before our mental vision.' I almost think that I would rather forget any other event of my life than the exquisite pleasure I enjoyed in hearing him preach on the last day of the Conference. . . . My mind was so absorbed with the theme that I was scarcely more conscious of surrounding objects than if I had been in a blissful dream. The uncomfortable seat seemed pleasant, and when at the close it was said that the discourse had lasted more than two hours, I knew not how to believe it, for to me the time had not appeared one-third that length.

But the same sort of opposition that had confronted him in Ohio, met him in Tennessee. The Conference was divided into two factions over the slavery question, and Bascom was known to have acted with the faction that favored moderate measures in dealing with this problem. The factions were quite evenly divided, and the more radical party were very jealous of any increase of the adverse party, and this fact entered into the matter of Bascom's ordination and advancement. When, in 1818, he came before the Conference for election to elder's orders, his election was very bitterly opposed, and he was elected by only *one* majority! In 1819 this Conference was almost rent asunder by the slavery question. The General Conference had allowed each Annual Conference to adopt its own rule in dealing with persons in any way connected with slavery, and, by a very small majority, this Conference adopted a rule not to receive any one into its membership, or ordain any local preacher who was a slave-holder, notwithstanding the fact that the laws of Tennessee did not permit of the emancipation of slaves. Gilbert D.

Taylor was this year refused admission because he was in possession of slaves, even though it was impracticable for him to free them. This action called forth a protest in the part of the minority, which protest was drawn up by Bascom and signed by sixteen of the leading men of the Conference. An address to the General Conference, setting forth their grievances, led to the repeal of the rule allowing the Annual Conferences to legislate on this subject. The question was becoming more and more acute in every part of the Church. Bascom suffered in both his standing in the Conference and in his appointments by reason of his *moderate* views upon this subject. He always insisted that he owed it to Bishop Asbury that he had espoused these moderate views. While he was opposed to slavery he did not believe in extreme measures in dealing with those who might be connected with it.

From the number admitted on trial at this Conference, Martin Flint, Richard W. Morris, William Peter, Cheslea Cole, and William Gunn received appointments in Kentucky.

Martin Flint was a North Carolinian who was converted when eighteen years of age, joined the Methodist Church and was licensed to preach. Admitted this year, he traveled successively the Henderson, Salt River, Lexington, and Mt. Sterling circuits, but in 1824, his health failing, he was superannuated. He died in March, 1825. While in the service he made full proof of his ministry, and died in peace.

Richard W. Morris this year served the Franklin circuit, then gave three years to the work in Tennessee before locating in 1823.

William Peter was a most useful man. Before his admission on trial, he assisted Andrew Monroe on the

Fountain Head circuit during the great revival there in 1818, during which time the Church in Bowling Green was formed. He was assigned to Barren circuit this year, and remained a member of the Kentucky Conference until 1828, during which time he was very acceptable and did much good in the charges he served. He later removed to Illinois.

Cheslea Cole spent two years on the Wayne and Somerset circuits, then after two years in Tennessee, located.

William Gunn was for many years a prominent member of the Kentucky Conference. As we will have occasion to refer to him in another volume, we shall wait until then to give a sketch of the man and his labors. He was known as "the sweet singer of the Kentucky Conference," and few men had a more honorable record for faithful service.

Three others who had been previously admitted, came into Kentucky this year. Jesse Green was a minister, first in Tennessee, then for a short while in Kentucky, then in Illinois and Missouri. He died in 1846, a member of the St. Louis Conference, where he was held in high esteem.

James Witten and Samuel Harwell each gave one year to Kentucky, Witten on the Cumberland circuit, and Harwell on Wayne.

Redford characterizes the Rev. Jack Stith as a very remarkable local preacher. Born in Virginia, he married, came to Kentucky and settled in Hardin county. He did much preaching in that section of the State, and it was of the highest order. A Presbyterian judge said of him that he "never preached a little sermon."

Although he never entered the itinerant ranks, yet his zeal for the cause of God led him not only to preach regularly at Hardinsburg, Bardstown, Elizabethtown, and Louisville, but to seek out the destitute sections of the country. He founded the Methodist Church in Elizabethtown, and was the principal instrument in the great revival in Hardinsburg, in 1828, the first with which that place was ever visited. On that occasion he stood side by side with the distinguished Marcus Lindsey, and was regarded as the peer of that great and good man.

All honor to those local preachers who loved so well the cause of Christ and gave such splendid service in building the Kingdom!

The reader who has followed us in these pages has doubtless been impressed by several things:

1. The youth of the men by whose labors the victories of Methodism in the West were achieved. There were but few veterans among them. Many of them were mere boys—young men who had not yet reached their majority. The plan of putting an older man in charge of a circuit, and then placing one or two or three young men under his care and direction worked well, and great things were done by them.

2. The number of locations that occurred. The work was exceedingly taxing. The long rides, exposure to all sorts of weather, swimming swollen streams, the rough fare, the constant preaching, meeting classes, praying and singing—all these things placed a terrific strain upon men of even the strongest constitutions. They broke down under it. The lives of many were thus shortened and many others were doomed to suffer ill health through the years they survived. Then, but few married men could support their families on the meager salaries they received, and were forced to locate in order to care for those who were dependent on them.

3. But few of the men who labored in this great field had more than an elementary training in the

schools. But this is also true of their hearers. Few men in any of the professions in those days were other than self-made men. But these preachers were students. It was the constant habit of McKendree and other Presiding Elders to map out courses of study for the younger men, and on their next round to catechize them on the books they had read. What books they read they mastered. They thought things through. Without newspapers and magazines and other light literature to dissipate thought and confuse the mind, they dealt with solid and thoughtful books. Many of them were deeply read in theology, and more of them could read the Greek and Latin classics than can do it today! Schools are, at best, only crutches to enable pupils to walk with greater ease!

4. While these men were not angels, they knew the secret of sainthood. We fear sometimes that most of us have lost this secret in these latter days. The time spent by these men in prayer and meditation and the study of the Word, puts us to shame. They literally went from their knees to the pulpit, and then from the pulpit to their knees. They knew God, and carried with them a constant sense of the divine presence. They found places of solitude in the woods and canebrakes where they could commune with God and draw down the power from on high. Their fellowship was indeed with the Father and with his Son, Jesus Christ. The atonement they believed in and preached to others was an unlimited atonement, reaching to all men and saving from all sin.

5. Their faith was definite and heroic. The Bible to them was the Word of God, and they accepted it as they found it, and preached it without apology or misgiving. They had not the slightest doubt that the gos-

pel was the power of God unto salvation to every one that believeth. It had saved them. They knew it. Conversion and sanctification were not to them vague and indefinite experiences, but great and conscious changes wrought in heart and life by the Holy Ghost. If they found a sinner anywhere, they believed that Christ could and would save him, and that he could save him then and there. So, not only in the meeting-house or at the camp meeting, but at the fireside and on the roadside, they offered salvation, full and free. That which had saved them would save any others!

6. They preached the Gospel. Much of the preaching we hear today is good and true, but it will not save sinners. It might be preached by a pious Jew or Stoic as well as by a Christian minister. It does not convict sinners of their sins, nor teach them how to be saved. The burden of the preaching of these men was Christ the Savior, and the only Savior, of men. They told people of their wickedness, but told them further of a God who cares, and of a Savior who saves. Conviction, repentance, faith, conversion, sanctification, a new heart and a new life—then Heaven at the end—these were the things they talked about wherever they found people to listen. "And the Lord added unto the Church daily such as were being saved." These things account, in some measure at least, for the marvelous success that attended the ministry of these holy men.

END OF VOLUME I.

Made in the USA
Middletown, DE
24 March 2022